One Self

Satsangs with Nome

Published by
Society of Abidance in Truth (SAT)
1834 Ocean Street
Santa Cruz, CA 95060 USA
(831) 425-7287
www.SATRamana.org / email: sat@cruzio.com
Copyright 2015 Society of Abidance in Truth
First Edition
All rights reserved
Printed in USA
ISBN: 9780981940977

Om Namo Bhagavate Sri Ramanaya

Acknowledgements

Deep appreciation and gratitude are here expressed to those who transcribed the recordings of spiritual events at SAT during the years, especially Grant Summerville. Gratitude is expressed here for the proofreading efforts of Sangeeta Raman, Raman Muthukrishnan, and Raymond Teague. Appreciation is also here expressed to Sasvati for the layout and design of this book and seeing to the printing of it. Finally, deep appreciation is expressed to those devotees at the SAT Temple who, through their dedication and offerings, enable SAT to continue to make the teachings of nondual Self-Knowledge available to seekers of Truth.

Introduction

"1. By association with the Sages, attachment (to material things) is removed. When this is removed, the attachment of the mind also vanishes. Those who have got rid of their attachment of mind become one with That which is motionless. They become Liberated even while alive. Seek their company.

2. That Supreme State which is to be attained here through association with Sages and steady inward-turning cannot be obtained through a (merely) learned teacher or by (understanding) the meaning of sacred texts, or by merit or by any other means.

3. If one associates with Sages, where is the need for all these methods of discipline? When a pleasant breeze from the south is blowing, of what use, tell me, is a fan?

4. Heat is allayed by the cool (light of the) moon, poverty (is removed) by the wish-fulfilling tree and sin by (bathing in) the Ganges, but all three are removed by the peerless benign look of the peerless Sages.

5. Neither sacred bathing places consisting of water nor the images of gods made of stone and clay can equal those great ones. They take countless days to purify one, but know that the Sages do so by a mere look."

— Supplement to the Forty Verses, by Sri Ramana Maharshi, Collected Works, Sri Ramanasramam, 1968

". . . Satsanga enlarges one's intelligence (expands one's consciousness), destroys one's ignorance and one's psychological distress. Whatever be the cost, however difficult it may be, whatever obstacles may stand in its way,

satsanga should never be neglected, for satsanga alone is one's light on the path of life . . ."

—VASISTHA, THE SUPREME YOGA, CHAP. 2,
SWAMI VENKATESANANDA

"My children, if you want to practise yoga, you must remove all attachment from your hearts. If you cannot do this, keep the company of holy men, for holy company is the panacea for the disease of worldliness."

—DATTATREYA, AVADHUTA GITA, TRANS., SWAMI CHETANANANDA

"The firm Knowledge that I am Brahman / Is rare, indeed, in all the three worlds. / It is very rare to see and talk to a sage / Who is steadfast in the Knowledge of the Supreme, / Who is the embodiment of Awareness, / And has not come out of the samadhi of the nature of the Supreme Brahman. / If, by any chance, doing service to that supreme sage falls to one's lot, / The supreme state of Liberation will also result."

—SONG OF RIBHU, 19:23, SAT TEMPLE

"By the company of the good, there is non-attachment; by non-attachment there is freedom from delusion; from freedom from delusion, there is the immutable Truth; from the immutable Truth there is liberation in life.

—SRI SANKARACHARYA, BHAJA GOVINDAM, V. 9

"In satsang, doubts are resolved, questions are answered, the Truth is revealed, and the way to realize is shown." —Nome

One Self is a compilation of satsangs with Nome from May 4, 2003 to January 29, 2012. All the satsangs begin with silence, which reveals the true nature of the One Self—our true nature. Most satsangs then have a discourse on the nature of the One Self and instruction on how to practice Sri Ramana's Self-Inquiry. Each discourse is followed by questions raised by devotees regarding their own practices and Nome's response.

Satsang with a wise sage is more than just words floating through the atmosphere; it is the experience of Reality itself. Those attuned to this phenomenon understand the greatness of association with the sage and the power of satsang.

The wise tell us again and again the importance of satsang and keeping the holy company of the sages to destroy the disease of worldliness. We must heed their wise advice!

- Sasvati

Contents

The Perpetual Being of Reality, Satsang, May 4, 2003 1
Agreeable to All, Satsang, June 15, 2003 15
Perfection, Satsang, July 6, 2003 33
Silent Being Ever Is, Satsang, July 13, 2003 48
Everyday and Eternity, Satsang, July 20, 2003 62
A Few Dialogues, Satsang, July 27, 2003 79
Samsara and Mukti, Satsang, August 3, 2003 94
Knoweldge of Identity, Satsang, August 10, 2003 108
The Only Real State, Satsang, August 17, 2003 123
The Self and Yourself, Satsang, August 24, 2003 135
No Topic, Satsang, September 7, 2003 154
No Differentiation, Satsang, September 21, 2003 173
Action and Knowledge, Satsang, September 28, 2003 184
Silence and Self-Realization, Satsang, October 5, 2003 201
Being-Consciousness-Bliss, Satsang, November 2, 2003 211
Egoless Self, Satsang, November 9, 2003 227
The Question and the Answer, Satsang,
    December 14, 2003 238
Sri Ramana Maharshi Jayanti, Satsang,
    December 28, 2003 245
Boundless Wisdom, Song of Ribhu, Chapter 35,
    January 2, 2004 255
None in Bondage, None Liberated, Satsang,
    January 4, 2004 269
Always Real, Satsang, December 21, 2004 278
Being, Satsang, February 13, 2005 286
Eloquent Silence, Satsang, April 10, 2005 299
True Silence, Satsang, May 8, 2005 314
One Self, Satsang, July 17, 2005 324
Nonobjective Realization, Satsang, October 23, 2005 330
The State of Identity, Satsang, January 1, 2006 343

The Silence of Dakshinamurti, Satsang,
  January 8, 2006 356
Absolute Silence, Satsang, January 29, 2006 367
Determination of the Self, Satsang, February 5, 2006 379
Identity, Satsang, May 7, 2006 396
Silent Truth, Satsang, May 14, 2006 410
No Other, Satsang, May 21, 2006 425
Space-like, Satsang, June 4, 2006 439
You Are, Satsang, June 11, 2006 453
Sahaja Samadhi, Satsang, June 18, 2006 466
The Self Alone Is, Satsang, June 25, 2006 477
Real Identity, Satsang, July 2, 2006 488
Knowledge and Devotion, Satsang, July 9, 2006 500
Sri Ramana Maharshi's Self-Realization, Satsang,
  July 16, 2006, In celebration of July 17th 515
Purnam, Satsang, January 7, 2007 528
Nirguna Brahman, Satsang, September 30, 2007 539
Mandukya Karika 2:32, Satsang, March 30, 2008 549
Undifferentiated, Satsang, April 6, 2008 559
The Mind, Satsang, May 24, 2009 567
Meditation, June 19, 2009 578
Meditation, April 30, 2010 588
Self-existent, Self-luminous, Satsang, May 2, 2010 591
Only One Self, Satsang, May 9, 2010 599
Can and Are, Satsang, May 16, 2010 607
Being is Knowledge, Satsang, August 22, 2010 618
Immeasurably Vast, Satsang, October 23, 2011 628
The Self is Brahman, Satsang, January 29, 2012 636

The Perpetual Being of Reality

Satsang, May 4, 2003

(Silence)

Om Om Om

(Silence)

N.: The Reality is perpetually existent Being. It is silent. It is as it is, eternally. It is neither an object nor an individual but is infinite. It is itself always. It knows itself. If realizing it is needed, it realizes itself. It alone reveals itself to itself.

It is the essence of the teaching, the source of the teaching, and the one who comprehends the teaching, all of which are one and the same thing. The teaching is that of perpetual Truth, for Reality does not have an alternative. Any alternative to Reality would simply be unreal, which is to say not at all.

The Realization, or Knowledge, regarding this Truth is a state of imperturbable peace, which is as immutable as Existence, or real Being, itself. In the Vedas, it is declared to be the highest of joys. Really, it is not in comparison to any other kind of joy. It is thus called "ananda," bliss. It is a happiness that leaves nothing else to be desired and for which nothing is lacking. Because it is also great freedom, it is called "moksa," or Liberation. It is Liberation from all of the imagined bondage. It is immense freedom. It is the freedom in which nothing can afflict, nothing can cause bondage, and which does not depend upon objects, situations, events, or conditions of any kind. All of this peace, happiness, and freedom is inherent in this Reality known as Brahman, the vast Absolute, which is neither an object nor an individual.

The only way to realize it is to abide in identity with it. To abide in identity with it, you must know yourself, for what you are is always this Absolute Reality, or God. Thus, the Upanishads say, "Tat tvam asi," That you are. It is not that you become That, as if you had the power to break off from it and return to it at some later date, but, rather, That, the Absolute, is the solitary Existence always, and That is what you are. This is true to such an extent that you are not a part of it, nor is it a part of you, but rather the Self is the Absolute, and the Absolute is the Self; the Absolute is not other, and the Self is not other. Therefore, know yourself. If you know yourself, you know the Absolute, and what you know is what you are.

In order to know yourself as you truly are, which is Being as you truly are, inquire in such a manner that you cease to misidentify with anything that can give rise to the illusory bondage. Such is any ignorant conception, whether that conception, or definition, be of an object or of an individual. If you regard objects as real, you do not know the true Existence. When one knows the true Existence, there is nothing objective created anywhere. As long as you regard yourself as the assumed individual being, or entity, your real Self is not known. If you inquire and know yourself as you are, there is not a trace of individuality, or ego, anywhere. There is just Being, which is simultaneously Consciousness and Bliss. It is utterly nondual in nature, without birth, and without death. The individual has not been born. The objects have not actually come to be. One Reality actually is. That should be known as your Self.

If you abide steadily in such Knowledge, all of the bliss, peace, and Liberation alluded to earlier are your natural state. Inquire and accept only that as a definition of who you are which is perpetual Existence. Do not accept as a definition, do not misidentify with, anything that is not perpetual, that comes in and out of existence, or that has birth and death, such as your body. It is particularized and is an object. It has birth and death. You cannot be an object. Who are you? Inquire into yourself, "Who am I?"

Discard what is objective, such as the body and the thoughts that constitute your mind, which are things that are known. Who is the knower? None of those things shine always. Something shines and exists always. It is you. What is that? Know that within yourself. I am speaking of Self-Knowledge, not a knowledge of ideas and perceptions through your thinking and your senses. This is something nonobjective. It is more subjective than thoughts, inclusive of all conceptions and perceptions. It is something known immediately, just as you know that you exist, without thinking about it and without seeing, hearing, touching, or using any other sense to know it. Existence should know itself. Existence, or Being, already is itself, so there is no question of attaining something anew, obtaining something new, producing something new, or transforming yourself into something other. There is no need for God to be transformed into anything else. This God you already are. Knowledge reveals it.

The method of inquiry to reveal this Knowledge is primarily one of negation of the ignorance. If we remove the illusory superimposition, the substrate is self-revealed. If false definitions about yourself are rejected, by this wisdom, the Knowledge of your own Being shines in its own Light. That which is said to shine then actually exists now and always, beyond the idea of time. It is without any particular location. It just is as it is, always.

(Silence)

Q.: Part of the grace of the Absolute exalted is that it serves to dwarf the significance of anything illusory. The word "infinite" is in the realm of illusion, just as people think that the universe is infinite. To be in tune with the Absolute, humility is natural, for the Absolute would be ultimately humble, because there is nobody else to whom to show off.

N.: The Maharshi says that your greatest glory lies where you cease to exist. Where you cease to exist, real Existence is self-revealed. We attain to it by means of humility, rather than by proclamation, let alone pride. Not making a big deal of ourselves is a good step. If we take the second step to see that there is no one to make a big deal about, it is complete.

Infinite is alright. There is nothing wrong with the Infinite. Truth is ineffable, so, as the Upanishads declare, before it all words and thought turn back, unable to grasp. Adi Sankara, the great sage, declared centuries ago, if the meaning of instruction regarding the Absolute Brahman is comprehended, the power of that instruction is none other than the power of Brahman, the Absolute. So, we should dismiss all words, yet we should listen very carefully to what they are saying. If a person knows that this word, "infinite," does not grasp the Reality, such is fine. If another person meditates on what it really means when the Self is said to be infinite, and thereby his mind is blown away like the clouds before the wind, that is alright. I have never seen anyone hurt by infinity, have you?

Q.: No, mine was a silly question. Yet, the Absolute is even more than infinite.

N.: Yes. (Silence)

Another Q.: Agreeing with you on a mental level is just not enough. I need to stop the idea that at the mental level I must agree with this truth to realize it. Why do I need to mentally try to do this? I am trying to become deeper than that.

N.: Truth is utterly impersonal. Reality is not waiting for anyone's opinion, whether such would be to agree with it, express it, or otherwise.

What I am saying, though born of direct experience, is merely a reiteration of what countless sages before have said. I have not added anything to it. It is just that I have not subtracted anything from it. There is nothing personal. So, there is no need for you to worry about whether or not you agree with what is being said.

That which is necessary is for you to dive within and realize the real Self, which is what you truly are. The Maharshi points out that it is the mind that seems to wander away from the Self. In Absolute Truth, the Self being infinite, there is no place for it to wander. For guidance of the spiritual aspirants, practice and instruction consist in restoring the mind to its proper place. In its proper place, it loses its form as a mind and remains only as pure Consciousness. That is without limitation or form. If the mind has wandered away, the mind must come into agreement with the Absolute Self. This may manifest in any number of ways. It may manifest as your powers of reasoning that you employ to come to terms with the instruction. The mind is left with the choice of either retaining its previous way of thinking or relinquishing that way of thinking so as to enter into a state that is in accord with the Truth. That is a state in which the experience related by countless sages and scriptures before you becomes your own experience. So, do not carry your personal ideas, but rather see how your mind can become wedded to the Truth. It is a good use of the mind and the process of introversion. It is introspection.

In the mind, doubts arise. There are no doubts for the real Self. Spiritual practice is concerned primarily with the mind. The body does not have ignorance, though thinking that you are the body is ignorance. The body, itself, is an innocent party. So, do not worry about the body. The Self has no ignorance. So, do not worry about the Self. It is the mind that conjures up the ignorance, and it is the practice that occurs within the mind that destroys the ignorance at its root. The efforts that you apply with your mind to listen, to reflect, and to deeply meditate are very worthwhile. Continue with sravana, manana, and nididhyasana, which are listening, reflection, and deep, continuous meditation. The result is samadhi, or absorption. When what is experienced in samadhi is realized to be the Reality without any alternative, such is Self-Realization.

Continue to practice turning your mind inward. It should question its own ideas. Find out why you think the way that you think. It is not random. When you so question, such will lead you to, "Who thinks?" You will find that all the delusive ideas have their root in a single idea, "I." That is the ego, or individual. As the Maharshi explains, it is the first thought to arise and the last thought to subside. It is integrally connected with every other thought. Who is this "I"? Inquire. Turn your mind inward, trace your thinking back to the "I," and inquire "Who am I?" Thereby, verify Truth within yourself. You will find it shining in yourself, but there is nothing personal about it. It is not anyone's opinion, for it is not a set of ideas. What you are is not a set of ideas. Inquire.

Q.: There is nothing more to say. The Maharshi said it all. You said it all. Sankara said it all.

N.: The Maharshi made it clear even in his Silence.

Another Q.: Last week I had the experience that I was aware that I was not the body, even though I was working. The next day, it disappeared. How can I keep it?

N.: Observe how it disappeared.

Q.: I was not aware.

N.: Yes, you were unaware, while the previous day you were aware. Did the awareness feel natural or contrived?

Q.: It felt natural.

N.: Something was contrived later. It may feel like the return of an old habit.

Q.: Yes.

N.: Undoing the habit requires effort. The effort is spiritual practice. When there is good experience, it is natural to want to remain with it. If it slips away, it is natural to want to return to it.

How did you get into it? Such questioning will give you a hint as to how to return to it. How did the experience come about?

Q.: From meditation and listening to the teachings.

N.: So, you were giving your mind to listening and meditating. Then, the experience came about quite naturally.

Q.: Yes.

N.: If that happened once, it could happen again, could it not?

Q.: Yes.

N.: If it happened twice, it could happen three times and so on. After a while, there would be more of the right experience and less of the delusive, bound experience. At some point, there would be more holes than substance in the delusion. Continue to meditate and inquire. In the course of practice, you will find that what now seems as if an experience that came and went is actually of the nature of the Reality, while the bound state that seems to hem it in before and after is transitory, coming and going. You do not come and go; ignorance comes and goes. Look in this way. Is this clear for you?

Q.: Yes, it is.

Another Q.: When I get good experiences, I doubt them, because I am trying to get away from something to escape into this experience. Maybe, I imagine that I am connected to this fullness. Am I just in a state in which I numb myself? Am I creating a bliss state?

N.: Is the suffering of the divided state also made up or imagined?

Q.: (laughing) Oh, it is "true."

N.: You have two states, both of which you feel are merely imagined. What is not imagined?

If you imagine pain and suffering, you naturally try to remove yourself from such. It is just your nature not to be unhappy. When there is unhappiness, you naturally move toward happiness, like any sentient being. Where this is bondage, you move toward freedom.

What is it that is not imagined? What is it that is not produced by thinking? Is there something?

Q.: (smiling broadly) This is true.

N.: When you reflect on this, even as this question is asked of you, there is a certain element of happiness.

Q.: Yes, there is.

N.: Did you imagine that?

Q.: No.

N.: Did you think, "I am now going to imagine happiness," or was it just naturally there?

Q.: I see now.

N.: Yes, it is not so complex.

Q.: When I am not thinking about it, I can really surprise me.

N.: Great obstacles do not confront you. You do not trick yourself into bliss. If you have a keen interest and an ardent desire to know yourself, it is sufficient that, to the best of your ability, you consistently try to know yourself. Inquire deeply within yourself. Get to the very root, or center, of your mind.

Trace existence. You are, and you know that you are. It is a fact, and you cannot even imagine otherwise. If you try to imagine that you are not, you still are. If you try to imagine a non-knowing state, you know that state, as well. The Knowledge essence and the Existence are not imagined. It is better to say that the entire world is imagined than to say that the Existence-Knowledge is imagined.

If you are in bondage, escape to Liberation. You go to Liberation by knowing yourself. When you know yourself, you see that there has not been any coming or going. That which was imagined, from the "I" to the formed world, is no more. One Existence remains. It is Purnam, perfectly full.

Another Q.: I am trying to meditate by negating what is objective. How could I be something objective? Anything that is objective must be eliminated. How do I proceed with this meditation? Is it that one has an inkling of what the Self is and meditates from there?

N.: You know that you exist. Existence and Consciousness are self-evident. The instruction is to negate all that is objective. This includes all that has name, has form, that you perceive, and that you conceive, and the instruments of those perceptions. Negation is not just of the objects but of the body, which is another object; not just the body and the objects, but also the senses, which are also objective to you; not just the senses, but the prana, being alive or animated, which you know about, as well. Not just all of that, but any idea or aspect of the mind should be negated. Even those modes of mind in which there are no thoughts are still known by you. Set aside as not being yourself everything that is objective. The sense of identity should return to just pure Being. In your identity lies Reality. The sense of reality returns to your Being. Happiness is likewise, as we have spoken of previously.

When it is said, "neti, neti," not this, not this, it means the sense of identity and reality return to their rightful place. That is your real Being.

You may say that, in deep meditation, you can see that what is objective is not what you are, and you negate it. It is probably the other way around. When you negate what is objective, your meditation is deep. You do not enter into a deep state and then have good meditation. Rather, you meditate in a profound way, and the result is a deep state. Is this clear for you?

Q.: Yes, I see it clearly now.

N.: Otherwise, you would need to wait for some state to come over you. It is far better to inquire than to wait.

Q.: Is the negation of what is objective similar to Self-inquiry?

N.: Yes, such are just different ways of describing the same inward turning of the mind. It is the same coming to know your Self. The essence of the meditation is one of Knowledge. We expediently speak of it in various ways in order to overcome various forms of delusive bondage, but it is truly one inquiry, whether you are negating what is objective or inquiring, "Who am I?" In a path of nondual Self-Knowledge, there are not truly a great variety of meditations, though there is a seemingly limitless application of the one essential meditation. The principle by which you transcend the body is the same principle by which you transcend the mind. The principle by which you know yourself is the same principle by which you come to know ultimate Reality. It is one, very simple, formless essence that you find to be universally applicable.

Q.: The applications may vary?

N.: If you are addressing different experiences, the applications are different, yet all the experiences depend on you. You must be there for any experience to occur. This "you" is of the essence. So, we start with that, and we end with that.

Q.: I start with that because there is a supposed existence that I then examine to find out what it is?

N.: You start with it because your existence is self-evident, even if, at first, it appears to be individualized or limited. The existence cannot be denied. It seems to be an inquiry into the bound one, but, when you inquire into the bound one, you find the One who is liberated. It seems to be an inquiry into the individual existence. The Self has no inquiry. It seems to be an inquiry into the ego "I." When you inquire into the ego "I," no ego is found. Only pure

Existence, or the real Self, is found. The one who so inquired is swallowed up in the process.

The applications are numerous. You might meditate in such a way as to transcend the body or to transcend the mind or to see the nonexistence of the ego or to comprehend what is meant by, "there has been no creation, there is no objective thing." You might address some particular form of bondage in order to free yourself from it. You might address some particular attachment in order to liberate your Bliss from it. The essence, though, is always the same. All your experience, what is apparently inner and outer, in whatever state—waking, dreaming, deep sleep—entirely depends on you. To change your experience requires a change in the knowledge of yourself. If, though, you know yourself entirely, there is no such thing as an experience. There is just one Self everywhere.

Another Q.: In Self-Realization, even the devotion, the renunciation, the inquiry cease or are not required? Do these things cease of their own accord by abiding in the Absolute? There is no meditation and no renunciation, for it is all the Absolute?

N.: We may say that Self-Realization is beyond meditation, renunciation, and so forth and so on. Or, we may say that it is the state of perpetual meditation in which the inquiry has fulfilled itself. It is the state of supreme renunciation. The state of supreme renunciation is that in which nothing adheres to one and one adheres to nothing. It is that in which there is no attachment to anything, from thought to the objects. The supreme renunciation is found in Self-Realization. It is to abide eternally renounced. Similar is it with meditation. When it is applied with effort, such is practice. When what is sought with effort is found to be innate, everlasting, and without an alternative, and thus nondual, it is called, "Realization." The same thing that was at one time called sannyasa (renunciation), yoga, jnana (Knowledge), bhakti (devotion), etc. is later called

"Realization." These are simply different terms to explain it in the course of practice. The essence remains by itself.

When one meditates, it is never in vain. When one renounces, it is never in vain. It is the supreme good. By that effort, the mind dissolves. That which is supreme remains. Then, and then only, one can say that the Supreme alone was existing the entire time, and nothing else has ever happened. Until that is the permanent, abiding, doubtless experience, one should continue devoting himself, meditating, renouncing, and so forth and so on.

Q.: That makes it easier. (laughter)

N.: In Realization, it is natural to be as one really is. That is the Absolute alone. In practice, it is natural to apply oneself fully.

Another Q.: If a mosquito comes onto the arm, it affects my body and mind. I slap it, and I have then just killed a mosquito. If somebody says something or behaves in a way that he should not, which makes me feel sad, how should I behave in those situations?

N.: We should first recognize that no one else makes us be in a certain state. One's sadness and happiness, his bondage and his liberation, are entirely internal. Neither the mosquito nor anything else can alter that. The mosquito bites your arm and receives the karma of the slap as described by you. This eliminates that particular mosquito as a factor in your experience. However, that, in itself, has provided you with neither bondage nor liberation. The slapping of the mosquito will not prevent your Liberation. Nor will it give you Liberation. One cannot gain the Bliss of Brahman simply by slapping mosquitoes. Nor does one necessarily gain the Bliss of Brahman by refraining from killing any mosquito. It is something entirely internal.

If someone says something to you that is disagreeable, you do not need to suffer thereby. If what is said has a useful component in it, if there is some degree of truthfulness in it, you may accept it self-critically and use it.

Q.: It is not ethical.

N.: The person is doing something unethical?

Q.: Yes. The person is saying something that should not be said and does not require to be said in that way. It is being mean and vicious.

N.: Are you forced to discuss it with that person?

Q.: Yes, I am.

N.: If the person says something unethical, you do not have to join in and also say something unethical.

Q.: What if I am closely related with the person who says this or behaves in such a way?

N.: You can always show a better way by example. If that person is open-minded to receive an alternative view, you may say what you have just said here, that it is not right to speak in such a manner, and there is a better way. If the other person is too close-minded, you may need to quit the conversation in silence and not carry it with you. That person will bear the karma of his or her speech. What we do with our body, speech, and mind has karma. There is a cause and effect relation. You cannot necessarily stop another person from using speech in a way in which it should not be used, but you can take care of your body, speech, and mind. You help the other person to the degree that you do not use your own body, speech, mind in ways that are not right, even if you cannot correct him or her by explicitly stating so. At least you set a good example. Sometime in the future, that person may think about it.

It depends on the person. The analogy presented by the Maharshi is that some people are like cotton wool, which ignites quickly, for they comprehend the lessons right away.

Q.: Yes, after some time.

N.: Some are like cotton wool and ignite at once. Others may be like wood and take some time longer. Some may be like a piece of hard coal that requires a long time to heat up.

Still, we do what is true, good, and beautiful for the sake of the source of what is true, good, and beautiful. We do not do it because someone else is going to agree. A person may be very much embroiled and entangled in his or her way of thinking, saying, and doing and may not see the better example. It will have its effect only a long time later. We should, though, continue doing what is true, good, and beautiful just for the sake of what is true, good, and beautiful. We do what is right because it is right, and not because someone else agrees with it or someone else will follow the right way. We do it for its own sake. Yet, it does set an example.

You, though, do not need to suffer when someone else does something wrong. Are you the intended target of the wrong?

Q.: Yes, that is how it is.

N.: Something is said to you that is not true about you. What is the aim or intention?

Q.: It is to degrade me.

N.: To degrade you or to ruin your reputation with others or make you feel bad?

Q.: Yes, that is what is occurring.

N.: You can still be totally indifferent. Be like a diamond that is unscratched by whatever touches it. Be detached. You have read, "Be detached from name, fame, etc."

Q.: Yes, I have.

N.: Everyone reads it in scripture. This is the practical application. It is not just that in those days people said what was not right. People say what is not right even today. (laughter) Turn your mind inward. Remain detached. When some person says something that is degrading of you, you have not been degraded. What has been degraded is the image in that person's mind, that person's idea about you. That person's way of thinking is degraded. You are not degraded. If those thoughts are put into words, those words are degraded. You are not degraded. If a third person believes what has been said about you, by accepting such bad rumors, that person's mind has been degraded, but you have not been degraded. Truth remains as it is. The facts stand as they are. All this degrading, which is only noise-making—just sound waves that are interpreted—does not affect the Truth and does not affect the facts. Remaining indifferent, we should go on pouring ourselves into what is true, good, and beautiful, living in and from that state, letting all else pass by like flowing water.

Can you now see? Is there more you wish to ask about this?

Q.: Yes. It is now clear. The mosquito is gone. (laughter)

(Then followed a recitation in Sanskrit and English from *Taittiriya Upanishad.*)

(Silence)

Om Shanti Shanti Shanti Om

Agreeable to All

Satsang, June 15, 2003

(Silence)

Om Om Om

(Silence)

N.: The Maharshi says that the state in which the ego is not is agreeable to all. Why is it agreeable to all? Because of its Bliss, the happiness of which leaves no other happiness to be desired, because of its immense, imperishable peace, and because it is our natural state, which is the state of the Self when it is not overshadowed by some delusive notion.

It is the non-ego state that is agreeable to all. Who is this "all"? If it is the non-ego state, how can there be "all"? What is the nature of "all," yourself included? That state is natural in which there is no ego notion, no assumption of being an individual entity, a limited individual, or an embodied individual. By what means do we know "all" as if they were multiple? Is it not according to the limitations superimposed upon what really is the Self? If we think in terms of individuals defined by bodily attributes, which is the form by which we say that this is one, this is another and this is still another, there appears to be a multiplicity conceived as "all." However, who are you? Can you be the body? If you deeply, penetratingly inquire within yourself "Who am I?" you find that you cannot possibly be a body; nor can you be an individualized or separated mind; nor can you be the idea of "I," which is just an idea and not your essential Being, or the quintessential Consciousness.

The Maharshi says that all find the non-ego state agreeable. Vedanta declares that all are the Self. We could say that the Self is agreeable to the Self and that the Self is the Self. If we inquire to know who the "all" is, yourself included, it is not mere body and not a mere ego.

Is the egoless state agreeable to the ego? I suppose you could say, "no," because why would it want to destroy itself? On the other hand, you could say, "yes," because that is where its happiness lies. On the third hand, if you are endowed with such, (laughter) you could say neither, because the ego is simply that which is not. Something which is not has neither good nor bad nor anything else pertaining to it.

The egoless state is agreeable to all. It is the natural state of the Self, of the nature of pure Being-Consciousness-Bliss, unveiled and not shadowed by anything else. To reveal that state within yourself, discern finely what you are, discarding the misidentification with what you are not.

Inquire, "Who am I?" If you inquire in such a way, you will know yourself. When you know yourself, you know "all," without there being a separate self and a separate "all." It is for this reason that the Maharshi was so well known for his seeing everyone equally. Of course, there was the example of his treating all equally, but this equality went beyond even that. He saw everyone as Himself. You, also, should see everyone just as yourself.

If you assume the wrong identification, thinking in terms of "I am the body," there seem to be differences. If you lift your vision, you may say that there is an essence that is the same in all. There is still "all" in terms of the different bodies, though there is an essence that is the same. If you pursue the essence to its core to see what it is, it is completely unrelated to a body. It is bodiless and not to be defined in any bodily terms, from birth to death and everything between. If you cease to regard yourself as an individualized "I," or ego, this bodiless, egoless equality is seeing all as the Self. Of course, you treat others as you would have them treat you, or you treat others as you would treat yourself. That is the correct way. What I am speaking of is the knowledge of "all," which is really the Knowledge of oneself. If the characteristics, or definitions, that are falsely imposed on oneself are set aside, one finds the state that is agreeable to all, agreeable to the Self, for the Self is all.

The bodies here this morning do not make for a multiplicity of selves. The idea of "others" exists only in one's mind, as does the entire world. Trace this mind to its source. From where do its ideas originate? You will find that they originate from a sense of "I," which is integral to every one of its ideas. Inquire further to see the core, or nature, of this "I." You will find its real "I"-less nature, the non-ego state, which is agreeable to all and which is the state of Reality.

(Silence)

The state that is thoroughly agreeable to yourself is the state in which you cease to obscure the Knowledge of yourself for yourself. That state of Self-Knowledge is Consciousness unobscured by any idea. It is just Being, not regarded as any kind of defining form. Because you are not the body, you are everyone and you are no one. The state which is agreeable to yourself and thus agreeable to all is the state in which "I" have never been born. It is the state in which the ego is impossible.

That should be known as Self-Realization in which no alternative is possible, in which there is just one infinite, unconditioned, eternal, homogeneous, formless Self, which is not the cause of anything, which is not the effect of anything else, in which there is nothing else, but which is infinite, with no division, no separation, and which has no parts within it. It is absolute and not in relation to anything else, but just is as it is. As for anything else, it also is just the same Absolute. To realize this is very simple. It is simpler than even a thought. It is simpler than the idea of "I." That divine simplicity lies where you are alone with no "I" to disturb you.

Again and again, inquire within yourself, "Who am I?", disidentifying from all that is objective and all that is transient. Trace the sense of "I" to its "I"-less real nature. The simplicity and directness of the inquiry merge with the utter simplicity and the nonobjective nature of the direct experience of oneself, which has neither beginning nor end. (Silence)

Q.: You are saying that the ego could never be the subject of the senses and could never be the object of the senses, whereas I was considering that it was an illusion, but still a thing, though not a real thing, but an unreal thing. As I listened, I could not see any point in making it the object of the senses. In some practical sense, it is an illusion to be worked with, but it seems that it is not even that.

N.: How do you work with an illusion?

Q.: You dispel it.

N.: Yes, like water in a mirage. You do not really work

with it, do you? You do not drink it or drain it off. You do need to know that it is not water, lest you fear drowning in it.

Q.: So, one works with his own mistake?

N.: If ignorance is examined in the light of Knowledge, what happens to it?

Q.: I would no longer fear the mirage.

N.: If you look for darkness with light, what happens?

Q.: I would find that it is an absence.

N.: It is an absence. "Illusion" does not mean something that is temporarily appearing, though a temporary nature is a sure sign that something is an illusion, for Reality always is without exception and without interval. Although illusion is temporary, and all temporary things are illusion, this does not mean that something that is temporary really exists, whether such be the ego, the mind, the world, or anything else. In your quest for Liberation, consider how real the Reality is, how absolute the Absolute is, and also how illusory illusion really is. Know that ignorance is really just ignorance. It is not partial knowledge. The illusion is not partially real.

Q.: There are other words such as "relative."

N.: Even your relatives are unreal. (laughter)

Q.: If there is a sense of reality attributed to such, even if seen incorrectly or partially, the reality part of that is the Absolute?

N.: For purposes of spiritual discrimination, you should discern how unreal the unreal is. There really are not any degrees of reality and degrees of unreality. The Maharshi says that there are no such things as degrees of reality. The Real ever is, and the unreal has never come to be. If you see the truth, you can draw the right conclusion. Nothing is partially yourself. There is the Self, which is what you truly are.

It is of the nature of immutable Being-Consciousness-Bliss and transcends every description and every idea. It is utterly nonobjective. That which is objective and superimposed upon it never becomes part of it. If you would forget that you are a human being and start to regard yourself as some other creature—you may pick one…

Q.: A mouse.

N.: You would never become a mouse. The mouse would never become a man. (laughter) Mousehood would be just a delusion. The man would still be a man, whether he imagined himself to be a mouse or not. No change in the man would take place. The recognition, or the realization, that he was always a man would be all that was necessary. This is simple yet very profound and very thorough.

The mouse would not merge with the man. The mouse would not attain manhood. The mouse would not put up a fight to stop manhood from occurring. The mouse would not be partially real, a temporary occurrence, or an arising mouse. (laughter) There just is not any mouse. It is only a product of imagination. Now, you know the truth of mice and men. (laughter) Apply this internally; it is not really a study of rodents.

Inquire and divest yourself of everything that seems to mark you off as a limited ego. Every time you do that, bliss is revealed all the more. Ignorance vanishes. If ignorance seems to return, inquire more thoroughly, until you are no longer scared of the mouse, even if it is supposedly a fierce mouse. (laughter)

Another Q.: Why is inquiry considered, in this teaching, more potent or efficacious than simply dropping off thought?

N.: Because one can drop all thought or be in a thoughtless state, such as in deep sleep, which everyone has practiced thousands of times, yet no Self-Realization is forthcoming.

Q.: What about being in a thoughtless state while being awake and aware of it?

N.: That would be beneficial.

Q.: Would that give a result different from inquiry?

N.: It would depend upon what the experience would be for the seeker. If that state would come and go, inquiry would be needed to find out for whom it comes and goes.

Q.: It seems that the inquiry also comes and goes. That is why we need to re-inquire.

N.: Does your existence come and go?

Q.: No.

N.: Once the inquiry is off the mental level, it is no longer contained within thought, it does not come and go. It is a path of Self-Knowledge and not a path of thinking.

Q.: Do words such as "Who am I?" still exist?

N.: They are not necessary. The Maharshi says to just put the question to yourself once. If you lose track of it, you can do so again and follow the significance inside.

Another Q.: The Maharshi talks about dissolving the ego-"I." Sometimes, the reference is to the hridyam, the heart, on the right side of the chest. He also refers to it as being without location. He also said that one should concentrate upon the place from which the mind arises. So, that seems to be a point upon which to concentrate the mind. What is your understanding or your teaching about it?

N.: The instructions from the Maharshi that you are quoting, at least in a segmented or partial way, are applicable to different seekers at different times. He said that the heart has no location and that it is neither right nor left. Right and left are an orientation for the body. The description of the heart is found in the Upanishads of the Vedas and is for visualization purposes. When asked whether one should concentrate on such a place, the Maharshi indicated emphatically that one should inquire to find out who he is. Right and left are conceived in your mind. You have no idea of right and left when you are in deep dreamless sleep, in which there is no mind or mental activity. So, the mind cannot be said to rise from that which is its own effect.

When it is said that you should find that place where the mind arises, something else must be meant. It cannot be a place in the body, because the idea of a place in the body is within the mind. This idea occurs in your waking state of mind, could occur in your dream, and definitely does not occur in your deep dreamless sleep. Those are three states of the mind. From where does the mind rise? That is the inquiry. If you find where the mind rises, you find the Heart, which is the quintessence of Being. Being is unborn and consequently imperishable, is not a body, is not in a body, and does not even possess a body.

If you find some kind of meditation with reference to the body as helpful for you, you may feel free to use it. Whether you use such or not, it is essential that you know yourself. When you know yourself, you realize that you have never been born. So, then, what is all this reference to the body?

Another Q.: What has transpired so far in this satsang makes me so keenly aware of the necessity of an authoritative, well-proven in time, well-supported by sages who lived it, teaching that is reliable. That is the guidance to know what it is one is looking for plus how to get there. The further one follows the steps, especially the inquiry, the more one enters into one's Being in which distance disappears. It is a matter of recognizing correctly what still blocks and is next to be released. Without this, it would be next to impossible, unless one has a pattern already setup that has so many experiences preparatory. In the Maharshi's case, who can tell? I do not know what shortened his inquiry to twenty minutes. It was not sheer luck.

N.: No, it is not luck. Luck is a peculiar idea that some people have. While, on a phenomenal level, perhaps, not many duplicate that duration of practice, if one can call such direct experience a practice, it is standing proof of how self-evident and immediately present the real Self is and how there is nothing really obstructing one. If viewed as a goal, the goal is space-like; the path is in the same space and made of the same space. We ourselves are that space-like Consciousness. We should see the space and not the illusion of the vessels or the borders of the apertures.

Sri Bhagavan mentions that inquiry alone does not contain the dualism one is attempting to transcend. It is not necessary to think, "I will inquire, and then I will know what to do." Rather, you inquire, and nothing remains but the one Self, which has been there the entire time. If we inquire, there is no further relinquishing. Who would do any such thing? Who would release what and where and how? The inquiry is simply the self-revelation of the Self. In practical application, it is the negation of everything that is not oneself.

Q.: In your example of the dropping of the cloth or something similar on the wooden platform and asking what would be required to reveal what is really underneath: just removing the cloth, and it is there. That was one of the simplest and most direct revelations one can have from the inner plane.

N.: We simply remove the ignorance, and Knowledge becomes self-evident. We do not attain something new, but that which does not really exist is done away with. If it were really existing, it could not be done away with. Because it has no reality, no actual substance, it can disappear.

Q.: We need the teaching to see what is ignorance in us, because we tend to cling to a thought just because we have been with it for long time. It is a ridiculous reason to cling.

N.: Yes. One thinks that what she thinks is true because she thought it, as strange as that is when you consider it.

Q.: Maybe, somebody told us, and we elected to accept it.

N.: Yes, one cannot really blame others for her ignorance. Even if others presented the idea, you accepted it. You are presented with plenty of ideas, some of which you accept and some of which you reject. One's own delusion and, consequently, one's own suffering are always one's own fault. You cannot blame anyone else.

Q.: That is why we need to discover that it is a thought, and it is not a wise decision. When we are convinced, we are ready to throw it off.

N.: Exactly so. We see something as not our Self, and the identity is clear. When we see that something is unreal, we no longer cling to it. When we see that something is not our happiness, or not the source of our happiness, we are no longer attached to it. Knowledge is all-important. When we regard ignorance as knowledge, we are immersed in it. When one no longer views ignorance as knowledge, but sees ignorance as ignorance, one does not cling to it. The comprehension must be deep. The depth comes by inquiry. The teaching is there. It has been there for ages. You mentioned some "authority." The Absolute Self is the supreme authority. What more authority can there be than the authority of Brahman? There is the authority of all the sages who have gone before.

Q.: Maybe, because we go to school for so many years learning the unreality and systematizing it, one hesitates without a true teacher, a sage. The importance of an ideal teacher is held very high through the ages. It is the confidence that, indeed, the Truth really is.

N.: It is revealed by deep inquiry. If we did not have schooling, the ignorance could still be there. People who have somehow avoided going to school are not necessarily wiser. They might be wiser, but they are not necessarily wiser. Ignorance does not arise from outside, and knowledge does not arise externally. Bondage is not caused by external conditions, and Liberation is not caused by external conditions.

Q.: When everyone seems to represent a certain view, we can still deeply look at the real nature and can see the eternal simplicity?

N.: Yes, but is not "everybody" existing in the same mind that is conjuring up the ignorance?

Q.: That is right. (laughter)

N.: It is like saying everybody in the dream is insisting that the dream is real. When we wake up, we see that it is all our own mind.

Another Q.: The ego springs up and grabs whatever it can muster, whatever the concoction is, and then I start believing it. The root cause is the sense of egoity. I do not think that I can trace that. In my meditation, I do not think that my discrimination was keen enough to see how all of this comes from the ego.

N.: Are you in meditation now, or are you talking about it as if it were an occurrence that disappeared?

Q.: As the observer in the meditation.

N.: Who is the observer?

Q.: (laughter)

N.: Is it the thing that you are trying to get rid of?

Q.: Oh yes, the culprit!

N.: That is the culprit, the thief. He is the one who has no form of his own but who latches on to anything to give himself a semblance of form. The Maharshi refers to it as the inchworm going from twig to twig, or the ghost with no form of its own. Do you believe in ghosts?

Q.: No. (laughter)

N.: How about yourself? Who are you?

Q.: Yes, that is interesting. It is all this complicated stuff.

N.: All the complicated stuff hinges on one thing. One point is the pivot. Can you perceive this? All the ideas and notions in the mind are for you. Clarify the understanding of what that "you" is.

Q.: That means to trace it back to the ego, the individual, or the sense of "me."

N.: You exist, and you know that you exist, now and at all times. Where is the individuality in this existence? Who are you?

Q.: It is a discrimination between Being, or Existence-Consciousness, and the individuality.

N.: The discrimination between what is the Self and what is not the Self, between pure Being and the ego, is inherent in the inquiry.

Q.: Can you say a few more words?

N.: How few?

Q.: (laughter) Let us say forty.

N.: Reality in forty words? (laughter). It has already been given graciously in forty verses (ed. note, refers to the text by Sri Ramana Maharshi), and there is nothing that is going to surpass that.

Be in search of your own existence. If it seems individualized, inquire into the individualized existence, and the individuality, being unreal, vanishes. Whether you perceive your existence as individualized or as something vaster, inquire into the existence, itself. Your aim is to know the Existence. Existence can be known only by itself, because Existence and Consciousness are one and the same. The Consciousness is, itself, the Knowledge. Being is, itself, the Knowledge. Being is its own Liberation.

Inquire to know what Being is. It cannot be known objectively. You cannot stand apart from the Self in order to know, as if it were a known or an unknown object. This is Self-Inquiry, Self-Knowledge. There is no distance to traverse. There is no obstacle between yourself and yourself. If there seems to be a duality, such as of the Self and yourself, the duality rests on the idea of "I," which is some idea of differentiation. Inquire into what appears to be an individualized existence. The Self does not need the inquiry. It already is as it is for all eternity. Who am I? The ego, being completely unreal, vanishes, like darkness in light.

Q.: When I meditate, it seems that it takes time to actually notice what is really the case.

N.: It is of no significance. Time is a figment within the mind. The inquiry and Knowledge take you beyond the mind and show you that in which the mind is not. Self-Realization is not an event. We are not concerned with whether it is slow or fast, sudden or gradual, or takes a long time or a short time. There comes a point at which you see that all the ages are about as long as a daydream lasting three or five seconds.

Q.: It is a matter of driving my mind deeper and relinquishing its forms and misidentifications. When the meditation does not seem to go deeper, is it a matter of noticing what I am holding?

N.: Yes, you can observe what it is to which you are adhering, but then discriminate. Upon discrimination, detach yourself from what you just discriminated as not your happiness, not Reality, and not the Self. All this should be fueled with an intense desire for Liberation. If you have an ardent desire for Liberation, your meditations will be deep. If you are not distracted by your own attachments in your mind, your meditations will be deep. If you keenly discriminate, the meditations will be deep. Other aspects could be added to this, such as the fourfold sadhana or requisites.

Q.: It is the energy or the determination to go past whatever are the obstacles.

N.: If the determination to go past the apparent obstacles to reach Self-Realization is intense enough, everything works out fine. If you intensely desire Self-Realization, in order to find that to be the real state, you will find it natural to sacrifice the contrary notion.

Another Q.: I do not want to go through the rest of my life just having glimpses but seeing through.

N.: What you are saying is within a personal context. Make your vision impersonal. Then, you will view all of this very differently.

Another Q.: Even if we have some insight into Absolute Reality and the Self, the existence of delusion still occurs. We still have thoughts that are limited in order to speak and in order to relate to the world. Do you find that, at one specific point, there is no longer any feeling of attachment or any belief in words or in those forms, or is it just an ongoing process in seeing deeper and deeper?

N.: The question presupposes that the ongoing reality is the forms of experience, whether detached from them or becoming involved with them. Detachment is beneficial in every way, but the ongoing reality is not forms. If you have deep experience or insight—or insight that has become deep experience—and forms recur, it is worthwhile to see which is actually enduring and which is not. From the superficial point of view, it seems as if the deeper experience comes and goes. It would be better to see that the forms come and go. If you then inquire to whom they come and go, you see they never were born to begin with.

Q.: But the existing experience is not identified as the forms.

N.: Experience implies an experiencer. Who is he? According to the form he defines himself by, he experiences a mirror image in what he apparently experiences. If there is an individual "I," there is "this." If he is embodied, the forms are the world. If he is in a mind, the forms are thoughts. Are you in the world? Are you in the mind? Are you "I"?

Q.: But there is still "this."

N.: For whom? Does this declare it exists, or do you say it exists?

Q.: It is just a way of speaking. There is all.

N.: For the realization of Nondual Truth, you may want to examine that more closely.

Q.: You still use dualistic language. All of us still use dualistic language.

N.: Does language make for reality? Whether a phrase or a sentence, a Mahavakya—a great aphorism of the Vedas—is dualistic or nondualistic will be according to the perceiver. If we stand in dualism, everything looks dualistic. If we do not stand in dualism, what then is seen? Words depend on you; you do not depend on words. You give them the validity; they do not give your existence validity. As it is with the words, so it is with all the other experiences that seem—only seem—to come through your senses and your thought. They do not declare their own existence.

Q.: It is just a habit of seeing things as real and declaring their existence. A habit can be seen as a habit, but that does not mean it stops the habit.

N.: When you wake up from a dream, do the dream occurrences continue?

Q.: Not if I wake up. They might go on if I fall asleep again.

N.: What would be the case if you could wake up and not fall asleep again? If you fall asleep again, the dream occurrences seem to continue. They do not necessarily continue from where they left off, but they resume in some form or another. They are dependent upon your state of mind, and they are composed of nothing but your state of mind. Wake up from the present waking state. As the dreaming state of mind composes the entire dream, so your waking state of mind composes all of the waking state experiences, including the subject and the object, you and this. Wake up from the present state of mind. If you want to wake up from the present state of mind, cease to misidentify with and cease to take as real anything in your waking state, such as your body, senses, and your waking state thoughts.

Q.: You say do not take them as real. How?

N.: You see that which exists only by the eye of Existence. There is no more "them." If they appear to be "them," they depend on the "I," for the perceived depends on the perceiver. If the perceiver loses his ego, or individuality, you can determine what is what.

Q.: Where does motivation come from?

N.: Motivation for what?

Q.: For anything.

N.: Such as?

Q.: Why are you giving this talk?

N.: Questions are asked; answers are given. What do you mean by "you"?

Q.: When you are spoken to, you respond.

N.: Yes, but what do you mean by "you"?

Q.: This object in my experience that I see.

N.: A body perceived by the senses. Is that the reality for you?

Q.: It is not the reality, but it is part of the reality that I perceive.

N.: From where does it derive its reality?

Q.: Which?

N.: From where does the part get its reality? It is not there all the time in your experience. If you close your eyes, you do not see a body in front of you. If you were blind and deaf there would be no such experience. From where does the reality come?

Q.: Thought.

N.: When you have non-thought states, do you still have the same experience?

Q.: No. There is a play between seeing Truth and also realizing that the mind works in a certain way. I do objectify certain things but do not believe in that. It is not a complete ceasing of functioning or of perceiving things. It might be a ceasing of believing in sense perceptions?

N.: It is the same idea as before.

Q.: Seeing through is essential, but I do not think it eliminates the working of factors, and dualistic perceptions still occur in the mind.

N.: Self-Realization eliminates the very idea of an existing mind that would hold dualistic perceptions. However, it should be understood that this is a state of Knowledge, and not a state of the senses. It is not an alteration of your senses. It is not a bodily state. So, it is not that you will physically not see the world. You will see that there is no such thing as the world.

Q.: Motivation is not an issue from that perspective?

N.: What motivates the entire universe? Motivation is a personal idea. With the abandonment of the idea of a person, the question also subsides. If you want motivation, act for the sake of all that is satyam-sivam-sundaram—the true, the good, and the beautiful.

Q.: Do you experience desire or motivation to do things?

N.: Things are done. The entire personal orientation is not true. One constant Being is the Truth.

(Silence for a time, then directly to this Questioner:)

Now, you have asked this series of questions, for whatever benefit that you derive from them. If you apply the answers to discrimination within yourself, it will be useful. The purpose of satsang is that we know ourselves. Questions and answers occur because, expediently, they are useful for inquiry. Aside from that, there is no particular value in them. What is comprehended should be realized by direct experience within.

Someone comes here, and it is assumed that he is humbly sincere in finding the Truth. For that purpose, conversation occurs. As for any personal orientation, it is insignificant. What is important is that you know yourself. What has been pointed out to you in the conversation is that it would be worthwhile to question the fundamental premise of the idea of two realities, a higher or absolute spiritual reality, called the "Self," "God," or "pure Consciousness," and some relative reality, thought of as ongoing. That is a concept in the mind. It is not the final Truth. When sages, from the Upanishads forward, spoke of "One without the second," they meant such literally. Rather than adapt the meaning to match a present concept, it is far better to relinquish the present concept, the present state of mind, to experience the original meaning.

(Then followed a recitation in Sanskrit and English of verses from Gaudapada's *Karika* on the *Mandukya Upanishad*, which, describing the Unborn and the Truth of No-creation, proclaim that the Immortal cannot become mortal and the mortal cannot become Immortal, that no modification of one's nature ever occurs, and that birth and diversity appear only because of maya, or delusion.)

(Silence)

Om Shanti Shanti Shanti Om

Perfection

Satsang, July 6, 2003

(Silence)

Om Om Om

(Silence)

N.: Perfect is Being. It is the body that has seeming imperfections, subject as it is to birth, growth, decay, death and the various faults of its activities. Perfect is the inner Consciousness. It is only seeming thoughts that can appear as if imperfect. Perfect is Realization. It is only the imagination of another state that gives the false sense of imperfection.

The imperfect can never actually be tied to the perfect. Otherwise, the perfect would not be perfect. It would be stained; it would be marred or flawed in some way. Perfection is, by itself, eternal, infinite, the Self, and invariable. There is no other beside it. Perfection is realized by the perfection itself. The perfect alone is.

Nothing other than itself can rise from itself. Because it is invariable, actually nothing arises. If we speak of something appearing, arising, etc., from the perfect, only the perfect can be. If it is only the perfect, we again return to its invariable nature. In truth, nothing appears and nothing arises. There, just perfection—infinite, eternal, unborn, uncreated, indestructible, phaseless, and conditionless—is. The perfection is the Self. Realization of this is Self-Knowledge.

At one time, Sadhu Arunachala, who is also known as Major Chadwick, spoke to the Maharshi, raising some doubts and questions he had about reality and unreality, the waking and the dreaming states, and how to examine them to determine what is real and what is unreal. At one point in the conversation, the Maharshi responded to him, saying, "You are attempting to discern or to know the unlimited from the limited. This cannot be done. You must be the unlimited to know the unlimited."

The unlimited is the perfect, the real Self. You must be that in order to know that. Being is not an action. The instruction is not an injunction to do something. Otherwise, the question arises, "How do I be the perfect, or how do I be the unlimited?" Such implies an imperfect entity, called an ego, an individual, attempting to become the perfect. He said, "You must be it," not "become it." What is implied here?

The perfect can alone know the perfect. Brahman alone knows Brahman. The Self alone can know itself. Nobody else can do so. The significance of the Maharshi's statement is that you are not somebody else trying to know the perfect Self. Self-Inquiry reveals the innate, that you are the Self. It is not a transformation of your "self" into the Self, but realizing, in a state of inner Knowledge, the Self as the only identity, the only true "I." Who is the one who now seeks to know the Self, or to attain Liberation? If that one removes the imagined bondage, Liberation is already attained. If the unrealized individual inquires as to what his nature is, the realized Self will be found to be the only existence. The unlimited will know the unlimited.

When you practice inquiry, "Who am I?" what occurs is a resolution into Truth, a dissolution of the false sense of individuality, so that in realizing the Self, the triadic illusion of knower, knowing and known entirely vanishes. It vanishes because it is unreal.

The unlimited knows the unlimited. The unlimited is Consciousness, which is, itself, the Knowledge. The unlimited is the Absolute Being, and unlimited is the Self that so realizes.

What is to be done for spiritual practice? A steady, penetrating, profound inquiry to know who you are. Seeking to know the Self, you inquire as to who you are. In doing so, you, yourself, come to be the Self that you wish to know, and what you wish to know is what you are. The knower, the knowing, the known, the realizer, the realizing, and that which is to be realized, all resolve into a single thing. That single thing is the infinite and the eternal, and it is the Perfect.

What knowledge rises from the perfect? Only the perfect Knowledge of the perfect arises from the perfect. It is full. The characteristics of the illusion of another state other than the perfect fullness of the real Self are the false sense of being bound or limited in some way, starting from the notion of an "I," the thinking that you are bound by any thought and defined by any thought, and being defined in terms of the body, that is, to be misidentified with the body. Consequent on such misidentification come suffering, attachment, and all the rest of samsara. The characteristic signs of turning inward is the dissolution of all that which has just been mentioned. Therefore, inquire within yourself, "Who am I?"

Coming to know yourself, perfection alone is. We do not manufacture or newly compose the perfect. Indeed, if you want to realize the perfect, examine the imperfect. Wherever there is bondage or suffering, examine what is seemingly imperfect, whatever the limited identity appears to be. If you examine the limited identity, it falls away as being false. It is maintained only by the lack of inquiry. When you inquire, your connection with it vanishes, upon such examination. It is light used to examine darkness. The darkness vanishes wherever you place the light. The result: the unlimited, the perfect, remains.

(Silence)

Q.: It is discouraging when I notice the sense of being the sensory being in the center of the senses. I still feel bound by this sense of being a sensory being. I am also able to see this seeming individual and ask who knows this individual. When I take that path in meditation, it is not remotely frustrating. More thoroughness is called for.

N.: If you wish to transcend the seeming present state, there is nothing disappointing or frustrating in being able to perceive some tendency of ignorance or some continuing delusion. If you do not perceive it and go on living in it, that could be frustrating. What you can perceive, you can step beyond. Is it not so?

Q.: Yes.

N.: The ability to perceive the presently appearing delusion is the doorway to your freedom or Liberation. So, from now on, whenever you perceive some misidentification, tendency, or attachment, rejoice rather than be frustrated, for you can address it more thoroughly than previously. That means much more freedom is going to be yours.

You speak of being a sensing entity, as someone who is at the center of all the senses. Ask yourself if this is true. Are you a sensing entity?

Q.: It seems to be so, but, at the same time, there is this distance from where I am looking at this sense of being a sensing entity.

N.: You know the sensed, what is seen, and what is heard, etc. You also know the sensations, the seeing, the hearing, etc. Such are subtler than the things seen, but you know if seeing is occurring or not. Who knows about that? He is not the senses. He is not even the mental cognition of the senses, which includes the idea of being located in relation to them. You are aware of that. You cannot be what you are aware of. So, where is the sensing entity?

Q.: The sensing entity is something in the imagination, and there is still this knower that is always present, regardless of what is happening, sensing or not sensing.

N.: There is this perpetually existent knower, who is not anything seen, heard, touched, tasted, smelled, or anything cognized in thought. This one knows all of the senses as they come and go. He also knows all of the thoughts about the senses coming and going, including the fictional notion that his identity is tied to the object portion. The knot is an illusion. It is the illusion that the knower is what is known, that the Self is what is sensed or what is thought of in terms of the senses. You can cut the knot by inquiry. Be thorough.

You know about your senses when you are awake. Isn't that true?

Q.: While dreaming, I have my dream senses.

N.: So, they correspond to the particular state of mind.

Q.: Yes.

N.: When your mind is in deep dreamless sleep, there is no sense activity. What you refer to as your senses is really a kind of mental activity, isn't it?

Q.: Yes, and that is very clear.

N.: Then, you never have sense activity. It is just a particular way of the mind.

Q.: Yes.

N.: There are thoughts that are abstract and thoughts that are seemingly concrete. The seemingly concrete ones are your senses. They are just a mode of mind. The entire universe is in your mind. If the entire universe is in your mind, where are you located, since you are the knower of the mind? Meditate upon this, until the vast Truth is so realized that you never take up residence in such a transient thing again.

Another Q.: There is some confusion for me. I used to have something to practice. Now, I look at the individual, and he is still there, but there is nothing for him to do.

N.: What do you mean by "he is still there, but there is nothing for him to do"?

Q.: The reality seems to be readily available and timelessly there.

N.: What of the individual? Which one are you?

Q.: Wishing for it to go away must be of the individual, which gives confusion.

N.: Then, the individual is himself his own confusion. He is the source of it. He is the container of it. He alone suffers in it. If, by any means, he subsides, a blessed state without confusion shines. How are you going to get the individual to disappear?

Q.: Some structured relationship to the world is necessary. Without the individual, everything would be wide open, and no one would be in control. That goes against everything the individual is structured upon.

N.: Does the individual control the world?

Q.: He seems to.

N.: The whole world?

Q.: He compartmentalizes everything to reduce it to a logical thing that works, but it does not.

N.: How would the individual control the world? Does he choose the moment of his birth?

Q.: He imagines that there is some kind of structure and that he has a part in all this.

N.: What is his part?

Q.: A very small part, but that is important for him.

N.: How small? Considering the eons and the universe, exactly what is the significance of the individual?

Q.: The reality is so immense, so unfathomable, and wondrous that the individual says, "It is too good."

N.: Is that individual you?

Q.: It is the one who is asking the question, but it is not the one I really am.

N.: Are there two of you?

Q.: No.

N.: Continue inquiring into the singular sense of existence, and you will see what the value, the worth, the importance, the significance, the power, the size, etc. of the "individual" is. If he is all-important, the ruler of the world, certainly this will become evident to you. (laughter) If he is not the ruler of the entire universe, this will also become self-evident. If he does not count at all in the scheme of things, this will become obvious. There is no sense in talking about the individual as if he were an established institution that goes by its own power, that it is self-existent, or that it is another entity with an awareness of its own. All of that is theoretical. Just find out who you are. Then, we will see if there is an individual to plague you or the rest of the universe. Put the question again, more deeply than before, to yourself, "Who am I?" so that you realize the singular Existence, which can be neither an object nor an individual, and which has no duality in it.

Q.: I have had the experience of being quiet in which everything is fine.

N.: Yes, in the silence in which there is no "I" is perfection.

Q.: After that, the individual says, I must be doing something wrong.

N.: How can the individual arise from the silence? How can the imperfect arise from the perfect?

No one obligated you to be the spokesperson for the ego. (laughter) You do not have to explain him, excuse him, or devise theories for his existence and his potency. All that you need do is to find out who you are, and that ghost-like illusion vanishes.

Another Q.: I think of being a mother, a wife, a grandma, and such. I should see these to be just thoughts and remove my identity from that. Eventually I will get to a point at which there is no identity. If I identify with these patterns of thoughts, I create an individual.

N.: The individual, or ego, is a falsehood. God is the Reality; the ego is a superstition. It is attributing power and existence to something that does not exist and has no power. Since it is a fiction, an absence, what gives it a semblance of being solid? The Maharshi says: vasanas (tendencies). The tendencies are composed of various thoughts. When those thoughts are repeated, such is a tendency. When you think the pattern and give it reality, identity, and you think that your happiness or peace is connected to it, you have a vasana, or tendency. The Maharshi says that you must destroy all the vasanas, or tendencies, in order for there to be Liberation. When you examine these tendencies, these various identities, what happens? You remove all the supports of, or the attire wrapped around, this empty phantom. It becomes apparent to you that there is no one in the center of them. Then, the inquiry, "Who am I?" penetrates to the core, to the heart, and what you really are becomes obvious. The destruction of tendencies is inherent in the inquiry.

Someone puts on all the identities. That one is none of the identities. If an actress finds that she is not any of the parts and ceases to be the actress, will the play go on?

Q.: No, the play would not go on because there is no one there to play it.

N.: Similarly, if the identity is clarified, the tendency will not be there, and the various actions that came forth from ignorance no longer occur. Rather, there is knowledge based on the Truth, and everything that is true, good, and beautiful manifests, but you, yourself, remain transcendent of such manifestation.

In inquiry, emphasis is placed on negation. You negate what is not the Self, and the Self knows itself. It remains as the residuum. Remove the covering, and the residuum, which was the substrate, is already there, known by itself.

We do not attain the Self. The Self is already attained. It already exists. We simply remove the confusion of mistaking the Self to be what is not the Self, "I" with what is not

"I." Destroy the tendencies. You destroy them by inquiry. There is really no difficulty in this. Any apparent difficulty is only prior to the commencement of actual inquiry. When you inquire, whatever the obstacle and however tenacious its grip seems to be, it dissolves.

Another Q.: How to increase the devotion towards realizing the true Self? I read scriptures everyday, think about it, try to repeat mantras. Even when I am working, I try to keep it in the background. How to take it to the infinite?

N.: The yearning you now express will bring it about in due course. You do all these good things, yet something is not quite satisfied. You yearn for the infinite. The yearning will make itself come true. Let that yearning be very strong. It should be like a fire.

Q.: It comes on and off. Sometimes, the intensity is strong, but most of the time it is not.

N.: But it has risen to the point that you now ask this question.

Q.: The question is going on for quite some time.

N.: So, it has some enduring power. (laughter) Generating the present line of questioning, this yearning, already has root in you. It is not possible to accurately measure it while one is engaged in practice. By the time it causes you to raise such questions, to approach this teaching and to give yourself to it, and to read scriptures and keep them in mind, it is already doing its work. Verify what you read in the scriptures within yourself. The prime method of verifying the truth of the scriptures is Self-inquiry. In meditation, attempt to see where in you what the scriptures describe is true. The scriptures describe the nature of the Atman, or Brahman, as infinite, eternal, etc. In meditation, attempt to find that in you which is infinite and eternal. You may find some discrepancy and think that you do not feel infinite. The scriptures tell you, "That you are. You are the infinite." What causes you to be apparently finite? Because of the yearning to be the infinite, you become ruthless in the destruction of the finite, which means ruthless in the destruction of the ignorant tendencies, the vasanas, that perpetuate the illusion of being a finite being, a limited jiva, when actually you are Brahman. You are familiar with the method of inquiry, so put it fully into practice. If there is great desire for Realization, to be the infinite, and you are blessed with the knowledge of inquiry, you are well equipped. Use what you have.

Q.: Every time I go to Tiruvannamalai, Arunachala Hill, I cannot make much difference between a normal hill like Santa Cruz and Arunachala hill. Is there something wrong in what I perceive?

N.: Just attend to the Self, and the significance of Arunachala, Siva etc., becomes obvious.

Q.: I am trying that, but it is not going far enough to differentiate.

N.: It is not essential that you have a particular experience when being at Tiruvannamalai. The Maharshi said, "Where is Tiruvannamalai?" Isn't it in the same Self as all else? That Self ought to be known. He proclaimed in a verse that A-ru-na stand for Being-Consciousness-Bliss. Being-Consciousness-Bliss, which is unmoving, achala, is to be known. If that is known, Arunachala Siva will shine as "I-I" within your heart, even if you never see the hill again.

There is the outer manifestation or symbol, and there is the inner significance. If we have a particular experience with the outer symbol, it is all right. If we know the inner significance of the outer symbol, this is what is important. If we realize ourselves to be the inner significance by a path of Self-Knowledge, we are at the very origin of the symbol. You are yourself the symbolized. This is the state at which to point yourself. This is the pilgrimage to make.

If you realize yourself to be the immovable Self about which all the universes spin, that is the pradakshina. If you realize your nature to be Consciousness, which has no beginning or end, no top or bottom, but which is ever shining with the Light that cannot be grasped by any mind or the senses, you, yourself, are Arunachala, the infinite column of Light wherein you have merged with That. This is the subsidence of the false, limited individual, so that the perfect, the unlimited, alone remains. Dive within. You will find everything you need there.

Another Q.: I want to proceed like I am waving away smoke and fog with vigor, but not that there are solid things that tug and pull against my investigation. I want to see their unreality but never attribute to them a separate solidity that I invented in the first place.

N.: If that can be done, it is all well and fine. If some illusion seems to be as if solid, you still must overcome it. However solid the fog seems to be, you still must remove the fog from your mind. Of course, to see that it is not solid, that it is only a figment of your mind, is one of the best steps you can take to remove it.

Q.: I pick some little guy in the center of the tapestry. I invest things with the real, the happiness and its possible loss.

N.: The gain and loss are for the pseudo-individual. Is he you?

Q.: I certainly hope not. (laughter)

N.: Find out. Do you observe him from somewhere else? Is the individual your continuous experience?

Q.: No. The tapestry comes in a way that it is different every moment.

N.: Like a daydream and another daydream and another. There are different scenes, but the scenes occur within you. Within the scene, appear the seer, the seeing, and the object, and you are identifying with one part. The entire scene, though, is in you, like a movie on a screen. What are you going to do to abandon the misidentification with the particular character who has gain and loss, pain and pleasure, and such?

Q.: I can investigate that directly, but I want to always wonder who and where I am really.

N.: Use close examination, accept only the facts that are well proved, and use good reasoning. Apply such to your mind, and see who you are. It would not be reasonable to conclude that something that is not continuously present in your experience is yourself. Since you already have, as a basis of fact, the continuous Existence that you are, do not accept anything that is just a hypothesis. (laughter) You would not build a structure very theoretical in character without any experiment to prove it. You have already conducted experiments; such are all the experiences of your life thus far and anything that came before, if you remember. All you need to do is to draw the proper conclusion. Science marches inward. (laughter)

Q.: I enjoy your humor on this. Another principle in this is to respect the independent corroboration of other investigators when it is a preponderance. If sages and seekers, throughout all places and times, keep coming to the same conclusion, that is worthy of much respect.

N.: Then, you need only repeat their experiment. (laughter)

Another Q.: I take myself to be two things. I take myself to be an entity, and there is the first and the second.

N.: Can you be two? Can you be the Self and be another self? Can you be the individual, who is apparently limited, trying to get to the Self? If you inquire, this limited identity and the mind that so conceives are blown away like clouds that disappear into the sky. What remains is the vast space of pure Consciousness, which is not two.

Q.: When I meditate, I see that I cannot be what is

objective. Yet, all the rest of the time, I take myself to be this illusive, objective stuff. It is only certain, not all, objective stuff.

N.: Which certain objective stuff do you think yourself to be?

Q.: The body and the mind.

N.: Are you the body?

Q.: No.

N.: You just said that you take yourself to be that. That was a quick turnaround. (laughter) A moment ago, you said you take yourself to be the body. I asked a simple question, "Are you the body?" and you said, "No."

Q.: I think that I am the body sometimes. (laughter)

N.: At which times do you think you are the body?

Q.: I do not know which times.

N.: You said sometimes. Do you have it marked on your calendar or on your computerized schedule as the time to misidentify with the body? (laughter) When do you become the body?

Q.: When do I become the body? This sounds like a trick question.

N.: It is actually matter-of-fact. You said that there were times when you misidentify, or become, the body. So, I asked when do you become the body. Point out any time when or any incident in which you actually become the body. Do you ever become the body?

Q.: I only think that I am the body.

N.: There is no change in existence and no change in the actual identity. You can think a thought that you are somehow connected with the body, but that is just a thought of such. It is made of imagination and does not change the fact of your existence. It does not modify your existence. Is this evident to you?

Q.: I try to meditate on it. It does not seem that I am anything finite.

N.: Whatever is your nature is ever the same. You do not change your nature. If Existence would become anything, even the least bit, other than what it is, it would be destructible, and it would not be actual Existence. Existence does not cease to exist. The Real does not become unreal. The Self does not change into something that is not the Self. If you are bodiless at one time and apparently endowed with a body at another time, that state of being endowed with a body is nothing more than a delusion. That which you are always remains. What comes and goes cannot be your identity, cannot be yourself. The body obviously comes and goes. The idea of being associated with it also comes and goes. None of that can have anything to do with your Existence. Know the truth of it. The same holds good with everything else objective. You mentioned the mind. It is not with you all of the time. Only that which is with you all of the time is you or yours. What is it that is there all the time, while waking, dreaming, deep asleep, living, and dead? What is it that is there all of the time? The unalterable is the immeasurable.

If you are trying to eliminate what is objective from your identity, do not harbor the idea that the Self you wish to realize is objective. Make your vision nonobjective. Do not treat the Self as if it were something objective, removed from you, as if it would come about at another time.

Q.: Can you explain more how I would do that?

N.: Consider the perspective with which you initiated the dialogue. Look at the stance of your mind, in the manner in which the question was raised. Can you see how you treat the Self as if it were something objective or removed from you? You ask the question from the position of the limited individual, who is sometimes caught in the body, sometimes not, etc. but are you such? There is nothing wrong with raising the question. Make your vision nonobjective.

Q.: It is a matter of trying to remove ideas. One idea is that the Reality comes and goes, and another is that, in practice, I try to get from one point to Reality.

N.: Do not artificially put a distance between Truth and yourself and make believe that you are some bound person at a distance from it or imagine an obstacle between you and that which you are seeking to realize. If you know better, dwell in that better knowledge. If you really know that you are not the body, that you cannot be the body, there is no necessity to pretend otherwise.

Q.: Acting, talking, I think that I cannot have this knowledge of not being the body or the mind when they are active.

N.: You are talking right now. Are you becoming the body?

Q.: I am not becoming the body.

N.: You are not it even while speaking right now. So, where is the difficulty? Speaking, you are still silent. You are not the body; you are not a portion of it called the mouth, which does the talking. The same holds true with all of the other limbs, etc., for action. You blinked the eyes just now. Did you become the body?

Q.: (laughs)

N.: Now, you are laughing. Did you become the body?

Q.: I should inspect the experience. It cannot be that any bodily experience changes it.

N.: If you thoroughly inquire, you see that no bodily experience changes your nature, that you are not the body, that you are not in a body, and that you do not have a body.

Q.: That makes it complete.

Another Q.: That is because he realizes that he never becomes the body?

N.: His Existence has not changed. He only needs to know his Existence as it is.

Q.: In all of these questions, you were asking him if he ever became the body, and he was not able to answer.

N.: Because it does not happen. We are never born.

(Then followed a recitation in Sanskrit and English from the *Prasna Upanishad*.)

(Silence)

Om Shanti Shanti Shanti Om

Silent Being Ever Is

Satsang, July 13, 2003

(Silence)

Om Om Om

(Silence)

N.: Being always is. This is the Self, and this alone is. This Self is of the nature of unformed, unending Existence, nonobjective Consciousness, and perfectly full Bliss, which is utterly nondependent.

The Maharshi has said in a verse, "What is the use of knowing all else without knowing oneself? What else is there to be known or to know when the Self, itself, is known?" One real Being ever is. It is all in all at all times. Truly, it alone is. There is no alternative and no other thing.

To know that there is no alternative to the Self, that it is One without a second, is Liberation, which means the absence of all the imagined bondage. All that is necessary is the Knowledge of Being, which is silently present always. Silence is indicative of its unborn, uncreated state, or nature.

As it is Reality, it is invariable. It does not undergo any kind of modification. Nothing rises for it, and nothing sets for it. Nothing comes out of it. Nothing goes into it.

If you attempt to know anything else, through the senses or the thoughts of the mind, what do you actually know? Without knowing yourself, won't your view of yourself go into the view of anything else? According to the definition ascribed to yourself, so is the view of everything else, be such the world, God, or anything else.

If you know yourself as the real Being, which is Consciousness, you realize that you have no form, be such of a body or of a mind, and not even so much as a trace of individuality, or an ego. The more your definition diminishes by virtue of an inquiry to know yourself, the more expansive you find yourself to be. If there is no definition, you, yourself, are infinite. Being infinite, there is nothing apart from you. You find yourself to be the one Existence, which solidly is, as Ribhu says, "A mass of Existence, a mass of Consciousness," yet which is space-like. It is all-pervading to such an extent that there is no pervader and pervaded. It saturates everything everywhere.

Just this nondual Reality must be known. Realization of it is Knowledge of it. Knowledge is that which transcends what is sensory and what is conceptual. Knowledge of the Reality, the infinite and eternal, comes by Knowledge of oneself.

If you know yourself, there is no triadic division of knower, knowing, and known. That which is to be known and the one who seeks to know are the same. When you know yourself, Reality comprehends itself. Brahman knows itself.

The direction in which to proceed is immediate, for it is yourself. What is to be practiced is direct inquiry to know the Self: "Who am I?" The result is utterly nondual, which is that which is always. Examine yourself thoroughly. Commence with your existence, for that is most immediate. Where you commence is where you wish to end.

Commence with your existence and examine it. You cannot see it as something objective. Indeed, you must give up the objective outlook in order to know it. Negate everything that is not a true definition of yourself. That much being accomplished, all is accomplished.

Spiritual instruction serves the purpose of revealing the unreality of the perpetually unreal. The Reality just is. When you see the unreal as unreal, the Reality knows itself. The nondual conclusion about this should be self-evident.

Q.: I have experiences of the world and discerning truth in it. I am puzzled about the relationship between the real part of it and the unreal or transient part of it. What is the relationship between Reality and unreality?

N.: How can there be a relation between the unreal and the Reality, since one never exists and one always exists. Whatever is transient is unreal. Whatever is dependent is unreal. Whatever is not self-evident but is known through something else, such as the mind or the senses, is unreal. Whatever is divided or differentiated is unreal. Whatever has a beginning and an end is unreal even in the middle. Whatever is objective is unreal. Whatever depends on or comes after an "I" is unreal. Discriminate along these lines while inquiring.

There cannot be a relation between that which always is and that which never is. Jaganmithya (jagat-mithya), the world is false. It is also declared to be asat, nonexistent. The two statements mean the same. If we can see that it is utterly nonexistent, for one Existence alone is, that suffices, as it is clear, simple, silent Truth. For others who want to know what "this" is, it is taught that there is some existence that is not seen through the senses and not cognized in the mind, just as there is existence even in your dream state, but the actual existence is the one thing that is invisible and not perceived in your dream. The one thing that composes it entirely is the one thing that cannot be perceived. Likewise is it in the waking state, which has the identical mental fabric of subject and object and the means of perception and such. It is a different state, but the modes of mind are very similar.

The world is said to be false. There is existence, but it is not seen. What is seen is what is not there. What is not seen is what is there. Existence is. The direct way to realize the Existence is to know that that which you regard as the "world"—which you may view as real, partially real, temporarily real, or something similar—depends upon you. You try to determine what it is. The Maharshi says, "It does not declare its own reality. You must say that it is real." All the light and the quality of reality in an experience comes from you. The reality quality comes from your Existence. The light that knows it is your Consciousness. The happiness that appears in it, at any time, is your own Bliss. When that which is objective is mingled with it, such is superimposition, which is characteristic of delusion.

See that all that is referred to as the "world" depends on you. Who are you?

Q.: So, the question is, "Who?"

N.: Exactly so. You want to know about it, but there is no "it" to be known. Realize this by asking, "For whom is this?" and then, "Who am I?" The sense of reality, the sense of identity, and happiness return to their rightful place. They never actually leave that place, but, in illusion, they seem to be elsewhere. Dispense with the illusion by the direct inquiry, "Who am I?" Seeing the Self, Reality is seen. The Maharshi declares, "What else is there to know or be known when the Self itself is known?" Therefore, there is no relation to be established. Such could be only if there were two. Can there be two?

Q.: I have the idea of One but the experience of the world, too.

N.: The world cannot be without the Self, but the Self can be without the world. The Self is formless. It is not the body. How can there be form in the formless? How can there be unreality in the Reality?

Q.: The one light is Sat. The world rises for the Self. I want to see clearly that the world is unreal and to see that there are not so many selves.

N.: The invocation to the *Supplement to the Forty Verses on Reality* says, "That in which this universe is established, to which it pertains, out of which it arises, for which it exists, by which it comes into being, and which it really is, that is the self-existent Reality, the Truth. Let us worship That in the heart." You may wish to meditate on all the aspects of the verse.

If we say that the world rises for the Self, how does this change occur to the Self? If the Self is changeless, what rises? This is to be experienced. There is no use attempting to figure out what it is. The "this" part of the experience is utterly dependent on the "I." This is so whether "this" is regarded as the world or as thought. Attain clarity regarding the nature of the perceiver, and then you can be concerned with "it," if there still is an "it."

Another Q.: If there is something else, it is only from That, of That, for That, and returning to That. In Reality, there is nothing out there.

N.: All such description is to resolve the view into nonduality and does not indicate the existence of something else. Because the aspirant comes with the idea of something else, nonduality is revealed. The purpose is to bring about the Realization of That and not to give a new name to "this."

Q.: The experience of That is intermittent for me. If I contemplate and meditate upon it, inquire into it, the experience is present. There are notions and misidentifications to be removed.

N.: Yes, you are giving yourself good advice. (laughter)

Q.: I need to be more intense in my questioning.

N.: Determine, by fine discrimination, what causes your higher experiences to come and go. You will find that what you experience, now regarded as coming and going, is actually continuous. That to which you think you return as if it were a continuous reality is discontinuous unreality.

(Silence)

Another Q.: Sometimes my inquiry to trace the chain of ideas and misidentifications is successful and sometimes not. Usually, I trace the misidentification to a personality, with some history or with a body sensation. Does it need to be more specific?

N.: Your discrimination should be at least as specific as your illusion.

Q.: When I discriminate, it is very clear that this is unreal. I do not think that it needs to be more specific than that to disidentify from it. Does it?

N.: Does the misidentification continue?

Q.: No, it usually does not.

N.: Then, it is sufficient. Experience becomes the validation. Where exactly do you keep these chains?

Q.: I do have a notion that they have a location and that they come in and out of it.

N.: Where is the location now?

Q.: It isn't anywhere. As soon as I look at it, it disappears.

N.: What remains?

Q.: It is more a sense of oneself. A sense of peace.

N.: Where are you bound?

Q.: Somewhat by the body.

N.: In what way does your body bind you?

Q.: By connection with some of the things that it does.

N.: You are scratching your neck right now. Are you connected to that?

Q.: No, no.

N.: In what way are you connected to the actions of the body?

Q.: There is no connection. I want to stay there.

N.: When you say that you are not, do you actually become connected?

Q.: No.

N.: So, what is your relation to the body?

Q.: None.

N.: Are you sure of this? Is there certitude?

Q.: Hopeful certitude. (laughter)

N.: Hopeful is good. It leads to faith. Faith becomes conviction with the addition of Knowledge. Are you the body?

Q.: No.

N.: Then, how can its activities be connected to you?

Q.: Something says that they are connected.

N.: What is that something?

Q.: It must be the mind, the ego, that gets into the picture.

N.: Is that your experience?

Q.: I am left with asking who it is that says it. I say it. I am trying to figure out why a real "I" would say that.

N.: You have a sense of existence. It is not caused. It was not born when the body was born, and it does not die when the body perishes. You exist. Its knowledge of itself is, likewise, uncaused and one with the Existence. You exist, and you know that you are. Is that Existence a body?

Q.: No.

N.: Is it located in the body?

Q.: (after a long pause) No, but…

N.: You need to inquire into this.

Q.: Yes.

N.: Is this Existence your senses? Does this Existence continue unmodified whether there is seeing or not seeing, hearing or not hearing, touching or not touching, and so on?

Q.: It is clear to me that it is separate and not dependent on such.

N.: So, it is not the senses. It is not the physical body. Your senses appear to be located in a body, which is perceived only by the senses.

Q.: I also have a concept of a "body" that is separate from the senses.

N.: Yes, there is a mental concept that puts the disparate parts together.

Q.: Yes, it glues them together.

N.: Like in a dream. Return to the Existence. Though the senses perceive the body, apart from which there is no body, they seem to have their abode in the body. An imaginary nexus point for those senses is your supposed location. Is it true? Inquire deeply into this so that you know it experientially through and through.

Teachings of final Knowledge, Vedanta, as nondual, or Advaita, as they are, are yet very reasonable to the intellect. With the intellectual apprehension, go into the experience. Trace your identity. Trace your very existence. See if it has any relation to a body. Is it in a body, out of a body, located in a body, equated with a body, or does it have any of the characteristics of the body? Inquire in the same way with the senses.

Q.: How would I inquire in relation to a bodily sensation?

N.: You feel the wind on your face. You do not feel wind on your Existence.

Q.: The Self is said to be simple. I keep trying to identify with something. That is the objective view.

N.: Maya (illusion).

Q.: In my existence, there is just nothing.

N.: It is not mere nothing.

Q.: Yes, it is not nothing, for the experience of it is very clear, but it is not an "it." That is the only way I can speak of it.

N.: Who is apart from it that he now tries to speak of it?

Q.: This person.

N.: That is the "spurious ghost with no form of its own," as the Maharshi says, which seems to tie the pristine Being, or pure Consciousness, with the body. That is known by the name, "ego."

Can you be two? Existence is innately singular. Be thorough in your inquiry and as specific as is necessary. Let your discrimination be precise. What now seems to be of the nature of fine precision will later be seen to be self-evident and so simple.

Another Q.: The Self seems solid, but not like a material thing.

N.: (Silence)

Q.: I should keep removing everything until there is nothing left except the Self?

N.: Can there be an outer confirmation?

Q.: There is none.

N.: It is self-evident Self-Knowledge.

Q.: I thought that I have certain things that I need to work on. Is there nothing to work on?

N.: Be thorough. Be deep. The Maharshi says that, for Self-Realization, we should eliminate all vasanas (mental tendencies). That means all the tendencies to misidentify and to become attached. When the tendencies no longer hold sway and you no longer conjure them up, and thus such have ceased to exist for you, your freedom is there. While scriptures and sages reveal it and confirm it, it requires no outer approval. It is self-evident, just as, now, you do not ask anyone, "Do I exist?" It is obvious. When the knowledge of your freedom and your peace is identical to the knowledge of your Existence, and equally self-evident, there is completion and perfection. In the removal of any particular vasana, the same should be the case. The path-knowledge and the end-Knowledge are of the same nature.

Another Q.: Traditionally, one should have a guru. The Maharshi says that one must have a guru. What is your view? Did Ramana Maharshi, while he was alive in the body, have recognition of a Guru Purnima day?

N.: I do not know if the day, Guru Purnima or Vyasa Puja, or to what degree the day, was celebrated at Sri Ramanasramam. You say the Maharshi has stated thus, and you ask my opinion. My opinion does not matter.

Q.: Oh!

N.: Sadguru (Sat-Guru) is one who is a true Guru who reveals the Truth. Sri Bhagavan is such a Sadguru. When there is such Truth, what is the point of anyone else's opinions?

Q.: "Sadguru" refers to one's own inner guru.

N.: Sadguru exists where "one's own" no longer exists. The idea that there is an outer guru and an inner guru, as mentioned in some teachings, is just expedient instruction for the mind of a seeker who is still dualistically conceiving. The division is made on the basis of the body, isn't it? Once the "I am the body" idea is gone, what is the case? If you are not the body, certainly it is allowable that he is not the body. If you can be infinite and eternal, it is allowable that he is infinite and eternal. If all Knowledge, bliss, and peace come from the real Self in you, it is certainly allowable in his case, too. The distinction vanishes. The disciple vanishes. Is it clear for you?

Q.: Clear.

N.: The Maharshi said that the responsibility of the Guru is simply to reveal his own Existence. That Existence being revealed, there is no other and no duality. No one remains to be confused.

Another Q.: I am unsure of the direction to take for gaining certitude about reality.

N.: Self-inquiry yields certitude. What other direction would you wish to take? What is revealed by Self-inquiry is that which is utterly nonobjective. It deals directly with your own Existence. Since it is your own Existence, it is undivided. Since your own Existence is nonobjective, it is not multiple. By whatever name it may be called, by whatever thought patterns it may seem to be embellished, the Knowledge of Reality and the Knowledge of one's Self are identical. The Maharshi says, "How else is one to realize except by inquiring 'Who am I?'" The meaning of this question should be traced inward. It is completely nonverbal and non-conceptual.

Another Q.: The reason I wish to be very specific in my meditation is so that I can know what is actually occurring. Is this a valid reason?

N.: Yes, discern the confusion that you have conjured up for yourself, which consists of the ideas by which you have bewildered yourself. Then, examine to see if the ideas are true. Who are you really?

Q.: Truth has to prevail.

N.: It always does. At the moment, in the mind, just as in situations in the world, untruth may seem to prevail.

Really, the Truth solidly exists always. The mirage of untruth does not drown anyone. In illusion, it seems as if otherwise. Yet, the Truth is present all of the time. Self-Knowledge reveals it. Untruth never makes so much as a mark, stain, or impression of any kind on the Truth. Nothing has impinged upon your nature. If you are confused, such is only delusion and not a change in your nature. Bliss has not gone elsewhere. Suffering seems to be present in the fruitless attempt to gain happiness in an inverted manner. The illusion seems to be present as the inverted attempt to find what is real. Inquire, and the inversion is destroyed. Blissful Reality reveals itself.

All the misidentifications start with the idea of "I," to which is added the misidentification with the mind, body, etc. Dissolve the delusion from top to bottom, from the root to the branch.

Q.: Whatever comes in the mind is that upon which I meditate.

N.: What comes to the mind?

Q.: All sorts of things.

N.: From where does the mind come?

Q.: The Self? I do not know. It seems like another hallucination.

N.: From one hallucination springs another. The illusion does not come to the mind. It comes from the mind, doesn't it? It comes from the mind to the mind in the mind. It has no outer cause. "Outer" exists only in the mind. There is, therefore, no "outer." All is in the mind. What is conceived as the mind is the erroneous combination of pure, infinite, space-like Consciousness with the imagined, objective forms.

Q.: Go a little slower. I understood, yet I did not understand.

N.: I am not going anywhere. (laughter) We will more slowly remain still. (laughter)

Q.: My mind did not understand.

N.: Which part did you not understand?

Q.: I cannot remember the words.

N.: What is your experience?

Q.: With thought or without thought?

N.: Now, are you with or without thought?

Q.: It seems that there is thought.

N.: Are these thoughts in your mind?

Q.: What do you mean by "mind"?

N.: (laughing) Yes, that is just the question I was asking you: What is meant by the mind? Pure, space-like, infinite Consciousness plus the idea of objective notions or appearances, which exist only in the mind, comes out as "a mind." The idea of "a mind" is only in the mind. It is like a picture of a wall painted on the very wall that is depicted, and the wall has not even yet been built.

Q.: So, what is the nature of thought?

N.: The same nature as that which holds it within it. If the mind is the container, what is the nature of your mind? Everything is in the mind. There is no outside, and outside is only in the mind. The idea of a mind is also in the mind. What is your mind?

Q.: I don't know.

N.: Not knowing is a good state.

Q.: Knowing something is not a good state?

N.: It would be only in the mind.

Q.: As soon as imagination rises, there appears to be someone to have a mind.

N.: Who has the mind?

Q.: That I need to inquire into.

N.: (Silence)

Another Q.: I am fascinated by the teaching that there is no compromise. The one hundred percent quality is fascinating. It is easy to fall into a partial approach, thinking a little percent won't hurt, but it does. I think that I can hold on to this partial view a little longer.

N.: But it will hurt.

Q.: It will prevent Realization.

N.: Will that cause you to suffer?

Q.: There is no advantage to it, at all. It will result in dullness, at best.

N.: Is that dullness a kind of suffering, or are you content with the dullness?

Q.: It is, at least, disappointing.

N.: Are you happy with the disappointment?

Q.: No, not truly. (laughter)

N.: So, your intuition that happiness is your real and natural state will drive you further inward to be complete. I can tell you that there is no purpose in suffering, but I think that you can figure that out for yourself. (laughter)

Q.: So, there should be an alertness to prevent one from having that compromise tucked away somewhere?

N.: Your desire for happiness, which you cannot get rid of but which you can fulfill, prevents you from staying with anything partial. If you meditate to a certain depth and retain some delusion, the desire for happiness, which transforms itself into the desire for Liberation, will cause you to go beyond that remaining ignorance, as well. You will enjoy the greater freedom, but you will not stop until it is complete. In practice, this manifests as a clearer and clearer discrimination, a deeper and more profound inquiry, and a more thorough detachment.

(Then followed a recitation in Sanskrit and English from the Upanishads.)

(Silence)

Om Shanti Shanti Shanti Om

Everyday and Eternity

Satsang, July 20, 2003

(Silence)

Om Om Om

(Silence)

N.: The natural, innate, and only true state of the Self is completely formless, timeless, locationless, unborn, and eternal. It is absolute, and it is the only Reality. Utterly impersonal, undivided, undifferentiated, it ever abides in its own silent peace and its own perfection.

There is no question of anyone realizing it as if it would become more real later. There is no individual who is unrealized, who is other than That, who exists in some other way, as if there were a second reality. For the Self, which is the Absolute, Brahman, is one without a second. Utter non-duality is the simple fact.

All kinds of trouble come from conceiving oneself as an individual and as embodied. As perfect bliss lies in the Knowledge of the Self, the root of all kinds of suffering and bondage is not knowing the Self, or misidentification. Regard yourself as an "I" or as a body, and you have the trouble of bondage and suffering of some kind or another or the possibility of these.

If there is suffering, naturally there is the desire to be happy. If there is bondage, naturally there should be the desire for Liberation. Yet, this blissful Liberation is an impersonal state. The person, that is to say the "I" with the body, does not become the Bliss, does not become perfect, does not become the Absolute, or Brahman, and does not become the Self. The person does not become liberated. You can, though, liberate yourself from the person, from the body, and from the false notion of "I," and realize the Bliss and perfection as innate.

The perfect, blissful Self is not created, and, consequently, it is not destroyed. It is not newly obtained, and, consequently, it is never lost.

Inquire deeply within yourself and perceive what you regard yourself as being. Is it as a body? Or is it as located, or cooped up, inside a body? Is it as with the attributes of body? Is it as of the senses? Is it as with the activities of the body, from birth to death and everything between? Does any of that pertain to you? Inquire deeply and examine yourself. See what seems to constitute the individual identity. There is no liberation for the individual, but, fortunately, you are not that individual.

There is Liberation from the false sense of individuality, which, through mere imagination, has been superimposed upon your real Being. Your real Being is space-like Consciousness, without form, and, consequently, with no boundary. It has no division, so it is homogeneous. There is nothing apart from it, but there is nothing inside it.

Inquire deeply to know yourself. Set aside anything pertaining to the body, whatever is objective, and whatever is sensed as not "I," as not really the Self. Set aside as a definition for who you are everything that depends upon the notion of "I." Sri Bhagavan points out that first there is the "I," and that is integral to every other thought. So, set aside whatever you think about. It does not make a difference if it is past, present, or future. Regard all of that as unreal and not your Self. Who are you?

What you seek to obtain in seeking Self-Realization is not objective to you, and it has not a trace of individuality, of ego, in it. This egoless real state, or real Self, which alone is, is the only actual topic in this teaching. There is not anything else real. The Self is the Self-Knowledge, and there is not anything else that is you. So, it is all about you, from you, and to you.

Because what you are can neither be expressed in a word nor conceived in a thought, for it is nonobective, the Silence for which the Maharshi is so well-known is the most eloquent explanation. All other instruction is merely expedient or auxiliary argument.

Dive deep within yourself and silently realize this singular Truth regarding your Being, the One without a second.

(Silence)

If what has just been stated makes sense to you, dive within and realize its significance by knowing yourself. If what has just been said does not make that much sense to you, do not worry about it, and just make the attempt to know yourself.

(Silence)

Q.: Ribhu says that whatever is known is Siva, and Siva am I. He brings together a variety of definitions and thoughts and shows the common denominator. They are the same in Knowledge. So, after reviewing various helps on the path, he wants one to seek total identity. Is this the purpose of his statement?

N.: Everything that is ever experienced at any time in any state of mind, waking, dreaming, or deep sleep, with thought or without thought, with the senses or without the senses, in life or in death, without exception, is known only in Consciousness. Since nothing is ever known outside of Consciousness, it is only within Consciousness. What is within Consciousness is Consciousness itself, since it does not harbor anything of another nature. Consciousness is the Reality. The Reality does not harbor within itself anything of the unreal. Consciousness, itself, is Knowledge. It is the Knowledge of Self-Knowledge, and, if one thinks of knowing something else, it is that knowledge also, without that other thing ever actually coming to be.

All, without exception, are only Consciousness. The emphasis is on Consciousness. All is just a figment of the imagination, the stuff of dreams. That Consciousness, inherent in which is the power to destroy all illusion and delusion and which, upon such destruction, remains as absolute, forever unmodified, nondual Being is the significance of Siva. Literally, the name means "the auspicious, the good," because of its blissfulness and its perfection. Everything is only That. There is no everything. There is just That. That is Consciousness, and That is what you are. That is the only identity, or "I." So, "I" is the name for Brahman, or pure Consciousness. It is the only identity and the only reality. It is the only lasting happiness. This is the significance of what Ribhu says.

Q.: You have referred to the fact that the path is not like a razor's edge and that it does not become more and more difficult, but rather, at the end, it becomes simpler. Why?

N.: Since ancient times, and as stated in the Upanisads and other texts, the spiritual path has been said to be like a razor's edge. The purpose has not been to make the aspirant feel diffident, but it is to indicate the keen awareness with which one should discriminate between the real and unreal, between what is the Self and what is not the Self. It is indicative of the careful attention that should be given to it. If we consider what careful attention has been given that such teachings have been passed down for millennia, not only through the written and spoken word, but through the minds of those who realized it, the aspirant should meet it with at least the same amount of care, along with humble thankfulness. So, like with a razor's edge, there should be keen awareness and care. Since, though, there is only one Self, and there are not two of you, it is difficult to go astray if one is guided by Self-inquiry and Self-Knowledge. Where would you go? Who would go astray? In light of that, it has been said that it is not like a razor's edge, for it is a path so wide that one cannot fall off. In truth, it is more like space emptying itself into infinite space.

Another Q.: When I take a class about anything, I understand things completely, but the attempt to put Self-inquiry completely into my daily life has not happened yet. I really want it, but the mind goes out, and the ego shows up. I sweep it out, and it shows up again. There are so many gaps.

N.: What constitutes the "daily life"?

Q.: What I want to do is just be. I used to meditate to get rid of thoughts, but I have given up that approach.

N.: Have you abandoned the meditation or abandoned the misidentification that made you previously think that thoughts were real?

Q.: (looking confused)

N.: If you abandon the meditation, but leave the "I" intact, this is not necessarily helpful. It would be better if you abandoned the "I" and remained in meditation all the time.

Q.: I would like to be in meditation all day long.

N.: Then, what makes up "all day long"? This is the meditation right now. What composes the "daily life"? Where does it take place? If you say that it is in the world, where does the world appear?

Q.: When the "I" shows up as the mind.

N.: So, your "daily life" is a product of misidentification?

Q.: (laughing) It would seem so.

N.: If you would eliminate the misidentification, what would happen to your daily life? Would you have one?

Q.: I would not have a life. I would just be.

N.: That is what you want.

Q.: My life would disappear. I am confused at the moment.

N.: You are clearer in your present confusion than you were before in your so-called clarity. (laughter) You said that you wanted to be, and that all that would be left of you would be just your Being, if you eliminated your daily life. You said that your daily life was composed of, or rooted in, the misidentification. It does not occur in the world. The world and your interaction with it occur only in your mind. You must assume some definition in order for all of that to evolve. Trace your way inward, and thoroughly abandon the misidentification.

Q.: When I inquire, everything comes down.

N.: Why not inquire without interruption?

Q.: That is what I want to do. I can do it while cooking and while driving in the car, and the world does not even feel real. There is a being that is dropped in there, perhaps by mistake. (laughing) It is a matter of remembering to do Self-inquiry all day long.

N.: If the inquiry is there, there is clarity. If the inquiry is not there, there is cloudiness. The Maharshi says, "When Atma-vicara, or Self-inquiry, is abandoned, loka vicara, or world inquiry, begins." That is what you call your "daily life."

How did the eternal, infinite Consciousness get a daily life? (laughter)

Q.: That is a good question!

N.: How did God get caught up in the cooking and the driving? (laughter)

Q.: I forget, so many times, that whatever I see and whatever I feel I just conjure up. How can anything happen for the "I" that is illusion?

N.: It is all for "I." As often as you can, trace the experience of whatever appears by inquiring, "For whom is it?" Your view becomes nonobjective, for you give up the objective outlook. "For whom is this?" returns the sense of reality and identity inward. Then, inquire, "Who am I?"

The Maharshi said that, if one would just inquire without interruption, that alone would suffice for complete Self-Realization. If you have a strong enough desire to inquire, it will manifest. Your inquiry will be off the mental level. It is not possible to have your mental attention upon it all the time. It is the nature of mental attention to flit about, to move, even if it is well-concentrated. Just as it is not possible to have thought all of the time, it is not possible to have no thoughts all of the time. Likewise is it for any other mental state. Yet, you exist all of the time. The inquiry must be at the same level as your Existence.

Make the inquiry non-mental. Stay focussed on the "I." Every time that you seem to slip from it, use such to your advantage by having it prompt a deeper, more thorough inquiry. This is especially so if you find yourself returning to the same misidentification as you had previously. A mere break in the thinking pattern is not the goal, though it is fine when such occurs. Cut the misidentification that is at the root of it.

You are not someone who has just been dropped into the world. The "I" and the "world" are both false appearances rising and setting together. Regard both as an illusion, and inquire as to who you are.

Q.: I used to think that it was impossible for me to handle my bank account and do Self-inquiry at the same time.

N.: This is a path of Knowledge. Jnana means Knowledge, or Wisdom. It is not a matter of thinking one way or another. It is not thinking about the Self. It is the inquiry indicated by the phrase, "Who am I?" It is a path of Knowledge. It is a state of Knowledge that you practice.

Q.: That is what I now see.

N.: The Knowledge is one with Being. So, it can be as continuous as Being.

Q.: But I do not do it all the time.

N.: You should inquire into the nature of the "I" that does not do it.

By habitual ignorance, the ego-notion returns. Inquire. If you persevere and are drawn by an intense desire for Liberation, the obstacle of this habit will turn out to be full of holes. It is not the experience of Reality that is full of holes. Though it is space-like, it is solid and enduring. It is the maya, the illusion, the ego, that is just a hole. It appears as full of holes.

Q.: That is true.

N.: It is a joy to go hunting to see just how many holes there are.

Q.: I can see how much debris I have cleared up. The illusory "me" felt good about it.

N.: From where did the good feeling really come?

Q.: From who I am.

N.: Yes. All the happiness lies in one place. The ego has no part in it.

Q.: You have said that love is Knowledge. I understand that now.

N.: (remains silent)

Another Q.: The habit with which we are involved is the misidentification with the senses.

N.: Yes, it is a "bad habit." A habit must belong to someone. Who has the habit? The Self does not have any habit. The body is innocent in all this.

Q.: So, it is a matter of it attaining its own commitment. Becoming aware of that, I should let it disappear.

N.: Yes, but how can that happen? How can something create itself? It does not make sense, does it?

Q.: No.

N.: That is the problem with the ego. (laughter) It just does not make any sense.

Any explanation for ignorance, illusion, or samsara is alright if it prompts us to destroy the illusion, etc. If you say that it is a habit, it is self-perpetuating, it is broken off from the Self, it comes from something else, etc., as long as you wind up taking full responsibility for it and examine it to destroy the illusion, it is all right. In the final analysis, such are only theories for something that has not come to be. All of them are explanations for the snake where there is only a rope.

(Silence)

Q.: The discovery that there really is no individual entity to be enlightened or unenlightened, to be purified or transformed and such, is in itself the wonderful release from the bondage and liberation at the same time. It is just to know that it is a nonexistent entity that has created all this imagination that has never existed in the first place.

N.: The Maharshi says, "Inquiring into the nature of the bound one and discovering his real nature (which implies the absence of the ego), itself is Release."

Q.: Friends of mine say to me, "Now that you have come to this deep understanding, what are you going to do about the suffering in the world? What are you going to do with your life? What are you going to create?" I do not know what to say to them.

N.: It does not really make much difference what you say to them. It is like being responsible to answer the questions of your fellow dream travelers after you have awakened.

Q.: Yes, it is difficult.

N.: It is not difficult. Do you have a difficulty in answering the questions of last night's dream characters?

Q.: (laughing) That is so.

N.: When a person has the doubt that now that he is realizing the non-ego state, what is he to do, there are two

"I"'s in the doubt, or even three, even though one's Existence is utterly singular and indivisible. Such is just a matter of someone not understanding what is meant by "the non-ego state." He has the words but not necessarily the experience, even though their meaning is true about his own nature. Otherwise, such doubts about creating, doing, re-entering into life, etc. would not arise. If the ego would really be gone, all those definitions of doing, creating, etc., and their opposites, active and inactive, life—however it is being defined in the question or doubt—would have vanished. All of that is based on delusion. The realized have no problem with any of that.

It is not important what you answer to the questions of others. It is important that you abide within yourself in Being beyond life and death, as pure Existence, which is neither active nor inactive, as the Unborn, which does not create anything and is, consequently, impershable, in which there are no others—whether they agree with you, or they do not agree with you.

Q.: So, the question is if there is anyone there to agree or not.

N.: Abide in that state which is like waking up from a dream. After you wake up from a dream, the dream happenings, the dream characters, the dream thoughts, the dream subject, and the dream objects are no more. Only the Consciousness, which is the one thing that was not visible in the dream, remains. Consciousness is what is real. That was never bound in the dream. There is no free individual. Remain free from the individual. The dreamer does not wake up.

Q.: That character cannot do anything about it.

N.: It is not a question of whether or not he can do something about it. The dream character never wakes up. Do everything you can do to wake yourself up from the dream character. That is the reason for spiritual practice and Realization.

Q.: Thank you. It is a joy to hear you.

Another Q.: That question, "What is your daily life?" struck me. There are all these things that make daily life. I need to draw the sense of identity away from the body.

N.: After a deep meditation experience, do you actually return to a daily life, as if it were waiting there for you? What is it that is called "daily life"? Would that definition match that of any other living being, or is it just a peculiar set of ideas and sensations?

Q.: The latter definitely.

N.: In the attempt to give such apparent, greater authority or validity, such is called "daily life" or "the world."

Q.: Yes, it is totally my particular perspective. As a body and a mind, I am in the world. It is a combination platter.

N.: A particular perspective in the mind is your combination platter. The ingredients are the misidentification of "I am the body," mistaking the sensations to be real or valid, the imagination that there is something outside—while outside exists only inside—and the mere idea that the outwardly projected, or imagined, so-called life as a personal entity in the world is an on-going reality.

In deep meditation, you are with yourself. It is your own Existence. The delusion is that your Existence is sporadic and the "daily life" is continuous, even though the daily life relies completely on your Existence, but your Existence does not rely on it at all. How can that delusion be?

Q.: It is a big hallucination. I reflect on how these ideas can have any strength at all for they are objective. They are not who I am, but I lend reality to them. I put the energy into the dream. The ideas become real and spin this entire dream world. It then seems real and solid.

N.: Then, do you think that it would be spiritually worthwhile to bring that which is spiritual into your daily life, though not realizing where or what the daily life actually is?

Q.: It is in my mind.

N.: Some people may make a big deal about that. It would be better if they gave up the entire idea of "a daily life" and found out who they are. Whose conception is it?

Q.: I have the idea that, after satsang, I have my daily life.

N.: What constitutes the daily life? What is the definition?

Q.: A body going about in the world.

N.: Is that you? Can you call an animated corpse "you"?

Q.: (laughing) That would be a sad definition for me.

N.: If you mistake it to be yourself, you are going to be sad.

Q.: Yes. It would be grim.

N.: If you abandon the misidentification with the body, what happens to the sadness or grimness?

Q.: There is a big difference.

N.: Your own experience proves the fact as to what is natural and what is unnatural. It is self-evident.

Q.: There is a kind of gravity here drawing all into the infinite. It is definitely a great aid to be here. I want to be sure to take that with me and blow away my "daily life."

N.: If you want to take what you experience in satsang with you, just continue inquiring as to what that "you" is. "Sang" means association. "Sat" means Existence, Truth, or Reality. The Reality always exists. The Truth of it is to be found by constantly knowing who you are. Since who you are, the Self, is nonobjective, to know who you are, negate everything that you are not. Hence, the process of Self-inquiry is primarily negation. It is a negation of that which is unreal, since the real cannot be negated. Continue questioning who you are.

The idea that there is some period of time marked off for meditation and another period of time for the daily life, the Maharshi says, is for the merest novices. A man who enjoys the deeper beatitude experiences it completely differently. Why did he say so? Is not the division into what you refer to as daily life and what is otherwise quite arbitrary? Is it just the body's activities? You are not the body. So what effect could its activities have? For someone who is correctly pursuing a path of Knowledge, activity represents no obstacle, for he is not the body. Active and inactive states are identical.

Even now, that is true for you. There is no alteration in your Existence. An hour from now, your Existence will still be with you, no different than it is right now. Likewise will it be several hours from now, tomorrow, and so on. What is it that seems to change? Your Being does not change. What is it that seems to change?

Q.: My mind changes.

N.: Examine how it changes. See what tendencies it conjures up. Go back the way you came.

Q.: Sometimes I see more clearly, sometimes I do not. The longer the misidentification goes on, the more delusion is piled up.

N.: Yes. If delusive thoughts are not checked, they lead to more delusive thoughts. Do not wait for delusion to wear itself out. You may get a brief respite from it, as in deep sleep when you are not thinking about anything, but that will not, in itself, eliminate the delusion. The longer it goes, the more it multiplies. Do not pursue it, but rather inquire. Do not think that this is your daily life so it is time to be bound. (laughter). The clock does not say that it is time to be ignorant. (laughter) Should we post a sign by the exit that says, "Now entering maya. Now entering samsara."?

Q.: It should read, "Population Zero." (laughter)

N.: It would be ridiculous, for it is the same space inside and outside. There is the same Existence.

Q.: When I meditate that I am not the body, it seems obvious that that is not the case. Yet, I need to take this further, so that I do not become re-attached.

N.: You can see that there is no one at the center of illusion. You can also strip off the various vasanas, or tendencies, of the illusion to see that there is no one at the center. That is what was meant by "more and more holes in the illusion" until you see that there is a vacuum in the center.

You can see that you are not the body. Is there, then, anything external to you? You used to mark off the exterior by your body, the body being the dividing line. Your thoughts you regarded as interior, while sense-perceived objects were regarded as exterior. Now that you know that you are not the body, is there an exterior?

Q.: I need to meditate more on how the senses do not say anything about me.

N.: What do they say about you?

Q.: If I accept them as true because I do not discriminate between the sense experience and where I am located, I start assuming that I am in the body.

N.: Are you in the body?

Q.: No. (laughing)

N.: That was quick. (laughter) So, what do the senses say about you?

Q.: Ahh, nothing really. They are just different pictures on the screen.

N.: Yes, like pictures on a screen. When the show is enacted, nothing really happens to the screen. You are the screen. The sense impressions are the images. They do not stand up on their own, but they never become the screen. Whatever happens with the images does not happen to the screen. Can you be seen? Can you be heard? Can you be touched? Can you be a seeing, hearing, or touching entity?

There is no inside or outside. Or, everything is within.

(Silence)

Another Q.: Scientifically, one's body is never the same from day to day. The cells, tissues, and such are changing even while we are sitting here. It is just an assumption that this is the same body as yesterday or last year. It is a constant flow of change until it finds its end. All these things are so temporary and unreliable in the long run. My main assignment in life is to know who I am. I must get on with it and be done with the illusion that this body will be a reliable friend in the long run.

N.: The body is transient, and we never step into the same river twice. The mind, though, has a contrary idea. All of it changes. Something does not change, but it is not the body. The misidentification with the body is not a safe haven. Sankara described that as being similar to trying to cross a river on the back of a crocodile, mistaking it for a log.

Changeful and transient, we call it ourself, but such is not ourself. We refer to it as our possession, but how long can we hold it?

Existence is guaranteed. If you seek to know yourself, Existence reveals itself to itself. Of that you can be certain. Everything else does not come with any guarantee.

Another Q.: The quality of my daily life is similar to a news broadcast in that it has ongoing drama from one day to the next. It may last for a few days, and then a new story arises. It always has the same star character and the same headline. What is its solution? One of its solutions is to go on vacation, which is an escape from daily life. The vacations turn out to have all the same misidentifications that daily life has. (laughter) It is the same, fruitless, inverted search to get out of the bondage and the suffering by doing the same thing. I fool myself and say maybe I should go very far away to New Zealand, because that is the spot that everyone says is the place to go.

N.: Except those who live in New Zealand. (laughter)

Q.: All of them try to come to California! (laughter) All of this is made of misidentification with the body and with doership. There is a list of things to do.

N.: If you take a break from the circumstances by going to another place, your routine is interrupted. How long does it last until the same mentality returns?

Q.: Sometimes, there is no break. That is a really bad vacation. (laughter)

N.: What you really enjoy is a break from your so-called self.

Q.: Yes. The one I am trying to get away from always shows up on the vacation. (laughter).

N.: The problem is that you always pack that in your luggage first.

Q.: It is a hopeless solution for the problem. So, that question regarding what is my daily life is very powerful.

N.: What truly exists the entire time? What you are thinking of as daily life is not really the ongoing existence. Rather than treating daily life as if it were some sort of established institution, as a reality to which one can add spirituality, which is a completely inverted approach, it is far better to find out whose life it is. Who exists the entire time? From where does all this start? Where is the source of all this?

According to the shape of your mind, so the experience occurs. In whatever state your mind is in, that is the state you enjoy, or otherwise, wherever your body is. Find out what exists every day. If you are trying to go on vacation, you should find out that which is quite beyond the daily life every day.

Q.: What is there before the daily life is conjured up is what I need to ask myself.

N.: Yes.

Q.: That is what I can see when I first wake up in the morning. There is not yet much daily life formed.

N.: So, it is a product of your thinking in the waking state.

Q.: Yes, and tying that to the memories of what was going on in the previous daily life.

N.: Everyone knows how unreliable memory is. Most of your daily life has been forgotten. If you consider how many moments there are in any day and how many days you have lived, how much of it do you remember?

Q.: Essentially, nothing, given the quantity and the memory.

N.: So, you build up a fantasy upon something that is essentially nothing.

Q.: Then, I act upon such.

N.: From where do the continuity, solidity, and identity come? All of that comes from some real source, but the reality of that source is projected upon those impressions in the mind. Those impressions are regarded as if external to you. Then, one has the audacity to declare that such are "daily life." Actually, such have nothing to do with life.

Trace the identity. From where is the sense of reality? From where is the continuity? Such is borrowed. Who is the lender?

If you trace in this way, you will find something that exists always. It is not small. It is for all eternity, in which daily life and the moments thereof are utterly insignificant. It is not sporadic. It is continuous. Realizing it, you find that every single moment is profound. It is bliss, so it need not get away from itself; nor can it. It is you. So, you must know yourself.

(Then followed a recitation in Sanskrit and English from the *Katha Upanishad.*)

(Silence)

Om Shanti Shanti Shanti Om

A Few Dialogues

Satsang, July 27, 2003

(Silence)

Om Om Om

(Silence)

Q.: As I meditate, I find myself caught up in a daydream. I play a part in the daydream. When I remind myself to ask for whom is this thought, the daydream dissolves, yet I am still there.

N.: The waking state experience is like the daydream. The mind functions in the same way, with subject and object. Some portion, which is actually objective, is regarded as if it were your identity. It seems to have a relation to an object. There is an "I," a "this," and the relation between them. As long as the misidentification is there, the daydream of the waking state experience continues. When you inquire "For whom is this?" and your attention is brought to that which is nonobjective, the "I," the daydream vanishes. So it is with the present waking state experience. Consider all this experience as a daydream lasting a few seconds.

Q.: The sense of sight is difficult for me. Meditation with my eyes closed makes it easier for everything to dissolve.

N.: In a daydream, you are endowed with daydream sight, aren't you?

Q.: Yes.

N.: Is it real?

Q.: No, it is not.

N.: It may be your predominant sense within the daydream.

Q.: That is true.

N.: That sense activity is really a function of your mind, isn't it?

Q.: Yes.

N.: Likewise are the present senses. The sensory experience is a mode of mind. When you are not in the waking state, as in deep, dreamless sleep, what happens to your senses?

Q.: They are not there.

N.: Your sight, as well?

Q.: It is not there.

N.: But you are still there.

Q.: Yes.

N.: Are you missing anything? You are peaceful and happy.

Q: Yes.

N.: Whatever existed in deep sleep and which was without sight is even now the same. Existence does not change. It does not cease to exist. If it changed even in the least, it would be destructible. There is something that is indestructible. That is you. That does not change and is not destroyed regardless of whatever state your mind enters, be it waking, dreaming, daydreaming, or deep sleep. That something should alone be regarded as you. The Upanishads call it eyeless, yet the eye of the eye without eyes. Likewise, it is the ear of the ears, yet without ears. Similarly, in relation to the sixth sense of your mind, it is the unknown knower of all that is known. Why should sight be difficult?

Just because you see something does not mean it is there. Have you ever seen an optical illusion or a mirage?

Q.: Yes.

N.: Was what you saw actually there?

Q.: No, it was not what I saw.

N.: You see things in daydreams. If the daydream is sufficiently vivid, the quality of it is the same as now. Yet, it is entirely just a figment of your mind.

Q.: Yes.

N.: Something is not conceived in the mind. That is real. The one thing that actually exists in the daydream or dream is the one thing that is invisible. It is your Consciousness. The present state is similar.

You may either keep your eyes closed all the time in order to maintain your meditation to make it perpetual (laughter), or you can see that this in which the senses are contained is your mind, and find that in which your mind is contained. All this that is seen by your eyes is in the space of your mind. The space of your mind is within the space of Consciousness. You are the space of Consciousness. You are not what is seen by the eyes, and you are not a seeing entity. With this knowledge, it will make no difference whether your eyes are open or closed.

Another Q.: Noticing how the senses are in the mind, I then see that there is no connection between that and my Existence. Is this the way? Can you clarify this more for me?

N.: The approaches are only expedient pointers to your real nature. Sensing is an activity, isn't it?

Q.: Yes, it is.

N.: Are you an activity?

Q.: No.

N.: So, what association can there be?

Q.: An hallucination.

N.: If the senses, including the sensing and whatever object is sensed, are merely a tiny hallucination, of what concern are they to you? In what way do they offer bondage?

Q.: If seen as an hallucination or if not seen as an hallucination?

N.: The way that you see it.

Q.: When I see it as an hallucination, obviously there is no difficulty, but when I put energy into it, it seems that I project some happiness out there.

N.: These are two alternating states: one in which you are beyond the senses and one in which you seem to become entangled with the senses. For whom are the two states?

Q.: (quiet)

N.: Can you see him? Can you hear him? Can you touch, taste, or smell him?

Q.: The one who has these two states?

N.: Yes.

Q.: No.

N.: Can you even think of him?

Q.: If I did, I would need to ask for whom that is.

N.: So, go ahead and ask that.

Q.: (after a pause) It is something before thought.

N.: Which exists now and always.

Q.: That always exists. I can think of something else.

N.: Who is the thinker?

Q.: That I do not know.

N.: You know that you do not know. Consciousness is perpetual.

Q.: What does that mean? I do not understand.

N.: You have the mental state of not knowing. Some Knowledge knows about that not knowing. Thus, in the *Forty Verses on Reality*, the Maharshi makes it clear that that which is real, true Knowledge has nothing to do with knowing and unknowing. In Self-Knowledge, the Knowledge is actually Consciousness. Not-knowing is a conception.

Prajnanam Brahma, Brahman is Supreme Knowledge. Brahman is the Supreme Consciousness. This is Self-Knowledge and not an objective conception or mental mode, however subtle. Consciousness, which is what you are, is, itself, the Knowledge. Thus, Being is Knowing.

If you say that there are thoughts, for whom are they? Can there be thoughts for the infinite, ever-silent, unborn Consciousness? How would it divide itself? Where would it get the desire to do so? If it is homogeneous, it is indivisible. If it is formless, it is infinite, and there is no thought, or anything else, outside of it. It is the undifferentiated essence. So, for whom is the thought?

Q.: It seems that it can be only for this individual.

N.: Inquire to see what he is. From where does the individuality come? It cannot come from the thoughts, because the thoughts come after him. It cannot come from the Absolute Self for the reasons already stated, such as its formless, homogeneous nature. It cannot come from itself, for that would presume its pre-existence. So, from where does this "I" come?

Q.: Are there any other choices? (laughter)

N.: You must say so. Are there?

Q.: I do not think so. It is becoming very plain.

N.: When you think, "I," what do you mean? Who is this "I"? If there is the assumption of "I," everything else follows. The thoughts follow and, if you are misidentified with the body, so does the belief in an external world. If you are not misidentified with the body, you know everything to be in your mind. But the mind must be for someone.

From another perspective, if everything, including "I," is in the mind, what is the mind? What is its nature? If the mind seems to be a combination of Consciousness plus something objective, for there is no such thing as a nonobjective thought, remove the objectified portion because of its unreality. What, then, remains of the mind? (Silence)

Q.: This is very deep.

N.: Is how to inquire in relation to the senses and the mind clear for you?

Q.: It seems clear, yet I am not sure how my mind got here and if I will forget.

N.: What are you trying to understand?

Q.: This meditation is not on a mental level. There is a certain clarity even on the mental level. It is the part that starts the meditation. The experience is actually at a higher level, but there is the drive that manifests in the mind.

N.: The drive to inquire and to know yourself manifests in the mind. From where does it derive?

Q.: It must be from something deeper. It is strange that it drives to dissolve itself.

N.: Why do you yearn to dissolve the mind?

Q.: To not suffer.

N.: So, happiness is the driving factor. Where is the source of happiness?

Q.: In myself.

N.: The desire springs from the same place that the happiness does. It is an intuition of your natural state. Which part was mental?

Q.: The discrimination between what is unreal and what is real.

N.: Can the unreal do that?

Q.: No, definitely not. (laugher)

N.: If you discriminate between thought and your Self, is that mental?

Q.: It seems as if the initial part is mental.

N.: What is the initial part?

Q.: Discrimination between thought and the Self.

N.: How can the discrimination between thought and your Self occur on a mental level? You may have the thought that you are going to meditate in such a manner, yet how does the actual meditation experience occur?

Q.: The essence of it cannot be mental, but deeper.

N.: It is a path of Knowledge that results in Self-Knowledge. It is not thinking about it. You may, though, think about it as much as you wish. Listen to it, reflect upon or contemplate it, and meditate on it. Sravana, manana, nididhyasana—listening, reflection, and deep, continuous meditation—samadhi, absorption.

You may think of it, but the Knowledge, itself, is not mental. The inquiry is not mental. This is the reason for inquiry becoming continuous, as well for its depth. This is, also, the reason why inquiry does not include the dualisms that one is trying to transcend. Dualism is a product of thinking. Thought is discontinuous. Even a concentrated train of thought will not continue forever. Self-Knowledge, though, is perpetual.

Does the Knowledge depend on thought, or do the thoughts depend on the Knowledge? Which is the support, and which is the supported?

Q.: The Self does not depend on thoughts. How do thoughts depend on Knowledge?

N.: In the same way that the print on a piece of paper depends on the paper. Does the print stand up on its own?

Q.: Yes, I see. It is because I am always aware.

N.: Consider the Maharshi's analogy of the screen with the movie images upon it. Do the images stand up on their own?

Q.: No.

N.: The analogy is from before the age of holograms. (laughter) The images depend on the screen, and the words depend on the paper. They cannot stand apart. All of your thoughts depend on you. You do not depend on any of them. It is silly when we think that the experience of the Self, or our Existence, depends on our thinking about it. It is the other way around. All of your thoughts depend on the certain Existence, or pure Consciousness, which is the spiritual essence.

Q.: This is actually very amazing to recognize.

Another Q.: Reflecting upon the instruction of last satsang, it is clear for me that the "daily life" is a combination of misidentification with the body, thoughts, and the individual. In *Ribhu Gita,* it is said: That state of being full of changeless Awareness is the unparalleled Liberation. Those who have attained that great state will never again be in sorrow, never again have any blemish, shall attain joy, shall be the ones who have accomplished all they have to do, and shall remain ever the one Supreme Nature.

I can see that my desires to accomplish in the world, to acquire money, etc. are inverted attempts to find happiness.

N.: If you can see that you have been looking for your happiness in the wrong places, asking something else to give you what is actually yours, your mind turns within, and you become detached toward all else. A man who is unattached is at peace, regardless of circumstances. Though his body may be engaged in various apparent accomplishments, from the onlooker's point of view, he has no concept of doing anything, because he is not the body. Nor is he attached to the success or failure of the activities, because he is carrying his happiness within him. He is no longer demanding from others to be filled up by what is his.

Q.: This applies to anything: individuals, objects, circumstances, or events.

N.: Exactly so. How could an event give you to you? How could another person give you to you? You, yourself, are the happiness, though you were looking everywhere for it. The Maharshi refers to an analogy of a woman, with a necklace around her neck, who thinks that her necklace is lost and goes about searching everywhere for it. Eventually, some kind friend points out to her how close it is. She recognizes it. Such is spiritual practice. She realized that it was never lost. Yet her happiness is mysteriously regained, as if it had been lost. So it is with Liberation from all of the imagined bondage. It seemed as if one were bound. One is liberated from the seeming, and sorrow, or suffering, turns to happiness.

What you expect to attain at the end of ever so many accomplishments exists always. Pretending that it does not exist does not help you in any way, spiritually or phenomenally. There is no advantage to delusion. There is no disadvantage to Knowledge.

Continue reading and meditating with Ribhu until what he says is self-evident within you.

Q.: Forgetting to inquire takes me out of who I am. What I want is satsang all day. How can I forget something that I want more than anything? Someone was speaking unkindly toward my husband. With the inquiry, I could remain quite peaceful with that. The peace comes from neti, neti (not this, not this). It is a matter of remembering to inquire.

N.: The desire is there. There is no state of forgetfulness waiting for you. The desire prompts the inquiry. Observe your mind. Examine closely, and see in what ways you assume yourself to be something that you are not. There is no other state for you, other than that which you conjure up. When you conjure it up, you have still not left the real Self.

Someone, whom the Maharshi calls a spurious, ghost-like entity with no form of its own, an ego, seems to rise, only due to lack of inquiry. If you inquire, there is no such one.

As long as there is the possibility of alternative states, rather than One without a second, the inquiry should proceed. You know the answer to your own question.

The Self is said to be beyond forgetfulness and remembrance.

Q.: The ego shows itself again and again. I awakened from my dream last night. Why can't I just wake up from this delusion? Why can't I wake up (snaps her fingers) just like that?

N.: Where do you measure the time?

Q.: Oh!

N.: The ideas of quick and slow, abrupt or gradual, fast or developing, and such are only in the mind. You are not that. There is no time for your real Self.

Q.: I now understand that the mind cannot possibly know. It is when the mind stops that the Knowledge appears. That is really knowing. It is not a willful stoppage of the thinking, but the thinking is not in operation. The next step must be to perfection.

N.: Whether there are many thoughts, few thoughts, quick thoughts, slow thoughts, thoughts present or thoughts absent is not of great significance. When thoughts appear, has anything actually been created?

Q.: They are an illusion.

N.: Therefore, in *Avadhuta Gita,* it is stated that "the absence of thoughts makes it no clearer."

Q.: It amazes me how quickly I can go off.

N.: The one who now sees that she is going off is no longer going off. When we recognize ignorance as ignorance, no longer regarding it as something truly known, it ceases to be ours. Only we sustained it. When we do not create it and do not sustain it, when we do not adhere to what we, ourselves, created, what happens to it? Someone who recognizes ignorance as ignorance will not remain ignorant.

Q.: That is encouraging. (laughing)

N.: It is just the simple fact. The apparent obstacles of yesterday now seem superfluous to you. Similarly will the presently appearing obstacles be. The obstacle appears prior to the inquiry and never afterward.

Another Q.: The obstacle appears?

N.: The obstacle appears before the inquiry. There is no actual obstacle to inquiry. When the inquiry commences in the attempt to know yourself, no obstacle proves to be there. A tendency in the mind seems to have power. From where does the power come? When you seek to know your Self, what power do the tendencies have? Of course, the one that you have already transcended seems easy, and the one that you have yet to transcend seems difficult. Similarly, the other person's tendencies seem easy to get over, while your own seem to be insurmountable, (laughter), yet it is an illusion.

Another Q.: So, it is a matter of continuing with Self-inquiry. It is the answer to every question.

N.: All the questions resolve themselves in, "Who am I?" The answer to the inquiry is the inquirer herself. There is no other answer. Sri Bhagavan has said that if one would, without hesitation or interruption, just continuously inquire, that alone would suffice for spiritual practice for complete Liberation.

Q.: I completely believe that.

N.: Then, understand this. In this context, experience plus the idea of time is belief. Without that idea, it is just experience. What you believe, that Self-Realization will be, is the fact already.

Q.: The belief in time is the problem.

N.: Eliminate the "I am the body" idea, and time will take care of itself.

Q.: Why should I inquire about the senses, when I can inquire as to how I am not the body and take care of it all at once?

N.: Yes. Sometimes, the instruction is that you are not the body, not the mind, and not the ego, but for those who find it helpful, more detail is given such as being not the body, not the senses, not the prana, not the mind, not the intellect, and so forth. As much detailed instruction about illusion as is necessary for various aspirants to destroy the delusion has been given as expedient teaching.

Another Q.: Desire often has a negative connotation, but the desire to practice Self-inquiry, in opposition to the desire to acquire things, has a positive connotation. There is no contamination in that desire?

N.: No one has ever been hurt by the desire to practice.

Q.: I objectify the desire in my spiritual practice into a desire to accomplish, to obtain a state, to get Self-Realization.

N.: What is the desire when you desire to accomplish Self-Realization?

Q.: It is the desire to attain some blissful, eternal state. It is above this world, and this separates me from this worldly experience.

N.: So? What is the problem with that? (laughter)

Q.: It is escapism.

N.: Escape from what?

Q.: Escaping from the world, running away from it.

N.: What do you mean by escaping or running away from the world? Do you mean such running physically? Wherever your body would go, it would still be in the world. What do you mean by escapism?

Q.: Not dealing with it. Not addressing it. Trying to hide in my meditation.

N.: Hide from what?

Q.: Delaying the negative experiences and challenges of the world by trying to go away from it internally.

N.: Where is the "it"?

Q.: This experience that I am having of this world.

N.: Where is that experience?

Q.: Within me.

N.: The entire world is within you?

Q.: My experience of it and my feelings.

N.: What of the world itself?

Q.: It is out there.

N.: How do you know "out there"?

Q.: (quiet for awhile) How do I know that? My thoughts.

N.: When you have thought, you have "out there," and, when you have no thoughts, there is no "out there." Is this what you mean?

Q.: When I am still, I am not involved or trapped in it.

N.: Physically still or mentally still?

Q.: Mentally.

N.: So, when your thoughts move in a certain way, there is the world. When you become overly attached to that world, looking for your happiness, you have the various emotional responses to which you referred a few moments ago. Is this so?

Q.: Yes.

N.: Then, not being satisfied with that, you wish to escape from that. It is a very healthy desire. Make your escape foolproof. (laughter) Who would want to remain caught in egotistical emotions based on false interactions with an unreal world that is imagined within his own mind? To criticize yourself for wanting to get away from this, after having made such a mess in your mind, is not necessary. There is nothing wrong with getting away from that, but you must get away from it in a much more intelligent fashion. You must recognize its source.

If you think that the world is a negative place and that you must become accustomed to it, what does that spiritually accomplish? If, further, you deride your inspiration to attain a blissful state of Self-Realization beyond it, what is really gained thereby? At that point, you have merely taken up a materialistic, atheistic approach, which is not necessarily supportive of deeper spiritual states. It may masquerade as nonduality, but it is thoroughly dualistic. The terms sound deep, but what is stated is not deep. See this for yourself.

What is it that you desire? If you innocently question what it is that you desire, you will be led back into yourself.

There is really no question of escapism from a world; nor is there a question of a world. One who knows himself finds the whole world to be himself. Then, again, there is no world. He is neither drawn to nor is he running away from any supposed thing. He is not caught in desire and fear.

Q.: I was also trying to escape from addressing fears.

N.: Of what are you afraid?

Q.: The death of the body and the pain that will occur with it.

N.: You know that death is inevitable. Why do you fear the inevitable?

Q.: I do not know.

N.: As long as to any extent you mistake your Existence as being the body, there is fear of death. This same fear of death can drive you to inquire. Consider the story of the Maharshi's Self-Realization.

Q.: Yes, I agree.

N.: The same is alluded to in the second invocation verse of *Saddarsanam*. "For those who have taken refuge, out of fear of death, in the Conqueror of death…" The verse concludes, "How again can there be space for the thought of death?" If you are born, there is death. Find out the real remedy. If you are not the body, your Existence does not begin and does not end with the birth and death of the body.

Far from not dealing with such things, when you dive within yourself, you actually deal with these things. It is the outward-turned mind that is merely distracting itself, making believe that the inevitable will not come. Every day, life is shorter. Death comes quickly and even unexpectedly. You know that this is going to happen. The outward-turned mind is the mind distracting itself, even if it is a conception of, "just being with it" or some similar notion. An inward-turned mind really deals with it at its root.

Q.: By transcendence.

N.: By Knowledge of the Self, which is the Knowledge of Reality. If you want to face Reality, face yourself.

(Then followed a recitation in Sanskrit and English from the Upanishads.)

(Silence)

Om Shanti Shanti Shanti Om

Samsara and Mukti

Satsang, August 3, 2003

(Silence)

Om Om Om

(Silence)

N.: The Being that is seemingly individualized is actually always infinite and undifferentiated. In the very space in which appears samsara, the repetitive cycle of birth, illusion, and death, is the infinite, the eternal. The very nature of the one who seems as if bound is Liberation. At the moment that you were born, no one was born. At the moment a thought arises, nothing actually occurs.

Where samsara seems to be, there is really only Brahman, the infinite, eternal Being-Consciousness-Bliss, which, in Self-Knowledge, we know as our real nature. Always, there is just this one Existence, which perpetually is just as it is. Samsara, or the illusion of duality and its consequent suffering, is the result of imagination. That imagination is constituted primarily of misidentification. If misidentification, which is ignorance, ceases, samsara, or illusion, ceases. The illusion, or samsara, and any of its bondage and suffering, depend entirely upon misidentification. Such is ignorance regarding one's own nature.

If ignorance is done away with, samsara is found not to be anywhere. This is why it is said that maya, or illusion, is inexplicable, for, when we find its nature, it ceases to exist.

For the purpose of Self-Realization, or Liberation from all of the imagined bondage, inquire into the nature of your Being. If it seems to be individualized, inquire into the individualized being, and the individuality, being false and an illusion, will cease to exist. What has not really come to be ceases. That which is has neither a creation nor a destruction. It is not produced, but just is, and what is does not cease to be. Inquire into the one who seems as if bound. If you inquire into the one who seems as if bound, examining your existence and of what the bondage is constituted, you find no bondage.

At first, you find just a mistaken impression, a misidentification. Being plus misidentification appears as the individual, who is at the root of all that is of the nature of suffering, futility, and bondage in life. It is the root of unhappiness. Consciousness plus some misidentification results in the illusion of a thinker with thoughts and a perceiver with perceptions. Bliss with misidentification manifests as attachment, which does not cause happiness, but results in just the opposite, which is unhappiness.

Turn inward in search of your Being, the Existence that you are, now and always. Turn inward and inquire into the nature of your Consciousness, which is that which is perpetually aware in life and death, in states of thought and non-thought, and when the senses are active and inactive.

If you examine samsara, you find Nirvana. If you examine bondage, you find Mukti, Liberation. If you examine the "I," which is the most direct path—thus the Maharshi's instruction to inquire, "Who am I?"—you find the Self alone. The Self being found, there is no further thing to find, for it is One without a second. There remains no individual finder, so there cannot be an individual loser later. There is neither a realized one nor an unrealized one.

The Realization is Self-Knowledge. It is Consciousness devoid of misidentification. Even the very mechanism of misidentification, the very power of ignorance, also, does not have a separate existence. There is nothing apart from this one Self. Other than the Self, there is nothing else.

To understand, deeply inquire as to who you are.

(Silence)

Q.: What is a tendency? It seems to be a repeating thought pattern. Misidentification must also be a part of it. The biggest tendency is identification with this person. I also have little tendencies, such as not liking when I do not get cereal in the morning. I want to hear more from you about this so that I can clearly discriminate.

N.: Yes, it is repeated imagination. They are ideas to which are attributed your own Being, your own identity. There is confusion concerning your happiness, as well, such as in the example regarding cereal.

You see that the tendencies come in all sizes and shapes, though, in reality, they are vaporous and really of no substance.

Q.: Yes.

N.: In satsang and when reading holy books, you become aware of what your true nature is. It is that which is without birth or condition, without difference, always blissful and at peace, space-like, bodiless, non-individualized, and free from all thought. A tendency is whatever makes your experience seem to be other than that.

What would be your experience if the vasanas, or tendencies, from those that seem to denote a person to the form of the desire for cereal, were not there? Most of what you usually, though not wisely, call "life" would not be there. What would remain? What would be the experience?

Q.: It would be the best of my meditation, with an open, unbounded freedom. It is difficult to see how, without tendencies, it could be anything other than that open space.

N.: To abide in illimitable freedom as that space-like Being, which is Consciousness, the Maharshi advises the destruction of tendencies, or vasanas. He says that if you can be still, or silent, which is the state in which even the tendency of "I" does not arise, that is fine. If the doubt is that this does not seem possible, his rejoinder is, "That is why the inquiry is advised." The inquiry is for the purpose of destroying tendencies.

We do not create anything anew. The real Self is not something to be newly attained. Where there is the real Self, now you seem to be experiencing everything from personalities to empty cereal boxes. You must examine within yourself as to how this happened. How did the infinite, formless, all-blissful Brahman become reduced to the experience of the individual and cereal boxes?

You must go back the way you came. Find the ways in which you misidentify.

There is no tendency that is so large that it cannot be easily overcome through direct inquiry to know yourself. There is no tendency too small that you should let it remain.

Do you have a clearer view of what is a tendency and how to eradicate such?

Q.: Yes, I do. Chapter twenty in the *Song of Ribhu* says something to the effect that by certitude the mind attains courage. I understand that the courageous mind is the willingness to deal with these tendencies directly.

N.: The courageous mind is one that dissolves its own form.

Q.: Yes.

N.: Finally, the state of courage is the state of no fear. That is the duality-less state. Where there is a second, there is fear, as the Upanishad declares. Where there is no second, no duality, there is no fear. Some call this courage. When someone once said to the Maharshi that he alone had the courage to speak in such a direct way, he replied, "Where is the courage in just saying things as they are?" So, it is also natural.

Another Q.: How to go deeper?

N.: Where do you want to go?

Q.: Where I should be.

N.: Where are you now? Are you in the body?

Q.: No.

N.: Are you certain of this?

Q.: Quite.

N.: What has happened to the previous ignorant notion of being connected to a body?

Q.: The experience is such that where the ignorance went is not an issue or what happened before.

N.: So, the unreal does not go anywhere, does it? This is so because it is unreal. It is the same with all ignorance. Just as the relation of Existence with the ignorance of being in the body, so it is with the ignorant notion of an "I" in Existence.

Q.: There is a tendency for these things to recur. Is the practice to clearly see what is true and what is not?

N.: Yes. What recurs and why?

Q.: Ignorance recurs, but nothing is really going on. Even the revelation is not really happening.

N.: It is true that the purpose of ignorance is for the revelation of Truth. Nevertheless, that understanding, in itself, will not be the primary factor in the elimination of this formal, or unreal, ignorance.

Q.: Could you say that again?

N.: It is true that ignorance is not a power separate from Truth. The only purpose of it, if we can say that it has a purpose, is the revelation of Truth. Nevertheless, that understanding, in itself, will not be the primary means to eliminate the unreal ignorance.

Q.: The means is, "Who am I?"

N.: The ignorance, the ideas that are the form of such, are always based upon misidentifications, the prime one of which is the notion of a separate individual. Whatever is appended to the individual gives him some kind of definition or form. When you perceive what that ignorance is, in whatever manner the tendency manifests, and when you perceive why it has occurred—that is, the misidentification—and you then inquire, "Who am I?", the very root of the ignorance turns out to be rootless. Then, no one can say where it has gone, but there is no more bondage.

Q.: Then, there is the experience of Existence and unity with it? And that is Liberation?

N.: As the rise, or apparent birth, of an individual "I" in the mind, in imagination, is the cause of the samsara, its disappearance is the revelation of Liberation. If you are attempting to have unity with Existence, which is the Absolute and which is without form, beginning, or end, the question is, "Who is it that seeks such unity?" Whatever his definition is should be eliminated.

Q.: It is very subtle.

N.: Yes, it is the subtlest discernment. The *Katha Upanishad* describes such as being like the razor's edge. Yet, as the Maharshi expressed, it is just seeing things as they are. This does not mean physical things. It means Reality as it is. In one sense, it is subtlest. In another sense, it is self-evident. At one point, you feel that you must discern in the subtlest way possible. So, then, discriminate, endeavor, and persevere, but you will come out laughing at how you ever could not have seen that which alone exists the entire time.

Q.: The subtle becomes all that we perceive.

N.: (Silence)

Another Q.: I see that my job and that of those who work with me are not secure. I have a feeling of compassion for them.

N.: Yes, the job is not secure. Even the body that holds the job is not secur.

Q.: I informed two of them that their jobs were over, for I felt that it was better to be honest than to tell them that everything was fine.

N.: You would appreciate knowing in advance, would you not?

Q.: Yes.

N.: We should always do unto others as we would have them do unto us.

Q.: There was a lot of emotion as I explained it.

N.: The emotions were on your part or theirs?

Q.: Both. I felt I was affected by this.

N.: In what way were you affected? Their emotions will be taken care of by whatever spiritual path they follow. You must take care of your own emotions.

Q.: I felt responsible, because I make the decision as to who goes and who stays. Sometimes, it is arbitrary and does not have anything to do with the person.

N.: So, your motivation is not personal?

Q.: No, it is not. But they want to know, and it is difficult to say that they are great, but they must go.

N.: If you are truthful and your motivation is not personal, what is the difficulty?

Q.: I worry about how they feel.

N.: To what degree do you have control over how they feel?

Q.: Being a manager, I care about how they feel. I become personally wrapped up in their lives. They are good people.

N.: What is the goodness in these good people?

Q.: It is not their personalities, for sure.

N.: Is it ever destroyed?

Q.: No.

N.: Is it determined by outer, phenomenal things?

Q.: Sometimes, I think that it is.

N.: Is it?

Q.: How could it be?

N.: Is that which is good inside you determined by outer things and events? Do other people give it to you or take it away?

Q.: I must admit that I sometimes believe that.

N.: Is it true? Does someone else give to you or take way that which is good?

Q.: (laughing) No. The mind comes in and believes that.

N.: Is the mind the goodness, or is the goodness something deeper? Does the mind give you that which is the source of peace or which is truly good and auspicious?

Q.: No.

N.: Then, the mind cannot take it away. Since all beings are the same Self, as it is for you, so it is for all others. It is not that you are superior or that you have a unique perfection that others do not have, as if yours would not be determined by the mind and outer events but theirs would be. The perfection of Real Being is the source of all happiness and peace. Obviously, outer events cannot deliver such. Can you see this?

Q.: Yes. Because I have this teaching, I feel that I have an advantage with dealing with this. I wish I could express this to them, but I do not feel that I can.

N.: If you can find a way of doing so, it is good, yet each one has the responsibility for his own spiritual state.

Many people become more spiritual when a situation has gone poorly. At a funeral, there are often more spiritual people. It is not because spiritual people gravitate toward funerals, but those who are not spiritual a moment before suddenly become so. Similar is it when some disaster is about to happen. When it is found that something is beyond the control of one's individual mind or body, there is a call for greater help. Prior to that point, the ego is in charge. At that point, God is considered responsible for this, and there are pleas for help. It is wise to not wait until an event, such as losing your job or losing your life or that of a loved one, occurs but to be deeply spiritual and know the Truth in a way that is not dependent on circumstances. Then, if circumstances are favorable, it is fine, and, when they are unfavorable, everything is still fine. There is not a real difficulty.

Otherwise, the person becomes more spiritually inclined only for the moment, and when the situation changes, the samsaric, deluded tendencies return. Even though one sees the alternation of good and bad events and that there is a death for every birth, one does not give attention to such. Everyone sees such every day, yet they do not notice it. Not noticing, in the very place where there is Bliss, they wind up suffering, and they think of differentiation where there is really only one undifferentiated Existence. They take themselves to be a small entity in a body wrapped up in a dream-like adventure, when, all the while, they are comfortably the real Self. Such is maya. Recall the story of Narada, Vishnu, and the vessel of water.

Q.: The deeper I know that the beatitude of the Self does not come from any sort of mental state and that happiness is not procured externally, the better.

N: Yes, the clearer you are, and the more at peace you are. The same clarity and peace will be conveyed in your communication. Then, it is in the hands of the recipient to do with it what he wants.

Another Q.: I am trying to see the moment of differentiation. I am trying to see this "I" that causes all this trouble.

It seems that I will never see this "I" because it does not exist and is only an assumption. Is it so that I will never see the "I"? Have I understood clearly?

N.: You should inquire, "Who am I?" to know yourself. The "I" or ego is a false assumption with no substance or reality. The Maharshi said that the assumption is like a ghost with no form of its own. So, another assumption is appended to it. Something real is not appended to the unreal assumption. It is another unreality, such as the assumption of being the mind, the senses, the body, and so forth and so on. All the assumptions are based on one assumption. The inquiry sweeps away all the assumptions, including the root one, so that there is no recurrence of the delusion.

You will not see an "I," just as you have never seen the actual connection between you and the body. You examine the connection between the Existence and the body, and you find that there is no such limiting connection. Likewise, you examine the very notion of "I," and you find that there is no one answering to that name.

Q.: I can see that it is an illusion and that there is no creation of it. There is no "I" there to begin with to assume it to be.

N.: If you know this and are convinced of this in your mind, follow through with thorough inquiry so that your experience is steadfastly the Truth in which there is no assumed individual "I" and none of the delusions following it.

Another Q.: Is taking things personally always an egotistical notion? I see that it is so when I take offense at something. If I get my feathers ruffled over something, is this always an egotistical tendency in my mind?

N.: What do you think?

Q.: Yes! (laughter)

N.: Then, you have answered your own question.

Q.: When I have taken something personally is when I should do Self-inquiry?

N.: You may do so at that point, yet you can also inquire before. When your feathers are ruffled, you can inquire and find out that you do not really have feathers. (laughter)

Q.: Well, then, fur. (laughter)

N.: Then, you can inquire further so that you realize that you do not have fur, either. (laughter) You do not need to anticipate a particular moment or a particular place in which to know yourself. Understand that it is important to know yourself and that all suffering, however it appears, is completely unnatural to your Existence. It is always a delusion and cannot possibly be what is innate or your real nature. You need not wait for a circumstance to act as a trigger for your mind. You can proceed even now. Recognize that the circumstance is, also, only in your mind. Therefore, you do not need to wait for it.

Q.: These events point out tendencies that I have, so they are actually beneficial. Yet, it usually starts out by being defensive about that egotistical entity. That is what I want to eliminate.

N.: That the tendency arises is not so great of a difficulty in practice. Where you wind up matters more. If, each time you find yourself in some kind of bondage of a personal state, you use it as an opportunity to merge with impersonal Truth and to destroy the tendency, such will be good. You do not, though, need to wait until the tendency finds you. You can go hunting for it.

Is there really anything over which you should become angry?

Q.: Often, I am called into action in a situation in which someone needs help because of an injustice.

N.: Can you right that injustice without feeling personal anger?

Q.: It is possible.

N.: Would it be better?

Q.: Yes, absolutely.

N.: If you know what is better, follow your better knowledge.

Q.: Yes, I will.

N.: There comes a point at which you recognize that all the personal feelings, which some refer to as their negative emotions, have all been to no purpose. None of them have any basis. There is one unmarked Perfection, Purnam, the Perfect Fullness of Brahman, and you are That. All is only That, and you are That.

Q.: All my ignorance is based on the unreal individual conception of being embodied, all my thoughts, and memories of my thoughts. I know that, though I do not truly embody it and live.

N.: So, the knowledge is not steady yet. How is it made steady?

Q.: Practice, practice, practice.

N.: What is found in the end to be natural and the only way it can be is attended with effort in practice until the illusion rises no more. You know the Truth and the way inside to realize it. If you give yourself to it, heart and soul, and persevere, everything comes out right.

Another Q.: What is meant by going deeper in Self-inquiry in the course of practice?

N.: By "deeper" is meant the elimination of those identities or ideas that seem as if more interior to you. It is not that you obtain a different Self, for the Self is already present. It means that those misidentifications that at first seemed subtler are inquired into and are found to be grosser than first supposed. They are set aside and no longer connected with your Existence. The result is greater freedom, greater bliss, and greater peace.

Q.: What is the place of detachment in this?

N.: When you eliminate attachment by clarification within your mind as to where happiness is and where it is not, you are said to have gone deeper.

Q.: Is it possible to be free from thoughts?

N.: Yes, it is possible to reach a state in which thought is of no consequence, in which, whether thoughts appear or do not, you are certain of your identity, and you no longer take yourself to be a thought. You can reach this depth by inquiry. How else would one find himself beyond the domain of thought, except by inquiring deeply, "Who am I?"

Q.: When a thought arises, I inquire again. Is that wrong?

N.: No, of course not. Continue to inquire, "Who am I?" until the very sense of "I" is absorbed in the Absolute and does not reappear. Then, everything is complete. If you are inquiring, "Who am I?", you are on the right path. Pursue it to its ultimate goal.

Another Q.: While I am meditating, I get the thought that it is time to end the meditation. My eyes open, the body becomes active, and I go into the kitchen to start making breakfast. Shortly after that, the meditation starts again as I detach myself from the meal. I need to look at the times of transition from eyes closed to more input of the senses and actions.

N.: Transition is between two different things. What are the two different things?

Q.: Maybe there are not two different things, and I am making up the difference.

N.: That is the nature of illusion. One just makes it up. Does your Existence change?

Q.: Once the meditation takes hold again, nothing changed.

N.: Even in the interim, did your Existence change?

Q.: No, it could not.

N.: Does your Consciousness change? That which is shining in the meditation and when active in the kitchen, as well as in the interim—not what you know, but that by which you know—did that change?

Q.: No.

N.: So, what is the transition?

Q.: I think it is just the misidentification with the senses when they turn on.

N.: Misidentification gives rise to the delusion of different states, when actually one is always in the same state.

Q.: The transition is just taking on the misidentification, the idea that I am this body and something is actually happening, so that I am moving into the kitchen.

N.: It is a two-fold misidentification that you are a body that moves and that you are an individual who navigates through various domains or states of mind. Are you for the mind, or is the mind for you? Are you in the mind or is the mind in you?

Q.: The mind is for me, and it is my tool. It is the ego that can go into different states of mind. It is the states that change.

N.: How many existences do you have? Do you have an ego-self and a real Self? Or, is there only one Self? Verify this experientially within you by the deepest inquiry, the deepest meditation, regardless of where your body is. Dive into your own existence, and see if it is bifurcated.

Q.: It is clear now that it is not. I was just making it up and believing in it.

N.: Yes, like a dream. First one dreams of it, and then one thinks one is in it. Then, whatever you assume yourself to be seems to be afflicted by what occurs in it.

Q.: Misidentification means suffering and being bound in my attempts to gain happiness.

N.: If you do not misidentify, what happens to the dream? If you do not dream of illusion, is there an illusion?

Q.: I would like to know the true meaning of "Existence." I know the dictionary meaning. What is the true, real meaning of it?

N.: (Silence for a long time, while the seeker smiled blissfully) So, you know something more than the dictionary meaning. If we seek to describe it, such is mostly done through negation. It is Existence, without beginning or end. It is Existence, but it never becomes nonexistence. It is Existence, but not the forms of things. What the Existence is in itself—who could stand apart from it to say anything about it? You are it, and you know it only always. (Silence)

(Then followed a recitation in Sanskrit and English of verses from an Upanishad.)

(Silence)

Om Shanti Shanti Shanti Om

Knoweldge of Identity

Satsang, August 10, 2003

(Silence)

Om Om Om

(Silence)

N.: One indivisible, perpetual Existence, unborn, uncreated, and imperishable, is your Self, and that alone exists. There is no second self. This unconditioned, absolutely formless Existence is what you are. It is Absolute, for it is invariable, and there is no second thing to which it could be in relation. It has not a trace of individuality. There is no form for it, yet it alone is always.

Abidance in That as That is Self-Knowledge, or, as we call it, Self-Realization. Such is not a separate state, but the nature of Existence as it is and always is.

Your seeming experience is by what you assume yourself to be. According to the definition assumed for the "I," so, in a mirror-like manner, "this," the experience, appears to be. If you know yourself as you are, that which alone is, there is no mirror-like illusion, there is no separate "I" or "this," and there is just one undifferentiated Existence, which is simultaneously infinite, pure Consciousness.

If it is perfect peace and complete happiness that you desire, you must know yourself as you really are. Whatever you assume yourself to be, that determines what you refer to as being real. All hinges on your identity. If you mistakenly assume yourself to be a body, you assume the senses determine reality, and you view your experience in bodily terms. You consider that which is of a bodily character to be that which is existent, and that which is non-bodily seems to be an enigma, or you think that such does not exist. Such is the way of illusion: you take the real to be unreal and the unreal to be real. Actually, the unreal never is, and the Real always is and alone is.

If you misidentify with the body, you also assume an identity as a sensing entity. Then, in a mirror-like fashion, the illusion of what is sensory appears as if real. Are you the body? Inquire within yourself and know your nature, your own Being, as it is.

The idea of being the body does not alter the nature of your Existence. The idea occurs in the mind. Are you what you think? When you cease to think these thoughts, what remains? Who are you? If you assume that your identity is of thought, the mind, you appear to be bound, defined and confined, by thought and states of mind. Sometimes seeming to be in waking, sometimes dreaming, sometimes in thoughtless, dreamless sleep, and sometimes in various modes of mind, who are you? Are you the mind?

Is the nature of your Being individualized? Have you ever seen the individual, or only the "footprints" of that delusion, which are the effects or tendencies? Who am I? If you deeply inquire in this way, all the forms of ignorance vanish, because they are not real. What is unreal can vanish. What is real has neither appearance nor disappearance. Your Self is the Reality. Your Being has neither appearance nor disappearance. If you continue to inquire, "Who am I?" all the forms of ignorance disappear.

If you inquire as to who is the one who assumes such ignorance, who imagines this illusion, ignorance disappears. There is, then, no one who is ignorant or who becomes bound. There is not a state of bondage or of ignorance. If there is no one who becomes bound, it would be absurd to speak of someone who is liberated or to treat Liberation as if it were a different state other than the perpetual Existence. It is the real nature of Being, which is not a body, not a mind, not an individual, and not anything objective whatsoever.

The unborn, uncreated state and similar descriptions of Brahman are descriptions of your own nature. What is this nature? What is your Self? Inquire. If, listening to this, you think in terms of "the Self" and "yourself," inquire, "Who am I?" The Maharshi says, "Can there be two selves, one to realize the other?" It is absurd, but if you find yourself in such an absurd position, inquire, "Who am I?" If you so inquire, you abide in Knowledge. Knowledge, itself, is the abidance. Being does not change its nature. There is not a second one to depart from Being or to re-enter Being. Sri Bhagavan says, in that state, "Knowing is Being." Knowledge and Being are not activities. They are not activities of the body, the senses, or the mind. Reality comprehending itself is alone true Knowledge.

As for anything else of which you might think: inquire into the knower. Who knows? Who am I?

Questions will naturally arise, yet all of them boil down to one: Who am I?

Q.: I have been contemplating how all that I know is within me. From there, I inquire. The mind becomes very quiet. You have said, "Go back the way you came." I have been trying to determine the meaning of that in my own meditation experience.

N.: You are able to discern differences in the states.

Q.: Yes.

N.: You exist in all states.

Q.: Yes.

N.: When you utilize spiritual discrimination so that you see that all is within, this leads to a greater sense of peace and a quieter mind. When you say that all is within you, this cannot refer to the body. Even if you assume a position of the mind and say that all is within you as the mind, you also observe those thoughts from some position of an unconceived witnessing Consciousness. The witnessing is innate to Consciousness and not some position you assume.

To go back the way you came means to relinquish the misidentifications that have been superimposed on your real Being. If going outward is believing in the mind's own imagined projections, which are projected into itself, such as you are located in a body, the inward path is to relinquish those very misidentifications.

When you have deeper experience, it is imperative to understand how you arrived at that and how you seem to leave from it. If you do not see how you come down from it, the Reality is viewed as if it were an experience, the experience becomes a memory, and, later, it is forgotten, perhaps leaving some tell-tale mark. If you go back the way you came, you inquire to see what it is that brought about the experience. You find that such is not random. It is not caused by the will of the ego. How can that which is eternally existent happen as an event?

Continue with the meditation upon all being within you, and understand that you are not in some thing. The body and mind appear within you. You are not in a mind or a body.

Q.: It would be helpful for me to observe the apparent transition when diving into what seems to be an uncaused meditation state.

N.: The depth is uncaused in the sense that Being is not produced by something else. You can, though, determine what exactly brought about the merger of your experience with it. Such is useful not only when the plunge is about to occur, but it is useful even now.

Another Q.: I have been experiencing waves of bliss. How should I differentiate bliss from Silence as described in meditation upon the five sheaths?

N.: You need not differentiate bliss from Silence, for Silence is of the very nature of Sat-Chit-Ananda, Being-Consciousness-Bliss. It does not depend upon the modes of mind that are reflective of bliss, just as pure Consciousness does not depend on what is commonly thought of as "being aware" and just as Being does not depend upon any objective thing.

Anandamaya kosa, or bliss sheath, which is among the five sheaths, is said to be discarded. If bliss rises and sets, it is not real Bliss, Sri Bhagavan teaches. It is a reflection. Trace it to the original light. You will not lose bliss, but you will lose the wave-like pattern.

Q.: Seeing the wave of bliss, one can trace it back to the Self-source.

N.: Exactly so. He who sees the wave of bliss come and go is himself the source of all bliss.

Q.: Since, really, all beings have that Existence, they have that steady bliss. Even if they suffer, really there is Bliss going on.

N.: Bliss is identical with Being. When you think, "beings," there is the possibility of suffering.

Q.: Yes. Duality.

N.: Where all beings are just one Being, there being just one indivisible Being, suffering is no longer possible.

Q.: So, the jnani does not see anyone suffering. They just see jnani-s.

N.: Do they see jnani-s?

Q.: They see themselves, but it is not seeing.

N.: Okay.

Q.: I have a dumb question.

N.: The only dumb question is the one that you retain in your mind and do not ask. Otherwise, there is no such thing as a dumb question.

Q.: The snails are eating my garden. I am vegetarian and try not to kill things.

N.: Then, at least, you are not going to eat them.

Q.: (laughing) No! Even if I were not vegetarian, I would stay away from the slimy stuff. (laughter)

N.: What is the question?

Q.: Do the snails deserve to die for eating the plants?

N.: Death is with everyone every moment.

Q.: Yes.

N.: Now, the plants are dying because of the snails.

Q.: Yes.

N.: You may or may not cause the snails to die. Later, the snails and such will feed on your body.

Q.: Perhaps, that is appropriate compensation. (laughter)

N.: It is in the very nature of things that forms are destructible. Whether it is perceived or not, death is with every living being all the time. People are apt not to notice it. If they do notice it, they try not to deal with it. You tend to be swallowed by that from which you run from fear. If you inquire deeply to see what dies and what does not die, this will answer your question about your own life and death and that of the snail.

Q.: I will pursue the sadhana to get the correct answer. I toss and turn at night and wake up from my sleep. I am aware that the body is turning, but there are not thoughts occurring. It is pleasant for I am not waking up into ignorance.

N.: Yes, there is no rule that states that we must wake into ignorance.

Q.: If one is meditating and unfamiliar images appear in the mind, is that a sign that one is meditating correctly or incorrectly?

N.: It would depend on the content of the images, but most important is it to inquire as for whom are the images.

Q.: In deep meditation, there is no effort. The images might continue. If I remain focused on Existence without becoming interested in them, would I be really doing inquiry?

N.: The images continue?

Q.: Yes.

N.: It would be better to apply effort in the inquiry as for whom are the images, lest a sattvic state turn into a tamasic one. You are skipping from Consciousness, which is the ever-free, unidentified witness and absolutely formless, to a mental observation post, which sees images of thought patterns passing by. Why do you think the way that you think? If you trace this, you will see that all of such is determined by your identity.

It is not that you take thought before you think that you are going to think this way. Otherwise, you would have twice as many thoughts as you do presently. Inquire from where does the thinking proceed? If it is natural to the Self, everyone should think that way. If those images are innate, they should be with you always and common to all. If that is not the case, inquire.

Q.: So, whatever appears can only be a thought.

N.: Yes, and it is better to apply effort than to remain indolent.

Q.: Yes, yes.

N.: If you think that you do not wish to err by applying effort, it would be better to err, if that is conceived as error, by applying effort than to err by being indolent and calling such indolence "effortless."

Otherwise, dissolution or destruction may be conceived as states of laya, or temporary abeyance of thought. That is not advantageous for Realization. Of course, if effort is not an error, and you rid yourself of any trace of that dualism, you are free to apply effort. Indeed, you are so free to apply effort that there is no one supplying any resistance.

Q.: Do thoughts that do not seem to have any meaning still arise from the same source as ordinary daydreams?

N.: What is the source?

Q.: Everything arises from the Self, and there is really nothing else.

N.: How does something arise from the Self?

Q.: Oh, that is on a different level.

N.: The answer to a question is always on a different level than the one upon which the question came about.

Another Q.: I had a good meditation Friday evening. Later, my ignorance seemed more intense.

N.: More intense or more obvious?

Q.: More obvious. (laughter) It seemed more intense, though.

N.: Which is it? If it is more intense, you will want to stay away from those deeper meditations. (laughter) According to that idea, the ultimate meditation or Self-Realization would mean that your ignorance would reach an all-time peak. (laughter) That doesn't make any sense at all.

If it is more obvious, that means that as the background becomes clearer, the inconsistencies stand out more blatantly.

Q.: I do not see it clearly. It is not as if the ignorance became more intense. It was just that I was seeing it for what it was.

N.: Where is the ignorance? Can you show it?

Q.: In my mind. I cannot show my mind, so it must be top secret. (laughter) I was concerned about a situation, and now it is not much upon which to look back.

N.: They never are.

Q.: It seemed that the world was real. At home, I was making a drink, and nothing I was doing was working well. Half of what I was using was frozen solid. This was for a drink I was to have ready in a half-hour. I was very frustrated. I was curt with the woman for whom I was preparing this, though later I apologized to her.

N.: To apologize is good. Why were you frustrated? Are you frustrated now?

Q.: No.

N.: Where did your frustration go?

Q.: I do not know where it went. It went away. Everything was going wrong, I did not know what I was doing, and I was trying to prepare this for other people. I was thinking how this came out and tasted was important.

N.: Did your frustration help the physical things to come out better?

Q.: No, definitely not.

N.: Was it related to the physical incident? You recount the frustration that you now say you do not know where it went and claim that it was caused by the circumstances. Is it true? Is anger caused by circumstance or by other people?

Q.: It seems that the cause is my superimposing my happiness on something.

N.: That is clear discrimination. Nothing causes you to become ignorant. This makes the difference between a worldly-minded man and a spiritually-minded man, doesn't it? The worldly-minded man thinks that his happiness and unhappiness are determined by things external to himself: the objects, the people, the events, the circumstances. The spiritually-minded man knows that such is not the case. He knows that happiness is within, and unhappiness is one's own imagination at work.

If you now know that the cause of the unhappiness, or frustration, is only your superimposition, which does not exist in reality but only in your mind, will you fall into that delusion? Go further with this. Who suffered? Who became bound?

Q.: There are a number of fictitious players involved.

N.: Yes. A phantom man experiences fictitious daydreams in which he imagines himself to suffer due to unreal things. What about you?

Q.: I assumed that I was suffering.

N.: Is that what you are? Are you a suffering entity?

Q.: That would be a grim identity.

N.: Is it continuous?

Q.: No, definitely not.

N.: Then, it cannot be your identity. Only that which you are always can be your Existence. Everything else is merely an accident or a product of illusion.

Q.: How does that become permanent?

N.: It is permanent.

Q.: Oh, that is the Self.

N.: How could your Existence be impermanent?

Q.: Hmm.

N.: Is there a second one of you, who breaks off from Existence and assumes a different identity?

Q.: (laughing) Yes, that is the one!

N.: Inquire as to who he is. See if you can catch hold of him. (Silence) Is it clear?

Q.: Yes, definitely clearer.

Another Q.: I have glimpses of not being the doer. Then, there is a great sense of freedom. I am considering this in relation to the real and the unreal, the body, and how others view my actions.

N.: In practice, the method is primarily negation-oriented. You eliminate the "I am the performer of action" idea and the "I am the body" idea. Not being a body, you do not do anything, even when the body is active. Reality is not eliminated, and such is not possible. Spiritual practice aims only at the elimination of the belief in what is unreal.

Even if you assume yourself to be the body and the performer of action, that is not the truth about you. All that we are doing here is clarifying everything in Self-Knowledge.

Q.: An anchor for me is to be cognizant of the intense desire for Liberation.

N.: It is the fuel for spiritual practice. Adi Sankara placed emphasis on it when speaking of the four-fold sadhana, or requisites for Realization. Without it, the others do not work well.

Another Q.: I have a question about a passage I read in *Talks with Sri Ramana Maharshi*. "There is no being who is not conscious and, therefore, who is not Siva. Not only is he Siva, but also all else of which is he aware or not aware, yet he thinks, in sheer ignorance, that he sees the universe in diverse forms; but if he sees his Self, he is not aware of his separateness from the universe. In fact, his individuality and the other entities vanish, although they persist in all their forms." How do they vanish but persist in all their forms? If there are forms, or objects, left, there must be some subject.

N.: That is not the meaning of what he says. When you awake from a dream, do your dream senses cease to perceive the dream objects?

Q.: No, they are gone.

N.: Both the dream character and his dream senses, along with the dream objects, are entirely gone, aren't they?

Q.: Yes.

N.: But they are not gone at their own level. Your dream senses do not cease to perceive dream objects. Rather, the dream character, along with his entire dream world, vanishes. It would not be proper to say that the dream body ceases to experience dream objects. Likewise is it with the present waking state.

So, he says, "the diverse forms," altough he has already stated that all the diverse forms constituting the universe are only That, Siva, which is Brahman. Siva is already defined as absolute, nondual, and One without a second.

So, to say that Siva alone is, I am Siva, and all this is only Siva conveys the identical meaning.

It does not mean, though, that your senses cease to perceive objects. Rather, in That, there are neither senses nor objects. Are you following?

Q. Yes, I am following what you are saying, but it seems different from what I read.

N.: Let's try it again, sentence by sentence.

Q.: From the beginning?

N.: If you can be before the beginning, that is Siva. (laughter)

Q.: Before the beginning, there was?

N.: That is the Unborn. There is no question there.

Q.: "There is no being who is not conscious and, therefore, who is not Siva."

N.: What is mistaken as the everyday awareness is actually pure Consciousness. Every being, then, is only That. This means that there cannot be "every being." Tat tvam asi, you are That. Thou art That. The "thou" must be That, else there cannot be the connecting middle word. So, what is the definition of "thou" or "you"? What is the definition of "living being"? Casually, we say that every living being is conscious. The living being is actually pure Being, beyond life and death, who is Consciousness. Therefore, they are, themselves, the Reality and the Realization. Please read the next sentence.

Q.: "Not only is he Siva, but also all else of which he is aware or not aware."

N.: This is said taking into account the apparent experience. Not only is he Siva, the Absolute, but, if we say that something else is experienced of which we are aware or of which we are not aware, the existent and the nonexistent, the moving and the unmoving, the living and the dead, and so forth and so on, he is all that. All that is Siva. The emphasis is on Siva and not on "all that."

Q.: "Yet he thinks, in sheer ignorance, that he sees the universe in diverse forms."

N.: In sheer ignorance, one conceives of the universe, all the world of experience, with all of its diverse forms. Such is only ignorance. If there is no ignorance, there is no creation. Since ignorance is not a reality, nothing has ever occurred. Only Siva is.

Q.: "But if he sees the Self, he is not aware of his separateness from the universe."

N.: If he sees himself, he is not aware of any separation from the universe because both the jiva (the individual) and the world have vanished. Indeed, the division of the triad of jagat-jiva-para, the universe, the individual, and what is regarded as the Supreme has vanished, because he has seen himself. Again, the emphasis is on Self-Knowledge. If the stand is as the ego, there is something else, a universe. If there is no ego, there is no universe. So, there is no division. How can there be a division between things unreal? How can there be division when there is only one Existence that was previously misperceived as an individual and a universe?

Q.: "In fact, his individuality and the other entities vanish, although they persist in all of their forms."

N.: The individuality and all the other individuals vanished because they are unreal. Yet, there seems to be a persistence of forms. You do not see the body turn invisible when one realizes the Truth. Yet, such a one may rightfully say that there is no body. He would be speaking the Truth. An apparent onlooker would still see a body. We can never measure or determine Reality, or the Truth as proclaimed by such sages as the Maharshi, using the senses. The same is so for the intellect. They appear to go on for the onlooker or at the level at which such is taken into consideration, that is, being alive with prana, senses, etc. They do not cease in ultimate Truth, either, because they did not come to be. That Knowledge of their not-coming-to-be is spoken of as their cessation. So, there is no creation of illusion and no cessation of the illusion, because such has not come to be. That is the final conclusion.

Is there still confusion about the passage?

Q.: A little bit. I have had the experience of all the forms being gone and there being no subject or object. I am progressing to a unified, absolute state.

N.: Did your senses need to cease to operate in order for you to perceive that formlessness?

Q.: No. They were not connected.

N.: You have, then, just said the same point.

Q.: Oh! Now I understand. Thank you.

N. Thank Him.

Another Q.: You have questioned as to who has a concept. Is there a reason why you proceed in this way?

N.: Yes. But what is your state right now?

Q.: (Quiet)

N.: I have asked this of you not because there is any such thing as a "now moment," as if that were real, but why objectify or place at a distance the Truth of your own Being? Why speak of meditation and instruction as if it were a past event or future event? Why postpone?

Q.: Is it better to ask something from direct experience?

N.: Yes, direct experience turned inward toward the Realization of one's own Existence. Although we use speech to communicate about Self-Knowledge, there is no objective topic involved. It is not necessary to treat your Being-Consciousness-Bliss as if it were an event in past, present, or future time. You are not an event. For

Nonduality to be, Realization of the Self must necessarily be of the same nature as the Self itself. Otherwise, there would be a duality of you, the realizer or un-realizer, and the thing to be realized. There is no such division. That is why you do not inquire into "it" but inquire into "I." The way is nonobjective.

Q.: I am meditating upon how everything, this whole satsang, is happening in my mind. Your questioning has pushed me even beyond that.

N.: Your meditation is in the right direction. Everything appears in the mind, even the present question. In what does the mind appear? (Silence)

Q.: It is very interesting how, when I take myself to be the body, I think that the senses determine reality.

N.: If you want to know reality as it is, know yourself. (Silence)

(Then followed a recitation in Sanskrit and English from the Upanishads.)

(Silence)

Om Shanti Shanti Shanti Om

The Only Real State

Satsang, August 17, 2003

(Silence)

Om Om Om

(Silence)

N.: Silence is the state of Existence as it is. It is absolute, invariable, perpetual, and nondual. The Maharshi defines Silence as that state in which no "I" arises. It means that no ego, or separate, false sense of individuality, arises. If no false sense of ego arises, nothing else arises or is imagined. That which is the unborn is the state of no-creation. What is required to realize this is Self-Knowledge, which is not something of a perceptual or conceptual nature. It is not a knowledge through the senses or through thinking. It is transcendent knowledge that is Self-Knowledge, which is nonobjective knowledge. This is the one thing that is necessary for the Realization of this Absolute Existence.

For Self-Knowledge, inquire within yourself to know yourself as you are, not as imagined as something objective, but as you are. The Maharshi says that the egoless state is our real state, the only real state there is.

That which proceeds from an ego is of the nature of illusion, or imagination. The egoless state is our real state, the only real state there is. That which you seek in Liberation is not something apart from you, but your own nature. Real Being, infinite Consciousness, and unconditioned Bliss are not apart from you, but are of your nature, the only real nature that there is.

If you mistake yourself for an individual, it is imagining yourself to be something that is nonexistent. What is existent, the real Being-Consciousness-Bliss that you are, is ever as it is. To assume yourself to be an individual, something other than pure Existence, is to take up a stand—through imagination only, for your nature does not change, as the Real ever is as it is—as something that does not exist. Everything that proceeds from that nonexistence is similarly nonexistent.

If the delusive notion of "I" is unreal, just so unreal are the ideas that you are an embodied being, that you have a birth, a life and a death, that you have a form that pertains to you, and so forth and so on. Everything that proceeds from an ego is of the nature of suffering and bondage, and it is of the nature of an illusion. The characteristic of an illusion is that it is unreal.

If you want to know your real Existence as it is, start with that which is real within you. That is your own existence. Existence can alone know itself. The Real alone can know Reality. The unreal cannot do so. So, none of this is addressed to the ego or the ego-mind. All of this is addressed only to the real Self within you, which alone is capable of knowing itself. Inquire into the very fact of your existence, and cease to regard what is objective, and thus other, as your Existence. If you do not know who you are, whatever stand you take up through imagination, everything that proceeds from that is imagination. If you want to know Reality as it is, know yourself. If you want to know God, know yourself. If you are to know yourself, truly inquire, "Who am I?" and penetrate into the depths of pure Existence as it is. Cease to regard anything objective, transient, dependent, with form, or sporadic as being who you are. Cease to regard the body or anything in relation to the body as who you are. Similar is it with anything appearing within any state of mind, be it waking, dreaming, or deep sleep. What is objective, what is a product, and what comes after "I" has seemingly arisen is not who you are and is not real.

Your real state is the silent state that is "I"-less. It is the only real state there is. It is not that now you are in one state called "bondage" and will find liberation, but rather that which is found in the state of Liberation exists all of the time. It is the only existence. Liberation is not removed from you; it is bondage that is removed from you. It is not the Realized State that is abstract or theoretical; it is the unrealized state that is abstract and theoretical.

To understand what is indicated by these words, deeply inquire and know who you are. Start with the fact that you are. You exist. This existence and the knowledge of your existence do not depend upon anything else, such as your senses, your body, the thinking of your mind, or the idea of "I." Start with the existence and inquire deeply to know it as it is. This is where you start, and this is where you end.

(Silence)

Q.: If the meditator becomes satisfied that the unreal is unreal, could there be attachment of egoity that was aside from the incorrect information? Or is it that, once the incorrect information is settled, the other aspect collapses?

N.: What would be the other aspect?

Q.: It seems to be a kind of incorrect information. I do not wish to be complacent in my meditation and think that dispelling the unreal is all that needs to be done.

N.: If you dispel the unreal, because it is unreal, how do you do so? It can only be by true Knowledge. The unreal has no existence. If you would dispel the unreal by Knowledge, so that no more ignorance remained, what would bind you? What would give rise to duality? Do you assume that there are two realities?

Q.: Are you hinting that there is no other attitude that need be of concern, if the incorrect information is settled, for then the ignorance collapses of its own weight?

N.: If you have an incorrect attitude, from where does it arise? It is from some idea, is it not?

Q.: Yes.

N.: If the idea is wrong, the attitude that follows is wrong. If the idea is false, the attitude or mode of mind that comes from it is a further delusion based upon that original thought. All the permutations of ignorance are still just ignorance. From where do the various modes of mind, such as wrong information, wrong attitude, etc. arise?

Q.: They must be thoughts that seem to arise in Consciousness, but they cannot be fundamental.

N.: Do the thoughts declare their reality or do you declare them to be real?

Q.: I do not know this from experience, but it seems that the teaching would say that the only thing...

N.: No, let's proceed from your experience. All the teaching comes from pure experience. However, you should have your experience align itself with the original teaching and not regard imagination as experience.

Q.: I attribute reality to these, but that does not make sense, for that is not who I really am.

N.: Do the thoughts stand up on their own, or are you the knower of them?

Q.: I am the knower of them.

N.: What happens to the thoughts in the course of waking, dreaming, and deep dreamless sleep? Are any of the thoughts continuously with you?

Q.: No.

N.: If they are not continuously present, can they be real? Can something that is existent go out of existence? The thoughts are discontinuous, but you are continuous, for you do not go out of existence.

Q.: So, I attribute more power to them than they have.

N.: You exist, and the thoughts come and go. You determine them, but you suppose that they determine you. If you would inquire for whom the thoughts are, the identity and reality would be retrieved from their superimposed position with the thoughts and would return to their origin. Then, who would be ignorant?

If there is no one in ignorance, can ignorance be there? Does it come to you, or do you conjure it up? If you inquire into that "you" and it vanishes, being unreal, will ignorance appear again?

The Maharshi says, "Your greatest glory lies where you cease to exist." When you cease to exist, another Existence, which is truly you, alone remains. This is Consciousness. In Consciousness, there is no ignorance. Although ignorance cannot arise outside of Consciousness, there is really no such thing as ignorance truly coming to be within Consciousness. The same holds true for thought.

Q.: Thank you.

Another Q.: I am leaving for India. I want to dispense with the individual so that my practice can go on without hindrance. May I have some silence to take with me.

N.: What do you mean by "some"? (laughter) If your goal is Truth, and if you aim at it by inquiring, "Who am I?", or by surrendering and seeing that the "I" simply does not count in the scheme of things, all is for a noble purpose. As for Silence, it is already there. The Self is not brought in anew. You need not ask for it. (Silence)

Another Q.: Once one becomes egoless, does one merge with God and become God? Or is one an extension of God?

N.: If the individual being, or ego, is inward turned, he will naturally desire to merge with God. After due practice, it becomes evident that this split, or breaking off, never actually occurred. What was sought as merger is the perpetual, undivided state. For this one undivided Essence, which is infinite and eternal, there are no states, stages, phases, or conditions. There is nothing apart from it, and nothing extends from it.

Q.: Then, the state, itself, is there all alone?

N.: Reality does not change. It does not start at any time, and it does not change its nature. Knowledge of it is of the same character, which is perpetual.

Knowledge determines the experience. If there is no inquiry, the individual seems as if solid, and God seems remote, theoretical, or even nonexistent. If there is some spiritual practice, God seems real, but the individual also seems to be real. The more the practice, the less the individual is there, and the more there is the presence of God. If the practice is complete, and all are agreed that the egoless state is the aim of the practice, there is only God. God knows God; the Self knows the Self.

Another Q.: I would like to ask about using our bodies as the means for Self-Realization. The inquiry, "Who am I?", tends to be on the cerebral side. According to other opinions, we can use our body to observe the impermanence of sensation and let go. Can we use the physical existence as a means to Realization?

N.: Let us say that you observe the transient nature of the body. The observation is not so much sensory but of a subtler knowledge. It is the knowledge that makes such contemplation work and brings the spiritual benefit. Without the knowledge, what is left? There is the knowledge that this is transient, yet there must be something within you that is other than the body, because your existence does not change. The knowledge of this existence is essential. In any spiritual experience, regardless of the path taken, it is the knowledge essence that makes it fruitful. The greater the knowledge-essence, the more fruitful the practice is. When you look at the body in this way, is this not part of inquiry? Is this not still the path of Knowledge?

Another Q.: I want to save the world. There is a body that does things that can make a change in the world. If the real is always real, and I am always aware of the real, why do I become high in your presence? Is that a subtle thing that is not so important? Is it related? When I am in the world having sensory experiences, should I ignore that difference? I feel high here. I do not feel high when I am saving the world.

N.: What makes the difference? It cannot be just passing through the doorway. There is no sign that says, "Now leaving satsang hall, please cease to be high." How do you determine the distance, the being here or there? The one you are now is the same one there. You are here, there, now, and then. Even in the unborn state, you are the same. So, what makes the difference?

Q.: Is the nature of the Self effulgent so that I become a light bulb?

N.: You say that you are here and high. You say that you are in the world and that you are helping the world. Are they the same "I," or are the definitions of the "I" different?

Q.: The experience is different. The identity can be with the Self, but there is a difference in experience. There is the effulgence of the Self, but I just don't know.

N.: The effulgence of the Self does not change. The Self is just as it is. It is not brighter at one time and dimmer at another time. Being an infinite effulgence, it does not really shine upon something else, but if we look upon something else as something else, the effulgence is the universal light that shines on everything equally. It is not brighter or dimmer at any place.

What changes in your experience? The Self does not change. Do you think that the outer conditions change your experience, or is such due to something else?

Q.: I can't answer.

N.: Look deeply. If you think that outer conditions change your experience, you are left with two options. One is to control the outer situation as much as you can to stay in a better position; the other is to throw your hands up in despair in a fit of worldliness and declare that everything external determines your happiness and suffering. I do not recommend these options. If you determine that what changes your experience is neither the Self nor the apparent outer conditions, but rather the change of your own state of mind, and you look deeply to see what actually constitutes that change of state of mind, you will trace the changes to your misidentification. You will seek to change what you regard as yourself, the way you think of yourself.

You say that you are high and later that you are not high. Eamine the definition of yourself. High is your natural state. When you add something to it, you seem to come down from it. What do you add to it? Examine this finely. On the one hand, you will be surprised at what you see. On the other hand, you will not, for, inside, you will say to yourself that you knew this all of the time, so why did you fool yourself?

Another Q.: The Maharshi says that, if one would inquire unceasingly, that alone would suffice for Realization. It seems that continuous inquiry is the state of Realization. When I really inquire, it is not an action, and it is off the mental plane. It is an inward direction. When I go through my day, or whatever you wish to call all that...

N.: Your dream.

Q.: (laughter)

N.: You said that I could call it anything, so I accepted the invitation. (laughter)

Q.: When the inquiry become steady, it loses the form of inquiry and just is the same state.

N.: Yes, the end, itself, appears as the means.

Q.: Whenever I inquire deeply, that is very clear.

N.: In *Saddarsanam*, the Maharshi says that the idea of dualism in sadhana (practice) and nonduality in Realization is not true. Who is there but the tenth man the entire time? (alluding to the Vedanta parable of the ten men who ford a stream). The end appears as the means.

He also says that holding on to the Self with effort is practice. When it is effortless, it is called Realization.

What is this "holding on to the Self"? Obviously, there are not two of you, one to grab another. So, what does he mean?

Q.: There is nobody holding on to somebody else. There is no other.

N.: Remaining in the otherless state is "holding on."

The inquiry can be continuous. If we regard it as a mental activity, like any mental activity, it will be discontinuous. Practices that rely on the senses or on bodily activity are obviously discontinuous. No one holds a thought all of the time. That which knows thought is not determined by the limitations of thought. The discrimination between thought and your Self is an aspect of the inquiry. That which knows always knows. It is not different from your Being. As continuous as Being is, just so continuous is Knowledge. As continuous as Being-Consciousness is, just so continuous is Bliss.

If, at any time, there appears to be an interruption, determine what gives rise, what conjures up, the illusion of such interruption. This will return you to the same inquiry.

Q.: Desire seems to cause the interruptions. In the waking state, there is this urge to satisfy it by finding something in the world or by arranging circumstances. By that point, the ego and misidentification have occurred.

N.: If there is misidentification regarding Being, the illusions of an ego and the "I am the body" idea seem to flourish. If there is misidentification regarding Consciousness, you then believe in a separate mind and suppose yourself to be wandering within it. If there is misidentification regarding Bliss, you project the innate happiness elsewhere and seek for it.

Does searching for happiness externally ever succeed?

Q.: No.

N.: Never?

Q.: Never.

N.: So, is it necessary to do that anymore? Just answering, within oneself, this simple question regarding happiness is enough to make an extroverted, worldly-minded person an introspective person. It turns the mind inward naturally. One always desires happiness. It manifests as so many forms of desire. Find that which fulfills. One who so knows becomes desireless.

In deep sleep, do you have these desires?

Q.: No.

N.: Yet, you are happy. The experience tells you something.

Q.: The part about the misidentification regarding Being I did not understand.

N.: The "I" that did not understand it is the misidentification. Do you see?

Q.: Yes. (laughing)

N.: If you recognize Bliss is within, you become detached. If you negate the objective portion of what you refer to as your "mind," your mind is, itself, Brahman, or pure Consciousness. If you inquire into your Existence, "Who am I?", and find no one to be named "I," Being stands self-revealed.

Another Q.: Recently, I noticed my misidentification with the body. I exercise, and sometimes I overdo it. The body runs out of energy and aches, and I become grumpy. I feel trapped within a tired, worn out, hungry body. My mental capacity diminishes.

N.: Are you the body, or are you in the body? Where is your location?

Q.: No, I am not the body. At times, I have thought I was in the body.

N.: That thought that you were in the body was in you, just as, in a dream, you may have the appearance of a dream body and think that you are inside that dream body. You might feel that your limbs and such of that body are sore.

Q.: (laughing) Yes.

N.: Perhaps, you become grumpy with your other dream characters. (laughter) Where is all of that occurring?

Q.: In a dream mind.

N.: Did becoming grumpy help to relieve the suffering?

Q.: No.

N.: You know that you are not getting any younger. (laughter) So, you are headed for either much more freedom or much more grumpiness. If that is the fork in the road, which way are you going to go?

Q.: I do not want to take the road to more grumpiness. I aim for freedom, for that is natural for me.

N.: You know that what you have described does not feel natural. Proceed by your better knowledge. You are neither a body nor in a body. It would be better to say that the body is in you than you are in it. Your real nature is utterly bodiless. It does not commence when the body begins, and it does not cease when the body ends. It does not become tired or old. Your real Being is entirely bodiless.

Q.: For most of my life, the body is not an issue. Most of the time, the limbs are functioning without pain, at least for now.

N.: In what does your life appear?

Q.: (Quiet for time) It is a dream.

N.: Then, where does the dream appear?

Q.: In my mind.

N.: Where is your mind?

Q.: Of that I am not sure.

N.: It is good to be not sure. When we are not sure, we can find real certainty. If all this is in your mind, where is the mind?

(Then followed a recitation in Sanskrit and English of verses from the *Taittiriya Upanishad*.)

(Silence)

Om Shanti Shanti Shanti Om

The Self and Yourself

Satsang, August 24, 2003

(Silence)

Om Om Om

(Silence)

N.: The Self is the nondual Absolute. It is perpetually silent. Even in the midst of speaking, it is perpetually silent. It is unformed, unborn, eternal Being. Even in the apparent midst of bodily life, one can realize oneself as that unborn, eternal, unformed, real Being.

It is infinite Consciousness. Even in the midst of ever so many thoughts and states of mind, it remains as unformed, boundless, undifferentiated Consciousness.

It is also Bliss, behind and beyond any state, mode, or mood of the mind.

The Self is only one. There is not a plurality of selves. There are neither many selves apart from you nor is there a multiplicity of selves within you. The Self is only one. It is impersonal, infinite, eternal, and without conditions, phases, or changes.

If to you there appear to be the Self, in which you have faith or conviction, or of which you have some knowledge, and yourself, it is necessary to inquire into what yourself is. If it appears as if individualized, personal, or in a body, all trouble and samsara—the repetitive cycle of illusion, birth and death—come from that. Inquire within yourself as to who you are.

Find out if you are the body or if anything pertaining to the body, from its beginning or birth to its end or death, from its attributes to its activities, has anything to do with your real Being. The body is a transient form dependent upon your senses and your waking state of mind even to appear in your experience. What is your Being? Inquire as to what your real Being is.

What seems to mark you off as an individual? If you are not the body, how do you determine your individuality, or the ego? What is it that is named, "I"? Inquire.

The Self and yourself: what is yourself? What is this "I" that could be apart from the absolute, true Self? If you inquire in this manner, the individuality, or "I"-ness, will vanish. What vanishes is unreal. Reality neither appears nor disappears. What is unreal seems to appear and disappear. With the absence of inquiry, an "I" seems to appear. The Maharshi referred to this "I" as "a ghost with no form of its own." Upon inquiry, it cannot be found. All of illusion is like this. It survives due to lack of examination. If you inquire, bringing the lamp of Knowledge to search for the darkness, the darkness is not to be found anywhere. If you inquire to find what this "I" is, the "I" is not to be found anywhere. The inquirer, himself, is not to be found. What remains is the impersonal, true Self, which alone exists throughout all of eternity.

Since the most ancient days, the instruction has been: tat tvam asi, That you are. What is this you? The "That" is clear. It is the Absolute, Brahman, which is the real Self. That you are. What is this you? If you determine what this "you" is, the "are" part makes perfect sense.

If it is Liberation from all of the imagined bondage that you desire, know yourself. How else are you to know yourself except by constantly, deeply inquiring within yourself as to, "Who am I?" If you so inquire, you find that the end itself appears as the means. Knowledge, itself, appears as inquiry to reveal itself.

This much has been said just to point out the nonobjective outlook that is necessary for Self-Realization.

Q.: When I come out of deep sleep and have the sense that I existed, that is from some place much different. The Zen Master Bankei says that, when you hear a bird behind you, there is no intention or anticipation, but the sound is registered spontaneously. He says that, when people are walking in a crowded street, both the thief and the saint equally manage to mill through the crowd. When I make major life decisions about my family or livelihood, or to pursue the Truth, there is an absolute place from which these decisions come. That place seems so different from the black space I might imagine sleep is. It seems very impersonal and promising. I want to get a better understanding.

N.: What are you trying to understand?

Q.: How my identity and the source of awareness are more akin to that spontaneous place.

N.: How many identities do you have?

Q.: I have only one, and the other imagined space of the mind is just a fantasy that is created.

N.: Who creates it?

Q.: That is the way the spontaneous awareness is, too.

N.: Does this spontaneous awareness come and go? Is it there at sometime and not another?

Q.: The particulars come and go, but the place it comes from does not seem to come and go.

N.: So, it has nothing to do with bird sounds?

Q.: No. It is not the particular sound or the crowd.

N.: Well, we do not have bird sound just at this moment (note: the usual bird singing during satsang had ceased momentarily), but we do have some remote highway noise. (laughter)

Q.: Yes, and sometimes there is the sound of an ambulance, and that is a wake-up call.

N.: What is it that knows the noise?

Q.: It is some spontaneous, unintentional knowing.

N.: There are times when you do not hear the noise.

Q.: But the potential to know, as I know I exist in deep sleep, seems to be the same knowing.

N.: That you exist in all the three states of waking, dreaming, and deep sleep is self-evident upon examination. That this existence cannot have any of the forms attributed to it in any of the states is also evident, upon inquiry. You hear the highway noise in your waking state. The sensory perception occurs only in this waking state of mind. Sensory perception is not present in deep sleep. In deep sleep, there is no thought. There is no bird sound, no highway noise, and no spontaneous knowing. All of that vanishes. Bankei could not have been referring to something so transient.

Q.: Hmm. He was giving hints of something very different.

N.: What is that different thing?

The ever-existent is important to know. That it is here, now, forever, there, and everywhere is also important to know. It is omnipresent. It should not be defined in bodily terms, for no body can be omnipresent.

You know about those spontaneous moments and their coming and going. What is it that so knows? To confound that knowing with sensory perception would be an error of discrimination.

What knows, whether you are awake and hearing bird sounds, dreaming and hearing highway sounds, or in deep sleep and hearing no sounds? What knows both things apparently sensed and the sensing, to which the things sensed and the sensing are equally objective? The mental cognition of the same is equally objective. What never becomes an object? All that is objective, in the realm of experience, appears and disappears and thus can be only unreal. The nature of Reality is to be invariable. So, it is without beginning and without end. That which has no beginning and no end is alone the abode of eternal Liberation. To know that is to be that, and that alone is

Liberation, whether we call that the state of being Brahman or the state of Buddha-hood or by any other name. It cannot be some transient thing. It cannot be a mere objective appearance within the mind, which is, itself, imagined.

Deep, spiritual decisions come from some profound source. What makes them deep, spiritual decisions is that they are decisions that turn you inward to the source. It is not blackness or blankness of the intellect's interpretation. It is colorless, not a thing, and not a blank. You are not a thing, and you are not a blank. If there is a thing, you are there, and, if there is a blank, you are also there. What is this "you"? If you pour your mind inward, every idea that you have about "you" and about "this"—from the world to God—will vanish for you. Consciousness, which is your real Being, which can never be conceptual in character and which can never be perceived, is directly realized. Direct means that no other instrument is necessary. It knows itself. Do you see the direction being pointed out?

Q.: It is the direction that I truly wish to follow.

N.: As for walking in a crowded place is concerned, consider such to be your mind, and do not bump into people.

Another Q.: I have been studying with (mentions a contemporary, local teacher) and reading Nisargadatta Maharaj and Ramana Maharshi. I do not know how to get to what is. I simply fall backward into a sense of non-identity. It is just nothingness. I go through this process as much as I can during the day. Then, my ego comes back to me. It shrouds. Why is it not permanent? I know that there is no doing but simple being.

N.: It is because you view this as states.

Q.: Hmm.

N.: As for "there is nothing to be done," you may want to examine that doctrine.

Q.: In what way?

N.: How do you know that there is nothing that you can do? Physical action may not be what is needed, but what makes you think that there is no spiritual practice?

Q.: Certainly, the act of falling is doing.

N.: So, there is practice.

Q.: Yes, that is my practice.

N.: There is plenty that you can do.

Q.: Is that enough? Should I just continue?

N.: What is it that returns?

Q.: The sense of a little me.

N.: To whom does it return?

Q.: My consciousness. It begins to populate my awareness.

N.: How does that happen?

Q.: Some type of gravitational, magnetic force. (laughter)

N.: The force is perceived by you. It depends on you. Ignorance does not come to one; it is self-conjured.

Q.: I am unaware.

N.: Then, it would be worthwhile to examine this. The Maharshi refers to such as vasanas, tendencies. The tendencies are for an ego entity. The "I" has no form of its own, so it manifests in various forms. One tendency may be to misidentify with the body. If the misidentification with the body is carried into the deeper experience, though you will think of yourself as being Consciousness, you will still think that there are other things to be seen, as a panorama or show. Can you see those things without the body? You may not notice this during the experience, but, later, the "I-am-the-body" idea manifests more and seems to bring you out of the experience. The seed was there in the experience.

Q.: Even more so, concepts in the mind.

N.: Yes, the "I-am-the-body" idea is such a concept.

Q.: Yes.

N.: If your orientation is to disidentify from the mind and the ego, but you still believe that there is a real world perceived by a body, you are trying to relinquish something subtler yet holding to something grosser.

Q.: Is there some part of me that still believes it to be real?

N.: (laughing) You are answering your own question.

So, let the inquiry become continuous, which means that it must be off the mental level. Let the inquiry be deep and thorough. Get to the very root of "I." Wherever there is a "somehow," such as somehow ignorance returns and somehow you fall into it and somehow fall out of it, examine. No one is nearly unaware as he pretends to be. (laughter)

Another Q.: I become bogged down in doubt. I am looking into the various routes to That. If I could see conceptual thought for what it is, that is it? It has to do with paying attention or concentrating. Sometimes, there is a natural way to pay relaxed attention. When I try to pay attention or concentrate deliberately, I let thought in and try to catch up with it.

N.: Try giving your attention to something impersonal. Make the orientation impersonal, rather than personal. If you examine the mode of mind from which you made the various statements, you will see that all of them pertain to the person, which is the identity.

The verses recited at the conclusion of last satsang are from an Upanishad. The word translated as "concentration" is tapas. Tapas indicates a fiery intensity of practice. The root of the word signifies heat or the ability to burn. It indicates the quality of meditation. It can be translated as "concentration" as was done in that book.

Concentration upon what? Do you want to concentrate on the real Self? The real Self cannot be objective. This focus upon the Self manifests as a negation of the identity and reality that are wrongly associated with anything of a personal nature, that is to say, that which pertains to the ego. If we approach in an impersonal way, what we hear of the teaching, what we remember of the teaching, and what we absorb of the teaching, whether here, elsewhere, or in ancient texts, changes dramatically.

The instruction here is not actually that of paying attention or paying attention in a relaxed manner rather than in a tense manner or of trying to catch up with your thoughts. This is so because you are already that space that can be described as neither still nor moving and that knows all thought. That is your nature. There is no difficulty in this.

You cannot say that you do not know your own thoughts. Of course, you know them. Otherwise, they could not appear for you.

You should inquire deeply and thoroughly as to who you are.

Q.: That is the thing that flashes forth?

N.: It has none of the problems and none of the breakthroughs from the problems. There is nothing like that. The teachings of the Maharshi and Vedanta speak of that which is beyond the three states of waking, dreaming, and deep sleep. What is the purpose of such instruction? It is to point out that which is utterly impersonal and transcendent and that that is what we are. Start with that, and put your focus upon that. Make your vision impersonal. Practice based upon the impersonal. The inquiry is entirely impersonal. Self-Knowledge is entirely impersonal. It has nothing to do with the individual, the attributes of the individual, and the difficulties of the individual, but eradicates all of that. Think about this deeply.

Another Q.: Would you speak about surrender? One has to apply effort, but, at some point, the ego must give up, and there is no choice involved. Then, there is release.

N.: How does this release occur?

Q.: (shrugs his shoulders)

N.: Do you feel that it just happens? Is there a cause for it?

Q.: I don't know.

N.: Then, how do you know that it will happen for you?

Q.: There is a sense that it is there. It is present. It is a matter of letting go.

N.: How do you practice letting go?

Q.: I don't know.

N.: What do you mean by "letting go"?

Q.: (quiet for some time) Allowing the space where there is no holding on to something, no attachment, and there is relaxation.

N.: Thus, there would be the real Self, the letting go, and the ego "I" who makes the decision being in charge of all of it. Why should that be so? Why would the Absolute not be in charge, the practice be subservient to the ego, and the ego be the lord of all? With that arangement as the supposition, would Liberation ensue?

Q.: No.

N.: Some discrimination is needed. A re-evaluation would help.

The Maharshi, indeed, speaks of surrender. He says that there are two ways to bring about effacement of the ego. One is to inquire, "Who am I?" and find that there is no ego; the other is to feel, "Not me, not mine," and renounce the possessing of anything whatsoever. That he calls "surrender." In that, God is all, and you have no existence, desire, or will of your own. The ego is thus effaced. Both indicate a precise method of practice.

"Letting go" is common enough. You have heard many other people speak of "letting go." If you ask how this release works or what is really meant by "letting go," it becomes exceedingly vague. It is not formless; it is just vague. Formless would be good; vague is due to lack of actual experience and Knowledge.

You should have this Knowledge. Inquire and know who you are, and you, yourself are the Moksa, or Liberation, or Release, for such is not an activity or a kind of practice but is a way of describing the ever-unbound state of the real Self. Or, surrender, but surrender must be to the Supreme. It cannot be to events and circumstances or to the vagaries of the mind. Surrender is to the Supreme, feeling that God alone matters, and the ego does not count in the scheme of things whatsoever.

Q.: There is still this sense of being in time and moving in time to the experience. Then, there is the Self, where there is no time.

N.: Where is time apart from us? Do you depend on time or does time depend on you?

Q.: Time depends on me.

N.: Have you ever had an experience in which time was not?

The exclusion of thought will eliminate time. You must be thinking in order to experience time. So, you need not worry about time; you need only disidentify from thought. Do you see?

Q.: Yes.

N.: You are not in the grip of time. If, though, you misidentify with the mind and body, time is becoming shorter in this ever-narrowing window of time called a "life-span." Use it very wisely to fulfill life's ultimate purpose. That is Liberation, or Self-Realization. Go about that in an intense manner. Don't wait for something to happen. Self-Realization does not happen. It is not an event. It is not in time. It is real. Find it by knowing yourself.

Is the direction now clear for you?

Q.: Yes.

Another Q.: Even if we don't acknowledge true Being, it does not mean that it doesn't exist. At a certain level, it does not exist in the sense that we do not care about it. Is that what you mean about time, too, or do you mean that it just does not exist?

N.: How many levels are there of reality? Is Reality undifferentiated or is it divided?

Q.: Oh! It is undifferentiated.

N.: If it is undifferentiated, can we speak of levels or degrees of reality?

Q.: No.

N.: What is real ever is; what is unreal never is.

Q.: (Smiling and laughing) Oh!

N.: If, in the course of aspiration, one says that he knows something that is truly real, yet, on another level, something else is going on, there must be someone who is shuttling back and forth between these levels. If one inquires, "For whom are these levels?" everything is answered. There is no multiplicity in Reality. This is the distinction between qualified nonduality and unqualified nonduality. Qualified nonduality means nonduality but with some difference. Unqualified nonduality means Reality as it is, with no limitations placed upon it.

Q.: That is the Self?

N.: Yes.

Q.: Everything else is not the Self. So, qualified and unqualified are useless.

N.: For the sake of aspirants seeking Self-Realization, it is a description of degrees of ignorance or Knowledge. Knowledge mixed with a bit of ignorance is nonduality mixed with a bit of duality. If the aim is utter nonduality, which is the seeing of Reality as it is, when one comes across notions, or perspectives, in the mind that there is the Self and also something else going on, he should examine what this "something else" is.

Another Q.: I accidentally injured someone, poking him in the eye, over the weekend while playing a sport. It bothered me. I meditated upon losing my senses. I am unsure if I resolved that feeling. The sport is somewhat dangerous for the body. My practice went down after that happened.

N.: Did you feel concern for the person whose eye was poked?

Q.: Oh yes! I also knew that, in this sport, such injuries are bound to happen.

N.: You did not intend to do it, but still, you felt badly that it happened.

Q.: Yes. He became very upset and then became angry.

N.: Did his upsetness bother you, or did your action in the accidental injury bother you?

Q.: I am unsure. He became extremely upset. I contemplated how I would feel if I lost my vision. It is an important function to have.

N.: If you lose your vision, what happens to your existence? If you closed your eyes and never opened them again, what would that mean for your existence?

Q.: The world, or my attachments in it, would be gone.

N.: Not necessarily. When you enter into dream, you lose all of the five senses, yet you create an entire other world in your mind, endowed with appropriate senses, with a body, and such. The attachment is still there. Liberation from attachment comes by Knowledge. It does not come by elimination of the senses. Otherwise, long ago, the ancients would have advised cutting off the ears, eyes, the nose, and anesthetizing the skin to make everything fine, but that is not what is advised. (laughter) Nor are the senses some great, universal, cosmic flaw. If eyesight caused attachment, whoever created eyesight is the one to blame for all this. (laughter). That which created or made eyesight even possible would be the guilty party. Is that reasonable? Eyesight does not create attachment, though you do need to be detached from your senses. If you had no eyesight, from where would you obtain your happiness?

Q.: I would need to get it from the same place, with or without eyes.

N.: That is clear seeing. Happiness always comes from within and is the very nature of the within-ness. It never comes via the senses. Neither your existence nor your happiness would be disturbed. Existence which is the source of happiness is already detached from the senses. It has none of the qualities of the senses. It is not a sensing entity, and it is not a sensed thing. This blissful Existence, which is also Consciousness, does not act, for it is not the body. So, it does nothing, either good or bad.

Q.: It seems to be sensed indirectly.

N.: What do you mean?

Q.: Not through a sensory function, yet it is somehow sensed.

N.: How do you experience it? Do you see it?

Q.: No.

N.: Do you hear the Self?

Q.: No.

N.: Do you smell the Self?

Q.: No.

N.: Do have a tactile sensation of the Self?

Q.: No.

N.: How do you experience it?

Q.: The less I am in the picture, the more it is experienced.

N.: Yes. Whether you think that you are in the picture or not, don't you exist?

Q.: Yes.

N.: Does the knowledge that you are vary, or is that the same?

Q.: The knowledge that I am?

N.: Yes. Not what you think about yourself, but the knowledge that "you are."

Q.; I think that it varies.

N.: How does it vary?

Q.: When I think or become involved with the world, it varies. It is when I believe that a world exists out there.

N.: Out where?

Q.: Hmm.

N.: Does the knowledge of your existence vary, or is it that you have an addition of other ideas?

Q.: It is an addition of other ideas.

N.: Does the existence disappear or become less?

Q.: It seems as if there is a variation.

N.: Is it a variation in your existence or of what comes and goes? Is it variation in the knowledge of existence or variation in the imagination of a mind, which is, itself, unreal?

Q.: I need to see that more deeply. How do I do that?

N.: Who is the one who wants to do it? You exist. You do not do anything to exist. You know that you exist. It is not an action of your body or your mind. Therefore,

Knowledge is referred to as the means for Liberation and not any kind of action. Action cannot lead to Liberation, says Sri Sankara in the beginning of *Atmabodha*. The Self cannot be anything sensed. Therefore, the Upanishad says, "the unseen seer of all that is seen, the unheard hearer of all that is heard. He is the unknown knower of all that is known." It cannot be sensed or conceived. You do not think or sense anything in order to exist or to know this existence. To know anything else, the mind and senses seem to be necessary.

What you refer to as the world and the senses is just as much inside the mind. It is just as in a dream, in which you seem to experience inside and outside, but both are inside your mind. The subject and the object are within the mind. The present waking state is similar.

Whether waking or dreaming, or both states vanish along with their subjects and objects, still you exist and you know that you are. You do not think that you are, but you know that you are. This you that you are cannot be anything that appears in those states of mind and cannot be anything that appears in the senses, which are nonexistent in sleep. You cannot be anything that appears in a mind that ceases to be.

The Knowledge of Existence is of the same nature as Being. This is the first point elucidated by Sri Sankara in his *Svatmanirupanam*. He makes it clear that Existence is. If you know your existence, that knowledge is the Existence. If you doubt your existence, that knowledge is of that real Existence. You may wish to look at those verses.

Q.: How does one go about determining this without a shadow of a doubt? I need to wear down the ideas.

N.: Who builds them up?

Q.: I am not sure of that.

N.: From where do they derive their solidity? From the same one?

Q.: Yes.

N.: How would you wear them down?

Q.: By investigating their nature.

N.: Yes, that is so. Wearing them down or demolishing them at once makes no difference, as long as the focus is the inquiry into your own real nature. If you proceed along these lines, you will see that you are not the body, not in a body, and that you do not have a body. So, you did not do anything. Loss of the body is no loss for you. The same applies to the senses. Detach yourself by the knowledge of where happiness is. You should further detach yourself by inquiry and arrive at innate detachment. That is of the Self, the One without a second, which cannot be attached to anything, for there is nothing else to which it could become attached.

Q.: Misidentification occurs quite often if investigation into my nature is not made. My meditation usually begins with that, and, often, I come back to that.

N.: In his teachings, the Maharshi so frequently makes reference to freedom from misidentification with the body. Without the "I am the body" idea, do you do anything? Without the "I am the body" idea, are you endowed with the senses?

Q.: It then reduces itself to the mind.

N.: Yes, the "I am the body" idea appears in the mind. Spiritual practice occurs in the mind for the mind. The body has no need for the practice, as it is an innocent corpse. The Self has no need for the practice because it is just as it is.

Q.: What is the experience of all the senses being in the mind?

N.: It is your present sense perception. Is such occurring now anywhere else but in your mind?

Q.: I could think otherwise.

N.: When you think something is some way, does it make it so?

Q.: No, it is just a matter of thinking.

N.: Do you have sense perception without the mind's activity?

Q.: That is interesting. If there were no thoughts at all, I would not sense anything.

N.: Yes, you experience that every night in deep sleep. It is also experienced in samadhi. There is no sense perception then. Where else could the sense perception occur? You may think that you sense something, but the something is in the sensing. The sensing is in the mind. It is only a mode of mind connected with the idea of something external, your own mind playing all the parts, as in a dream. Where is the mind? If all is in the mind, where is the mind? If you inquire deeply, you will find neither world nor mind, but just nondual Consciousness.

Another Q.: With the "I am the body" idea, there is never anything spiritual. The senses do not give anything spiritual.

N.: That is so. Even when some holy thing is sensed, such as a holy person, an altar, a temple, etc., the holiness is not in the sensation. Sacredness comes from something else. The senses do not give anything spiritual; nor is spiritual experience to be equated with anything sensory.

The senses live in the body; there is no body apart from the sense perceptions. Within that circular illusion is the realm of sense activity.

Another Q.: How can I stop creating suffering, so that it is not necessary for me to surrender? How to stop identification with the body, the mind, and thought? I ask, "Who am I?" and I go through stages of boredom in which I do not have any experience of knowing who I am. The subtlety is lost, and I am in a dense state. Suffering comes, and then I let go. Should I answer the inquiry question with "I am"? If I have a certain answer, it will bring a state of peacefulness and surrender. Those answers seem to work for a period of time, and then they are no longer effective. That leads to a state of suffering. I think Bhagavan once said to Yogananda that suffering is part of the process.

N.: To which process was he referring?

Q.: I can't remember that. He said that suffering was part of the teaching, part of the process.

N.: He was asked why there was suffering in the world. He first gave instruction about who sees it. When the question was reiterated, then he said that suffering was part of the process. In what way? Suffering drives a man to look within, for he cannot find an answer outwardly. Looking within, he seeks God, in which case he surrenders to God. What is surrendered cannot again be claimed or picked up. So, the roots of suffering are burned and destroyed. Or, he looks for the Self within, and that Self is God. He inquires, "Who am I?" and the sufferer, along with all his attributes that created the suffering, are understood to be unreal. They cease to exist and can no more sprout into new suffering, just as the waters of a mirage cannot cause you to drown.

If, in meditation, you give an answer as described by you, such as "I am," or "I am the Self," because of what the answer signifies, you feel a certain degree of peace. This, though, is not the actual inquiry. It is a noble thought that reflects something of Truth. You feel better because of the reflected light of Truth.

Sri Bhagavan indicated that no answer is to be supplied for the inquiry. There is an answer, but it is the nature of the inquirer himself. It is of the nature of direct experience. You need not supply an answer in your mind, in the form of certain words or ideas, because whoever has those ideas still remains unknown. As long as one is on the level of thought, there are some thoughts that are of a suffering nature, which are denser and represent more bondage. You need to be off the mental level entirely.

It can be put roughly like this. The Self, which is of the nature of Being-Consciousness-Bliss, is always there. The more ideas that you pile on top of yourself, the more veils you are putting on and, thus, the absence of bliss, the missing of your own being, and the overlooking of your own consciousness. This is called suffering. To remove the suffering, remove the misidentification that causes that thinking. If you simply remove the thoughts, this is what you are doing every night in deep sleep. You have successfully practiced deep sleep hundreds of times (laughter), each time enjoying the peace of it, but the suffering returns. There is no wisdom in it. Wisdom, or true Knowledge, consists of the loss of the ignorant misidentification with what you cannot be. The inquiry is the most efficacious in this. Inquiry includes none of the misidentification that you are trying to dissolve. So, it includes none of the duality that you are trying to destroy.

If you surrender, surrender to God, but then you cannot pick up what is God's. If you surrender, there is nothing that is yours. Or, inquire directly into the "you." Either way, it should be complete. If you merely have a thought as described by you, you may obtain some relief, but it will be transient. If you merely relax the mind and don't think about it, that should not be called "surrender." Even a casual glance at the records of the great bhakta-s (devotees) throughout history shows you that a superficial, momentary, relaxation technique has really nothing to do with surrender. It is merely a temporary mental mode. There is nothing wrong with taking a brief mental respite, but that is not going to further your liberation. Surrender, or deep devotion, is much more profound and readily available. Similarly, inquiry is more profound than suggesting an idea to the mind, and the inquiry is readily available as your own Existence is already there.

Boredom cannot occur in Self-Knowledge. The Self is of perpetual fascination. Your ideas become boring. If your practice seems boring, try the elimination of some ideas, especially the ideas about yourself. That which is Bliss can never become boring. You cannot find any bored sages.

(Then followed a recitation in Sanskrit and English of verses from the *Isa Upanishad*.)

(Silence)

Om Shanti Shanti Shanti Om

No Topic

Satsang, September 7, 2003

(Silence)

Om Om Om

(Silence)

N.: The nondual Absolute Reality, Brahman, is the true and only nature of the Self. There is no one apart from it who could know it or be ignorant of it. For this reason, the Truth is not something that can be discussed like a topic, even though that alone is what we speak of here. When questioned about the nature of Truth, the Maharshi and other sages remained silent. In this silence, there is no "I" apart from the Truth to know it or to be ignorant of it.

In the absence of a separate individual, or "I," Truth knows itself, God knows God, the Self truly knows itself. Therefore, if you want to know the Truth, the Absolute, you must know yourself.

Your own Self is nonobjective in nature, whatever is objective is not yourself. For Realization of the Absolute, Self-Knowledge, which is equally nonobjective, is required. It is not a matter of knowing about the Truth, the Absolute, or God. Rather, the light of your innermost Consciousness shines upon itself without anything objective whatsoever. It is your very Being reposing as it is.

How does Being come to repose as it is? In truth, it ever is as it is. It is not a doing. That which is real always is, without variance, without change, without creation or destruction, without birth, and without death. That which is really the Self is as it always is, without change, without variance, without condition or phase, without creation or destruction, without birth, and without death. So, what is this "Being the Self"? It is just what is actually always the case.

In spiritual practice, this knowing of the Self manifests as a negation of misidentification. If only what you assume yourself to be is set aside as being only so much delusion, the Reality shines of its own. There remains no one to be ignorant of it; nor is there anyone apart from it to grasp the knowledge of it. Rather, the thing in itself, Reality, the Knowledge, and the one who realizes it are identical. It is nondual.

Set aside from your identity everything that is not actually you, be such the objects, circumstances, and events of the manifest world or your body or the thougghts of your mind. Set such aside as having nothing to do with your real nature, and see what remains. Inquire within yourself, "Who am I?" Inquire deeply, giving up the objectifying outlook. Cease to regard what is objective as yourself, what is not your Self as yourself.

The body is something that you know. If you call it you or yours, you are simply mistaken. What do you do when you find that you have made a mistake? You give up the mistaken approach. Cease to regard the body as you, yours, your encapsulation, or any such definition in relation to you. If you are not the body, what are you? If you are not the body, what can define you and consequently confine you? If you are not the body, where is your beginning, and where is your end? Where is your location, what is your birth, and what is your death? If you are not the body, can you be active or still? If you are not the body, can you say that you do this or do not do this, that you are here or there, or that you are now or then?

There is existence and the sense of "I." From where does it come? Question yourself, inquiring to know what your nature is, and give up that which is objective as having nothing to do with who you actually are. Attempt to determine what is actually your identity. (Silence)

Consider your thinking. Which thought or pattern of thought is actually you? Whether a pattern of thought appears while your mind is awake or dreaming, is it you? If a thought cannot be you, can a bunch of thoughts be you? Does more of "not you" make up you? Inquire. Your thoughts are as objective as your sensations are. It is simply a mistake if we regard them as subjective. When you find a mistake, you abandon it.

You are not the thinking and not the object of thought. Every thought has some form to it; there is no such thing as a formless thought. If every thought is objective, and you are not what is objective, who are you? What is the Consciousness that knows thought yet is not known by thought? If you are not thought, can you remember yourself or forget yourself? If you cannot possibly be a thought, are you conceivable? If you are not thought, where is desire and where is fear? If you are not thought, where is ignorance? If you are not thought, have you, after all, made a mistake at all? Inquire and know yourself. Who am I?

Is the notion of "I," the idea of being an individual, you? If it is not with you all of the time, such as when you are in deep, dreamless, thoughtless sleep, can it be you? You exist continuously. Can the assumption of "I," that you are an individual entity, be you? If it is not you, where is bondage and where is liberation? Where is ignorance and where is knowledge? Knowledge and Liberation are your own nature. Who becomes bound? Who becomes ignorant to imagine himself as bound? (Silence)

No body, no mind, no "I;" so, no boundary, no time, no space, no bondage, and no limitation. The formless, the nondual, the forever undifferentiated, is alone you. Being formless, and thus boundaryless, being undifferentiated, and therefore with nothing apart, this is the sole-existent Reality. Though called, "That," can it be objective? Though known as the Self, can it be an individual or a particular thing?

The Reality, which is the Self, simply is as it is. It is not a topic for discussion, though it is that of which we speak here.

Q.: It is very clear that the "I" did not rise in the body, in the senses, and in the perceiver of the senses, though it is put in those places. Still, I find myself returning to the stand that I am so-and-so sitting here.

N.: What makes the change?

Q.: What I see as true.

N.: The inquiry, whether expressed as, "From where does the 'I' arise?" or as, "Who am I?" cannot be merely the intellectual recognition of such. The inquiry is experiential knowledge. It concerns what you feel or experience as being yourself. If you want Liberation from the bondage of thinking that you are the body, you must truly know yourself. For that purpose, there is spiritual practice. The real practice consists in the relinquishment of misidentification. If you stop short and say that you know that you are not the body, the senses, and the mind because you have heard such here and have read it in the Maharshi's teachings and in the Vedanta, so that you have the thought but still feel that you are there, this is not accomplishing the good for which you seek. What matters is what you consider to be your existence, your identity.

Are you here and now in a body? Exactly where in the body are you?

Q.: As soon as you ask that, it is obvious that I am in no part of the body. So, who am I?

N.: Certainly, you cannot expect an objective answer. If you remove what is erroneously thought of as being yourself, such is no longer your stand. See what you are; not with the eyes, of course, and not with the mind. See with something far deeper.

Do you really ever become a body? Are you not the body in this room, but, stepping downstairs, become a body?

You have known people who have died. Everyone eventually dies. This is obvious. Is it that, the moment before death, you are in this body, and the moment later, you are somewhere else? If you are here, and, then somewhere else, what is this thing that can be here, there, and in different places? If later you are not in the body, and Existence itself does not change and does not alter its attributes, for it is Existence and not an illusion, where can it be now?

Q.: Looking at my dead father-in-law's body a few days ago, it was clear to me that he was not his body.

N.: Did he only recently become other than the body? If you think so, you will think in terms of life and death. Usually, there will be grief at death, though people grieve during life, as well. If you look dualistically, you see differentiation. Then, as the Upanishad says, one goes from death to death.

Wherever he is now is where he was before. What you are before birth and what you are after death is the same as what you are now. The temporary appearance does not alter your Existence.

When you are in deep sleep, there is no experience of a body. Now, in the waking state, there seems to be an experience of the body. Your mind has become active, and there is an experience of the body. With discrimination, you can derive the appropriate conclusion regarding this. Certainly, your Existence continues throughout, with and without the body.

There was no idea of being here and now in deep sleep. Something that is so fragile as to be utterly vanquished just by going to sleep cannot be the abiding reality.

Q.: I experience some other ideas heaped on top of the experience of the Self.

N.: Distinguish between the appearance and the substrate in what you feel that you are. Right now, you feel that you are. The same feeling was present many years ago and will be there in the future.

Q.: The same experience has been there since the earliest memories I have. There is not a bit of difference in that experience.

N.: Even before memory, you did know that you are. You have never known a time when you ceased to exist, but you have known many times when your body was not a factor in your experience and times when only a part of your body was. Reflect on this. Become clear about what is the ongoing Existence, which is the substrate, and what is merely a temporary, illusory appearance. Come to this knowledge in certainty. Continue to inquire until the habit of delusion of conceiving yourself as that thing, in that thing, or possessing that thing—the body—has vanished and no longer binds you. To realize this, what more direct approach could there be than inquiring, "Who am I?" and proceeding by the direct path of Knowledge? The Knowledge reveals that you cannot possibly be the body. Since the state of Knowledge is that in which you wish to end, standing by itself, being self-supported, why not practice that? Is it clear for you how to proceed?

Q.: Yes, it is. Thank you.

Another Q.: When I hit my hand with a hammer, I experience physical sensations of pain. Yet, if somebody else's foot is smashed with a hammer, I do not experience the physical sensation of pain. Is it a misidentification with my own body that I do not feel somebody else's pain? There is a connection with my body and not a connection with somebody else's physical discomfort or pain.

N.: Examine the misidentification with the senses. If you presume that you are of the senses or a sensing entity, you regard those sensations pertaining to that body as somehow pertaining to you and, unreasonably, that the body is you.

Did you have any dreams last night?

Q.: Yes.

N.: If someone, another character, was injured in your dream, did you feel the pain?

Q.: No.

N.: When you awakened, where did the dream characters and dream bodies go? Who composes the entire dream? The bodies of the others were equally yours. In the dream, you selected one. You are actually all of them equally or none of them. It is just so now. You are, as the *Gita* says, the Self dwelling in the hearts of all beings. Yet, the same *Gita* says that I am not in all beings. All beings are in me, yet they are not in me. I am in all beings, yet I am not in them.

Q.: Is the experience of pain an individual sensation because of misidentification?

N.: The pain is there for that body and those senses if you bump it with a hammer as described by you. What, though, has that got to do with your nature? If you think that that is you, or that you are caught within it, you feel bound within the experience of pain, and, thereby, you suffer. If you are endowed with Self-Knowledge, you do not suffer. The body, the pain, and such, seem to be and to occur, but there is no suffering. It is just as now you are not suffering due to the pains or pleasures that may be happening for the dream character, if you regard him as still continuing now that you have awakened.

Q.: Is it likewise for the mental conception? If there is a disagreement with someone and I feel anguish, is this also a misconception that I am the one so feeling?

N.: What constitutes the anguish?

Q.: I committed a mistake. Someone became upset. Then I felt bad. I am identifying with the feeling of anguish. In the moment of the emotion, how do I deal with that with the practice of inquiry?

N.: There are two misconceptions. One is the "I" that is caught in the anguish, and other is the "I" that is the very core of that anguish. If both conceptions of the ego were gone, would there be anguish? You say that you have a disagreement, that you made a mistake, and that you have anguish. Who is the "I" in your statement?

Q.: My unclear practice of that tends toward disavowal of my actions.

N.: It does not do you any good. The law of karma still holds sway, and you experience the results of your actions. Theory does not change the reality.

Q.: I try to learn from the experience and not repeat the mistake.

N.: How do you learn? How do you guarantee that you do not repeat the mistake?

Q.: That is my problem. I repeat the same confusion.

N.: So, that is what you actually have a problem with and not with the inquiry.

Q.: No, not with the inquiry.

N.: Do the mistakes in your mind just happen or do you conjure them up? Who is responsible for your own thinking?

Q.: Me. I make the mistakes.

N.: Why do you think the way that you think?

Q.: I am not sure.

N.: The man caught up in complete worldliness hardly notices that he is thinking. He says that events are happening, some people are being disagreeable, and such. If he becomes angry, he says that someone else made him feel so. A more spiritually-minded person notices that it is his own thinking. Yet, why are you thinking the way that you are thinking?

Q.: Because of ignorance and conceptions of such.

N.: If you know it is a misconception, why do you repeat it? Or, do you not know that?

Q.: I am not sharp enough and am lazy at times.

N.: How sharp do you need to be, considering its your thinking? It is not someone else's thinking. (laughter)

Q.: Yes, that is so. (laughing)

N.: Do objective circumstances, inclusive of the activities of other people, generate your thinking or does your thinking come from you?

Q.: It comes from me.

N.: From what you regard as you.

Q.: Yes.

N.: What you regard as you determines the way that you think.

Q.: This goes back to the core, ignorant thought of my individual self.

N.: Yes, and whatever definition that you give to that individual self, since, as the Maharshi says, the ego is a ghost with no form of its own. It feeds on forms in order to appear.

Q.: I want to live more fully in this way. I know that I am not the body. Now, that is only on the surface for me and not the deepest understanding level of living that.

N.: Only what you actually experience should you regard as knowledge. All that is said here about Knowledge is of a non-conceptual nature. Approach it by the interior experience of what you actually feel that you are. Mere phrases are alright for erudition but are not sufficient for Self-Realization. You must determine what you take yourself to be. Why? Who? If you notice what you are thinking, and you take full responsibility for your thinking, because that enables you to have full freedom, you then find out why you think the way that you think. You find that your thinking is generated from some identity. It is not the inert body. It is not the Self, for that has neither thought nor a body. That is only pure Being-Consciousness-Bliss for eternity. Something seems to be between. It is some definition. It starts with the core notion of "I," and other definitions are added to it. Trace your thinking to those definitions. Then, inquire, "Who am I?" and you will erase the definitions. When you erase them, they will be as if they never were. How to suffer will become a lost memory for you.

You must apply yourself and discern. Look within yourself to know who you are. It is not difficult, though you must persevere with it. There is nothing really that obstructs the Knowledge of yourself, yet you must be thorough and penetrating with the elimination of all that is not the Self. No longer regard as knowledge what is actually just ignorance.

If you approach in this way, will you have any anxiety or anguish? The very root of suffering will be dissolved, because it is unreal. The inquiry reveals just the Truth, the Reality of your own Being. Nothing new is created. Just that which really has no substance is eliminated. Consider it like waking out of a dream or the relinquishment of imagination.

You do not wish to live your life in imagination. When you see imagination as imagination, naturally, due to that which is innate, there is the intense desire to find reality. When you see that what you were pursuing in the name of happiness was actually causing suffering, there is the natural desire to become happy and secure your happiness. The desire is the intuition that happiness is your own Being.

Do you now know how to proceed?

Q.: Yes. Thank you.

Another Q.: We are manifested. We serve in the Reality when we are dedicated to the Reality. Is that what is considered devotion or seva (service)?

N.: The highest seva or selfless service is to abide in and as the Reality, with the ego gone. That is also the highest, or supreme, bhakti (devotion), parabhakti, in which there is no vibhakti, no non-devotion. This means that the individual ego has evaporated or merged. Likewise, it is the supreme yoga, the mahayoga, the great yoga, in which there is no viyoga, no division. That is the highest yoga or highest union. The same is Knowledge.

Q.: Are independence and freedom synonymous? One of the impediments of pure devotion is claiming my own independence.

N.: How can you have your independence apart from the Absolute? By what power would you do so?

Q.: By my sense of enjoyment or misidentification, claiming something that is false.

N.: When you claim something that is false, such does not make it real.

Q.: Yes, but it postpones any pure intention.

N.: With pure intention, then, eliminate as false that which is false, but God is never fractured. There is never a second power. The idea that there is a second power, or another entity, is maya, illusion. A principle teaching of Advaita Vedanta is that maya does not exist.

Q.: Is maya misrepresentation, misidentification, and going astray?

N.: Yes. If, though, it is misrepresentation, it does not really occur. If it is an illusion, it is not the truth.

Q.: In *Bhagavad Gita,* the Self is identified by the eternal, and the maya is another energy that is hard to overcome. This energy, which is not real, is part of "Me, the real, and is hard to overcome."

N.: Yes. As long as one remains as an individual, it is nearly impossible to overcome, but, if the ego is effaced, then we can see if it is hard or not. Can it be hard for God?

Q.: Is it by the Grace of Reality and not by effort that it is conquered?

N.: Even if one applies effort, it is the same nature as the Grace.

Another Q.: I think that I am misidentified and need to identify with something else. When I inquire, that idea falls apart. What is this process called "identification"? At a deep level, there is no identification occurring.

N.: In the practice of Self-Knowledge, you are advised to relinquish misidentification but not necessarily to conceive of another identity. You are not told to think that you are That. You are told to find out, "Who am I?", and the Truth declared in Tat Tvam Asi, That you are, becomes abundantly clear and self-evident. You are not to go on thinking that you are That.

Q.: I think to myself that, if this is a bad identity, I should get a good identity.

N.: Who is doing either? What is his identity? That is not a topic but is you. The mind is accustomed to dealing with "it," but this is you. Deal with the "I" directly.

Abandoning one identity and taking on another: who would do either of these? Who is this one that is taken for granted in your question?

Q.: It is an unexamined myth that lives on because it is unexamined. It is a superstition.

N.: The ego "I" survives due to lack of inquiry and vanishes upon inquiry.

Q.: There is always somebody.

N.: There seems to be somebody there, but you claim not to know him. Is it not funny? Everything revolves around this "I," yet you do not know who he is.

Q.: Yes, not knowing who he is. (laughing)

N.: How is it that you do not know who he is? How could you know anything else without knowing him?

Q.: He is the star of the show, and I am not finding out who that is.

N.: How could one not know himself? Seeing the absurdity of such a position, one inquires, "Who am I?" One arrives at a conclusion that seems similar to the beginning: how would it be possible not to know one's Self? One finds that it is not possible. In illusion, it seems to be the case, but you find that it is not the case at all.

Continue questioning what this "I" is. It is at the root of all of your perspectives, mental modes, thinking, and such. As long as the "I" is not known, or thought of erroneously, everything streaming forth from it is equally delusive. If you then give such the stamp of reality, which is borrowed from your own Being, such is illusion. Illusion then seems as if real. Then, you say, "I know this." Thus appear the "I" and the "world." Even the notion of the "Supreme" is like this. *Ribhu Gita* emphasizes a negation of jagat-jiva-para, the world, the individual, and the Supreme, as an illusion. There is something real, but the only way to know what is real is by knowing yourself. Once you know yourself, there is really nothing else to be known.

Do not continue with the misidentification. There is no need to attempt to produce or obtain a new identity or to transform yourself from one identity to another. Nor is such really possible.

Q.: I should inquire into who is the one who is trying to find a different identity.

N.: Who is the one who is aware of this now?

Q.: (remains quiet)

N.: Why discuss Truth or meditation as if it were an objective topic? Who are you? This is what is meant by turning the mind inward.

Another Q.: The senses are an activity. Because I give them attention, it seems to be a mental function. Yet, they are different from other thoughts, because I have more control over the other thoughts. I see objects, and there seems to be a non-volitional part of this.

N.: Volition is an activity of the mind, or a mode of mind, isn't it?

Q.: It is not clear for me.

N.: If there would be no thought, could there be volition?

Q.: No, it could not be.

N.: Would you have it or not?

Q.: I would not have volition if I had no thoughts.

N.: If that is the case, one mode of mind sometimes determines another mode of mind and sometimes does not. The causality may be true or not. It is insignificant. Sometimes, you seem to have volition over your senses, and sometimes you do not.

You seem to decide what it is to which you give attention. Now, you are listening, so you are not paying much attention to the tactile sensations. Now that I have mentioned them, you are thinking of them, but you are not noticing your taste.

Q.: (laughing) Yes! The senses are focussed. I have one or two active, and the others are not.

N.: Yes, the others are not in focus. Your mental attention is one of the factors that determine your sensory experience. Yet, you do not determine everything that you hear or see, for you often hear or see things that you do not wish to hear or see. That which produces volition, desire, and aversion is not necessarily the determination of the phenomena or the senses. This is good for it lends itself to a state of detachment.

One mode of mind is the volition, decision, desire, and so forth. Another mode of mind is the sensing. They are different modes of the same mind. What has this got to do with you?

Q.: There is a cognition of the sense perception, such as seeing.

N.: If you close your eyes now, there is a cognition, or awareness, of the cessation of that sensation.

Q.: Yes.

N.: So, the senses come and go. The cognition ability also rises and falls, as in the three states of waking, dreaming, and sleeping.

Q.: Yes.

N.: Thought and non-thought states, waking state and fainting state, or what is called being "unconscious," can occur. The sensations, their objects, and the mental cognition rise and fall. Something does not rise and fall. That which knows of the rise and fall does not, itself, rise and fall. It is inseparable from your Being.

How, then, could you be the senses or anything sensed? How could you be the mental cognition that knows about those senses?

Q.: For sensing, an identification must occur, or thinking that I am that sense and the body.

N.: In order to suffer or feel bound by it.

Q.: Yes. I must believe that I am those things.

N.: But are you those things?

Q.: I am trying to destroy these ideas about the body and the senses. The senses seem tougher.

N.: It is worthwhile to be thorough in your inquiry. You are trying to accomplish this. The "you" that is trying to do this cannot possibly be the body or the senses. It is not the body or the senses that is trying to destroy those ideas.

Q.: No, it cannot be them.

N.: What, therefore, do you already know about yourself?

Q.: I have nothing to do with them.

N.: Since you have nothing to do with them, your success is assured.

Q.: During the retreat, I acquired a deeper sense of what the inquiry is. Meditation deepened for me. The experience has given me more confidence. I question my identity, it breaks apart, and the strength of it reduces.

N.: By examining it through inquiry, the pseudo-strength of ignorance breaks apart. The strength of spiritual practice builds by more practice. For inquiry to be strong, inquire. The more you inundate yourself with the Maharshi's teachings the better.

Another Q.: Would you explain a sentence in a text, *Atmasakshatkara?* "You are that Siva, but not in the power to create." "You are in essence one, but you just are not that power to create."

N.: Look at it in context, with verse 57 of *Atmasakshatkara,* the *Direct Experience,* or *Direct Realization, of the Self.* "Becoming ethereal," which means space-like, "and pure," which means unalloyed, not mixing your identity with anything, "he merges in Siva." "He" means the yogi who so meditates. "Synonymous with omniscience," which is the perfect Consciousness, "contentment" for you are content only in one place, which is your real Self, "eternal Consciousness, independence," meaning freedom from all the bondage, "and eternal, undecaying, and infinite power," which is stated to be your nature. That is, such is of the Self. Verses 58 and 59 are a negation of what is no longer necessary for such a one who abides in Truth, who has such identity as Siva, the infinite Consciousness. In verse 60, "Drink of the nectar of Siva Knowledge," which is Knowledge of That which is the Absolute, the Auspicious, "and conduct yourself as you please." Then, he adds, "You are the same as Siva in immortality and purity, but not in the power to create, etc."

This verse 60 deals with the apparent individual. The previous verses deal with your real nature. Advice for one who meditates with this text is then given. "Drink of the nectar of Siva Knowledge." That is how you attain immortality, transcendent of the body, the mind, and such. "Conduct yourself as you please." This does not advocate being licentious in any sense. In verses 58 and 59, he has negated the various rules of conduct. If you abide at the very source of all that is satyam-sivam-sundaram, the true, the good, and the beautiful, you can expect that which is true, good, and beautiful to be the nature of the conduct. If a person is outward turned in mind and unruly, various regulations and rules are given according to traditions, in order to help keep the mind turned inward and in respect of karma. If, though, one drinks this Siva Knowledge, one is at the very source, and the rules are no longer necessary because he abides at the source of which those rules are but a faint reflection.

Then, he gives a further reminder: you are the same as Siva in immortality and purity, that is as Being-Consciousness-Bliss, but not in the power to create, etc., which deal with name and form. Of the five aspects associated with Siva, Being-Consciousness-Bliss, to which belong purity and immortality, are real. That which is name and form is characteristic of illusion, or the unreal. You, as an apparent embodied being, do not have the power to create entire worlds and galaxies like God. You do not decide even which way the electrons spin in the atoms of your own body. You do not choose your birth and your death. That power is not yours. You are the same in terms of immortality and purity, of Being and Consciousness. If you identify with this Siva Knowledge as Being-Consciousness and know that there is no other, this is Advaita, and the verse is no longer applicable to you. There can be talk of power to create only if there has been a creation. If you find that your identity is that which is unborn, the Reality, there has been no creation. This verse is advice for created beings, not for uncreated Being.

If, though, another approach to the translation is used, the question does not arise, for that which is declared in these verses of the Agama is devoid of any dualism or differentiation.

(The English translation by Dr. H. Ramamoorthy and Nome of the original Sanskrit verses:)

> 57. Omniscience, contentment, origin-less Knowledge,
>   Freedom, ever undiminished power,
>   And limitless (infinite) power, the affliction-less
>   Self,
>   [With] an immaculate body, he attains (reaches)
>   the nature of Siva (Siva-hood).
> 58. [There is] no japa (repetition of a mantra), no
>   worship (homage) or ablution (snanam),
>   No ritual sacrifice with fire (homa), no practice
>   (means), indeed (or: these are not the practice),
>   No result (fruit) of right and wrong action
>   (dharma-adharma),
>   [And] there is not the oblation to the ancestors,
>   [and there is] not the water offering (for the
>   dead).
> 59. Not for him are the injunctions [for observance],
>   No fasting is prescribed,
>   And no entering (proceeding, pravrtti) [into action]
>   and withdrawal [from action] (or: And no issuing
>   forth and no return),

And vows of brahmacarya (vow to live a life of study of and according to the Vedas, celibacy).
60. There is not entering into fire,
Falling from mountains (or: into crackling fire) or into water.
Having drunk the [immortal] nectar of Siva-Knowledge, [One] moves about just as one pleases (happily),
Like Siva, eternal, pure, Devoid of the dharma (codes, object) of creation.

(The English translation by Dr. H. Ramamoorthy and Nome of the Tamil version written by Bhagavan Sri Ramana Maharshi:)

57. Omniscience and bliss and mature wisdom,
Independence, un-withering limitless strength—
Attaining these, he shines ever, the Self without afflictions.
With immaculate means (or in an immaculate state), he, as the Self, merges with (dissolves in) Siva.
58. Japa of the name, worship, bathing in holy waters, ritual sacrifice,
None of these or others are needed.
The fruits of dharma and adharma (righteousness and unrighteousness), water oblations to forefathers,
None of these are for him.
59. No injunctions for observance, no fasts,
Nothing required of engaging in any activities or inactivity,
No observance of meditation, no vows of the brahmacari (moving in Brahman),
For him. Know this.
60. Not having recourse to falling into the fire or water,

Or falling from the mountain top,
Enjoy the feast (ambrosia, final Liberation) of the
     Knowledge of Siva, eternal and blemishless.
Rid of the rules applying to all creation, move
     about as you please.

(Then followed a recitation in Sanskrit and English from the first chapter of the *Avadhuta Gita.)*

(Silence)

Om Shanti Shanti Shanti Om

No Differentiation

Satsang, September 21, 2003

(Silence)

Om Om Om

(Silence)

N.: Undifferentiated is the nature of Reality. It is one indivisible, solitary Existence, without beginning and without end. Timeless, boundary-less, and utterly indivisible is the nature of true Being. Being is, simultaneously, Consciousness. It is indivisible, nonobjective, unformed Consciousness. This Being-Consciousness is, simultaneously, Bliss. It is the natural state of all beings. Abidance in this, as this, is known as Self-Realization, or Self-Knowledge. Some regard it as the highest state of love. The indivisibility and undifferentiated nature of Being is That. That is birthless, deathless, absolute Being.

This infinite, eternal, absolute Being is what you are. That is all that you are. It is not something removed from you. You are not removed from it. If this is your direct, continuous experience, yours is real Knowledge. You know your Self.

If, though listening to this instruction, reading this in an ancient text, or studying the Maharshi's teaching, there still seems to be some differentiation for you, what is the cause of it? If there seems to be some differentiation between your identity and the Absolute Self, why is it so? What marks you off as anything other than the absolute, real Existence-Consciousness-Bliss? Whatever it is that marks you off as such makes boundless Being appear as if bound, makes infinite Consciousness appear as if finite thought, and makes unconditioned Bliss appear as suffering or as an absence of happiness. It makes that which is undifferentiated appear as if two or a plurality.

What defines you? Inquire into this. If, upon such inquiry, you find that there is no valid definition that marks you off as some separate individual, the so-called experience of individuality, which is but a product of illusion, will vanish, because it is not real. Herein lies the efficacy of the Maharshi's inquiry, "Who am I?"

How do you define yourself? As a body or within the confines of a body or with the attributes of a body? If such seems to make a difference between you and the Absolute Self, inquire into that very "you." Find out if that "you" is a body or is defined by bodily attributes. Inquiring to discern if you are the body, know your Self as bodiless and undefined by the body. Then, where is differentiation? If you are the body, there is birth and death, which seems to contradict the birthless and the deathless. If you are a body, you are a finite form, which seems to be in contradiction to the infinite and the formless. If you are a body, you have activity for a limited time. The absolute, real Being is forever unmoving, actionless, and eternal. Are you the body? Plunge into your Existence with an inward-turned mind. Find out if you are the body or if all of the connection with the body is merely a product of ignorance. If you remove from yourself the misidentification with the body, what happens to your experience? What remains? What remains of you?

What makes the differentiation between you and absolute Being, the infinite Consciousness? Is it the thoughts, the ideas, about you? One of those ideas is a connection with the body. Question within yourself. Inquire. Can you be what you think? If you are not one thought, can you be a group of them or all of them put together? If you misidentify with the mind, which is thought, you seem to have a beginning and an end, and this is in contradiction to beginningless, endless Being. As every thought has a form, however subtle, you seem to be in contradiction to the formless, pure Consciousness. No thought lasts forever. Misidentification with thought contradicts eternal Consciousness, timeless Being. If, forever, wise sages have declared that your nature is absolute Being, Brahman or God, and the present state, which apparently exists for you, runs contrary to it in your mind, you are left with the choice of either all of those sages were wrong or you need to change your state of mind. By "to change your state of mind," I mean to cease to misidentify with whatever is the content of thought, whatever is merely a mode of mind or a way of thinking.

Inquire within yourself: who is this differentiated "I"? If the differentiation by the body is not true, can it be true in terms of thought? A thought comes, and a thought goes. It does not actually exist when it appears, but, starting at the level of observation, it comes and it goes. Can whoever knows about its coming and going and whoever knows about all those thoughts or ideas, be an idea?

Making your vision nonobjective, seek to know yourself. If the body does not give you individuality, because you are not the body, and if thinking does not make for an individual because your identity is not thought, what differentiates you? There seems to be the Self and yourself. What is this "yourself"? The more you question in this way, the less you will find of yourself. You will find that the notion, the assumption, of being a differentiated, individual, separated being is entirely false. It seems to exist only due to non-inquiry. Upon inquiry, it disappears. Make your inquiry so thorough that its disappearance is forever.

What is it that disappears? That which really has no existence. What remains, knowing itself? That which you have been the entire time. In Absolute Being, there is no such thing as ignorance. There are not two states of knowing and not knowing, or of bound and liberated. If you appear as if bound, gain release by inquiring into yourself. You will find only the Self. There is only one of you, which is why, I suppose, that you call yourself "I" rather than "we."

If there is only the Self, and there is really not a trace of an individual self, only Brahman and no jiva, there is no multiplicity of beings here. We cannot count on account of disidentification from the body. There are no higher and lower beings. We stop differentiating based on the content of unreal thought. Just as there is no multiplicity of beings, there is no multiplicity of things; nor is there any other kind of plurality.

There is just one unborn, imperishable, real Being. This alone regard as 'I." Examine yourself, until you are quite sure of what really is "I" in you. Not knowing what the "I" is, not knowing oneself, is the cause of all kinds of trouble. All the trouble evaporates by knowing who you are. Absolute Being, the infinite Consciousness, has no trouble, ever. The undifferentiated state is alone the real state. Do not regard differentiation as real. There is only one of you.

Do not regard a second as real. You need not, in your mind, declare to yourself the second is not real. All you need merely do is to inquire to see if it is real. In the light of inquiry, Reality will stand, and the unreal will vanish.

Q: Listening to your talk this morning gives me still another tool to use. I am looking to see if there is the sense of separation. It is clear that it is just the faintest wisp of an idea. It seems that there is a sense of time and place for that. I have a different way of looking at it now.

N: Alright. How are you going to approach this "I"? What are you going to practice?

Q: I see two different ways of looking at the same thing. One is to continue to look at what is real, which is what is always so. What is always so is here now. I want to discard everything that is not so. This is one part. The other part is the ongoing inquiry of "Who am I?"

N: The inquiry to find out what is real and the inquiry to find out who am I, identity and reality, are really the same thing.

Q: Yes, there are two angles of vision.

N: It appears as two angles of vision to the mind.

Q.: Yes, yes.

N.: The mind loses itself in either of these angles of vision. We are dealing with one and the same substance. Called "identity" or "reality," it is yourself. You look at your experience, and you determine that there is the substrate, which is present all of the time, and there are other things that are not substrate, which come and go. First, you should see the Reality of the Self as the substrate. Then, you should see that it alone is real.

If a rope has been mistaken to be a snake, first, we see the rope as the substrate of the snake; the snake is lying on the rope in the exact same pattern. (laughter) Then, we see that the rope alone is there, and there is no snake. It was merely a misperception. The Existence that you are is the substrate. It never changes. It is always so. Everything else comes and goes. What is always so alone is you and alone is real. What is not always so is but an illusion or a misperception of reality. What is not always so in your experience cannot possibly be you, because, when it is not so, you are still there to know that it is not so. Whatever it is that is always so in you is entirely formless.

Being always so means that it is ever existent. It is always real. It is the substrate upon which all unreality seems to come and go. If it is unreal, does it come and go? The practice of inquiry is the introspection to know your

Self. The real Self is the substrate upon which the "I" rises. With the rise of "I," anything else can rise; with its subsidence, everything else subsides. The "I" rises and falls on some substrate. So, the "I" is the temporary, and the substrate, the real Existence, is the permanent, or abiding Reality. Can you be two?

Q.: Not two.

N.: Then, if you inquire, you see that the secondary "I" is not only not the continuing reality, but that it is not real at all. Continue to inquire, in a nonobjective manner, into that very thing which is the substrate, into yourself, until the very sense of a second "I," a differentiated thing, is gone. The more you examine it, the less there is to see of it.

Another Q: I have a short period of time to make some big deals. My mind is active regarding this. My company has enough money to go to Tuesday, and they want me to sell all of these pieces for as much as I can get in that amount of time. They also want some exorbitant price. I get this assignment, and I have to concentrate on it. I become caught up in it.

N: Who becomes caught up in it? Your body is busy trying to sell stuff that you don't want to other people that probably don't need it (laughter) at a price that is outrageous (laughter), so that your company can keep going, in order that it can sell more stuff that the customers don't need. Whatever the situation may be, who becomes caught in that? Your body is active, but are you the body? Can mental attention be yourself?

Q: No.

N: Therefore, we don't place so much emphasis on the directing of mental attention. Meditation should be off the mental level. Regarding the entire experience, which is in your mind, for whom is it? Who is aware of it?

Q: The objective part goes away. I keep trying.

N: What do you mean by "I"? Yes, remove the objective part. The pure Self is Consciousness, when the objective part, being an illusion, is removed. What do you mean by "I"?

Q: It is assumptions of who I am.

N: You are aware that those are assumptions now. So, what is left for you?

Q: It seems that there is not much left. There are always these thoughts that come and go and that latch on to this "I."

N: What generates them? Where do they come from?

Q: I don't know.

N: Do you have them always?

Q: What do you mean?

N: When you are in deep sleep.

Q: Even in my waking state, they are not always there.

N: Yes. So, what brings them about?

Q: I don't know.

N: Why do you think the thoughts that you think?

Q: It has something to do with placing my sense of existence or my sense of happiness on something else.

N: That is clear seeing. "Random thoughts" are not nearly as random as one randomly thinks that they are. They start with some mistake about happiness, or deeper still, some misidentification. If there is no such misidentification, what, then, is your mind?

Q: It is definitely clearer.

N: How clear? If there is no misidentification, what form does your mind have? If it has no form, go deeply into this. Inquire as to where thoughts come from or where do they go or if they exist. If the real nature of your mind, liberated from misidentifications, is just clear, attributeless Consciousness, can there be thoughts?

Can there be the senses? If there is misidentification with the body, the senses and their corresponding objects are assumed to be existent. If there is misidentification with the mind, thoughts and the corresponding objective aspect are assumed to be existent. If there is no such misidentification, what is left of you?

Q: This is very amazing, because, considering my state of mind when I first entered this conversation, what you just showed me is how to trace to that deep, much more formless state.

N: Did you learn how to do this by just hearing it, or did your mind introvert?

Q: My mind became more focused on what is the center.

N: Real knowing and experiencing are identical. When someone is in satsang, he can hear about Truth. He can listen to the instruction. He can also experience the Truth directly because he is That. There is no reason to delay. The instruction can be followed here and not only later. If the instruction were just for later, I could say it later. (laugher) What you are shown is innate always. It is your own. Where is your mind now?

Q: That is an interesting question. There is no seeming location.

N: The location, if conceived, would be in the mind, but the mind, itself, has no location. Your place of work and the dealings with work are in your mind and are not outside it.

Q; Yes. You were just saying that the mind has no location, but all of the work and dealings seem to be located.

N: They are all located, but the location is actually entirely in the mind. The mind, itself, has no location. It is a false appearance, a semblance of something ghost-like, cloud-like, appearing in Consciousness. Consciousness is absolutely space-less, timeless, and formless. You may recall from *Yoga Vasishta,* the description of mahakasa, chittakasha, and Cidakasa. The great space is inside the mind-space, and the mind-space is inside the space of Consciousness.

Q: Can you explain that again?

N: The space of all experience occurs inside the mind-space. You know of all things and occurrences by your senses, but your senses are just one aspect of your mind, and they occur only in the mind. There is, therefore, no outside space, except inside of the mind. There are no external things. All is just in the mind. Do you follow?

Q: Yes.

N: The mind never exists apart from Consciousness. Whatever be the form of the mind, whatever seems to be its variegated content, Consciousness remains always clear, formless, void, and ever existent. The mind-space has no independent existence. If it does not have an independent existence, it cannot be said to really exist at all. It appears only within the Consciousness. Consciousness is what you are. You cannot possibly be the mind or the content of it, such as something that appears in this world.

Q: Can you go a little more slowly concerning the independent existence? It can't have any existence at all?

N: We can proceed slowly, until we are absolutely still. (laughter)

You have seen that the world has no existence apart from the senses, to such an extent that you can't say that you sense something, but only that you have sensations. You have seen, also, in your meditation and in previous conversations that we have had, that the senses don't exist outside the mind. All that is required is a change of your state of mind, and the senses correspondingly change or vanish altogether. Since they have no independent existence, they cannot be said to really exist at all. The senses are never seen apart from the mind, though the mind can be without the senses.

You exist, as the Self, without the mind, but the mind never exists without the Self. If the mind never exists without the Self, yet the Self exists always with or without the mind, can the mind be said to exist?

Examine your mind. There is Consciousness, which is what you are. There is the thought part of the mind. Consciousness and thought combined together seem to be a mind. The connection is entirely delusive. Even with that delusive connection, there is Consciousness, which is the knowing part, and the thoughts, whatever the thoughts may be. Not one of those thoughts stands up on its own, no more than the printed words stand apart from paper upon which they are printed. All of them rely entirely on Consciousness, which knows them. Consciousness can be without thought, but thought doesn't exist at all without Consciousness. So, we may regard thought as Consciousness misperceived. If the misperception disappears, there is just Consciousness, which is sometimes called the space of Consciousness, but it is not a physical space. All this manifested space is contained in the mind-space. The mind-space is contained only within the Consciousness-space.

The Consciousness-space doesn't really contain anything. Everything is in it, yet nothing is in it. It is in all, yet it is not contained in all. Now, identify with that space of Consciousness and not with the mind, which becomes deluded by its own imagination. Certainly, do not misidentify with the result of that imagination. Do not misidentify with anything that appears in your waking state of mind, from thought to the form of the body. Is this clear for you?

Q: Clear.

Another Q: I felt great peace and happiness when you spoke. I feel less burdened with assumptions, and I see a way to practice better. What is the best way that I can be with somebody who is suffering?

N: You must first perceive that which does not suffer. If you see the other's identity as that which does not suffer at all, that knowledge, even silently so, will be of the greatest benefit. Anything that you say will come from that. Where you stand determines what you manifest. What you say is the child of what you think. What you think is but the faint reflection of what you really know. So, knowledge is most important and most potent.

If you would approach the other person and feel that this person is a suffering entity, you would be trying to help with the one hand but accidentally pushing him back with the other, because you would be carrying the same misidentification. You must come to the conclusion within yourself that all suffering is missing a valid cause. There are plenty of excuses for it, but there is no valid cause.

Q: I understand and believe the instruction to identify with that which is not suffering. At what point should someone snap out of the suffering, if the person has knowledge of the teaching but still continues to suffer, as I do myself?

N: At that moment, do you really know?

Q.: No.

N.: You may have a memory of words and corresponding thoughts, but you don't really know. When we know, we don't suffer. That is real knowledge. At what point do they snap out? When they want to. If the desire to be free is strong, nothing binds, and nothing actually proves to be an insurmountable obstacle. If the desire to be free is not there, you could heap up all the words and give encouragement, but there is the old adage about horses and making them drink upon showing them water.

Q: Compassion doesn't necessarily mean saying anything. It makes for listening and coming from the place that is non-suffering.

N: The Maharshi was well known for the extent of his compassion, his Grace, as well as for the profundity of his Wisdom. When a woman, who became a devotee of his, named Echammal, came to him, she was suffering greatly. Several people close to her, including her husband, passed away in a rapid succession. She came to the Maharshi. He was still up on the mountain, I believe in Virupaksha Cave. She came to him and stood before him. He didn't say a word. He was abiding in Truth as the Truth. He was so silent one could not even tell whether or not he even recognized she was there. She also fell silent and did not say a word. Nothing was said for about 45 minutes, at the end of which she was completely transformed. A tremendous depth of spirituality opened for her, and her heart was at peace. If power resides in the words, how could that have happened? She received a better answer regarding life and death and the resolution of such than any words could have given. The knowledge is the key. What you know is what you are.

(Then followed a recitation in Sanskrit and English from an Upanishad.)

(Silence)

Om Shanti Shanti Shanti Om

Action and Knowledge

Satsang, September 28, 2003

(Silence)

Om Om Om

(Silence)

N.: Self-Knowledge is Self-Realization. It is Knowledge in which there is not a trace of dualism and in which there is no mistake about the nature of Reality. It is nondual Knowledge in which the knowing and Being are identical. Sri Sankara declares that Self-Knolwedge is Liberation and that no action can lead to Liberation. The Knowledge to which he refers is of one's own actual Being. Liberation is the natural state in which the imagination of bondage is no more and in which suffering is impossible. It is the state that is utterly devoid of duality. It is the state of imperturbable peace. This is the state that the Maharshi refers to as the state of Silence.

No action leads to Liberation. Self-Knowledge yields Liberation, but no action leads to Liberation. Most of the commentaries upon Sankara's writings say that the actions refer to the performance of various religious rituals and that religious rituals do not lead to Liberation but that Self-Knowledge leads to Liberation. This interpretation is fine, yet there is more to it.

Sri Sankara gives a hint of what he means, saying that the purpose or goal of an action is different than that of Knowledge. Action seeks to produce something, to obtain something, to transform something, or to purify something. Knowledge reveals, and its purpose is Liberation. He says that various spiritual activities and religious rituals can purify the mind or prepare it for Self-Knowledge, but that Self-Knowledge alone yields Liberation.

The path of Knowledge is formless, for the means are identical in nature to the end. If the end is nondual, it is necessarily formless. If the end is formless, the means are also formless. The practice must be of the same nature as the Realization, and this is shown by the Maharshi in his *Saddarsanam*. The attempt to describe the formless path, the Vedas say, is like trying to describe the track of the birds in the empty sky. Nevertheless, something is pointed out. It is the path of Self-Knowledge.

Actions occur with your body, speech, and mind. If we understand that which has been said by Sankara and the other wise sages concerning action and Knowledge, comprehending that action includes everything that occurs with body, speech, and mind, the depth of what is being pointed out opens for us in an interior, experiential manner. Accept this teaching as not so much concerning religious rites and spiritual activities with which you may or may not be involved, but as instruction about how one reaches Self-Realization, or Liberation from all of the imagined bondage. It is Liberation from the various misidentifications constituting ignorance, which alone gives rise to bondage.

Ignorance is composed of misidentification. Bondage is composed only of ignorance and is not real, for our real nature is innately Liberation itself. Only with bondage does one suffer. If you want to be free of suffering, liberate yourself from bondage. To liberate yourself from bondage, free yourself from misidentification. The Maharshi says, in *Who am I?*, that finding the nature of the one who is in bondage is release. Release is Moksha, Liberation. To eliminate misidentification, inquire, "Who am I?"

Activities occur with the body, speech, and mind. These are the very things with which you do not wish to misidentify in order to realize Self-Knowledge. An activity of the body will not produce Liberation or Self-Knowledge. Actions of the body bring results to the body. What is spiritual is non-physical. The body is physical.

The actions of speech also do not bring about Self-Knowledge. Learning to speak about Truth does not bring about the Realization of Truth. The Realization is deeper.

If we engage in some spiritual activity with the body, this core of Knowledge must also be present or else the desired deep spiritual experience will not be forthcoming. If we speak about spiritual matters, this experiential Knowledge must be at the core of such, or otherwise all such is only empty echoes, making sounds with no substance.

Action also pertains to the mind. There are activities of the mind that can, as Sankara says, purify or make ready the way to Knowledge, but they do not give Knowledge directly. However much you may think along spiritual lines, that is not the same as spiritual Knowledge. This is not to say that you should not think spiritually. If you must think, think spiritually.

The Knowledge that is Liberation does not pertain to the activities of body, speech, and mind. It is the Knowledge of your Self, transcendent of the body, speech, and mind. It is the Knowledge of your Self that is revealed to yourself by the inquiry as to whose body, speech, and mind it is. That they are instruments for you can be easily discerned. For whom are they appearing? If you inquire into this "I" that is seemingly individualized, Truth is revealed. Remove all the misidentification with the body, speech, and mind, inclusive of all that you think about, all relating,, and all physical forms of experience from birth to death. What remains of the "I"? Attempt to see the "I" as it is.

If you so inquire, the "I"-ness, being an illusion, will vanish. Individuality, being false, will "become" nonexistent. Silent Knowledge of this cannot be done, spoken, or thought. It is, as the Upanishads and *Gita* declare, where words and thoughts turn back unable to grasp. Before whom do they turn back? Before you. Who are you? This is the inquiry yielding Self-Knowledge.

Is inquiry an action? It is an increasing depth of Knowledge. It is not thinking or speaking along some particular line, and it is not having the body in some particular posture or engaged in some particular activity. It is far deeper and less objective.

Inquire, "Who am I?" This is the Knowledge that yields Liberation, showing that your real Self has nothing to do with the body or the mind and has not a trace of an ego, or a separated individuality. Then, where is bondage, and where is dualism? In the absence of one to be ignorant, can there be ignorance? If there is no actor, can there be action? If there is no possessor of the mind, can there be the mind? Find this out for yourself by direct, interior experience. This interior experience is the Knowledge.

Consider your existence. It is a basic fact that is doubtless for all. What do you do in order to exist? Breathing and such pertain to the body. Do you engage in any activity to exist? Existence ought to know itself, not as misidentified with what is objective, but as it is. This is nonobjective knowledge. It is not an action, but it is the knowledge that liberates.

Practice of Knowledge is not confined by any of the limitations that are present for action. Your mind cannot always be on the same thought. It has the limitations of time and interruption. The body needs to attend to various activities, and you need to speak about different things at different times. Knowledge alone has none of those limitations or interruptions. Knowledge is of the very same continuous nature as the real Self that is sought to be known. The means and the end are identical. The end appears as the means. That end is your Self. You, yourself, appear as the path to realize your Self. Who is treading that path? If you so inquire, the path disappears, and the goal is no longer a goal but the abiding Reality.

Let your meditation be of Self-Knowledge. When you read or listen, let it be for Self-Knowledge. When you are alive, let it be for Self-Knowledge. Death, also, is for Self-Knowledge. Everything everywhere is for Self-Knowledge. For one who turns inward to know himself as he is, there is no obstacle. Everything is for Self-Knowledge.

Q.: Everything is in the mirror of Consciousness, and none of that is who I am. I need to keep going until I see that nothing in the mirror is real and that I am Consciousness. It does not matter what I am doing, as the practice is not associated with doing in any way.

N.: Yes, doing is just the reflected image of the body in the mirror and pertains only to the body. For one who turns inward for Self-Knowledge, activity and inactivity, one place or another, provides no obstruction to the Knowledge. To see what is real, see yourself. What is said about the elimination of the superimposition of the unreal upon the real is for Self-Knowledge. If, having been instructed about the nature of Reality, there seems for you to be something else that exists, you must ask yourself for whom it occurs.

Whatever be the identity you assume, the reflection in the mirror corresponds. The analogy of the mirror appears in *Yoga Vasishta, Tripura Rahasya, Dakshinamurti Ashtakam* of Adi Sankara, and in your own mind. The mirror is Consciousness. Everything appears in the mirror, which is to say that it has no actual existence or reality. Identify as the mirror-like Consciousness, which has no border, no form, no shape, and no matter. An analogy can express this only so far. One may think of an external object reflected in the mirror to cause the image. In the analogy, there is no consideration of something external, but only of the mirror and the image. We realize that the image has no substance, no reality. Its depth is an illusion. Its substance is an illusion. There is nothing there but a mirror.

The apparent play of the Light of your own Consciousness makes it seem as if something else, other than itself, is there. To draw a conclusion to that play to see Reality as it is, all that you need do is to continue to clarify, in Knowledge, what you are. If there is even a tinge of the "I am the body" idea, there is some concern about the world, however it is conceived. If there is no trace of that misconception, there is no trace of a misconception of a world. If there is no "I am the body" misidentification, there is no trace of misconception regarding the world. Likewise is it with the senses.

If there seem to be different states, such as meditation and non-meditation, there is some misidentification with the mind. If you proceed to inquire to know who you are and disidentify from the mind, so that no thought pertains to you and, thus, no state of non-thought pertains to you, can the idea of an existent mind remain? The belief of an existent mind can occur only so long as you are misidentified with it.

Q.: I seem to confuse the image in the mirror with my Reality.

N.: Are you confused?

Q.: No. (laughter) The confusion is, itself, a confusion.

N.: Is the one who is aware of this confused?

Q.: No, he is never confused. (laughing)

N.: What particularly defines you? What is the "I" notion, and whatever ideas are appended to it, that gives the false impression of a separated, individual being? Is it you?

Q.: In confusion, it seems to be this body in this place. The confusion is not always present.

N.: If it is not always present, it cannot be real.

Q.: Yes.

N.: In which place are you now?

Q.: I am where I have always been.

N.: Is that in the body?

Q.: No. As you have said, it could be said that the body is in it.

N.: This does not sound very confused.

Q.: The specialty of this temple is non-confusion.

N.: Where are its walls?

Another Q.: How does sexuality fit into that? Some people claim that the sexual act is the most original experience that they can have because it is a point at which one surrenders the body.

N.: To what is one surrendering the body? Is it yours to surrender? Or is surrender the deeper Knowledge that the body was never one's own and one does not continue with the mistaken belief that it is one's own?

As for sexual activity, if that in itself would lead to Liberation, every creature, not just humans, with the possible exception of an amoeba, which seems not to need it, (laughter) would gain Liberation thereby. But we do not see that as forthcoming. If one supposes that sexual activity is against Liberation, that does not accord with facts, either.

Knowledge makes all the difference. The same activity appears as samsaric or nirvanic depending upon the state of Knowledge. The same activity is worthless or with depth depending on the state of Knowledge. So, Knowledge is given emphasis here.

Q.: Yet people who have a high level of self-awareness engage in sexual activity.

N.: Why would one suppose that it must be otherwise? Is sexual activity opposed to Knowledge of the Absolute? If it would be, whoever created it must be opposed to Knowledge, too, which would be absurd.

Neither engaging in nor refraining from it is related to the Knowledge of the Absolute. If you think that you will engage in sexual activity in order to gain the highest, the Absolute, will it bring about the desired result? If you think that you will refrain from sexual activity, and that, in itself, will bring about Realization of the Absolute, will it bring about the desired result? All of that is action-oriented. Knowledge yields Liberation. Action, on either side of duality, does not lead to Liberation.

When we speak of activities of any kind, inclusive of sexual activity, such relate to the instruments of body, speech, and mind. The Self is ever inactive. Being infinite, it has no activity. Being formless, it does not perform any action. Being all-fulfilling and blissful in itself, it desires nothing. It is neither with nor without anything. We should know ourselves as That.

Another Q.: So, this path looks to Knowledge and not to karma and its results.

N.: As long as we refer to bodies and minds, the law of karma is irrefutable. As you sow, so you reap. You may see the reaping as it occurs, as your state of mind, which is instantaneous karma, or you may see this in the phenomenal aspect. Karma continues. Self-Realization clears up the misidentification and leaves one without karma, because one stands as the Self. The body, etc. are considered to still have karma.

Q.: Intentional good action leads to the path of inquiry?

N.: In *Upadesa Saram,* the Maharshi says that karma is inert and cannot be God. We should not regard karma as the ordainer of our fate. He then indicates that selfless action helps on the way to Liberation. How does it help? It tends to turn the mind inward. There is some essential diminishing of the ego that occurs, and that is useful. It is not sufficient for Self-Realization, but, obviously, a selfless action is far more beneficial than a selfish action. What we do should be drawn from the source, which is satyam-sivam-sundaram, the true, the good, and the beautiful. That is our own nature. We should draw, in our activities, decisions, and motives, upon that which is true, good, and beautiful. If the motive is right, the action will follow accordingly. The results will also follow. If it is truly selfless action, one does not look for the results. The state of mind that occurs when engaged in the selfless act is the reward. That is what is sought and not the fruit of the action.

Q.: There is no karma for one who is realized?

N.: What do you mean by "one who is realized"?

Q.: For the one who becomes realized.

N.: Who is that one?

Q.: The Self.

N.: Yes, for the Self, there is no karma. There is, thus, no prarabdha karma, and no action or inaction. The only real Liberation from karma is identity as the Self. Otherwise, the law of cause and effect holds. For the Self, there is neither cause nor effect. For that which has never taken birth and for which there is no creation, there can be no karma.

As soon as you speak of "a realized being," you have added some other definition to the Self. You have supposed some individuality, some mind to make decisions and to think, a body with which to do the actions, and a world in which it is engaged in activity. Then, cause and effect still apply to those superimpositions and not to the Self. The key to freedom is identity as the Self. See for yourself that you do nothing ever. No matter what you are doing, you are doing nothing.

Another Q.: The teaching is that the Self alone exists and there can be nothing else, though it appears.

N.: The understanding is right. Make sure that it is thoroughly experiential. If you know that the Self alone is and that anything that appears does not actually exist, inquire as for whom it appears, thoroughly examining his identity until the identity remains just as the Self and not as the supposed experiencer, however he may be defined. Examine the identity as a mind in the waking state with senses.

Q.: I see the "I" that arises. I have a thousand lifetimes in a given day. The more one inquires to see what it is that comes, the more one sees that it is nothing more than an idea. From it, all the rest, which is imagination, spawns forth.

N.: When one looks for it, it disappears.

Q.: I can see it arising in my two grandchildren; one grandchild is a one year old, and the other is a two year old.

N.: How old are you? (laughter)

Q.: They have already mastered "me" and "mine." The inquiry seems to be the undoing of the habit of thousands of lifetimes of "I" arising, until that habit is no longer.

N.: Repetition of the unreal, even many times, does not make it more real. A falsehood uttered a hundred times is still not true. It is still just a bad rumor.

Q.: Very much so.

N.: So, it does not make a difference how many times the assumption of individuality has seemed to occur or how much has been appended to it. All that matters is the depth of inquiry.

Q.: And to see that all the time.

N.: Time is not a factor in this, and repetition is not a factor in this. Just depth of Knowledge is important.

Q.: Yes, certainty and depth without wavering, I can see, are needed.

Another Q.: In eyes closed meditation, I can quiet the mind, and the ego reduces. There is a deeper experience than being an individual in a body with thoughts. When I open my eyes and the senses are more active, I experience what I am looking at as a mirage. Who is looking at it starts to become mirage-like. It is the same experience as with the eyes closed, with detachment from the senses, but I can't hold it very long.

N.: What happens?

Q.: Misidentification with some of the sensory phenomena. Instead of remaining with the experience, I wander in my mind with the thought that this is some great insight.

N.: So, you treat the nonobjective as if it were an objective occurrence, that which is of your Being as if it were an event. It is mistaking a mere illusion, or a momentary "I," for the ongoing reality. Such is an inverted view. When you see that delusion is delusion, it does not continue for you. When you see the mirage as a mirage, you do not pursue it for water.

The subject and object rise and set together. The object depends on the subject. The Maharshi expressed this with the analogy of the movie. Upon the screen is projected a figure, a king. Before the figure is enacted a drama. The king watches the drama. The drama is unreal, being a mere projection upon the screen, and the king, also, is unreal. The screen alone is there.

Q.: He is the one watching it?

N.: Yes. The king watching the drama is the movie. The drama is unreal. The king, also, is unreal. The individual seer is unreal. His seeing is unreal. What is seen is unreal. The screen alone is real the entire time. The screen corresponds to the Self, which is real Existence.

If "I" rises, the rest rises. If the "I" subsides, the rest subsides. Find out who it is that cannot hold the good experience. If he dissolves, what you want is already existent. The king is gone, and the movie is over. The screen is already there.

Is there any difference in Consciousness, which is Existence, between your eyes open and your eyes closed? You are blinking right now. Is there any difference? Has Existence changed position?

Q.: No. That is something artificial that I am making up that is different. This reminds me of the reading on Friday night, during which the Maharshi spoke about the man in the shade where everything is fine and comfortable who goes out into the sun where he fries himself, and then, coming back into the shade, says how marvelous it is that he found himself again. The whole journey outward and the bondage were non-Self and was something that was... (pauses)

N.: Was not called for. (laughter)

Q.: Yes!

N.: The analogy is about creating the bheda bhava, the concept of feeling of difference.

Q.: Yes, and I am tired of getting sunburned! (laughter)

Another Q.: Why doesn't the Self come into the shade?

N.: The purpose of the analogy is a description of illusion and its destruction by the finding of one's real state, showing how unnecessary the illusion had been the entire time. It also reveals that illusion does not come to one, but is perpetrated by himself. One's ignorance, or bondage, is conjured. We should not attribute bondage, unhappiness, and such to things external.

Another Q.: It seems that there is really nothing that I can know.

N.: There is nothing that you can know, but still there is Knowledge. You do not doubt your Existence. Considering the Self as something objective, you may or may not know it. If you fall asleep, you may forget completely your thoughts of the Self and of all else, but, even then, Existence does not disappear, and, likewise, knowledge of it, though thought disappears. The knowledge of Existence is known for certain. Ascertain what you know for certain.

Q.: It is good to stay in that not-knowingness. When I focus on the "I" thought, it dissolves, and there is formless Consciousness. If the thinker is dispensed with, is the "I-I" Consciousness gone?

N.: What remains?

Q.: Not-knowing Being.

N.: Forget about not-knowing. What remains?

Q.: The Being.

N.: That Being is the Consciousness referred to by the Maharshi and in *Ribhu Gita* as "I-I."

Q.: In reading teachings of Nisargadatta Maharaj, I see that he speaks about the "I am" also. Would the "I am" be the "I-I" that the Maharshi refers to?

N.: Does it come and go?

Q.: (Quiet for a while) It would seem that if there would…

N.: In your experience, does it come and go?

Q.: I have not…when it seems that there is nobody there, there would be nobody there to see it go.

N.: What remains?

Q.: I am not sure how to label this.

N.: What really remains is known in silent Knowledge. It is the "I am" of the Exodus passage, "I am that I am." It is that which all great sages realize within themselves, knowing it in silent Knowledge. Different words are given to it. It has no trace of individuality, no particularization, no birth, and there is none other than it.

The silent, experiential Knowledge is the teaching. Everything else is only auxiliary argument or helpful instruction along the way.

Another Q.: It is said that jiva,, the soul, is manifest in the material world. There are so many impediments. Even animals attack me, and mosquitoes bite me. The ego constructs all this ignorance on so many levels. I try to meditate. In spite of the practice, it does not dissolve completely, and I become more sensitive to the attacks and to the mosquitoes.

N.: I can see that mosquitoes are high on your list of problems. (laughter).

Q.: It is a problem of vulnerability and sensitivity that increases.

N.: True Being is not vulnerable. Your body is vulnerable to mosquitoes.

Q.: How can I abide in Being when conservation of the body is so important?

N.: Temporarily.

Q.: It is important.

N.: Yes, but temporarily.

Q.: But it is many times temporarily. (laughter) It keeps manifesting. Sometimes, it is females, sometimes it is dog, sometimes it is a mosquito, etc.

N.: Is it necessary to conceive of the entire universe as being set upon attacking you?

Q.: Being a part of the entire universe, it is beautiful to see that it is temporary and imagined. Still, I keep coming back in a form.

N.: There is your problem. You keep coming back in a form.

Q.: Yes!

N.: The universe is not the problem, dogs and mosquitoes included. You should question your coming into a form. Either inquire or surrender that notion.

Q.: It is surrendered, but there is still the form.

N.: If it had been surrendered, that notion would no longer exist.

Q.: The notion may not exist, but look at this. (taps his hands against his body)

N.: That is one part of the body touching another.

Q.: It is a form touching a form.

N.: Is it yours?

Q.: It is mine until I let it go.

N.: Oh. From whom did you borrow it?

Q.: (laughing) From the Infinite.

N.: You took out a contract with the Infinite? (laughter) Did the Infinite say, "I give you this form"?

Q.: I made a bad decision by manifesting in a form.

N.: Is it necessary for you to continue with a bad decision?

Q.: No. It seems that I do keep coming back.

N.: That is not the fault of the Infinite.

Q.: No, but that's the contract I signed! (laughter)

N.: No such contract was signed. The Infinite didn't give you anything. You must cease acting the part of a thief, taking what does not belong to you. (laughter) Since you have indicated previously that the path of devotion is your leaning, your surrender should be along these lines: "I falsely took, or thought that I had taken, what I assumed to be my own. I now realize my mistake. I will no more make that mistake. I will no longer claim as my own that which is not mine at all."

Q.: It is my ego that claims these things. The claim is egotistical.

N.: Yes. If you cease to claim anything as your own, even the sense of "me" will go. When "me" and "mine" are both gone, Liberation is assured.

Q.: Okay!

N.: The universe is on your side.

Another Q.: I have been thinking about the analogy of going in and out of the shade related by the Maharshi. I settle for too little. I contrast my meditation with all that happens in my life.

N.: What do you mean by your "life"?

Q.: Running around looking for a job, interviewing, and such.

N.: Where does that life exist? In what does it appear?

Q.: It appears in my mind.

N.: Like dreams appear in your mind. While dreaming, a dream appears in your mind, and you seem to assume a position within the dream itself. The waking state is not dissimilar. All the while during the dream, you are not really in the dream. Likewise is it now.

Q.: (quiet for some time) When that meditation goes deep, there is then no difference between meditation and my life?

N.: Is there "your life" for you?

Q.: I am not sure if I understand your question.

N.: Your life is like a dream, as you said it occurs within your mind. You are the knower of the mind. Can you be something that appears in the mind?

Q.: No.

N.: Then, is it really your life? Are the sensory perceptions and activities that are mistakenly called "your life" you? Are those really yours?

Q.: Interesting. In the waking state, it is a recurring dream.

N.: The recurrence is in the mind.

Q.: Yes.

N.: The idea of recurrence is also in the mind. Where are you?

Q.: Definitely not there.

N.: So, do you run around looking for a job?

Q.: No, no. (laughing)

N.: The ever-existent Consciousness, which does not pass into waking, sleeping, and dreaming, and such, which never becomes embodied, is all peace itself because it is unchanging, and That you are.

(Silence)

Q.: I reflect upon the sense of ego. I do not really see it. In my meditation, I try to notice it, and I see that I exist somewhere.

N.: Are you in meditation now?

Q.: It seems that I am.

N.: We need not treat meditation as an objective occurrence. Is there an individual?

Q.: I do not know if I always perceive it, but I know that it keeps coming back.

N.: Coming back for whom? (Silence) The inquiry swallows itself, doesn't it? (Silence)
The non-ego state is the simple Truth. There is no one born, no one perishing, no one in bondage, no one striving for liberation, no one liberated. That is the Truth.

(Then followed a recitation in Sanskrit and English from the Upanishads.)

(Silence)

Om Shanti Shanti Shanti Om

Silence and Self-Realization

Satsang, October 5, 2003

(Silence)

Om Om Om

(Silence)

N.: Identity as the Absolute Self is the essence. Therefore, the Self is just Being; not being this or that, just Being.

Consciousness is forever nonobjective. Knowing itself by itself is the innate state. Therefore, Self-Realization is just Being. It is not being this or that; just Being.

Non-individualized, unformed, birthless, deathless, and without a trace of duality is the Reality of the Self. This Self is just Being. It is never being or becoming this or that; eternally, there is just Being.

The egoless state is the real state, the only state that actually is. Egolessness is identity with the Absolute Self. So, Self-Realization is just Being, not being this or that, just Being.

(Silence)

Being forever is. Consciousness ever knows. Bliss is never interrupted. To comprehend fully what has just been stated, know yourself.

Q.: I meditate on the substrate that I am. Even in the midst of conversation with others, I am able to see the substratum, rather than just the reflections that have been so much the source of seeming confusion. Consciousness is so vast, and I am seeing how small this idea of being an individual in the midst of this Consciousness is.

N.: Now, the individual is seen to be quite small. Just how small he is should be thoroughly investigated. It is like looking for a corner in space. The more closely you examine it, the smaller is the corner, until it reduces itself to a mere conceptual dot with no reality. See if the individual exists. Consciousness is vast and all-pervading. Where is there room for the individual? If the imagination of the individuality can be effaced, in any way, Reality knows itself; you know your Self.

Now, the Reality is considered the substrate. What if nothing ever occurred on it? If all the emphasis is given to the substrate, so that the sense of happiness, identity, and reality return to it, their rightful place, that which is appearing on the substrate will prove to be nothing but the substrate and will cease to exist as such.

Yes, this Self-Knowledge does not depend on circumstances, time, place, etc.

Another Q.: I wish to abide as the Self in union with the Absolute.

N.: If you wish to know and abide as That so that there is no alternative, eliminate the ego that seems to provide the alternative state. If the ego provides the alternative state of bondage, naturally you seek Liberation. In seeking Liberation, eliminate the bondage by elimination of the ego. Then, you find that what you were seeking is not a state, but the real Being, which is the only thing truly existent the entire time. Eliminate that which seems to constitute the ego that gives rise to the illusion of unhappiness in the midst of the Bliss and a limitation in the midst of the Infinite.

Q.: I know that, ultimately, it is a matter of looking directly into source of the ego or the source of ignorance. I have done that, but I need to do it again and again.

N.: Who is the one who has done it?

Q.: I have.

N.: Who is that "I"? That is what you need to find out. The answer is not verbal or conceptual.

Q.: Yes.

N.: If you find who you are, you will find that which is stateless and invariable. If you desire union with the Absolute, the ego must go. It is a false assumption, just imagination. It is not difficult to destroy the ego, because it is unreal to begin with. Nevertheless, if you continue believing in it, it will give you trouble.

To have the Realization of identity with the Absolute, the ego must vanish. In its vanishing, it is said that one has attained union with the Absolute. Sankara compares this with an image in a mirror. If the reflecting medium is removed, the image of the face merges with the original, he says. How does it merge? By its absence.

Another Q. (a Buddhist practitioner): Can I eliminate the ego by renouncing negative karma, becoming good, and seeing the Self in others as much as one can?

N.: That is in every way beneficial. If we are going to see the Self in others, the inquiry will help, for we tend to see others as we see ourselves. If you are aware of the divine Self within you, you will be aware of the divine Self within others. It is a natural corollary. If one says that he sees the divine Self within himself, but does not see it in others, whatever that notion or mode may be, it is not the divine Self and is not real. If there is, as you say, negative karma, know that doing that which is beneficial for all and purely good is natural for us. The negative karma is unnatural for us. The good tendencies will undo the bad tendencies, says the Maharshi. Those good tendencies should resolve themselves into an inner, natural tendency to know the Self. Thereupon, you become all-transcendent.

The ancient scriptures describe this all-transcendence as being beyond bad, good, etc. It is utterly impersonal. It is beyond action and the body. If you have the instruments of body, speech, and mind at your disposal, use them for what is true, what is good, and what is beautiful.

Q.: So, one should become a bodhisattva (ed. note: Buddhist term referring to a spiritually elevated or illumined being) as much as one can?

N.: Yes. The word bodhisattva has two parts: sattva and bodhi. Bodhi signifies Knowledge, an awakened understanding, or Enlightenment. Sattva signifies being luminous, inclined toward Knowledge, pertaining to truth, and leading directly to Knowledge. What is this Knowledge? It must be Knowledge of oneself.

If you endeavor to become a bodhisattva, or to be like one of the saints, certainly do so. What else should be done with the manifested life? You should know what the saints and bodhisattvas know.

Consider the word "Upanishad." Usually it is understood to mean that which is heard when sitting near. What happens when you spiritually sit near? Sankara says that the word "Upanishad" means that which destroys ignorance and leads directly to the Knowledge of Brahman. So, if you sit near and listen, you should eliminate all ignorance and directly reach the Knowledge which is within you. If you endeavor to be a bodhisattva, you should awaken to the Bodhi.

Another Q.: I used to think that renunciation was giving up the things that I thought gave me happiness. Now, I understand renunciation to be a return to the source of happiness. So, it is not really giving up, but a recovery. It is getting rid of the ignorance about where I used to look for happiness. It is a joy. That renunciation was suffering was my idea, but the truth is just the opposite. It is breaking the strings of attachment that bind the real source of happiness.

N.: So the notion previous to the experience was completely contrary to the actual experience.

Q.: One hundred eighty degrees.

N.: The thing to which you were attached seemed as if the source of happiness. Renunciation then seemed like a reduction of happiness, but the experience proves otherwise. Renunciation is a joy, and there is no happiness intrinsic to the thing whatsoever.

Q.: The teaching says that when one eliminates the "I"-thought, all the downstream objects and forms go with it. As practice deepens, there is more of the experience of being in the state of Existence without the "I"-thought. Even the activities of the body, speech, and mind can go on without my identifying with them. Why do I have the experience of not identifying with the mind and thoughts, but they still go on? If I would just get rid of the "I"-thought, those other things would not exist at all.

N.: Have you inquired as for whom it is going on? When you speak of Existence and when you say that you still have thoughts, etc. do such refer to the same "I"?

Q.: Well, no.

N.: Can there be two of you?

Q.: No, there cannot be two.

N.: You must inquire as to who you really are. The same Absolute Consciousness appears as the Supreme, the witness of all this, and as the Uncreated. This is determined by some notions, very few notions, and no notions about it.

Q.: Someone knows about all three of those.

N.: When you approach That as the Supreme, there is still someone who knows about it. When you stand as the witness, much of the duality has been erased. In the Uncreated, there is no one who knows. If there is no one who knows, there can be no one who does not know.

Q.: The not-knowing would be for the ego, for a second.

N.: To destroy ignorance, look into the one who has the ignorance. For whom does it pertain? All the ignorance is based on misidentifications. The forms of the misidentifications are based on the central notion of "I." This is the "I" thought, or "I" mode, aham vritti. Inquire into the "I." See what is there.

Q.: I understand to some degree. What if thought and the body occur?

N.: How do you know that thought is existent at all?

Q.: The only proof of it is another thought. (laughter) This leads to the questions, "From where are these thoughts coming?" and "For whom are they?"

N.: The cure is "Who am I?" for it gets rid of the samsara, the illusion. How do you know a thought? If its source and its ending place are not apparent to you, when you know a thought, how do you know it? What actually is a thought?

Q.: I thought that I knew that. (laughter)

N.: Ignorance is always like that. Delusion consists of stacked up assumptions. As long as we take them for granted, they seem solid, as if they were something experienced. Yet, they are made of the substance of dreams. You say that thoughts occur. Do they?

Q.: They seem to occur.

N.: Is there one who has them? Do thoughts occur? What do you consider to be a thought?

Q.: I talk about thoughts as if they are real, but I don't even know what they actually are.

N.: This is clearer.

Q.: I thought that I knew what they were. Who was thinking that?

N.: If you inquire into him, both the subject and the object, being unreal, vanish.

Another Q.: How is this Being different from the undifferentiated state of a child?

N.: If the child's state is truly undifferentiated, there cannot be a difference from an undifferentiated state.

Q.: You speak of Consciousness knowing itself.

N.: Yes. That does not require thinking. It is Knowledge of which we speak here, not thinking. This does not require thinking and does not require elimination of thinking, as if thinking were something real now occurring that would disappear in the future. This is Knowledge of Reality.

Another Q.: I understand now that I do not need to deny the existence of things and say that they are unreal, but see with what I identify and then ask, "Who am I? Who thinks this way?" Am I correct?

N.: Yes. "Who am I?" is the essence. If we come to the conviction that the "this" aspect is unreal, it may be helpful, but unless it is connected with the inquiry, it is of dubious worth. If one wanders in the mind thinking, "Is this world real? Is the manifested thing unreal? Is it half real and half unreal? It may be unreal, but I still see it. If it is unreal, why do I see it? If it unreal, why doesn't it go away?" and debates within his mind in this manner, without actually inquiring, such will not necessarily yield Liberation. If, though, one is deeper, one questions, if it is unreal, how could the unreal thing go away since it is not there to begin with? If we inquire, "Who am I?" which is the direct path as revealed by the Maharshi, since the "this" is dependent upon "I," and since "I" is integral to "this," with the subsidence of the "I," the entire question of "this" vanishes. First know the Self. Then, see if there is any "this" to consider existent or not.

Q.: So, the idea that it is unreal is okay, provided one connects it with the question, "Who am I?"

N.: That is correct. Countless aspirants who became sages, who, in the course of their practice, meditated on the unreality of the world, did not waste their time. It was time well-spent. In the beginning of the text *Who am I?*, the Maharshi first elucidates what one is not, starting with the body and extending to the state of residual nescience, such as what appears in deep sleep, saying that none of this I am. He says that the Awareness, which alone remains, is what I am. The nature of that Awareness is Sat-Chit-Ananda, Being-Consciousness-Bliss. Immediately thereafter, in response to a question of how the Realization of this will come about, he says that when the world, which is what is seen as real, is no longer taken to be real, like the example of the rope and the mistaken supposition of it being a snake, the Realization will be. If the unreal is still taken to be real, if one still sees the world as such, the Realization will not be.

So, if for you there is "this," inquire "For whom is this?" The perception of it, or the taking of it to be real, depends on certain misidentifications. Therein lies the efficacy of discerning its unreality, because you wish to see the unreality of the misidentifications that are the foundation that enables the dualistic, false perception to occur. To eliminate the dualism, go to the core: Who am I?

Q.: If Consciousness is nonobjective, how does this tie in with pujas (worship), which seems to be externally focussed?

N.: As soon as you relinquish the "I am the body" idea, what is inside and what is outside? To understand puja without outside and inside, without the distinctions of worshipper and worshipped, you may wish to look at *Nirguna Manasa Puja, Worship of the Attributeless One in the Mind.* The text corresponds to the third chapter of the Tamil *Ribhu Gita.* Read that first, and then we can discuss puja.

Another Q.: The confusion regarding reality and thoughts and identity and thoughts seems similar. Is it that my identity gives a thought reality?

N.: From where does the reality given to thought come?

Q.: From myself.

N.: There is no differentiation between identity and reality. One Self is all this. In maya, it appears as if divided between subject and object. Then, identity and reality seem distinct. Identity inheres in Being. Reality inheres in Being. Identity and Reality are identical. Do not attribute them to thought.

Q.: Once I identify with a separate "I," reality spreads out.

N.: Within one notion of "I," the entire illusion plays out, with all of its time, space, matter, energy, separate beings, the states of mind of those beings, the experiences of those beings, and whatever else there may be. Is there an "I"?

Q.: It seems as if there is. It seems to spring up in different places.

N.: What is it that springs? You say that "I" springs up. What is this "I"? It is not the body, for that comes later. Likewise is it so with the senses. The word and even the thought "I" come later. What is it that springs?

Q.: It seems like it is just thought.

N.: Do you actually think the thought, "I," or is it vaguer?

Q.: It is definitely vaguer. It seems that it is not a thought. It is an assumption, but an assumption must be something, doesn't it?

N.: Does it?

Q.: That assumption springs up and attaches itself to some thought, the body, and all of this.

N.: So, destroy the forms of that assumption by inquiry. What of the "I" itself? It is not the body, not the senses, and not a particular thought. It cannot really spring from the Absolute Self, because the Absolute Self can bring nothing forth other than itself. If it were otherwise, its undifferentiated, nondual nature would not be true, and Liberation would be impossible, but that would be absurd. So, what is this springing "I" assumption?

Q.: Sometimes, when I look, it may not be found.

N.: Why did you say, "sometimes"?

Q.: Sometimes, it seems there but very vague.

N.: Then, you did not look.

Another Q.: I hold the idea that there is conditioning. The conditioning may be by causation or something else. I have trouble letting go of the idea that things are conditioned.

N.: Just find out if you are conditioned or not. That events are conditioned by previous events or actions is prarabdha karma. You may or may not be able to perceive all the causal factors, for how many factors go into the making of any particular event! Yet, what is the case regarding yourself?

Q.: I am thinking of my own conditioning by my own past and memories.

N.: What is the nature of the one who is conditioned? This is to be examined. The real Self has no conditioning whatsoever. It is unformed. That events condition each other is so. Usually, one thinks of the preceding events determining the succeeding events, though, from Vasishta's perspective, (laughing) it may sometimes be the other way around. Similarly, the preceding thoughts generally influencing the succeeding thoughts. Those who cultivate a pure, inward-turned mind obtain results in the course of time, as is evident to anyone. Yet your Self is not conditioned by the world or by the mind.

Q.: I can see that it is just mental stuff that has no relation to the real Self.

N.: Yes, it is sufficient that you see that the conditioned have no relevance to your real Self. Those things with limitations, whatever the limitations are, have no relevance to your real Self. Your Self is beyond all such limitations because you are not of the world, not the body, and not the mind. You are not any form whatsoever. You have not been created, and you will not be destroyed. It is sufficient to see that this is your own nature.

(Then followed a recitation in Sanskrit and English from the *Hastamalakyam*.)

(Silence)

Om Shanti Shanti Shanti Om

Being-Consciousness-Bliss

Satsang, November 2, 2003

(Silence)

Om Om Om

(Silence)

N.: The Self is all in all at all times. It is everything. Forever nonobjective, for there has never been anything created, the Self is nothing. Though it is nothing, it is That which alone exists. Though it is everything, nothing ever happens to it, and it does not give rise to anything.

If you know yourself as you truly are, you, yourself, are everything and nothing simultaneously. Your nature is Existence—pure Being. This Existence always is. This Existence alone is. Your nature is Consciousness, apart from which nothing else exists. You, yourself, are the Bliss that everyone intuitively knows to be the natural, real state. Apart from this Sat-Chit-Ananda, Being-Consciousness-Bliss, there is no other kind of self.

If you apparently do not know yourself as you are, overlooking this Being-Consciousness-Bliss, which is your real nature, you assume yourself to have some nama-rupa, name and form. By "name" is meant all that is conceivable, and by "form" is meant everything perceptible. The entirety of one's experience consists of this Sat-Chit-Ananda, Being-Consciousness-Bliss, and this name and form, the conceivable and the perceptible. The first three, Being-Consciousness-Bliss, are Reality. Name and form, what is conceived and perceived, are unreal. The unreal, though, has no separate existence apart from the Reality.

You, Being and Consciousness, appear as if all the names and forms. You, yourself, are everything. Being everything, you cannot limit or injure yourself. Every name and form, everything conceived and perceived, vanishes, but your Existence, Consciousness, remains utterly unaffected. So, none of this is you.

Particularization is to be avoided. Such starts with the notion of individuality. Other definitions accumulate based on it. Such definition may be a particular form, such as the body, which is subject to birth, limitation, and death. The particularization may be some idea, thought, or group of thoughts. If you assume individuality is what you are and, further, attribute a form to that individuality, you appear not to be everything and not to be nothing, but appear to be something. That is not a good state. Birth as something spells samsara, the repetitive cycle of illusion, which is suffering and bondage.

Inquire and know that you are not anything. If you are something, you cannot be everything. To be everything, as is indicated by, "All is Brahman," you can't be a thing. If you are an "I," there is something other. If you inquire into the nature of this "I," and thereby bring about the destruction of its unreal appearance, in the state in which there is no "I," you are all that is. The only thing that exists is this unmodified Being-Consciousness-Bliss.

Examine your mind and inquire. Determine what things you assume yourself to be. With what do you misidentify? Further inquire, can you be those things, the body and whatever thoughts to which identity is lent? The less you find yourself to be, the vaster you find your real nature is.

If, inquiring, you find that there is nothing that corresponds to "I," the remaining Existence-Consciousness-Bliss, which is infinite, eternal, and forever immutable, alone is. It is the Reality. It has been always. The inquiry merely reveals the fact. It is the revelation of Truth and not the production of something. The Knowledge of the Self by the Self remains eternally. It is immortal Knowledge. There is nothing else like this.

Inquire. Determine if you mistake yourself to be a body, a mind, or an ego entity or individual. Find out, "Who am I?" Can "this" be "I"? Inquiring like this, you realize within yourself That which has no second, no other, no birth, no creation, and which just is, apart from which there is nothing. Since the first assumed separation from this is the notion of "I," commence the inquiry with the "I." Where you begin is where you end.

Q.: I was inquiring while in the midst of activity, and, for the first time, I had the strong sense that I was not doing anything. It is easier to identify with Consciousness and look at activities rather than identify with what is seen in the mirror.

N.: You are always still, and you never do anything. What would obscure this basic fact? What would cause you to believe that you were the performer of action?

Q.: Confusion with the stuff in the mirror. It seems as if real for it seems to be going on.

N.: Yes, but, like an image in a mirror, there is really nothing to it. One image in the mirror is the body. Can you be the body?

Q.: More and more, it seems to me that I cannot and that the body is in me.

N.: So, the body goes through the motions, yet you do not.

Q.: Yes, that is why it is easier to have the sense of not doing.

N.: Deepen the knowledge of not being the body. For one who knows that he is not the body, action and inaction are utterly insignificant. Inner and outer, defined in terms of the body, also cease to exist.

Q.: So, what is there to move?

N.: Moving and still, action and inaction, and inside and outside never apply to you. They apply to you only if you take up a false position as if you were an embodied entity, either the body itself or the inhabitant of a body. All those dualities exist only for those who continue to misidentify with the body. Such are never for the true Self.

Q.: I read in Ribhu (*Ribhu Gita* or *Song of Ribhu*) that all dualities exist only in the mind, and the mind doesn't exist in the first place.

N.: Yes, the dualities are only like the decorations on the snake that is only a rope. (laughter) Either see that the mind contains all and that there is no such thing as the mind, pure Consciousness alone being the reality, or proceed to the identical Liberation by the elimination of the various forms that, in the mind, seem to compose an identity, such as being a body. The result will be the same: still, silent, serene, and always the same.

Another Q.: You said that form, or rupa, is anything perceptible. You have also said that the world utterly does not exist and that the world is totally misperceived as if other than Brahman.

N.: Brahman misperceived is conceived as a world.

Q.: This refers to misperception.

N.: Ignorance appears as the veiling and the projection, or misperception, of Reality.

Q.: You have asked me, in the past, what is perception without a perceiver. Would you connect these three?

N.: In what way are they disconnected for you?

Q.: The connection regarding the perception is not clear for me.

N.: With perception, which is experience of any kind through your senses and, to consider name and form together, through the mind, there is the objective portion and that which knows. If you trace that which is known to that which knows, what is that?

Q.: There is only I.

N.: The objective portion is unreal, for it is utterly dependent on the "I" and has no separate existence. What has no independent existence has no existence at all.

Q.: That is why you say that misperceiving Brahman becomes the world. If the world is nothing but Brahman, there is only Brahman. Then, the world is utterly nonexistent, because everything is Brahman.

N.: It seems that you have very nicely tied it all together yourself. (laughter) Whether we say that the world is unreal and Brahman alone is real or that Brahman alone is all or that Brahman misperceived is all, still Brahman is just Brahman. There is no separate misperceiver, and ignorance has no reality. These amount to the same thing. I really did not think of anything new in all of those statements.

Q.: Yes, but you expressed them truly very well.

N.: It is the same old Truth.

Q.: I have been reading your book, *Self-Knowledge*, and it is very clear.

N.: Oh, now we have book reviews. (laughter) What about your experience?

Q.: You said that form is anything perceptible.

N.: Yes. When you read the ancient texts, such as the Upanishads, *Ribhu Gita*, etc., understand the references to form. Form means anything perceived. It can be something seen, heard, touched, and so forth. It can also apply to mental form, but to that the name "name" is also given. It is that to which a word or a name can be applied, that which can be conceived.

Q.: Both name and form arise from the Self?

N.: They cannot come from anywhere else. The source is the Self. The Self, though, is nameless and formless. How can the nameless and formless give rise to the name and the form? The Reality does not change its nature. If it were to do so, it would be unreal.

Q.: So, anything perceived is form. Perception without a perceiver is not really going on.

N.: The real nature of the perceiver is pure Consciousness. When something of the perceived is attributed to the pure Consciousness, it appears as an individual perceiver. That is the "knot of the heart." There is the false connection.

The perceiving is pure Consciousness plus the idea of objectivity. If all that is objective is abandoned as being unreal, all that remains of the perceiving is pure Consciousness, without "I" or "this," the perceiver and the perceived.

The nature of the perceived can be only the one Existence, pure Sat, which is identical with Consciousness.

When name and form are attributed to it, you consider it to be the realm of experience.

The real nature of the perceiver, the perceiving, and the perceived is only pure Consciousness, or pure Being, without any of the three.

For the purpose of inquiry, if you attempt to determine what the perceived is, it is likely that you will retain the objective outlook. You would be only spinning an illusion.

If you examine the perceiving, it is far better, but, if you don't question the identity of the subject, you are likely to wind up believing everything is of the mind, and you will have no Knowledge in your heart of what the Truth is.

If you inquire as to who is the perceiver, "Who am I?", you are already transcending the very dualities that would hinder you. Thus, the Maharshi advocates inquiring "Who am I?"

Q.: Getting rid of the perceiver would be the perception that the perceiver is nothing other than Brahman, which is Consciousness?

N.: The perceived is consumed in the perceiving, like ghee poured into a fire.

Q.: Yes.

N.: The perceiving is absorbed in the perceiver, like a river emptying into the ocean.

Q.: Hmmm.

N.: The perceiver has no existence other than pure Consciousness. This is like space emptying into space.

Q.: The perceiver arises. The perceiving then follows. The perceived follows. I need to take it back so that all of it dissolves.

N.: Alright. The arising is a bit of imagination. So, dissolution is generally the emphasis in one's spiritual practice, rather than evolving theories with the mind about "arising."

Q.: Yes.

N.: So, there is greater affinity for Siva than there is for Brahma. (laughter)

Another Q.: You say that I am not even the inhabitant of the body. I am confused. There is the connection of mind and body and action. I think that I am the inhabitant of the body and that there is a connection between thought and action. Where do I go from here?

N.: Are thoughts in your body, or is your body contained within your thoughts?

Q.: The correct answer is that the body is contained within the thoughts.

N.: Why do you say that that is the correct answer?

Q.: I feel that a thought comes from a certain place and that an action can occur from that thought.

N.: Where in the body are you supposed to be?

Q.: My confusion is the connection between action and thought.

N.: Do you have actions in a dream?

Q.: Yes.

N.: What is the connection between the dream character's thoughts and his dream actions?

Q.: Perception. It is perceiving the reality in the moment.

N.: Are they two different things, or are they the same mental state or mind-stuff endowed with different qualities, one apparently internal and one apparently external to the dream character?

Q.: Is it just an illusion that I think that I am moving my arm from thought?

N.: There may be a connection between them. The dream character has a thought and also dreams of causality within the dream. There is the dream thought, and action follows. Since thought moves much more quickly than the apparent manifest action, it is natural to consider thought as the cause and the action as the belated effect. Still, all of it is within the mind. If the dream character loses a dream limb, he can no longer perform dream actions.

When you wake up, what happens to the dream character? He is neither in parts nor whole. He is of no relevance.

Q.: What do you suggest that my line of inquiry should be at that point of confusion about thought and action?

N.: Where exactly is the confusion between thought and action? Action seems to be the effect of the cause, which is thought, but both are imagined within the mind. You, yourself, have nothing to do with either.

Q.: At times, I have felt that I am not the doer at all. It is not the case all of the time.

N.: But you exist all of the time.

Q.: Only if the Self allows it to be will something take place. If something is not to take place, no matter how hard I think that I, as an individual, am trying, it won't happen.

N.: Alright. Your effort is only one small part of a vast tapestry that is beyond your control, a single bubble in a vast tidal wave, or it is nothing at all. The standpoint of the individual is insignificant, or he is nothing at all. Your nature is Consciousness and not the individual with his preferences and aversions.

Always, you exist. The fact of your existence does not change. The actions come and go. Even within the context of misidentification, you can be a performer of action only while the action is occurring. The moment it stops, you are not that anymore. The idea of being a doer of action is just a temporary delusion when your body is engaged in some activity. Your unchanging Existence is with and without that activity. How can it be a doer? How can you be the performer?

Q.: Only according to the delusion that I think that that is happening.

N.: When you are confused and think that something is occurring that is not, such does not make it real, does it?

Q.: No.

N.: So, inquire to see that your nature is the unmoving Consciousness, or Being, that remains before, during, and after any activity. It never changes. This idea of being the doer, the body, or the inhabitant of the body will vanish for you. Before birth, where were you? After death, where will you be? Where are you now? Your sense of existence does not derive from the body. It does not well up in the body. The body is something that appears to you. It has birth and death. Continue to inquire, seeing the distinction of the Self from the body, the freedom from the body and the bodily definitions. That includes the bodily actions. Do you see how to proceed?

Q.: Yes.

N.: Then, you will do nothing, even if you are doing all day long.

Q.: I have been accused of that before! (laughter)

N.: Prove them right! (laughter)

Another Q.: I lose my focus in my meditation. What would you suggest to ignite my meditation?

N.: Eliminate the "my" part.

Q.: My concerns, my world, my body, and so on. I guess that I should truly question if those are really mine.

N.: "I" and "mine," the ideas of individuality and possession, compose delusion. Liberation is characterized by an absence of "I" and "mine." If you want your meditation to empty itself into the fullness of Liberation, eliminate the "my" part.

Q.: I observed someone caught in desire. Why someone does not understand where happiness is I just don't understand. When you asked, "Who has the daily life?" I couldn't answer. The mind has been much quieter since then. I am trying to clear up the debris covering who I am so that I can realize.

N.: If someone who meditates told you that some of the meditations dealt with the inquiry, "Who am I?", and some were upon the names and forms, full of "me" and "my," including daydreaming along those lines while meditating, and he wanted to know how to attain total peace, what would you advise him?

Q.: It is up to me whether I follow those ideas or go wherever they carry me. There are two doors. One is where the thoughts come in and one where they go out, with me in between.

N.: If that person spent a considerable portion of his time daydreaming all his vivid daydreams, becoming caught in them, thinking that he was someone in them and thinking that the things and experiences he dreamed belonged to him and affected him, you would advise him to give up the sense "I" and "mine" or to recognize that he was in meditation to start with. What causes you to think that you are not in meditation all of the time? Do you know that you have just been vividly daydreaming about this daily life nonsense? Is "daily life" now a term used as an excuse for why meditation is being done on things that are unreal rather than on the real?

Q.: Daily life just is?

N.: There is no one who really has a daily life. There is no thing called "daily life." Yet, if you leave such unexamined, then you can speak of such things. In reality, the Consciousness that you are always exists. In practice, every moment is the opportunity to have Self-Knowledge. There are not two separate existences.

Q.: Every time I have a dialogue with you, something goes blank in my mind. I believe that I am attuning myself more to your silence. All of a sudden, there was no "me" here. When you asked the question, "Who has daily life?" I somehow got it. When you speak, there is something that penetrates.

N.: The Self that is here is the Self that is there and everywhere. Its nature is silence. The Upanishads say that it is where words and thoughts turn back. The *Gita* says the same.

Sometimes, a question is given to you as part of your inquiry. You draw a blank. That is, what is pointed out does not correspond to the previously prevailing concepts. When an answer, even in the form of a rhetorical question, or anything that you are learning spiritually, corresponds to a preceding concept, the good it does is only a little. When it does not correspond to one's previous concept, which is when you draw a blank, it is doing the most good.

Many people, it would seem, approach the books that they read and those to whom they go for instruction for a confirmation of their present state of mind with their present views. If that present state of mind is one of complete Mukti, or Liberation, confirmation is not needed. If it is not so, the last thing that would be wanted would be confirmation. What is wanted is that which questions and uproots the very basis of the prevailing assumption. Inquiry accomplishes this. Every time that you inquire within yourself, "Who am I?", you are questioning at a level deeper than the very foundation of whatever the prevailing concept is. If you draw a blank, it is alright. Not having a verbal answer is fine.

Q.: I have been in a bucket all of my life. Clear water has come. The mud goes out and the water becomes clear.

N.: If the bucket is the mind, why not take away the sides and the bottom?

Q.: Yes, that would be great.

N.: So, if there is the idea of "daily life," whose daily life? Where does this occur? Why do you think that you are not in continuous meditation all of the time? You have just been meditating upon the wrong things at times. (laughter). It is upon the form rather than Being-Consciousness-Bliss.

Q.: It is like the story of whether or not it is a butterfly dreaming.

N.: The story of being unsure if one is a man dreaming he is a butterfly or a butterfly dreaming he is a man shows the interchangeability of the waking and dreaming state conceptions within the mind. There is something that is not of either state. It cannot be confused with the changeful states of mind. That something is true certitude. The certainty that people seem to have with their perceptions and conceptions is not true certainty. A mere change of the state of mind can turn such around, so that that of which you thought you were so sure you are not so sure. Yet, still, you are very sure of your Existence. Putting men and butterflies aside, pay attention to the Existence that is not altered in any way whatsoever, no matter what the state of mind is. Whether you are apparently convinced or in doubt regarding something, you still have the certitude of your existence. The Existence must know itself as it is. That is the certitude of which Ribhu speaks.

Q.: I would tell that person who is meditating that he is thinking about forms.

N.: Why not tell him to find out his own nature and realize the ever-present state? The purpose of the analogy is to indicate that you are in the opportunity of meditation all of the time. There is no such thing as "daily life" in which to "integrate" the meditation. You are always the same One, the same Existence. That Existence is infinite and eternal. When you say, "But my daily life," the "my" refers to a small, embodied individual with likes and dislikes and such. That is not you.

Q. It is just what I feel like.

N.: Dissolve all of it by inquiring into this very identity. See that it is false and take up your true stand as infinite Consciousness. It does not have even birth and death. So, how could it have daily life?

Q.: It makes a big difference when you say that.

N.: Continue to reflect and meditate along these lines. Inquire deeply. You will find it quite impossible to squish the infinite Being that you are into the finite form that supposedly has daily life, pleasures and pains, births and deaths, etc.

Another Q.: I participated in a formal meditation at a nearby Buddhist center. In the fifth period, I began to dive down. It was sinking into an experience. I had misconstrued what "bliss" meant. I thought bliss meant happiness, but I wonder if it means meditating more in that spaciousness than just in my mind.

N.: Bliss means something that endures. We can call it happiness, but it is not a temporary pleasure or elation or a good mood or a pleasant sensory experience. The Maharshi speaks of happiness, sukha, and also bliss, ananda. He uses these terms interchangeably.

We cannot be truly happy with what is superficial. A pleasant sense experience is just a pleasure and is not really deep happiness or bliss. A good mood is just that, and, when it passes, it is as if it never had been. Bliss, or real happiness, lies in that which is deep within, in which you become absorbed. It is not on the same level as the running thoughts. It is not on the same level as the senses and the breath, which rise and fall.

That in which we become absorbed, in Self-Knowledge, we come to recognize has been there the entire time. Now, it seems as if you are on the surface and recognize that there is something deeper. If you inquire as to who you are, you, yourself, are the depth of all depths. What is first experienced as sinking is actually a dissolution of superficial identity, which is not really you.

You are the screen, not the images projected on it. The sinking is the recognition of yourself to be the substrate or the screen. You were never those images, but, if, in illusion, you take up your stance there, you need to sink or go deeper. Sinking deeply, guided by Self-Knowledge, you recognize that the depth that you reach is actually subjective, is who you are. Where you thought you were you could not actually have been.

Do not run with the thoughts and do not contend with them. Sink into the depths and find that there is no such thing as thought.

Another Q.: When I take myself to be a body, I reflect and realize that what is true is deeper.

N.: Do you ever become a body?

Q.: I can only think that I am a body.

N.: If you think that you are a purple giraffe, do you become one? (laughter) So, why would thinking that you are the body be any more solid?

Q.: It seems as if it is solid.

N.: In what way?

Q.: If I think something, so it becomes.

N.: That is in the realm of becoming. What becomes and ends is not real. If you think it and so it becomes, that merely proves the unreality of the objective part, which is born of mental imagination. The one thing of which you cannot think cannot become, and that is you.

Q.: I need to meditate on how to dissolve my mind. All these thoughts that come up in my mind do not really connect to the body and the world. They are just threads of assumption.

N.: When unchecked, that to which they connect is other thoughts. All of this is in the mind, but you are not in the mind.

Q.: If I were a thought, that would be so bad.

N.: Can you be a thought?

Q.: No, because, if one were jumping from one thought to another, and if that were oneself, that would be very bad. One would feel scattered.

N.: And multiple.

Q.: Yes.

N.: But that is not your experience.

Q.: No.

N.: Since you are free from thought, where is bondage?

Q.: It is only when these notions come up.

N.: Where do they come up?

Q.: In my mind.

N.: Where is your mind?

Q.: This is something I must check out often.

N.: Often is also in the mind. The where and the when are in the mind. What is the mind?

Q.: I don't know. The mind arises when I believe in an external entity.

N.: Is that belief in your mind?

Q.: Yes.

N.: It cannot precede the mind if it is in it. What is the nature of your mind?

Q.: It seems that it is not found.

N.: Then, there are really no such things as thoughts, their arising, and their cessation. One forever-undivided

Consciousness is. That alone you are. There is neither connection with anything else nor anything else to which to connect. The infinite, space-like Consciousness is all that you are, not just often, but always.

(Then followed a recitation in Sanskrit and English from an Upanishad.)

(Silence)

Om Shanti Shanti Shanti Om

Egoless Self

Satsang, November 9, 2003

(Silence)

Om Om Om

(Silence)

N.: The Reality, which is the Self, of the nature of Being-Consciousness-Bliss, has no division, no form and no ego-entity in it. It is singular, without a second, alternative, mode, or any kind of condition or change. The Maharshi says that the egoless state is the real state, the only real state there is.

It is the state of your Existence. It is innate. All illusion and all consequent trouble in the forms of bondage and suffering arise from the idea of an ego-entity. The ego does not truly exist, the illusion does not truly exist, and the bondage is unreal. The realization of this within yourself by Self-Knowledge is Liberation.

The key ingredient is egolessness. That is the nature of Reality and the nature of your Self. Though it is commonly said that you should make yourself egoless or attain the egoless state, really it is a matter of the truth of your Existence as it really is, which is innately egoless. It is without any individual entity whatsoever.

In your inquiry, "Who am I?", to know the Self, egolessness, or the absence of individuality, is the key. This is the key for practice that yields Realization. Who or what is it that seems to correspond to the name "I"? This is what you ought to find within yourself. "I act," "I perceive," "I think," "I am unrealized," "I am going to be realized": who is this "I"? Inquire into the nature of "I." "I am like this. I am not like that. I am one thing. This is another thing. I am I, and Brahman is something different": who is this "I" in all of these conceptions?

If you feel that you experience something, that is, you perceive or conceive it, implicit in such conception is this idea of "I." It is the aham vrtti, the "I" mode, the mode of being an "I." Who or what is this "I"? All that is built upon this "I" is as false as the "I" itself. Find the truth behind this "I," and there is homogeneous, partless, indivisible Existence, partless, indivisible Consciousness, and causeless Bliss, the real peace of Reality.

All trouble comes from the assumption of the "I" as existent. All duality stems from it. To realize nondual Truth, in all its fullness, examine this "I." Who am I? Who is it that says, "My body, my mind, or my God"? Stay with the Knowledge of yourself, or stay with the inquiry to find the Knowledge. The silliest thing is to read, hear, or comprehend within yourself that there is really no ego in your nature and, with the next breath, suppose "I think this, I do this, etc."

The egoless state is the state of Silence. It is Reality as it is.

Q.: I feel that I am being told what is, and I am looking for what to do, how to change, and how to be. The theme seems to be to stay with the Truth or turn inward to the Truth so that an awakening occurs.

N.: What do you understand by "turn inward"?

Q.: Completely finding out how it is.

N.: How what is?

Q.: How what I consider to be myself is, what I am.

N.: Well, then, what are you?

Q.: I would like to fully know.

N.: What is the nature of the one who yearns to know?

Q.: On the good side, there is an awareness, and, on the wrong side, there is a separation, too.

N.: You are aware of the separation?

Q.: Yes.

N.: Then, it is objective to you and cannot be you. What remains?

Q.: I can't say, but the closer I turn to it, the more space-like it is.

N.: Is there one who turns and one to which you turn? Or is your existence singular?

Q.: To the extent that it feels space-like, it is more singular. If I break it up, I am looking at something objective.

N.: How and with what do you break it up?

Q.: With some figment that I project.

N.: Some figment of the mind, some mental activity, gives the appearance of breaking up. When you think something to be so, is it necessarily so?

Q.: No, that does not seem to be so.

N.: Thoughts do not determine reality. The Knowledge that is sought to be realized we thus know is not of a thought basis. Look for something that cannot be contradicted and is eternal. As thoughts do not really break up Existence, can there be more or less singularity of the Existence? Can you use your thinking to determine Reality? If you assume that thoughts determine reality, such an approach is as erroneous as supposing your senses to be the determination of reality. You see multiplicity and take that to be real. Whatever you conceive, so it appears, even though the "it" is entirely in your thought. You are not a thought. Your Existence does not depend on thought in order to be. There is no "how" to be. Being should know itself. Actual Knowledge is not a thought about it.

That which is basic is the substrate of all the thoughts. If you are not what you think, what remains?

Another Q.: The eternal is always the answer.

N.: Yes, the eternal alone can be and know the eternal. The infinite alone can know and be the infinite. The Self alone knows the Self. The ego has no part in it. Brahman alone knows Brahman. Nothing else can do so. Something finite cannot know what is infinite. The senses are incapable. Something non-eternal cannot know the eternal. So, thoughts are not capable. Thus, "Where words and thoughts turn back unable to grasp, there is my abode." That is your real state.

Q.: The thoughts and the "I" are stopped from knowing it.

N.: Illusion cannot know Reality. Knowledge is possible. Knowledge is all-important. Knowledge is of the Reality by the Reality. The inquiry does not manufacture some special thought, does not transform thought into Reality, and does not transform the ego into the real Self. It simply reveals the Truth of the Self as it is. It is nondual.

In practice, one does not look so much for a change in thought, though you might expect the patterns of thought to change as the ignorant tendencies that generate and drive them are obliterated. What is sought is the nature of your identity, what you are. You find that everything that you thought yourself to be you are not. What you are is something beyond the domain of imagination.

If, in your heart, you have the desire to align your mind to what the teachings that you read and to which you listen declare, such desire and the effort applied to such are fine, yet what will actually happen? The mind will lose its form in the attempt to do so. All that remains of it is pure Consciousness.

Pure Consciousness plus objective, false notions constitute the mind. When the false notions, or the objective outlook, are relinquished, all that remains of it is pure Consciousness. So, there is no mind, but only pure Consciousness, which is the Absolute. The mind is not. It is an illusion.

Q.: Sincerity will lead me to the Truth, not the thoughts?

N.: Whatever is done with a sincere, earnest desire for Truth will be beneficial, be it with thought or anything else. The end is, though, beyond all the means and is within.

Another Q.: It seems that it is only grace that allows Consciousness to see Consciousness.

N.: Consciousness is innately self-luminous. You may call that the power of the Light of Consciousness or the power of Grace. Pure means nothing mixed, being utterly unalloyed, and having no scope for "I" and "mine."

Q.: I feel that that is where the bliss is.

N.: As "I" and "mine" are the cause of all suffering and are the characteristic signs of samsara, "I"-lessness and "my"-lessness are the characteristic signs of Liberation. The result is complete peace, happiness without cause and, therefore, without end.

Q.: My misidentifications lead to searching for completeness in various things.

N.: Do they fulfill?

Q.: No. They are like the analogy of a squirrel running on a treadmill.

N.: When we see deeply that there is no fulfillment in the pursuit of the imaginings of our own minds, whether in the mind itself or outwardly in the world, which is also only in the mind, renunciation becomes natural. We find ourselves detached. Attachment has as its cause the false belief that happiness, or satisfaction, is to be found in some other thing external to ourselves. When we see that this is not so and the source of what we want is within, detachment is natural. Meditation on the mortality of one's own body also helps.

Another Q.: We superimpose all this stuff on the Reality, such as the body, the senses, thoughts, etc. Can I just stand back and leave all of that behind and go as deep as I can? It seems that it is also good to notice where I am misidentified. Meditating upon what we spoke about on Friday evening. I reflected on from where the sense of reality comes. It was very interesting. I was not focused so much on what it was I was misidentified with as where reality comes from.

N.: It is good. With what are you misidentified?

Q.: Many things.

N.: Such as?

Q.: I received a call about what I had done with some milk bottles in the car.

N.: Were you misidentified with the milk bottles? (laughter) With the car? (laughter) With what?

Q.: Feeling in a hurry and impatient because of all the work I have to do and the expectations of those at work.

N.: When you work on the computer, are you misidentified?

Q.: Yes, sometimes. I start to worry and think of the difficulties.

N.: Do you misidentify as the performer of the action?

Q.: Yes.

N.: Is that present for you all of the time?

Q.: No.

N.: Why not?

Q.: (laughing) Because it is not real and not I.

N.: (laughing) I thought that you said that you were misidentified.

Q.: Yes, it is a strange thing. Isn't this the way with all illusion? It is never always there.

N.: So, what are you? If we expediently speak of misidentification or superimposition, it is not intended for you to build up a concrete concept that such things actually exist.

Q.: Yes, that was also part of the teaching on Friday night. This is always amazing. It means maya is not even existing.

N.: With what are you actually misidentified? What does your identity become? Or does it become anything?

Q.: My identity really does not become that. It just somehow becomes caught up in the thinking about it.

N.: Your identity, or existence, does not change and does not become bound. Somehow, you become caught up in this play of imagination or ideas. What is it that becomes caught? If it is not your Existence, what is it?

Q.: It is a sense of person.

N.: What constitutes the person?

Q.: Imagination.

N.: Does one imagination become caught up in another?

Q.: That is hard to do. Can that happen?

N.: That is what I am asking you.

Q.: It does not seem that it can happen. How can one imagination get caught up in a different imagination?

N.: That is what you were supposing. Then, you were asking me if illusion really happens and if it happens that way.

Q.: There is one thread of it that seems to be there for most of it.

N.: What is that?

Q.: The sense of existence. I always exist, but I think that I am the individual and involved.

N.: Is the idea of being an individual entity synonymous with the Existence? Or do you, Being,, exist without that idea?

Q.: It is definitely without that belief. I was assuming those misidentifications to be true. When I examine them, they lose their power.

N.: If they lost it, they did not really have it, did they?

Q.: No, they did not.

N.: Is this more of illusion possessing illusion?

Q.: Yes, like a dream, thinking of false connections in a train.

N.: There is no track. (laughing) All the while, you exist, uninvolved and unaffected.

Q.: The other does not really have the cohesion.

N.: Does the other exist at all?

Do you have two states? We see waking, dream, and deep dreamless sleep. We can see states with perception and without perception, with thought and without thought, and even samadhi, but does the Existence change states? Or does it remain immutable throughout? Does the Existence change its own nature, its own state, or does it remain immutable regardless of waking, dream, and deep sleep and any variations within them?

Q.: This is very helpful. This is much clearer for me. When I don't remember that, it seems otherwise.

N.: Who has forgetfulness as his experience? Does Being forget its own nature? Is it somebody else?

Q.: Somebody else.

N.: Are there two of you?

Q.: No.

N.: If Existence is only one, can there be another existence, a second self?

Q.: It is not possible. With the meditation that we just had, will this illusion appear again?

N.: How does it appear, by what cause, and for what experiencer? Is it that there is an individual entity who is the continuum and illusion and reality come and go? Or is Being the Reality, and illusion has no basis?

Q.: No basis?

N.: No root, no starting place. Maya is beginningless.

Q.: I need to really examine this. (quiet for a while) That eliminates quite a lot of stuff.

N.: (laughing) Yes, the Realization of Truth eliminates all of the "stuff." (laughter)

Q.: So, how does someone make that happen permanently?

N.: Is there someone? All the ideas of permanence, cultivation, acquisition, attainment, loss, or non-attainment revolve around the idea of an ego-entity, don't they?

Egolessness is the Realization. Being and Knowing are identical. Can you lose your Being? As Being cannot lose itself, the Knowledge cannot be lost. If we assume the objective notion and treat our Being as if it were an "it," the realization then becomes an event and the individual seems to be the controller, the possessor, or, at least, the experiencer, going in and out of all of that. Inquire. Is that the truth?

Q.: I noticed the experience, but did not quite grasp what you were saying.

N.: Do not worry about what was said. What is your experience?

Q.: It was something very deep and formless.

N.: Is it the same now? Is it you?

Q.: It is probably more me than thinking would be.

N.: All right. How much "you" is it?

Q.: Hmm. (remains quiet for some time)

N.: In truth, there are no degrees of you. Similarly, there are no degrees of Self-Realization. (Silence)

Q.: This has answered my question.

N.: (Silent)

Q.: This is stronger and clearer, now at the end of this conversation.

Another Q.: How often I still think of myself as this individual! Apparently, I return to illusion. I feel that I am this guy in this chair. I know that this is not I, but those ideas keep returning.

N.: As long as the misidentification with the body is still there, it is more difficult to see how there is no ego. The body is the chief form for that definition. So, thoroughly and deeply meditate upon the bodiless nature of your Being. If you must meditate upon it again and again, it is all right. It is not so much the repetition that is effective, but, each time you examine deeply, the answer that you find in the form of freedom from the body will be deeper with you.

Q.: So, saying that I should be thorough is actually an understatement.

N.: If you consider how many times you have misidentified with the body, to say that it may require some practice to cease that bad habit would be common sense. Continue meditation along these lines until you are not seated in a chair, until the chair, the body, and all else are in you, but you are not in them.

Q.: That is very helpful and what I will do.

Another Q.: To my view, the thoughts appear to be apart, and there appears to be a mind, but I am finding that such is just not true.

N.: Either see that the mind and all else, which are products of the mind, are completely different from you and cast all of them off or see that you alone are all this and that there is no other separate "this." Or see both.

Q.: I was in a quiet, thoughtless state. Instead of trying to get rid of all, there was nothing that was not I. Thoughts did not really go on.

N.: You should be rid of such completely from your identity, but you should know that such have no separate existence.

Q.: Oh, that's it. When I start to identify with the thoughts and the body, separation happens. It is when I identify them as something separate.

N.: If you are individualized, "this" is distinct and differentiated. If you are not individualized, no ego, what can we say about "this"?

Q.: This becomes That.

N.: If, without clarifying the knowledge of your Existence, the Self, you attempt to embrace everything by saying that you are all this, eventually you will find some kind of "this" that you do not wish to embrace and the state will be partial, or, if you are successful, you will be in a lofty mental state, but not Self-Realization. You will still be regarding all these things as multiple. Who it is that is all these things will remain unknown. If he is unknown, trouble is sure to follow.

Q.: Unknown means that the identity is not where it belongs?

N.: (Smiles silently)

Q.: Who has the capacity for Self-Knowledge? Who is seeking Self-Knowledge?

N.: Just that inquiry reveals the Knowledge. You must, therefore, inquire into yourself, whatever you regard as yourself, deeply. Inquiring into yourself deeply, the less there is to call yourself, the more expansive your experience is. If there is nothing that can be referred to as yourself, you are boundless. Becoming egoless, you become space-like. Losing the falsely assumed individuality, there is nothing apart from your Existence. Finding your own Being unborn, there is no creation.

(Then followed a recitation in Sanskrit and English of the dialogue of Ribhu and Nidagha from the *Tejobindu Upanishad.*)

(Silence)

Om Shanti Shanti Shanti Om

The Question and the Answer

Satsang, December 14, 2003

(Silence)

Om Om Om

(Silence)

Q.: I think that I must identify with something that does not have name or form but that is some kind of identification with something outside of Brahman. Is there some duality in that? There is no duality in Self-Realization, is there?

N.: What is the nature of the one who is considering these?

Q.: The one who asks questions.

N.: What is the nature of the questioner? If you want to know what is Self-Realization, just know the Self.

Q.: I should forget about the rest of it?

N.: Forget everything that constitutes the unrealized state.

The answer to all questions lies in one place.

Another Q.: Sankara and others have equated vairagya with Liberation. When detachment is removed, the Self naturally shines.

N.: Jnana (Wisdom) and vairagya (detachment) are also equated by the Maharshi in *Who am I?* What does detachment or dispassion (vairagya) mean?

Q.: I have been attached.

N.: What in you becomes attached?

Q.: It is circular thinking, such as thinking my happiness is dependent on this, or some goal, but there is not real happiness there.

N.: The idea that happiness is dependent on some object, circumstance, etc. constitutes the attachment. What is it that becomes attached? The idea cannot have itself.

Q.: The idea cannot have itself?

N.: The idea cannot generate or possess itself. So, what possesses the attachment?

Q. It does not make sense that the Self would.

N.: Does Existence, which is pure Consciousness, become attached?

Q.: No. It definitely doesn't.

N.: Is there another?

Q.: I believe in another, those things.

N.: Does the Self have that belief?

Q.: No, the Self doesn't have that belief.

N.: Does another have the belief that there is another existence?

Q.: Maybe.

N.: Does it have a pre-existence to commence its own existence? Is that possible?

Q.: That is not possible.

N.: It should be understood that attachment is constituted of superimposition, or the mistaken notion, regarding where happiness is. A man who knows where happiness is becomes detached from everything. Upon deeper inquiry, what actually becomes attached?

Q.: It seems as though nothing really becomes attached. The ideas cannot connect to themselves. That is what attachment is. It is only circular thinking in which I think that I am separate from the Self, and there is an assumption of this different entity.

N.: To whom do all the ideas belong?

Q.: (Quiet for a while). It seems that they belong to this entity. Once I question for whom they belong, that disappears. It seems as though there is nothing there.

N.: Yes. To what does one become attached? Do you actually become attached to the object, or do you become attached to just the idea?

Q.: Definitely the idea. It is just thought or imagination most of the time. For example (laughing), job security: that's a myth. (laughter)

N.: It has proved to be illusory not only in the absolute sense but in the pragmatic sense, as well. (laughter) Attachment is an idea. What you become attached to is also an idea. The one who becomes attached is also a supposition. So, there is nothing to which you become attached, and you never really become attached at all.

Q.: Can you go over that more slowly?

N.: You never become attached at all. To what is your Existence attached? When you inquire to see if there is a second one, an "I," you say that he vanishes. That to which you become attached is an idea. Attachment, itself, is just the confused idea regarding happiness. The one who becomes attached is an idea.

To be free of ideas, to have no conception, is Wisdom. To have no attachment is vairagya. Do you now see the similarity?

Q.: They go hand-in-hand.

N.: They are the same state. Being is never attached to anything, be such a body or an object. It has no senses. To what would it become attached? How could it be attached? You, in your real Being, unborn, undying, not entering into any of the three states of mind, and having none of the attributes of thought or of the body, are always detached. How can that which is One without a second become attached and to what?

Q.: That is in meditation.

N.: That is eternal detachment. Meditation upon your nature yields such detachment and Knowledge. They are the same.

Q.: I must continually remind myself of that meditation.

N.: What do you mean by "remind yourself"?

Q.: Reflecting and meditating upon it.

N.: So, to remind yourself of a meditation, you meditate on it again?

Q.: Yes, that state.

N.: Of what is the meditation composed?

Q.: It is composed of deep understanding.

N.: Does anything else compose meditation?

Q.: Yes, sometimes, reflecting.

N.: What happens when you reflect?

Q.: Sometimes, the truth in the reflection leads on to, "Well, it's true."

N.: It becomes your experience. The experience is not a sensory one. Is it mere thinking?

Q.: No, the experience is different from thinking

N.: Is it deeper knowledge?

Q.: Yes.

N.: Does this deeper Knowledge really have a start in time?

Q.: I believe that it does.

N.: You can inquire even now. Does the knowing with which you are inquiring now have a starting point or ending point in time?

Q.: If I believe in something else, is that belief more powerful?

N.: Does the belief in something else make that something else actually exist?

Q.: Is this so for all the world?

N.: Yes. When you believe that you are in the body, do you actually become embodied? Reality is that which is not determined by conception. The knowledge now seen as sporadic will be found, upon deeper inquiry, to be a continuous, unbroken thread. That which appears as a continuous, unbroken thread in practice is actually the continuum of pure Consciousness, which alone constitutes the Knowledge. Pure Consciousness is attached to nothing. It has no ignorance.

Another Q.: Could you clarify more the nature of Consciousness without definition by objects?

N.: If you negate all that can be negated, there is something in you that is never negated. It is not a mere thought. It is not a thought that is called "an emotion." It is not a body. It is imperishable. It alone can know itself. Inquiry reveals that you are That. Thus, absorption of identity is that which is emphasized.

Q.: There is also a false identity.

N.: The elimination of the false identity means that what you regard as your identity stands as That and no longer as an individual.

Q.: So, there is no one who is realized?

N.: We can say that there is Realization, but no one who realizes. The Realization, itself, is not an event or occurrence. If it were an event, it would happen to somebody and would necessarily be transient. What is transient is not worth seeking. What you seek is something eternal. What is eternal must always be, without a moment's interruption. Nothing objective is such in our experience. So, the way is nonobjective.

Q.: Can you help me?

N.: What kind of help do you need?

Q.: With understanding.

N.: What are you trying to understand?

Q.: God.

N.: How are you going about it?

Q.: It varies.

N.: If we want to understand God, we should understand ourselves. Otherwise, the assumed definitions of ourselves will get in the way of the view. If God be somewhat mirror-like, by way of analogy only, and we want to see that mirror-like God as God is, it is imperative that we do not place our head in the picture. Otherwise, we see according to our image. Therefore, the Maharshi pointed out that, if we want to know God, we must first know ourselves and that any attempt to know God without knowing the Self results in a mental image, but not God as God is. If, though, we know ourselves as we are, we find God seeing God with God's own eye. That darshanam is flawless.

(Silence)

Another Q.: What is the relation of thoughts to the knowledge of the Self, and what is the relation of these to the world and God?

N.: You cannot be any notion. You exist. What is this existence? As long as you define it as "I," "this," or "that," such is not the Existence itself. According to the perceiver, so is the perceived, whether you speak of the world or of God. Of the threefold illusion of the world, the individual, and God, the individual is the pivot. According to the definition of the individual—what you regard as yourself—the others are defined. If you are considered a separate being, God is a separate being, and the world is a separate thing. If you are defined as a body, God is conceived in bodily terms and the world of objects is considered as real. The same is true regarding what is subtle.

You are not something gross or subtle. You are nothing finite and nothing transient. If the Infinite and Eternal knows itself as it is by a deep inquiry as to "Who am I?", so that every notion, from "I" to the forms of the world, is relinquished as having nothing to do with identity or reality, you may call the result God-Realization or Self-Realization. It is the same.

Without that Knowledge, what we think that we know is diversified delusion. With that Knowledge, which is the natural state, everything that needs to be known is known.

(Then followed a recitation in Sanskrit and English from the *Tejobindu Upanishad.*)

(Silence)

Om Shanti Shanti Shanti Om

Sri Ramana Maharshi Jayanti

Satsang, December 28, 2003

(Silence)

Om Om Om

(Silence)

N.: Today is celebrated as the jayanti of Sri Ramana Maharshi. Jayanti refers to birth, yet he is the Unborn. The Unborn is Brahman, the infinite, the eternal Absolute.

The jayanti celebrates his birth, so to speak, in us, that is, our becoming aware of him. Of what do we become aware? Who is he? In order to truly answer these questions, we need to answer his question first, which is, "Who am I?" Otherwise we will view him according to our own aptitude. The only way to view him properly and truly is to see him with what he has referred to as the "infinite eye." The infinite eye is the eye of pure Consciousness. To see with the infinite eye of pure Consciousness, you must abide as That, without the least trace of any misidentification with anything else whatsoever.

Who is he? It is not possible to place the ineffable in words. It is not possible to place the inconceivable in thought. It is not possible to place the "I"-less as an object of perception of an "I." In order to know him, you must know yourself. If you know yourself, you know what he is, but you can't say anything about that.

What do we celebrate? If we cannot actually celebrate his birth because he is unborn, and if we cannot celebrate him because he is the infinite and the eternal and there is no one apart from him to worship or celebrate, what are we celebrating? It is that which he reveals. It is Self-Knowledge that unfailingly puts an end to all of the imagined bondage, the illusion of samsara. The best way to celebrate this is to be immersed in the Truth. If you are blissfully immersed in the Truth that liberates you from the illusion that samsara exists at all, you are really celebrating, even silently so.

Consider how in all this maya, he, with his liberating teachings, has somehow appeared, so that you can come to know of the Truth and pursue it to its core. What greater miracle could you want? How is it that you have come to know about him and the Truth that is revealed? You didn't do so by your ego or will-power. It did not happen because of some objective cause removed from the Self. If we look at this from beyond the "I am the body" misconception, it is entirely the Self revealing itself to itself. It is one infinite Self, unborn, imperishable, nonobjective, and One without a second.

Liberate yourself from the "I am the body" misidentification, and he is not a body. Liberate yourself from the misidentification with the mind, and he is not a mind. Liberate yourself through Self-Knowledge from the erroneous assumption of being an individual entity, or ego, and he is not an individual. Then, who is who? Who reveals what to whom?

When we inquire in this manner and understand like this, it is said that something apparently at a distance has been restored to its proper place. This is the significance of upadesa, or spiritual instruction. Something that had seemed far away has been shown to be very close. How close? It is exactly where your Existence is. That is where he is. You should know yourself to be this Existence and cease imagining yourself to be otherwise. That you have a doorway, so to speak, out of the imagined samsara, the illusion of birth, death, and everything between, is a great blessing. To realize within yourself that there are not two sides of that doorway is also a great blessing.

Q.: In meditation, I have a timelesss experience for awhile, as I do in deep sleep. With misidentification with the body, it ends.

N.: If it is timeless, so that it cannot be measured in terms of duration with a start or an end, for such would be absurd for what is timeless, what stands apart from it in the attempt to measure?

Q.: There is no one separate ever in that experience.

N.: Has anything changed?

Q.: It would be a joy to know.

N.: There are three states of waking, dreaming, and deep sleep. They seem to pass before you or revolve within you. You seem to pass through them, but they appear only in you. Within those three states are contained all modes of mind. Each one appears and disappears in you. One thing does not appear and disappear. It does not wake when there is waking. It does not dream when there is dreaming. It does not sleep when there is deep, dreamless, thoughtless sleep. That which innately transcends all three states is timelessly existent.

You are not the one who experiences the waking state. You are not a dreamer. You are not a sleeper. Those three, with their respective spheres of experience, do not affect you at all. You are the unchanging, unborn, indestructible Consciousness. That is your Being. It does not enter into any state. It is in its own state always. The natural, innate state is sahaja. If you think that you are in a state, there is some misidentification with the mind.

The wise declare that your real state is like waking-deep sleep, to indicate the luminosity of Consciousness and the formlessness found in deep sleep. In deep sleep, there is no misidentification with whatever is objective. It is a causal state, for the subject is still there, but there is no object. Consequently, you are not advised to go to sleep, but abidance as the Self is like deep sleep in its formlessness, in its undifferentiated nature. Yet, it is being awake, more awake than what is commonly called the waking state. Thus, the description of "waking-deep sleep." It signifies that which is utterly transcendent.

That with which you should identify and know as yourself has no waking, dreaming, or sleep. It cannot be said to be with thought or without thought. It has no birth or death. It does not enter into anything and does not exit anything. To inquire "Who am I?" is to establish your identity as that which is stateless.

Q.: There is a Reality that is always the same. What is other than that is unreality.

N.: Yes, Reality is always existent. In delusion, that which is not is superimposed upon that which is, the unreal upon the real. This gives the stamp of reality to whatever experience that is regarded as "present" and the deluded notions of the "here," the "now," etc., as if they were real. That slips on, and the next experience gets the same stamp of reality. This can occur myriad times, and the "reality" is as vivid and as substantial as it was the first time. The stamp doesn't wear out, but the experiences of the past, present, and future pass away. The Reality is still there, and your Existence is still there, for they are one and the same.

The unreal never comes to be. The Real always is.

Q.: So, anything that does not stand is just unreal?

N.: The Maharshi says that what newly arises will disappear. Something that appears and disappears, arises and sets, cannot at all be real. Apply this in practice. Whatever is regarded as you or yours that comes and goes, has a beginning and an end, is not truly you or yours at all. What is yours is yourself. What is yourself is the perpetual, undifferentiated Existence. It never becomes other than what it is. A "second" has not been born. Neither the states of mind nor the worlds in those states of mind have come to be. Continue to inquire. Whatever can disappear, if even for a moment, cannot be you. The nonobjective, the uninterrupted, alone is what you are.

Another Q.: May I ask about the *Heart Sutra?* It says that form is emptiness and emptiness is form.

N.: What do you want to know?

Q.: How would the Maharshi view this.

N.: If we regard sunya, void or emptiness, as the Absolute, that one Absolute, itself, is the form and the formless, without there being any variation or differentiation whatsoever. It is similar to stating that Brahman alone is and all this is only Brahman, without giving any credence to the belief in "all this." The emphasis is the Existence of Brahman.

If we regard sunya, emptiness, as one aspect and form as another aspect, we need to inquire as to what it is of which they are aspects. If one thing appears as two different states, that one thing must be different from both states. If that one thing is one's own mind, we should then know the nature of our mind. To know the nature of the mind, negate the false attribution of content, state, condition, etc., on one side or the other, and know what the mind's nature is in itself. If you remove from your definition of the mind all of its modes, conditions, thoughts, and objective conceptions, what remains of it? If we call it "Void," such means that nothing can be said of it, yet it is not nonexistent.

Though it has been a long time since I read any Buddhist Sutras, I believe that the rest of that sutra goes on to a thorough negation of the senses, the sensing, the sense objects, etc. So, it must be indicative of something unborn and uncreated. If you are unborn, there is no creation.

Another Q.: Spiritual instruction is a pointer to Truth. What is the relation of that to negation?

N.: Reality is not a negation. If there is a belief in something else, a second or duality, by way of instruction there is negation, "This is not so." By your application in spiritual practice to know your nondual nature, neti neti, not this, not this, you cast off all of the illusion. The Reality stands ever transcendent. That is your nature. The Maharshi said that all of the sastras (holy books) were based upon the existence of an ego, the elimination of which is their purpose. The same applies to spiritual instruction.

In practice, you do not produce a new self. You do not transform yourself into the Self. You do not obtain a new self. That which was imagined to be the case in ignorance is eliminated. The imagination ends. Then, what is real stands self-revealed.

Another Q.: When interactions go smoothly with others, especially my relatives, I am fine. When there is friction and disagreement, I need to look closely as to what actually occurs. It seems as if there is something outside of me doing something to me. Then, there is a reaction. When I meditate, I see that there is no one there or here. Then, I experience deep unity.

N.: Yes, the individuals are not there to be a self or another. They are merely imagined. When you disagree with someone, with what do you disagree? What actually is disagreeing?

Q.: It seems that the ego is threatened or is unhappy with what is occurring and is fighting with itself.

N.: Does some physical activity need to occur, or can you enter a disagreement just by having a conversation?

Q.: A conversation, and the person does not need to be physically present for it to go on.

N.: So, the conversation goes on in the mind?

Q.: Yes.

N.: Even when the conversation occurs, it is just in the mind. If there is action involved, it is still entirely in the mind.

You have one idea, and the other person has another idea. The ideas have a disagreement. For your true Self, there can be no question of agreement or disagreement, because there are not two. What happens with those ideas when the suffering occurs?

Q.: The two disagreeing ideas spawn more ideas. The suffering happens with the downstream flow of these ideas or the fallout from them.

N.: Is that the case? The generation of multiple ideas may be multiplied ignorance, yet what causes the suffering?

Q.: The suffering is the thinking that I am those ideas.

N.: So, "I am like this. This other one is like that." This and that don't match, and there is conflict and division. Whether it is one, two, or a whole zoo of ideas, the suffering is your misidentification with them.

Q.: That is from where the pain comes. My experience shrinks from something incredibly vast.

N.: If you cease to misidentify with thought, is there a problem or bondage? The Maharshi often points out that the primary thought is the assumption of "I." That spawns all the other ideas. Inquiring and knowing within yourself that you cannot possibly be whatever it is of which there is thought, that there is no connection between you and thinking, and inquiring further to see that there is no "I" from which illusion can spring, will take care of your disagreements. You may still not have matching ideas, but you will not be bound.

Q.: As soon as there is the "I," there are others. Then, there is the potential for conflict. When there is no "I," there is no one with whom to argue.

N.: Cut the veil from top to bottom, that is, both the misidentification with thinking and with the notion of "I." To say that you will be free of the ego notion but still misidentify with various thoughts is absurd.

Q.: To say that I will get rid of the ego-notion is another ego-notion?

N.: It would depend on the approach. If you declare that you know that there is no one there, in terms of an ego, yet remain misidentified with various thoughts, such is absurd. Cut the veil from top to bottom, from the "I" that is the apparent subject to the thoughts that are the apparent object.

Be keenly aware of the nature of everyone else by being keenly aware of your own nature. You cannot expect to have agreement of all the ideas. Someone may have a ridiculous idea that you do not find agreeable. Perhaps the idea is too silly. It may even be your own. You do not agree with the idea, and there is no complete unity at the level of thought. In the Absolute Self, though, there is no division. So, there is no need of unity.

Consider the Maharshi's example. He did not enter into arguments, even when people came to argue with him. If there were some means, while in the midst of verbal discussion, to help someone to turn inward and eliminate delusion, he would discuss the matter with him, even in the case in which the questioner was a bit feisty. He had no interest in argumentation. As soon as someone arrived in the old hall, he knew who that one was through and through. More accurately, he knew who that one was even before that person arrived. Such is profound, spiritual wisdom. Not having any misidentification with the mind, he had no mistaken notion about identifying with thoughts and those of the so-called "other person." No matter what would be presented in the question, it was impossible to convince him that there was anything but the one Self. Who can count how many gave up their notions of another in the light of that continuous silent revelation that the one Self alone exists for all eternity?

So, if you are arguing with the relatives, give up everything that is relative. (laughter)

Another Q.: In dealing with the misidentification with thought, is it that I deal with the content of thought?

N.: What determines the content of your thought? Obviously, a thought includes its content, for there is no such thing as a nonobjective thought.

Q.: It seems to be my ideas and my beliefs regarding where happiness is.

N.: From where do your beliefs about where happiness is stem?

Q.: They stem from delusion.

N.: They do not stem from wisdom or from actual experience. Thinking has its source in more thinking. Where does all of it start?

Q.: Not knowing the Self. My problem seems to be assuming that I am something that I am not. I need to check what I am assuming myself to be and what am I.

N.: Your nature is Sat-Cit-Ananda, Being-Consciousness-Bliss. If Being is unknown, it appears as an ego, which can then be embodied. If Consciousness is unknown, it appears as a mind. If Bliss is unknown, it appears as the external search for happiness or attachment. You, yourself, are the Being-Consciousness-Bliss.

You say that the trouble lies in the assumption about yourself. This is accurate. Who is involved in the assumption?

Q.: That I do not know.

N.: Who is the one who now perceives that he does not know?

Q.: It does not have a form. All else has form.

N.: If it does not have a form, it was not born.

Q.: Do I need to deal with the content in meditation?

N.: Does the content exist apart from the one who knows it?

Q.: No. There must be a misidentification for there to be all the rest.

N.: Whether you regard the thinking itself or the content, such depends upon misidentification, according to your discrimination. It is the same false assumption. So, since you are not really dealing with two things, there is no choice. You have only to know yourself.

To inquire and know yourself, eliminate the false belief that thought exists, that there is such a thing as an existent mind, and all of its so-called content. Both the mirage and its waves vanish. The snake and his multi-colored skin vanish from the rope.

Q.: I am weak at looking past the notions.

N.: The ability for such self-appraisal is laudable and perfect for practice that results in Self-Realization. Since you already have the ability to self-critically examine yourself, proceed a step further. How do you know that you are weak?

Q.: Often, I do not see the ideas clearly. Instead of seeing that all the ideas were in the mind, I have been dealing more with the content of the mind, asking myself if I am taking myself to be a body. You have been driving these points deeper.

N.: How deep?

Q.: (laughing)

N.: The measurement of being weak is useful to the extent that it causes you to then become strong in that very aspect, but it is not a definition for you. It is not appropriate to say that, because you have not discerned until now, from now on you will still not discern. That would credit ignorance with an on-going reality or self-sustaining power, although ignorance survives only by your belief in it.

There is really nothing in you that prevents you from knowing yourself. Neither thinking nor its content do so. Nor is there an ego or anything else.

After all, the instruction, which is timeless Truth that forms the most ancient teachings, clearly revealed by the Maharshi, upon which you are now meditating, is about the Reality of the Self, and not the existence of the unreality. It is about Liberation and that there is no existence to the bondage at all.

For that which has no actual existence, there is no valid cause. So, there is no delusion and no cause of delusion.

(Then followed a recitation in Sanskrit and English of verses from Adi Sankaracarya's *Vivekacudamani*.)

Boundless Wisdom

January 2, 2004

[This chapter is a portion of a transcript of spiritual instruction imparted during commentary upon *Song of Ribhu*, the English translation of the Tamil *Ribhu Gita*, Chapter 35. The verses, which were read aloud, are not reprinted here.]

N.: The chapter opens with Ribhu's instruction about the intensely steadfast abidance. Abidance in and as the Self is steadfast, for that is nondual and without an alternative. It is also intense, as intense as Reality, itself, is. Nothing is more intense than Absolute Reality. Just so is Self-abidance. There is no state of mind that is as intense as steadfast abidance as the Self. The most intense mode of mind is very dull and trite in contrast. There is nothing as intense as pure Being, pure Consciousness, for there is nothing between the Self and yourself.

He says that it is steadfast abidance in the undivided Self, in the contemplation that there is not a trace of the appearance of this world apart from the universal substratum, the Supreme Brahman. All of this, whatever appears in your experience, rests upon some support and has no existence apart from the support. So, then, does it have any existence at all? This is the line of inquiry suggested. Nothing exists apart from the support, the substrate. If nothing exists whatsoever apart from the substrate, is there anything whatsoever existing except the substrate?

You should inquire to know Reality. When you know Reality, you know Brahman, which is vast beyond all limitation and eternal. Brahman, which you come to know, is not different from the Self. Its nature is Existence-Consciousness-Bliss. There is no name and no form. There is only pure Existence-Consciousness-Bliss.

In the absence of inquiry, name and form seem to be realities. Then, one says that he is one thing and this is another. Only when name and form are not inquired into to see what their real nature is does one believe the phenomenal world to be real. Then, one thinks something has happened, something has been born, something has been created, and then, of course, something will perish, too. If you inquire into what are all these names and forms, you find the substrate, or you find that there is really only one undivided Essence, which is pure Existence. You must see it as bodiless, as Ribhu declares. You must realize Existence as formless and bodiless. Otherwise, your mind is caught up in the delusion of false appearances and does not perceive Existence at all.

That bodiless, undivided, essential Existence, is the Self, and there is nothing different from it. If you endow, through delusion, the Self with name and form, and thus conceive of some particularization, there is undoubtedly something different from it. Everything is different from it, to some degree or another. If, upon inquiry, you find that you have no name, no form, no thought, no sensed attribute, or anything similar, can there be anything apart? If you want to see the divine Oneness of which all the sages and saints speak and sing, see your own nameless, formless, true nature. The true nature of the Self being perceived, the immaculate, indivisible nature of it becomes self-evident.

"Casting aside everything" means having no attachment, no misidentification, and not asserting in your mind that this is real, that is real, and such. Cast "aside everything with the blemishless certitude that all is the peaceful Brahman," in light of what he has already declared and "I am that changeless Brahman," for knowledge of identity is crucial, and thereby abide in your natural Self.

It is the mind that seems to have illusion. It is the mind that seeks to know. Ribhu declares that Consciousness, which is Brahman, alone exists. Your mind does not exist. It is very worthwhile to deeply meditate upon the meaning of this. If your mind does not actually exist, what is real? Who are you? If your intellect does not even exist, what are your doubts? What are your obstructions? Where are your hopes and fears? Where is desire? Where is aversion? All the ideas that you have about yourself and other things, of the past, of the future, and of the present, are entirely in your mind. Ribhu says that the mind does not even exist. Then, what of its content?

Nothing exists apart from Brahman, the perfectly full. Neither the world nor your mind is. Cast aside everything. Be detached. Renounce the unreal. Have the nondual certitude that any kind of appearance is only Brahman, Brahman misperceived as that, Brahman appearing as that. There is no second thing that comes to be. The emphasis is not so much on the mutability of Brahman, but on that nothing exists other than Brahman. Understand Brahman to be yourself, and everything is perfectly clear.

Once you have realized this within yourself, you see that there are no states of "darkness and light," the darkness of ignorance and a separate state of the light of wisdom. There is no such thing as this or that. However one conceives of objective appearances, there are really no such things. "You" and "I" do not exist.

Bewilderment, clear perception, and illusion are different states of mind, which does not exist. If you have a mind, there are "ramifications." If the mind, itself, does not exist, which can be realized by inquiry as to what its nature is, what ramifications are there? Likewise is it with form and formlessness. He says that one should "cast aside everything with the blessed certitude." It is a true, eternal blessing to have certainty regarding the real nature of the Self. If you pray for a blessing, pray for that one alone.

"All that exists is Brahman. That I am. Thus changelessly abide in the Self." Ribhu declares that all is only Brahman, Brahman is myself, and thereby one abides in Self-Realization. It is indicative of identity and reality being unobscured. When they are unobscured, they are one and the same thing. That is the Self. It is also called "Brahman." If we think that there is something else, it is only due to our having misconceived who we are. Then, the Absolute appears as if different, and there seems to be something else in our experience. If we cease to misidentify and know our own nature as it is, that one Self is Brahman, and there is nothing that exists apart from it.

Everything, from the first spark of creation to the seed notion of an individual and the idea that you were born, followed by growth, maturation, decay, and death, is an illusion superimposed upon your real nature. By inquiry to know yourself, gain a clear understanding of what your real nature is. Only the Self, which is uncreated and unborn, is imperishable. Then, blissful immortality is your direct experience. Otherwise, you live a life as a dream character in your own dream.

When, in the great scriptures, something is declared to be an illusion, you must look within yourself and determine just how illusory is the illusion. He says that the one, the many, the all, duality, existence and nonexistence, the troublesome, the new, the nearby, and the far off are entirely false. When you meditate upon the illusory nature of that which is not the Self, is it illusory to the point that it is a temporary appearance, to the point that it is dreamlike, or to the point of never having been? Just how illusory is illusion? If you determine that it is thoroughly illusory, Brahman, which was earlier proclaimed to be "the One, the taintless, and the mass of Bliss," remains as "I am." That is the changeless abidance in the Self, which is the theme of the chapter as indicated by the title.

"All the delusions of the mind": what are the delusions? "Wakefulness," the waking state, inclusive of the entirety of its content; dream, inclusive of the entirety of its contents, deep sleep, including the absence of any content, and the "fourth" state, that is, the Absolute conceived as a fourth state, or a separate state of samadhi. All of that, he says, is completely untrue and has no basis in fact. If you are not awake, not dreaming, not sleeping, and not even in samadhi, in what state are you? What is the state of the Self? This is what needs to be discerned.

In the waking state, you have a gross body, and there seems to be a waking state experiencer, which is presently identified as "I." In your dream state, you have a dream body, and there is a dreaming character and experiencer, who may conceive of things differently than the waking state one. In his time and in his realm, he is also called "I." In deep sleep, there is no content. There is a causal body and a causal state. Still, there is the "I." All of those experiencers and their forms, Ribhu says, are completely untrue. If none of those forms are your form, what is your state? If you are not the experiencer of waking, dreaming, and deep sleep, or any of the content, which means any of the experiences that occur in those states of mind, where are you? What are you? Unless you know this, you are just roaming about in a waking dream. You may think that it is real, but it is not. It is entirely untrue. If, casting aside everything, you divest yourself, by the "faultless, steadfast certitude that all is the great Brahman and that I am," of these definitions of waking, dreaming, deep sleep, and the experiencer within each of these, what do you find? That which you realize is imperishable.

If Brahman is motionless, if the Self is changeless, and that is what you are, can there be a fall into ignorance or a coming into bondage? If there is no coming into bondage, can there be the reaching of Liberation? If there is no motion in the Self, can duality arise? Question, like this, within yourself. If there is no separate meditator and only the unchanging Self exists, there cannot be qualities. Nor can there be the meditation on the qualitiless nature, for how could you meditate on yourself?

There can be no knowledge of an attributeless form. Every form has an attribute. If your nature is motionless and changeless, has form come to be? Do you have any attributes or qualities? What is your knowledge of that? If the knowledge of that is only imagination, have you ever moved from your original state? If only you know the primordial Being is still the same and has never changed, you know Reality. If not, you are only dreaming and need to wake yourself up.

If you believe in the nonexistent, discriminate between the existent and the nonexistent. But when you have so discriminated, is there still an "existent" and a "nonexistent" and a mind that so discriminates? If you are caught up in the motion of maya, you need to see that which is always still. When you so discern that which is always still, is there a moving and an unmoving or a mind that so discriminates? You need to know the nature of the innate Consciousness. So, discriminate between what is non-Consciousness and what is Consciousness in order to know yourself. When you know yourself as the infinite Consciousness, are there anymore the two things of the Consciousness and the non-Consciousness, and a mind that discriminates between the two?

If there is the non-Self, you must inquire to know the Self. The Self having been known, are there two, an inquiring self and something into which to inquire? If there are not two, is there really an inquiry? If there was never delusion, is there really an inquiry that reveals Knowledge?

Like this is the direct experience of Realization being explained. The essence of the real teaching is just the Reality itself.

Whatever you think exists or does not exist, what you have achieved and not, cast aside all your thoughts of these things and abide as you are. Know yourself as you are. Cast aside everything that makes for desire, anger, pride, ostentatiousness, arrogance, your ideas of duality, and cast aside even your ideas of nonduality. Such are nothing more than thoughts, which means they are nothing. Know yourself.

Everything that can be cast aside is just a thought. Recognize everything is just a thought and cast it aside. No longer regard it as reality or yourself, and see what remains. It is simple, but you must do so thoroughly.

The innate state, the natural state, is the identity of That and "I." It is unnatural when one considers duality to be true, even in the least degree. Negate all the conditions, as Ribhu describes them, which are all the limitations. The mind and the intellect, the body, the senses, the prana, the idea that there is a world, an individual, and a God apart from him—all this should be cast aside as mere delusion. Then, the natural, or innate, state of identity of That, the Absolute, and "I" becomes self-evident. Verse twenty is about this self-evident identity.

True Knowledge is differenceless. False knowledge, or ignorance, is characterized by differences. False knowledge, or ignorance, is characterized by a distinction between the knower, "I," and what is known. True Knowledge has no such distinction of and no division between a knower and a known. All of the false knowledge of all of the different things is merely superimposed upon something that is differenceless. It is superimposed like a snake on a rope, like the waters of a mirage on the sand of the desert. The thing upon which all this is superimposed is very real. Its nature is Existence, for it is real. Its nature is Consciousness. Consciousness, itself, is the Knowledge referred to as "differenceless." In the superimposed illusion, you are one thing, the knower, and something else is the known. In the differenceless real substrate, you are not one thing and "something else" is not another thing. The differenceless substrate should be realized as that which the "I" really is. You should cast off, or negate, the assumption that the "I," or your identity, is anything appearing amidst all the superimposition. You are only the rope and not the snake. You are only the real Self and not the illusion so appearing. The nature of this Knowledge is eternal. It is as everlasting as Being itself. As Existence does not cease to exist at any time, so the Knowledge of the Self cannot cease. Therefore, Liberation by Self-Knowledge is eternal.

"The 'I,' the expanse of Knowledge, and Brahman, abide changelessly in the Self" are the last two lines of the verse. Knowledge is not a small thing. It is vast beyond all of the thoughts of the mind, which he has already alluded to as having been cast off. It is eternal. It is infinite. The infinite, eternal expanse, or space-like Knowledge, space-like Consciousness, is what you are. It is referred to as "Brahman." The root of the word means expansive. It refers to Absolute Reality. The expansive, Absolute Reality, which is immeasurable, is what you are. You are not a small illusion. You are not a mere superimposition. Give up the ideas of being anything else, from the body to the idea of an "I," and experientially abide as That. For how long? For as long as That exists.

Changeless abidance in the Self is the one state of lasting peace and happiness. For the sake of your own bliss, for the sake of your own peace, you must abide changelessly as the Self. Since there are not two selves, one in which to abide and another to do the abiding, abidance in the Self is Knowledge of oneself as the Self. What you know yourself to be, that you are.

He says to consider "the dream and the waking state." Your, yourself, appear as everything in a dream. Likewise, you, yourself, appear as everything in the waking state.

In your dream, your dreaming state of mind makes up the dream. Everything in the dream is the dream state experience. The dream state experience is the dreaming state of mind. What is the nature of this mind?

Everything in the waking state is the waking state of mind. The perceiving awareness constitutes everything perceived. If we think that this is not so and that there is a difference, such is due only to the "I am the body" idea. When once the "I am the body" idea is relinquished, it becomes obvious that your own state of mind, or your own perceiving awareness constitutes everything perceived and experienced. You need to know the nature of the awareness or mind.

The mind loses its mindness, the awareness loses its awareness. What remains is the essential nature, which is pure Consciousness. You have never experienced anything but yourself. If you think that you are a body, there are many things held as other than you that you experience. If you think that you are an individual, there are many other individuals that you experience. Some of those individuals are animate, and some are inanimate. If, as discerned by Self-Knowledge, you are not an individual, there is not a single other thing existing anywhere. Nothing is apart from you.

Q.: There is a substrate of the waking state. I am projecting an idea upon it. With the dream state, there is not a substrate to be projected upon other than Consciousness.

N.: Likewise is it with the waking state.

Q.: It seems clearer to me with the dream state. In the dream everything is self-contained within Consciousness. Upon waking up, I can see that.

N.: Yes, likewise is it with the present waking state. The equivalent of waking up is leaving behind the "I am the body" idea. If you are not the body, everything is in you, in the same way that the dream is in you. If you are not the body, everything is a product of your mind, just as it is in a dream.

Q.: There is only Consciousness there. The substrate is Consciousness. Everything else is only imagined in that Consciousness.

N.: Yes, yet Consciousness has no capacity of imagination. Expedient teachings make use of "it is all of the mind," yet we then see that the mind, also, does not exist. The chapter begins with this.

Q.: If one says that there is a mind, he can say that there is imagining. If there is no mind, Consciousness cannot imagine, and this has never come to be.

N.: So, when we speak of appearances in the substrate, in any state of mind, what is meant thereby is that the substrate is real, but the superimposed is not real at all.

Q.: I think that everything is nothing other than Consciousness, which is the cushion for all of it.

N.: Yes, but Consciousness does not become a cushion.

Q.: It is not even misperceived as a cushion?

N.: That, also, is just expedient teaching. If you think that something is perceived, a cushion is imagined, it is Consciousness misperceived. If we inquire who it is that misperceives, there is no such ignorant being. Then, there is no cushion or imagining of it.

Q.: The perceiving is part of the misperception.

N.: (laughing) Alright.

Another Q.: In the waking state, it takes all kinds of adjustments to harmonize the thoughts that occur. Is any of this worthwhile?

N.: Are you in the waking state?

Q.: I imagine myself to be at the moment.

N.: Find out what your real state is. Then, the harmony that is sought in the waking state will be realized, but it will be of a transcendent nature.

Q.: As far as trying to do it in the waking state, none of it is worthwhile. Only the transcendence of the misperception is.

N.: The efforts to harmonize may be fine, but you will find the answer for which you are looking by utter transcendence. That is discerning Reality as it is.

"The inner faculties" refer to the mind, intellect, and such. In deep sleep, where is the mind? Where is the world? Where is the individual? No one experiences them in deep sleep. If just entering deep sleep can obliterate the experience of the world, the individuals, and such, can they possibly be real? Not a trace of these three, the world, the individual, and the Supreme, exists before the mind projects. After the projection is over, these things do not exist. Between, they are merely due to the projection of the mind. He says that if you inquire into them to see what is true, they do not exist at all. The projection is false. Thus, negate all else and "abide changeless." Negate all thoughts and abide as the Self, the changeless.

Q.: What is the obscuration of deep sleep?

N.: Why don't you realize the Truth by entering into deep sleep? Is this what you are asking?

Q.: Yes.

N.: Because it is still a state of mind. It is very useful for someone who is already inquiring to know the Truth of the Self to examine that state, comparing and contrasting it to the other states, because it negates what may otherwise be assumed to be real, what is objective. In deep sleep, the object is removed, but the subject is not known. Hence, the ancient Vedanta works refer to it as a causal state. The cause is there, but the effect is absent. The seed of ignorance is there, but the whole weed of delusion is not grown.

Q.: Then, I am not entirely ignorant but not in a samadhi state either. Are there degrees of ignorance in deep sleep?

N.: What is your experience of deep sleep? Do you have degrees of deep sleep?

Q.: There are nights when I toss and turn and wake up witnessing the body tossing and turning. Other nights, there is more identification with the dream characters.

N.: Are there nights when there is nothing to be said about it at all? That is deep sleep. There can be no degrees of it because the effect, the objective part, has been removed. Degrees mean how much of the objective illusion is present or absent.

Q.: I am thinking that there is a lessening of ignorance in deep sleep. If one lessens that and then enters the waking state, he might carry on with some of that clarity.

N.: Since you need to liberate yourself from the states, do you want to practice within the states, or do you want to practice the Knowledge beyond the states that sets you free from the states?

Q.: I want to transcend.

N.: The answer for which you are looking is beyond all three states. You want ignorance to be diminished, if not destroyed outright.

Q.: Yes.

N.: Earlier, he spoke of three experiencers, the sleeper, the dreamer, and the waker, with their respective forms and states of sleeping, dreaming, and waking. The Truth is that you are not any of those. So, inquire not to better the deep sleep experience, but to wake up from the cause, the ground, that constitutes the deep sleep. Do not look for a transient experience within the waking state. Obliterate entirely the idea that you are the waking state experiencer or in a waking state. The same is true with the dream.

Q.: In the waking state, there are the five sheaths. One can disidentify.

N.: In deep sleep, there is only the fifth sheath. In the waking state, there are the other four sheaths, too. In which sheath are you?

Q.: None of them!

N.: If you are not in any of the five sheaths, you are not in any of the three states. If you identify with the body, you seem to be bound in the waking state. If you are identified with the manomaya kosa or vijnanamaya kosa, the sheaths of the mind and intellect, you seem to be going through different states. Are you the mind? That is the inquiry.

Q.: So, anandamaya kosa is the form of ignorance in deep sleep?

N.: Yes, which is a cause with no effect. There is a veiling of yourself but no projection of false multiplicity.

Q.: One is either misidentified with that sheath or not.

N.: Like all else and like at any other time.

Q.: One can be in sleep but not misidentify with it. Then, though, one is not asleep anymore, but is in the fourth state.

N.: Yes. We may say that sleep is in you, and you are not in it. You can misidentify with the projected illusion of someone passing through states, or you can know yourself as that space-like expanse of Consciousness in which the states appear and disappear. You do not move. They arise and disappear in you. You do not arise and disappear in them. They travel through you. You do not travel through them. You are the space-like Consciousness, which does not wake, dream, sleep, etc. You do not move.

Q.: What is the mind in sleep of one who remains in full awareness of oneself?

N.: One who has no mind remains always aware of himself. Those who are misidentified with the mind think that jnani-s such as the Maharshi are always thinking of the Self even while asleep. In deep sleep, how do they manage to think that they are the Self, while not thinking at all when the waking state occurs? It is very perplexing to the misidentified viewpoint. The *Gita* says that what is night to the ordinary person is day for the sage and vice versa, but such an interpretation is not the meaning of that verse. The Maharshi and other jnani-s never sleep, never, dream, and never awake for there is no identification with the mind. There is no false identification with someone undergoing those experiences.

Q.: Is Sahaja Samadhi and the fourth state of nirvikalpa samadhi the same experience?

N.: It depends on the meaning ascribed to those terms. Samadhi means a state of absorption in which there remains no individual, and nirvikalpa means without differentiation and without doubt, implying absolute certainty, and without imagination. Sahaja means innate, inborn, though unborn in true sense, and natural. What is the innate state? Can it be something that comes and goes? If it did, it would not be innate. It must be without difference, which is nirvikalpa. Do you wish to call that "samadhi"? You may do so. The *Avadhuta Gita,* though, says that, if there were duality, how would samadhi be possible? If there is nonduality, how would samadhi be possible?

Q.: It is not a question in that state.

N.: Some call it samadhi; some call it the Self.

Q.: The mind would go through its three states, but one's experience would be undifferentiated?

N.: What would perceive the mind and its three states?

When you pose the question about a jnani having his mind pass through three states, but being beyond it, what is it in you that still considers three states and a mind? It is a mind in the waking state that you need to transcend.

Q.: It implies that there is difference or something that can be noticed.

N.: Yes. The mind in the waking state considers what mind there might be in others and in what state they might be. But are you in the waking state? Are you the mind?

Q.: It needs to be discerned.

N.: Keep your focus on that which is not in any state or which is the innate, invariable state.

Q.: What does not have the possibility of entering a state?

N.: It does not enter or exit.

Q.: Because there is no mind.

N.: There is no individual traversing such realms or states of the mind. Stay with the space-like Consciousness. That alone is real. That is Brahman. That alone is your Self.

None in Bondage, None Liberated

Satsang, January 4, 2004

(Silence)

Om Om Om

(Silence)

N.: None bound, none liberated: this is one way of pointing out the innate state of Self-Realization. This is the state of the Self as it is, Being as Being is, with no trace of individuality to give rise to bondage or its consequent suffering.

In the pursuit of Self-Realization, do you practice while presuming that you are in one state seeking to attain another state? Of course, you don't want to retain whatever state that you think that you are in now. Nevertheless, it is the nonexistence of the individual ego entity that is said to constitute Self-Realization, or Liberation.

Whatever you assume yourself to be is that by which you seem to be bound. Who is bound? The one who so assumes. The Maharshi reveals that the inquiry "Who am I?" is pivotal to know yourself and to be free of the "I" mode, or "I" notion.

However the "I" is defined, so is the corresponding experience. If you define the "I" and misidentify as an embodied individual, your waking state world is your experience. If you seek highest Truth, you need to vacate that experience, but how will you do so? Can the waking state individual vacate the waking state? Can the body vacate the embodied state? How is Liberation to be? How is Self-Realization to be?

If the misidentification, or the attribute of the "I," is the mind, inclusive of every kind of thought, the corresponding experience of that mental experiencer is all the realms or states of the mind, the mind's modes, and all of thought's permutations. Self-Realization is said to be the state of no-mind or Liberation from the mind. How is there going to be Liberation from the mind? Will the mind liberate itself, or will that be, as the Maharshi says, like a thief dressing up as a policeman to catch the thief which is himself? Will the thief be apprehended?

Turn to the Maharshi's quintessential instruction. Know yourself; Who am I? Find out if you are an embodied individual. Find out if you are the one who has mental modes or travels through mental states. Liberation comes by clarity of Knowledge regarding one's identity. This is not so much a transformation from one self to another, but knowing, which is realizing, the Self, or the real Existence, that you are and ceasing to misidentify as a second.

The Upanishad says that where there is One without a second, there is no fear. Why is there no fear? Because there is no possibility of disruption of one's happiness or one's Existence. Sat-Chit-Ananda, Being-Consciousness-Bliss, is the one Self.

Clear Knowledge is needed regarding your Existence. This is your very Being. As long as there is the assumption that you are an individual, there is bound to be bondage. Because bondage is not your natural state, you yearn for freedom. If you are spiritually-minded, you pursue this freedom and happiness in Liberation, Self-Realization. So, you should realize what your Self is. The Self is not a body, and it is not one who inhabits a body. The Self is not something sensed, and you are not one endowed with senses. The Self is not in the mind, and it is not something that possesses a mind. It is not an "I." The real nature of "I" is utterly "I"-less.

Self-Realization is described as neither bound nor free, no one bound and no one liberated. This is because the ego does not exist. In Self-Realization, the Self alone knows itself. There is no second thing capable of doing so.

You do not change from a bound state to a liberated state. At the start of spiritual practice, it may seem that way, but, if the practice is one of Self-Knowledge, inquiring "Who am I?", the very one who is bound proves to be nonexistent. In its place is That which is always liberated. So, none are bound, and none are liberated. There is no individual entity involved. The infinite Being-Consciousness-Bliss, which is your real nature, has never been born and has never been bound. The ego has not been born for it has not started.

To inquire means to utterly abandon the ego, which means the assumption of being an individual and all that is appended to it in the form of definition. The entirety of that is nothingness, and that constitutes the entirety of samsara, the repetitive cycle of birth, illusion, and death. You must deeply, thoroughly inquire within yourself, "Who am I?"

What do you take yourself to be? Your desires are for someone. Your fears are for someone. Who is that one? Your birth is for someone. Your death is for someone. Who is that one? Everything between birth and death is for someone. Who is that? Put the question to yourself in the innermost manner.

The state of Self-Realization is just the nature of Being as it is, which has no birth, is utterly nonobjective, is completely formless, and is forever undifferentiated. For it, nothing is created, and nothing happens. That alone is true. Therefore, it is absurd to say that you do not have Realization or that you do have Realization, as if it were a possession. It is absurd to speak of this Realization as coming slowly, as coming quickly, as coming in a piecemeal fashion, as coming in degrees, or in any other such manner. The Reality, which is the Self, does not come and go; nor is there anyone else for whom it comes and goes.

If, in your heart, you yearn for Self-Realization, with the recognition that it is the highest good and that it is the sole purpose of life, know yourself as you are. You are not waking, not dreaming, and not in deep sleep. You are not with thoughts or without thoughts. You are not with any kind of form. That which you are in Truth you are always. The characteristic of Reality is its being invariable.

If Self-Realization is true, it must be of the very nature of that which is realized. If what you understand yourself to be is true, it must be of the very nature of the Reality, which is nondual and invariable. If, upon examination of your mind and experience, what you take yourself to be is something other than the Reality, that is not you.

(Silence)

Do not assume about yourself. Know yourself. Do not imagine about yourself. Know yourself. If you know yourself, the Self is Brahman.

Q.: Disidentifying from the body and mind is akin to Realization. It is really renouncing all of this.

N.: "Me" and "mine" constitute delusion. Absence of "me" and "mine" is Truth. If you eliminate "my object," it is good, but it is better to entirely eliminate the possession quality that pertains to "my object, my body, my thought, etc." If you give up the "me," all of the mine is gone at once.

Q.: I confuse myself with thought. Disidentification and focusing on the truth of who I am are needed.

N.: What is the truth of who you are? It is ineffable. You must know it inside. To mistake an object to be yourself is ridiculous. Regard your body as an object. The thoughts, constituting the mind, are, similarly objective, though subtly so. They are not you. If you are not thought, inclusive of the content of thought, what remains? In this way, know your freedom from thought.

Another Q.: I am reading *Timeless Presence* and using each paragraph as a meditation. In it, there is a statement pertaining to stopping thought and quieting the mind in Self-inquiry. When inquiring, it seems that one becomes so focussed on noticing oneself that his thinking stops. I am wondering how there is something that runs deeper than thought.

N.: Do you have that book with you?

Q.: I will read the whole paragraph: "Who am I? If only the answer to this is known, there is then nothing more to be known or attained. He said, 'The inquirer himself is the answer, and there can be no other answer.' Who am I? At one point, it seemed the method to quell all other notions, and, indeed, it is ideal for that purpose. Yet, it is still more. It is the revelation of unobscured Being."

N.: Did you have a question about quelling thoughts or about the revelation of unobscured Being?

Q.: That is clear, but "at one point it seemed the method to quell all other notions, and, indeed, is ideal for that purpose."

N.: Yes, because it eliminates the superimposition regarding reality and identity.

If, with every thought that rises, you inquire, "For whom is the thought," that thought subsides, and the focus is entirely upon the "I." The sense of identity and reality have returned to the "I." It is not the subsidence of the thoughts that is the fruit to be cherished from the inquiry, but the revelation of Being, which alone is reality and identity.

Q.: So, it is the knowledge of oneself that is the key.

N.: The disappearance of the unreal is nothing great, because it is unreal! (laughter) Reality comprehending itself, atmasakshatkara, direct perception or knowing of the Self, is that for which inquiry is.

Q.: The knowing of oneself is also the effect of removing the misidentifications by that investigation into oneself?

N.: Yes.

Q.: It is clearer, and my mind feels unobscured by notions.

N.: Where do you keep your notions?

Q.: In my misidentifications. (laughing)

N.: Alright. Then, where do you keep your misidentifications?

Q.: In the mind.

N.: What is your mind?

Q.: (quiet for some time) My mind seems to be a bunch of thoughts running.

N.: Do the thoughts know themselves, or does something else know?

Q.: Something else always knows.

N.: That something else that always knows combined with the notions you refer to as the "mind," apart from which there is no mind.

Q.: One knows himself as he is without those thoughts.

N.: Can you be a thought? Can an idea be a definition for who you are?

Q.: No.

N.: Then, what is the true definition of one's own Self, svatmanirupanam?

Q.: It definitely cannot be a thought. I can't describe it as something.

N.: If it cannot be a thought, can there be multiplicity in it?

Q.: Thoughts are the multiplicity.

N.: Yes, there must be thoughts in order to have multiplicity. If this is That which is not a thought, there can be no multiplicity in it. Likewise is it with form.

Consciousness plus the notions is called "mind." Without the notions and the Consciousness, there is no mind. If you remove the notions, what is left of your mind?

Consciousness can exist without the notions. The notions, or thoughts, cannot exist without Consciousness. Have you ever experienced a thought apart from the Consciousness that knows it?

Q.: No.

N.: Then, there is no such thing as thought, for it has no self-existence. The only thing that exists is pure Consciousness. Consciousness is not multiple, not divisible, and is never modified at any time. What are the supposed thoughts? Inwardly wonder about this.

Q.: It is much clearer for me. I must have a misidentification to have them.

N.: Yes, starting with the primary misidentification of someone, of "I." Thus, the Maharshi's instruction that the "I" thought is the first of all thoughts. What is the "I"? In you, something seems to exist as "I." What is it? Who is that?

Q.: (quiet for a while) It is not these notions. If my mind starts to move, I need to find out if that is I or a definition for myself.

N.: Good. For whom is the mind?

(Silence)

Another Q.: I am trying to understand what Self-Knowledge is. I know that I have gained some Self-Knowledge. I ask myself who it is that is gaining that Self-Knowledge. It collapses on itself.

N.: Thus, you gain some more. (laughter)

Q.: The Self doesn't really gain Self-Knowledge. An ego can't know the Self. So, what is this Self-Knowledge? I know what it is, but, logically, it does not work out.

N.: What do you mean?

Q.: If somebody gains Self-Knowledge, it means that he lacked something that he has gained. The Self, though, has not gained anything, and the ego has not gained it. The more I think about it, the more confused I become. If I don't think about it, everything is fine.

N.: On the path of Self-Knowledge, you need to determine deeply within yourself who you are. Yes, the ego doesn't gain anything. What it has is an absence. The Self is not in need of anything. If, though, in your experience, due to ignorance, there seems to be some deviation from the pristine bliss and peace of the Self, Knowledge is needed. Self-Knowledge alone is needed, and it is essential. Without it, there is no Liberation. With it, there is none bound and none liberated.

You must know who you are. As far as the attempt to describe what happens in the path of Self-Knowledge is concerned, one of the Upanishads says that it is like tracing the tracks of the birds in the sky. An expedient description of footprints can be made, but they are not really there.

There is great precision in the practice on the path of Self-Knowledge, yet, it is a formless path to realize the Formless. It is questioning that which is most immediate. "The ego, the Self": who are you who knows about these? You say that everything collapses. The entire superstructure of notions and concepts in the mind collapses. That which is constituted of mere imagination and based on a foundation of a false assumption is bound to collapse. The inquiry is merely the revelation of what is real and an utter dismissal of what is unreal. To discern what is unreal and what is real is in keeping with Self-Knowledge. Thus, you come to the conclusion, as stated in the *Gita*, that the Real ever is and the unreal has never come to be.

This conclusion must be reached experientially. The experience is of your own Existence. Nothing could be more experiential than your Existence. Indeed, other than your own Existence, treat all else as merely theoretical—a mere hypothesis or a bad rumor.

There are not two selves in the one of you. For everyone, existence, itself, is singular. The ideas about oneself, which form the mind, personality, and such, and the bodies may be multiple, but Existence is singular and indivisible. It is most immediate. There are not two. Continue with the Knowledge of the Self, negating from your identity everything that is objective, discontinuous, conceivable, or perceivable. What remains is what is. It is not a thing.

Q.: I see now that, when I was talking about Self-Knowledge, I was speaking about it conceptually and not experientially. The actual experience does not collapse, though everything may collapse around it into a singular existence.

N.: Self-Knowledge is real and Self-ignorance is illusory.

Q.: Could one say that Self-Knowledge is just getting rid of the ignorance?

N.: Eliminate the ignorance, and then you can define Self-Knowledge.

(Then followed a recitation in Sanskrit and English of verses from the *Tejobindu Upanishad.*)

(Silence)

Om Shanti Shanti Shanti Om

Always Real

Satsang, December 21, 2004

(Silence)

Om Om Om

(Silence)

N.: That you exist is absolutely certain. Whatever you may conceive of this existence, including all that is perceptible, is entirely unreal. When the two are confounded, there is the illusion of bondage. If one, seeking Liberation, inquires to know his own existence, the Liberation that he has sought is his natural, innate state. It is the one state, without an alternative, for the Self, as it is, is the sole-existent Reality.

Duality is not true. There is no alternative to your Being, which is the Absolute, Brahman. There is no other state in which you can be, and there is not a second "you" other than the one, indivisible, illimitable Self to be in any such thing.

It is necessary to examine your existence. The supposition of anything else to be so or not so, to be like this or not like this, without knowing yourself is ridiculous. If you would know that which is reality, the first thing that you must do is know yourself. Likewise, if you wish to see God, the first thing that you must do is to know yourself. Having accomplished this first thing, it is also the last thing.

Examine yourself and observe what you regard as your identity. Set about determining what is truly your existence.

Whatever is truly your existence is so without a moment's interruption. Whatever is truly your existence cannot possibly be something objective, that is, removed from you, not even so much as the amount of a thought, which is subtly objective in contrast to those thought-forms that one takes to be physical, or grossly objective.

What is truly your existence can never be other than existence. So, look for that in you, that which is alone you, which is both unborn and imperishable. It cannot be the body. It cannot be the mind. Inquire to know yourself, not to create a new self, for that is not possible. It is not to transform your existence into something other than what it is, for that is not possible. Only know yourself. Realize your Self.

The Maharshi stated that we may speak of "Self-Realization," but how is one to realize, or make more real, that which is already real? By inquiry into yourself, abandon the imagined limitations. You do not make Reality more real, but Reality comprehends itself in Self-Knowledge. Do not regard whatever is objective, whatever is transient, whatever is perceptible, and whatever is conceivable as your Self. Whatever has a name or a form cannot possibly be you.

Search for your actual Existence. The Existence, itself, is Brahman with which one becomes One. That is the God that one worships and to which he devotes himself. That, in itself, is the Self to be known and the Self that is the knower, there being no duality.

If you proceed along these lines, you will find that your nature is indivisible, so that you cannot be separated from your own bliss. You cannot be separate from your own peace. You can never be other than what you actually are. The nature of such abidance is Knowledge. Such Knowledge is without end.

(Silence)

There is no separate individual, or ego entity. Abandoning this false assumption, know yourself as you are. If you think that you do not quite realize this, inquire into the "I" that does not quite realize it. If you are waiting for spiritual experience to dawn, find out who it is that waits, for Existence does not wait for an opportune moment. If you are waiting for teaching to happen, Existence, itself, is the essence of the teaching. It does not happen; it is. Profound spiritual experience does not happen; it is. You, yourself, are the nature of the Realization. For Nondual Truth, it is necessary that the Realization be of the identical nature as that which is realized. That, the Self, is not an event in time. Likewise is the Realization. It is absurd to say that you have it, and it is absurd to say that you do not have it.

Q.: I see now how ridiculous it is to try to hold to things other than the Truth.

N.: Spiritual practice consists in the elimination of mere imagination. If imagination continues, samsara and maya continue. The practice simply eliminates the imagination, since you cannot be other than what you are. Determine what you are, which is nonobjective, by the elimination of what you are not. What remains knows itself.

Q.: In my practice, there are times when the veil of illusion is not present. At other times, the misidentifications return. I can see that they are the mind's construct. The mind wants to know and will make up what it does not know.

N.: It will make up any amount of ignorance in the name of knowledge.

Q.: Yes.

N.: What is the mind that has this tendency? Remove the objectifying tendency from the mind, which is only an unreal function, and see what the mind is in itself. See its substance or nature. Without that tendency, what is left of it?

Q.: There is nothing that I can find. Not even one to find it.

N.: It is in the abandonment of those kinds of assumptions that the purpose of practice is fulfilled. As long as ignorance seems to return, see that of which the ignorance consists. It is misidentification. Inquire to discern if such is what you are. Can this be "I"? When the potential for ignorance is impossible, there is no longer an alternative state. If you know that there is really no one there, but someone seems to start the show going, inquire into him again and again. The more you look at him, the less you will see. You exist, but there is less of him.

Another Q.: When, in meditation, I drift, it is my mind drifting to something to which I attribute reality. My mind drifts to something at work. My mind returns to it to fix a problem at work, which is a contract that was wrongly negotiated in my absence.

N.: Within the mind's space, there are endless things of which to think. The entire universe exists within the mind's space. In what space does the mind exist?

Q.: It must be much larger than the mind.

N.: When the mind drifts, do you drift? From where would you start, and where could you go?

Q.: I must put together the pieces in order to have a place from which to start in that daydream.

N.: What is it that starts?

Q.: I start with myself as a body in the world.

N.: With this misidentification, mixing up the real and the unreal, there is the mind, its drifting, and that to which it drifts. All of that is contained within a single notion, "I." All the while, that which is vast and space-like remains unmoving. Where are you?

Q.: How can I be in those thoughts, because those thoughts change? Yet I don't ever feel that I am jumping from that thought of myself to another thought.

N.: You do not jump from thought to thought. You do not change from thought to thought, regardless if this is a single thought, a pattern of thought, or thought of an entire world.

You remain as you are, vast and space-like, within which the mind space appears. That which is vast and space-like is of the nature of Being-Consciousness. Since it always is as it is, the very nature of Existence, how does the mind space come to be at all?

Q.: (remains quiet)

N.: Once we look for explanations of illusion, there are as many as can be imagined. The explanations of illusion are as endless as the illusion itself. Is there illusion? Or are these explanations of how water came to be in the mirage? Is this the detailed biography of a man who was never born?

Q.: The meditation is coming back to what is real and there all the time. It cuts out this person.

N.: What person? Are you a person?

Q.: That is the question. (remains quiet for awhile) I don't know. This cuts out everything, including personhood.

N.: Are we cutting out anything? If existing, it is always existing. If it does not exist, it never exists. Apply this knowledge to your own nature. (Silence)

Q.: There is no other side, nothing I need to go against.

N.: That is right. There are not two shores or sides. There are not two of you.

Q.: Once I project duality, it is hard to get out of it.

N.: Once duality is imagined, there are all sorts of explanations of why it is there and all kinds of mental acrobatics to try to unify the supposed two sides. The two sides are yourself and the Self, or "I" and "this." If, though, the "this" does not exist, is there anything to unify? If the "I" has not been born, is there anything to put together and has anything become separate?

Q.: This is very different from the way I was meditating. I reflect upon this, having talked with you about this. Every time, when I think I am something else, I reflect upon this, it makes a difference.

N.: Meditation is yourself with yourself by the power of your own self. Meditation, if it truly be nondual and of the nature of the path of Self-Knowledge, is nonobjective in character. It is not thinking of something. It is certainly not just emptying the mind of thought, for that would be a temporary mental state. It is not feeling anything. It has to do with your very Being, which is, simultaneously, Consciousness. It is not something to be postponed. As you do not wait for your Existence to begin, as you do not postpone the very fact of your Consciousness, and likewise is it of Bliss, so the same is true with meditation, spiritual experience, and Self-Realization.

Another Q.: When the eye is on the goal of complete happiness as being the natural state and true nature, it seems that all the paper tigers that my mind would construct as obstacles and confusions are pushed away much more effectively than trying to create paper scissors to cut up the paper tiger. If I keep my eye on the goal, and not only that happiness is at hand but it is my true nature, that focus seems to be a generalized solution to what would otherwise be innumerable, detailed obstacles. Is this useful?

N.: It is all right. Is happiness useful?

Q.: No, not useful, but the purpose. It is not the purpose, it is the Reality.

N.: It is the Reality, and it manifests in life as the purpose. The happiness is the desired in everything that you desire, experience, and in every effort that you apply. The happiness is nonobjective and identical with your Being. Your constant search for happiness is really an intuitive search for your own Self.

Q.: In meditation, this seems to be an obstacle remover. I am not trying to create antidotes to the obstacles on the same level as that on which they occur.

N.: Most obstacles are easily removed by having your mind rest on the substrate that is the foundation upon which the obstacles are standing. The Maharshi points out that if we have a doubt and answer it, another doubt will arise, and then another, and one could go on answering doubts endlessly. It is similar with your obstacles. He says, though, that if you doubt the doubter, inquiring into the doubter, all the doubts are tackled at once.

If we know that happiness is within, and within must be the Self, so many obstacles to our happiness are removed, for how is something to intervene between you and your own Self? The obstacles are effectively removed by a perspective that is deeper than the one from which the illusion of obstacles arises.

Q.: So, the inquiry becomes the knocking on the most direct doorway. That is the only door on the way.

N.: So, you shall knock, and it will be opened unto you, because you are the One who opens it. (laughter) You are knocking, and you are already on the inside. Please come in. (laughter)

Another Q.: How is one to find God?

N.: The first step in finding God is to know oneself. In the Maharshi's *Upadesa Saram* and *Saddarsanam*, emphasis is placed on that the seeing of the Self, or Atmadarsanam, is the seeing of God. He says that seeing God without seeing the Self is just a mental image.

Of course, it is far better to see God than to see anything else, but if we want to see God as God is, we must see our Self. Otherwise, in a somewhat mirror-like fashion, we hold up our so-called self and see a reflection of what we, ourselves, hold up. If you want to see what a mirror is by itself, you must not get your head in the way to see it. It is analogous to the point that the ego must go. What we think ourselves to be must go. Something remains. That which remains is actually God. Before such inquiry is commenced, what one supposes oneself to be is an individual with a body and such. Then, God seems removed from us, because of thinking of oneself as a body. When we eliminate the "I am the body" idea, God's all-pervading nature becomes apparent to us. Yet, we may still think of our Self as an individual soul, or jiva. That is a combination of God and some ideas about the Self. The jiva, or soul, has some form, perhaps a mental one, such as mental attributes, hopes and fears, and likes and dislikes. If we continue to inquire and eliminate as not "I" those various attributes, we then find, in place of a soul, the Existence without boundary, the very same as God.

We want to make the soul One with God. The soul disappears. Soul is the conception of God plus some limitation. The limitations being cast off, God remains. Then, God sees God by the vision of God, which is the Self seeing the Self. Nothing remains of himself, says the Maharshi, but God. So, God sees God. God's Knowledge of God is true Knowledge, perfect Knowledge. Then, as God is never unhappy, so you are never unhappy. As God never loses peace, you never lose peace.

(Then followed a recitation in Sanskrit and English of verses from the *Tejobindu Upanishad.*)

(Silence)

Om Shanti Shanti Shanti Om

Being

Satsang, February 13, 2005

(Silence)

Om Om Om

(Silence)

N.: Nondual Being, the real Self, alone is. Being undifferentiated, it does not arise from anything else; nor does anything else arise from it. It is unborn and, for it, there is no creation, no second, at any time.

It is realized by Self-Knowledge. Yet, as the Maharshi reveals in his spiritual instruction, there is no second, no other self, to realize it.

In the inquiry, "Who am I?", to know yourself as you are, the inquirer is the focus, and the inquirer is the answer to the question. There can be no other answer.

In the attempt to meditate upon the Truth of your Being, the meditator is the focus. What is the nature of the meditator? What is the nature of the inquirer?

Self-Knowledge is nondual. Sri Bhagavan teaches that there are not two selves that one self could realize another self, for your Existence is always singular. So, what is meant by "I"?

To realize the Self, you cannot imagine a standpoint apart from it as your identity. If you do so, such imagination is termed, "an ego." From the ego arise all kinds of illusions and their consequent bondage and suffering. Liberation, which is the natural state, is the egoless state. It is freedom from such imagination. What is free from the ego is also free from the adjuncts of the ego, such as definitions in terms of the mind, the body, or the world. Inquire within yourself, "Who am I?"

The Self is of the nature of Being-Consciousness-Bliss, Saccidananda. There is no second existence, or being, to know it. There is no second consciousness to know it.

Between the Self and yourself, there is no chasm, no gap. If you imagine that there is such duality, inquire into what you regard as yourself. The Self is alright by itself. Inquire into the nature of yourself. If you do so, the false sense of individuality, and all of the adjuncts of the ego-idea, will be destroyed. They will vanish because they are not true. What remains is that which exists all along. Because it exists always, Self-Realization, though the only direct experience, is not an event in time. What comes goes. What is gained is lost. That which is realized in Self-Knowledge, and that which you seek to know through inquiry, neither comes nor goes. It has neither creation nor destruction. It is not gained, and it is not lost.

The Maharshi reveals the Truth of Being, the Truth of the Self, which is the very substance of Self-Realization, by Silence. As he explained, Silence is that in which no "I" arises. Where there is no "I," there is not anything else. Just Being is. It knows itself. Sankara said that Brahman alone can know Brahman. The Self, which is real Being, alone knows real Being. There is no second. Where there is no second, there is no suffering, no fear, and no death, but just the self-evident Reality.

To comprehend within yourself what has just been indicated, inquire, "Who am I?"

Q.: I noticed the effects on my body during some recent illness that was a form of pneumonia. I focused very much on the body and the impossibility of it being myself. It is objective to me, and I know that I am not it, though I was not convinced of this at the time. I could not breathe in or out and was stuck. The only thing that relieved this was to say, "Jaya Bhagavan." That produced a release from the inability to breathe. The chemical changes seemed real to me. Meditation on what my identity is showed me that all these things that were objective to me could not be myself. How am I to release all the things that I think about myself, including not being able to breathe? In order to release this impasse that relates to breath or prana, the only thing that

I can think of is "Jaya Bhagavan." Once I think of that, there is no more scope for the ego and all else that I think of as being true or not true. I am a fish in water complaining about being thirsty. So, Jaya Bhagavan.

N.: In the course of your description, you have answered your own question.

Q.: Not to my own satisfaction.

N.: Be sure that your identity is free of the body, inclusive of your breath, and everything of which you think. The very fact that you have a great variety of thoughts, some of which are contradictory, yet your Existence remains unchanged and uninterrupted, should be more than ample proof for you that your Existence is not thought. Remain free from thought.

The very fact that you observe the prana, the animating life energy, which seems to be connected with breath, means that it is objective to you. You see its changes. What changeless one sees all those changes?

You are not at any kind of impasse. Who are you? You are not bound. Who are you?

Q.: "Remain free of thought." Being free from thought means having thoughts but not being identified with them. How is that I become identified with these thoughts?

N.: Are you thought? Are you what you think?

Q.: Obviously not, but I hold them. This experience focused my attention more on identification with the body and all these misidentifications.

N.: What do you mean by saying that it focused your attention more?

Q.: More thinking about the body, worrying about the body.

N.: Are you the body?

Q.: I cannot possibly be the body. I don't know why I don't accept that.

N.: Is the one who says that he does not accept it a body?

Q.: (laughing) No bodies around here! (laughter)

N.: Thinking about the body does not make your Existence equivalent to a body. Wisdom has everything to do with the Knowledge of your identity, with who you are in your real Being. There is no similarity between your Being and the body. Your are not bound by a body. The same is true with thought.

Certainly, you have become more keenly aware of how experiential the Knowledge must be. What you think about will not save you when your breath is gone. What you know as your identity, fused with your Existence, remains. There is where you find peace, and there is where you find freedom. That does not depend on thought, breath, bodily action, or any state of the body or mind. With all the questions that you have ever asked about spiritual practice and Self-Realization, I have never placed any emphasis on the activities of your body, the activities of speech, or the activities of the mind. Self-Knowledge alone is Liberation. Action does not lead to Liberation, be the action subtle or gross.

Certainly, you can see how tentative and flimsy the bodily condition is. It is not something upon which to depend. Likewise is it with the breath or prana, the animating energy. Certainly, a train of thought in one direction or another is not steady. All the while, your Existence is steady. You never cease to exist, and you never cease to know that you exist. Abide in this Knowledge, free of misidentification. Do not give rise to the confusion that you are something else. If you have given rise, inquire, and the truth about your nature will become self-evident. Then, you see life and death with an equal eye.

Another Q.: I worry so much. I still become lost in thoughts. I know what I am not, yet I still can not get who I am.

N.: Who you are is nonobjective, so how do you suppose that you are going to obtain it? If you really know that you are not your thoughts, you will not be lost in them. If one really knows that the mind is nonexistent, there is nothing in which to be lost.

Q.: So, the knowing has to go much deeper for me?

N.: Self-Knowledge must penetrate to the core. There is not much sense in saying that you know that you are not your thoughts, when still they bother you.

If we really know that what we think we are not, we are neither bound by those thoughts nor will we continue to conjure delusive thoughts. You have seen, though, that outer conditions do not create the mind's suffering. The mind suffers due to its own productions. This point distinguishes a person who moves in a spiritual direction, in contrast to being worldly-minded. With worldly-mindedness, or extroversion of mind, one assumes that the external things are real, that they determine her, and they determine her happiness and, consequently, her sorrow. A spiritually-minded person knows that happiness is within, in which case there is no longer any superimposition of the outer environment upon one's own experience. The world neither gives you happiness nor gives you suffering. In truth, the world is not even real. Happiness, reality, and your sense of identity have their origin in you. If you overlook your true nature and suppose yourself to be something else, you confound the Real and the unreal, imagine happiness to be elsewhere, and consequently suffer.

Turn your mind inward. Know the place of happiness. That place is within. Within is the Self. So, one-pointedly seek the Knowledge of yourself. If you know yourself, you know Reality, and you no longer dwell, suffering, in an unreal dream.

Another Q.: Can you help me with "one-pointedly seeking it"?

N.: When you desire something intensely, you are one-pointed about it, aren't you?

Q.: Oh, yes!

N.: You are very familiar with this. (laughter) If you are out of breath, you become one-pointed. The Maharshi gives the example of a drowning man attempting to get to the surface. For some reason, he is not distracted on the way up. (laughter) He does not delay, thinking that he will get to the surface later. He does not think that he has all these other desires to be fulfilled. He does not think that he is at an impasse, wondering if he should or should not get some breath and save his life. Nobody has such ideas.

When we see the importance of Self-Realization, we become one-pointed. When we see the fleeting nature of life and the fact of death, we become one-pointed. When we see where happiness is, we become one-pointed. When we see the present opportunity to realize Truth for all eternity, we become one-pointed.

Try any or all of this. If you still have a problem with one-pointedness, you may ask again.

Another Q.: Since returning from Tiruvannamalai and Arunachala, I find a very deep desire to intensify my practice. I meditate more frequently, and, prior to meditation, I reflect on the desire for Liberation. Are there other things in practice that are worth doing to let this increase in focus bloom?

N.: You have stated the most important. Adi Sankaracharya has stated that of the fourfold practice for Self-Realization, the last, the desire for Liberation is the most important. Even though discrimination, detachment, and such are so intrinsic to practice, he says that the desire for Liberation is the most important. It is so because, if you have the desire for Liberation, even if you are lacking in discrimination, detachment, tranquility, renunciation, and the others, all those will come to you in due course, because of the intensity of the desire for Liberation. If that is lacking, even if you have a very sharp mind for discrimination and are renounced and such, not much progress will be made, for there is no motivation. Desire for Liberation is important.

You need to know why you meditate. The knowledge of why you meditate, the manner of approach, is as important as the content of the meditation. If just this much is kept in mind, the focus is there, and the practice blooms. The practice is of inquiry. If you desire Liberation, you destroy vasanas, tendencies, which manifest as misidentifications, attachments, and such. If the desire is present, you have the motivation to examine your mind and unravel it until there is nothing left to it.

If you have the desire for Liberation, naturally the spiritual practice arises, inclusive of its manifest activities that are suitable for you. You have the key. Keep applying it.

Another Q.: I have heard that this desire should not be the hankering for enjoyment by an individual. At the same time, any postponement of grasping the truth of Realization is not to be worried about as if it were the suffering of the individual. It is a matter of trust in what the Guru has pointed out and systematically disposing of the illusion. It is contradictory to be hankering for the enjoyment.

N.: Yes and no. The Maharshi is the Guru, and he states that you must be ardent for Liberation. He also says, "Who is to realize what?" He also says that there are none bound, none liberated, no bondage, and no liberation. How can you put together what, on the surface, seem to be disparate statements? In truth, there is no contradiction among them at all.

Let us say that you know of Liberation and hanker after it as an individual. There is no harm in that. In order to fulfill that desire, you need to dissolve the individuality. The individuality being dissolved, the desire is fulfilled. There is no casting off of the desire for Liberation. If you would do so, you would just desire something else, because it is in your very nature to be happy. As long as there is even a drop of suffering, you desire this happiness. Liberation means freedom from the imagined bondage, which reveals Bliss that is innate and perfectly full.

Q.: What you describe is the perspective from the depths. I see in my nature something more perverse. I think that maybe I won't get there or that I won't get there during this lifetime.

N.: Get where?

Q.: To freedom.

N.: Where is the freedom? What is the distance that you are to traverse?

Q.: That clarity is not there when the first thoughts are being entertained.

N.: Why not proceed by your better knowledge?

Q.: When it is seen to be something that can be won or lost, that is the occasion that I put on the shabby clothes of the individual again and lose focus.

N.: If you think that it can be won or lost, you had better win it.

Q.: (Laughing)

N.: If Realization is a matter of winning or losing a race against time, as it were, you had better win. Do everything in your power to win it, but, in doing so, you come to the point at which you see that it is imperative to dissolve the ego, or the false sense of individuality, with all his concomitant ignorance. How else can it be dissolved, or destroyed, except by a thorough, constant inquiry that reveals its nonexistent nature. That being destroyed, you see that what you desired to attain is not a new attainment but existent all the time.

There is no danger in your desire for Liberation, in whatever form it may appear. I have seen people wander much due to lack of that desire, for the same desire is dispersed among various worldly means and not focused on Self-Realization. I have never met anyone with too much of this desire for Liberation. Even if it is misapplied along a line of sadhana that is not as fruitful, though there is still the element of knowledge that yields some fruit, one refines that practice until it is one of pure Self-Knowledge, in which case, such a one realizes completely. I have never seen anyone hurt by this, though I have seen people wander about in mazes of their own creation in their minds due to lack of this desire for Liberation.

Q.: From fear of not succeeding, some one will commence to wander in despair, thinking, "I cannot grasp this, and I will not make it." Can even that be used positively?

N.: Surely, because you still want to attain it. You need to investigate the "I" that thinks that it is going to fail.

Even the least attempt does not go in vain. Krishna states in the *Bhagavad Gita* that not a drop of this Dharma is ever in vain.

Q.: So, one need not worry about seemingly futile attempts, because there are no futile attempts, if they are true, honest attempts.

N.: If there is sincerity, there is, in some way or another, at the core, an element of Knowledge and the fruit thereof. Whatever you do spiritually never comes to a loss. It is never in vain.

Q.: Thank you for this clarification.

N.: The Maharshi is not critical of the great variety of spiritual methods, but simply points out the quintessence of pure Knowledge and how that can be practiced directly. We, ourselves, are the Self we are trying to realize, for duality is not true at any time, as in the story of the ten men.

Q. It is good to be busy with the task of Self-liberation.

N.: Do you have anything more worthwhile to do? (laughter) It serves little purpose to anxiously think about whether or not you are going to attain it. You can use that valuable time that would otherwise slip by and which you would not recover unless you transcended time entirely. Why waste it? Spend the time in fruitful inquiry to know yourself.

For Self-Realization, there are no other factors in play except you. The apparent obstacles are of your own creation. Ignorance and adherence to the ignorance, which form delusion, are of your own doing. There is nothing that anyone or any God has set up as an obstacle for you.

Q.: So, I need not wait for anything else that has been imposed upon me to settle down.

N.: Nothing has been imposed on you. You may have superimposed various ideas and forms upon yourself, but nothing else has done that. The bondage is entirely of one's own making, and the Liberation is all of one's own knowing.

Q.: At times, I feel that I am not practicing as intensely as I could.

N.: If you have that observation, what should you do? Shouldn't you practice more intensely? There is nothing wrong with the observation about your intensity in practice. You may make that observation each day. Each day, you practice as fully as possible and then practice more intensely the next, because you realize that you can practice still more intensely.

Since practice is a sweet joy exceeded only by the Bliss of Realization, there is plenty of motivation. Do not waste your time bemoaning yourself. Nothing is in your way.

Another Q.: Upon my return to work, I found several people with hot tempers.

N.: Are the hot tempers helping things?

Q.: No, they are not! There is a belief in the company that such helps. I said that we could just solve the problem, and that quieted them down a bit. Yet, it weighs on my mind, as some of it was directed at me because I wasn't there.

N.: (laughing) Because you weren't there, they are directing the anger at you?

Q.: I become identified with the body. I am looking for another job.

N.: Are you inwardly indifferent to the opinions they may form of you even in your absence? There is a certain irony to their blaming you when you are not even there. It shows how much the problem is in the mind.

Q.: They were in a screaming match about the faults of someone else. It was not I, but I tried to find solutions to the situation.

N.: They were too busy enjoying their anger?

Q.: (laughing) Yes. That does not seem worthwhile. The problem is due to miscommunications between a woman and the others there. Why they become angry at me I have no clue.

N.: Does it affect you?

Q.: Yes, definitely, though not in a deeper sense. It affects my mind. I need to fix the situation, for it is my job to do so. When anger is expressed in my direction, the mind does not like that. I am worried about fixing this issue.

N.: So, you need to place your mental attention on fixing the issue. What has that to do with you?

Q.: I become overly concerned. I sit in meditation and think about it. It means that I am misidentified. I should be able to drop it.

N.: It could be. Just thinking about it does not prove that you are misidentified. You have something better to do in meditation, though.

Q.: Yes, for sure! I am not always thinking about it.

N.: When you are thinking about it, is that which is keenly aware of the thoughts bound? Are you a character in a dream that needs to work this out? Or is your nature the infinite Consciousness, which is entirely formless and never does anything, in which all this appears, in which all this disappears, for which this appears, by which this appears, and which, in truth, is the only Reality?

(Silence)

Q.: That helps. Whatever the mentality is there, it is not possible to appease such convoluted thinking.

N.: They probably need a little more spiritual practice. (laughter)

Q.: What about my being in that situation?

N.: Are you in that situation?

Q.: That is a good point. So, I am not in that situation.

N.: Stay with the facts, the Truth. It is far better to stay in the Truth, abiding in Self-Knowledge, which is natural and, indeed, the only thing that is real, than it is to imagine a situation, which is only within you, as is all this universe, and then imagine yourself as a character in that situation, and look for a temporary remedy at the level of the mind for the interaction between the character, who is in the mind, and the situation, which is also in the mind. Do you follow?

Q.: Yes. Yes. This is the key. I am seeing the distinctions between these imaginings and myself. The mind conjures this up, which is definitely objective, but somehow I think that that is I.

N.: If you think that you are this, inquire as to who you are. If you say that all this imagination has its source in the mind, discern the nature of the mind.

Q.: A "second" is thinking that the source of the mind is an individual?

N.: A "second" is the false assumption of the individual "I" and anything that follows thereafter. With the individual, God is viewed objectively and so is the world; thus jagat-jiva-para, the world-the individual-the supreme. The truth is that there is no second "I."

For all experience, there is an "I." If you inquire for whom is this, your way of looking becomes nonobjective. If you make your vision nonobjective, you see what the Self really is. It is indivisible, of a changeless, formless nature. It does not give birth to a second "I." When the Upanishads say, "One without a second," such means Brahman alone is. The Self alone is. There is nothing else. Nothing else has ever come to be. Neither you nor the world, neither a character nor a work situation—nor any other experience—has ever come to be.

Q.: Pain comes with the identification with the individual, the mind, the body, etc.

N.: The individual "I" is the source of all other delusion and, therefore, all kinds of suffering and bondage. With "I," comes "my," such as "my experience, my thought, my mind," etc. Bondage is said to be characterized by "I" and "mine." Liberation, or Reality, is characterized by the absence of "I" and "mine."

Q.: I wish I could say that I have the discrimination to always go to the inquiry.

N.: Who would be otherwise? You say that you wish you had the discrimination to always go to the "I." Who would do otherwise?

Q.: I would. The individual.

N.: By inquiry, swallow the whole of illusion. There are no excuses for bondage, for bondage does not exist.

Q.: This is just what you said to another questioner.

N.: I tell the same thing to everybody. (laughter) I have never thought of anything new. (laughter)

(Then followed a recitation in Sanskrit and English from the *Chandogya Upanishad.*)

(Silence)

Om Shanti Shanti Shanti Om

Eloquent Silence

Satsang, April 10, 2005

(Silence)

Om Om Om

(Silence)

N.: Absolute Truth is the continuous silent teaching of the Maharshi. Truth refers to Reality as it is, while "absolute" is indicative of it being invariable and of it not being in relation to anything else, which is its utter nonduality.

That which truly exists alone exists. It is of the nature of Being-Consciousness-Bliss. This is your Self, the only self that there is. This is what exists, apart from which nothing else exists.

According to what it is with which you identify is established your relation to the Absolute and all else. If you misidentify yourself with the form of a body, you are in relation to a supposed external world and God is distinct therefrom. If you know the truth that you are not the body and the body is not a definition for yourself, that you are neither a body nor embodied, can there be a relation to a universe? Can there be a relation to a God apart from yourself?

The Truth expounded everywhere in Advaita Vedanta is Tat tvam asi, That you are. How are you going to realize That? That is something that cannot be grasped and cannot be lost. It is ever existent. According to how you regard your identity, you conceive of your relation to That. So, if you misidentify with the mind, thought, you conceive of yourself as one thing and That as another, though the instruction, both in aphorism and in silence, is "That you are," and not "That you are not."

If you imagine yourself to be an individual, you are then, in some manner or another, in relation to the Truth, but the Truth is absolute and is not in relation to anything. How can the Real be in a relation with that which is unreal? Or the Self with what is not the Self? Where is the connection?

If you regard yourself as a thing, there is this distinction or difference. Non-differentiation, nonduality, is Truth. Truth is supremely blissful. To realize the Truth, you must set yourself free of all the imagined differentiation, the imagined duality. To do so is a matter of ascertaining your identity.

If you are distinct, even in the least, from the Self, from Brahman, and that is true even for a moment, it is true for all eternity, and there is no liberation, which is absurd. For everyone who feels bound seeks liberation as an intuition of the natural state, just as everyone who feels suffering seeks happiness as an intuition of the natural state. The seeking for happiness cannot be stopped, though it can be fulfilled.

Inquire, "Who am I?" If you thus determine, in Self-Knowledge, what your identity actually is, you yourself are the Liberation. You are the Bliss sought. You are the very Being, or Consciousness, of That. In order to find the Truth, realized experientially as That you are, Tat tvam asi, inquire as to who you are. See for yourself that you are not in relation to a body, to thought or a mind, and that you are not an assumed individual.

Though the Maharshi's answers to questions posed to him were always extremely relevant to the questioner, the glorious beauty of his answers is that they always uproot the imagined identity, thereby revealing absolute Truth in which he gives instruction silently all the time. That Silence still is. Absolute Truth is eternal. Realize the Absolute Truth as your very Being. It is Self-Knowledge.

If you misidentify as an "I," as a mind, as a body, and so forth and so on, you assume that you are, in some way or another, in some kind of relation to the Absolute. If you cease to misidentify with the body, the mind, or the ego, there is no relation. There cannot be a relation where there are not two.

(Silence)

Attempting to inquire to know the Self, do not regard yourself as one thing and the Self as another. If you do have that idea, "I am a self attempting to realize the Self," leave the Self alone, for it is fine, and inquire as to who you are. If you inquire, that which is unreal is revealed as such. What is known as unreal cannot bind and does not remain. Then, Reality knows itself, as the Reality, Brahman, the real Self, alone can know itself. Only the Nondual Truth can realize the Nondual Truth. Do you understand? There is nothing objective in this Knowledge. There is nothing objective, except that which is negated, in this inquiry. All is resolved in indivisible, nondual, absolute Reality.

(Silence)

Q.: From the teaching today I understand that there cannot be any relation of the Real with the unreal except in imagination, and the imagination is just not necessary.

N.: If imagination is not necessary, no kind of ignorance is called for, no kind of suffering is necessary, and no kind of bondage is needful.

(Silence)

Q.: No separation is there?

N.: Separation is only according to the one who perceives it.

(Silence)

Another Q.: I keep forgetting this aspect. I do not know why I forget. It seems clear at times. It is so important to investigate the assumption upon which everything is based.

N.: Do you ever forget yourself?

Q.: I can think that I am something else.

N.: But do you forget yourself? Do you forget your existence?

Q.: Probably not at that level.

N.: The Existence is the substrate upon which the thinking can even appear. It is by the Light of Existence, or Consciousness, that you can even be aware of the thinking. Can you remember yourself?

Q.: I have tried.

N.: Has your Self ever been an object of memory?

Q.: That is the confusing part. There is an experience of it. It is not a memory. It is the actual experience.

N.: Is the actual experience a thought or not a thought?

Q.: Not a thought.

N.: Memory is a kind of thought.

Q.: Yes. There is no question of that. I mix those up, though.

N.: In truth, you cannot remember the Self, but you cannot forget it, either.

Do you ever cease to exist or ever forget your own existence? That which is within thought can be subject to remembrance, forgetfulness, and other such mental conditions and modes. Are you a thought? Is it possible to really think of your Being? Even if you think "my Being," that is not the same thing, is it?

Q.: No, it is very bland and unexciting.

N.: It is not the actual experience.

Q.: No.

N.: Not the actual Existence. Your Existence is neither subject to being remembered nor subject to being forgotten. In addition, how would it be possible to have a memory that is steady and would survive not only the waking and dreaming states, but also the deep, dreamless sleep in which there is no thought activity? Self-Knowledge, though, transcends all three states.

Q.: If I would examine my meditation to see if it would survive the transitions involved in those states, so that the meditation is existing and continuous throughout those three states, it is valid.

N.: Are you existing throughout all those three states? If you are, what is the nature of this you? Who are you who transcend all three states? Whatever is limited to the scope of a state is merely a product of that state. All the dream perceptions and conceptions are just a product of a dreaming state of mind. The waking state world, perceptions, and conceptions are just a product of the waking state of mind and are equally imaginary. The apparent not-knowing or forgetfulness in deep dreamless sleep is just a product of that state. You exist, though, throughout all. So, your nature cannot be anything of those states. Self-Knowledge, Self-Realization, to be eternal and nondual, must be of the very nature of the Self that is realized. Otherwise, it would be dualistic and transient, and what is transient is not worth seeking, the Maharshi teaches. Only what is eternal is worth realizing.

You exist in all three states. The three states pass by and you still exist. That existence is invariable. Real Knowledge, the essence of deep meditation, is the very same thing. Examine your experience and discern.

Q.: I know that whatever is on a mental level definitely is not it. I become fooled by that mental level quite often.

N.: Does the real Self become fooled, or is there another one?

Q.: The other one.

N.: What is the nature of the other one?

Q.: I don't know the nature of it.

N.: Who is the one who does not know?

Q.: It seems that that one knows more specific things and is closer to myself. When I try to investigate it, that is more expansive.

N.: How expansive?

Q.: (quiet for awhile) I don't know.

N.: Find out. You will find that it is expansive beyond all ideas of expansiveness, and it is that which is formless. Whenever you actually inquire into the ego or individuality, no ego or individual is found, but just the expansiveness, Brahman, the real Self. If conceived otherwise, how many are there of you?

Q.: This is important. I never really feel that there are multiple selves. However, there is a confusion that there are multiple selves.

N.: Where does the confusion dwell?

Q.: Definitely on the superficial.

N.: Where is the superficial contained?

Q.: It must be contained in the notion of "I" existing as something.

N.: Alright. Within the notion of "I am existing as something" is all that is superficial, all that is just the thin veneer of illusion. It is all that does not actually exist. It is the stuff of imagination. One notion of "I" contains all the illusion and is the source of all the delusion. It, itself, constitutes the entire illusion. All of maya is just "I."

Q.: It is so important to know that which is aware and always before the existence as an individual.

N.: Is there a "before" and an "after"? Was the "I" born? There is the unborn, real Self, which is also imperishable. Was another one born? If you assume so, there will be a "before" and an "after," the "original Self" and the "break-off self." Then, you will attempt to determine the relation of this "break-off self" to the real Self, whether it is entirely divided, partially divided with some similarities, or of much similarity but partially divided.

Q.: It will all change.

N.: Yes, it will change.

Q.: Just like the weather or the ideas.

N.: The ideas usually change more quickly. (laughter) But, were you born?

Q.: The being born could be anything. It is just going from one state to another.

N.: There must be someone who traverses from one state to another. One "I" makes up all the illusion. It, itself, appears as subject and object. So, examine the "I." See what is there.

Q.: When you say, "examine," what do you mean?

N.: Inquire. Try to see the "I" as it is.

Q.: When you ask me that, my experience becomes much deeper.

N.: Whether described as deeper or more expansive, it is the same thing. The ego, which was never born, is said to cease to exist. Its cessation is really the realization of its utter unreality. The one Self that has been there alone all of the time knows itself.

Another Q.: I was reflecting on this sense of body-misidentification and the waking-state-misidentification as being the same. Certainly, they are known. This knowledge that knows the states is mostly the identity and seems to have no boundaries, edges, starts, or finishes.

N.: That which knows the body is utterly bodiless. That which knows the states is stateless. That which sees all the characteristics is nirguna, no characteristics or qualityless.

Transcendence of the body is not being in the body and going out of the body. There is nothing bodily about it. Transcendence is pure Self-Knowledge. Since the Self never had any relation to a body, it is naturally immortal. The Knowledge and the Bliss of one who knows his own bodiless nature is, similarly, of the same immortality.

Q.: Immortality implies some kind of duality that isn't present.

N.: In what way?

Q.: Immortality implies mortality, and that is dual as an idea, which the experience is not.

N.: Such is determined by how we understand. Immortality is just immortal. It implies a duality only for those who conceive of such. Likewise is it with body and bodiless, realized and unrealized, and all of the other terms that are expediently used to point out something that can be only silently expressed.

Another Q.: I spent most of yesterday working in the garden. I wanted it to be a day of meditation. I started from, "I know that I exist." It was not very long, though, until I was into the gardening, in a body, and, then, I had hands. I went from the formless to battling with the weeds. (laughter)

N.: How did that happen? Is it just intrinsic to gardening? In that case, all should renounce gardening. (laughter) I do not think that the Vedas say anywhere that one must renounce gardening. What happened? How did you go from being formless to having hands?

Q.: It seems that I made the mistake when I supposedly woke up. There was the thought that I am going to garden today. Then, I thought that I would try to meditate.

N.: Why would the earnest desire expressed in the idea, "I want to meditate, or am going to meditate," endow you with form and hands? You could eliminate the "I am going to meditate" attitude and see if it does you any good. Most likely, you would just be stuck with a pair of hands, and that would not be very impressive. (laughter)

What happened? Do you have hands now? Are you the body?

Q.: I am trying to answer the question from an identity that is in a body.

N.: Where in the body are you? Are you in a particular place or all over it?

Q.: All over it, but more focused right about here.

N.: So, there is more of you there and less of you elsewhere?

Q.: It's silly.

N.: You shaved this morning. Did you lose part of your existence? If you are all over, such includes the hairs that...

Q.: Went down the sink. (laughter)

N.: You literally went down the drain? (laughter) Is that what happened, or is that absurd?

Q.: That is so absurd. I would have had to feel less after shaving.

N.: Right now, your body is endowed with hands. If your body did not have hands, would you have less existence?

Q.: No.

N.: So, how can you say that you are all over the body? The same thing would apply to a particular spot. If something would happen to that particular spot, would something happen to your Existence?

Q.: In deep dreamless sleep, the spot and everything are gone.

N.: Yes, and that is due just to a change in mind. The idea of being a body, or an entity in a body, is only an idea in your mind. It is just like in your dreams last night, in which you seemed to occupy a body, but the body, the occupation of the body or the inhabiting of the body, and the things beyond the skin of that body, inside and outside—all of that was just the dreaming mind. The dreaming mind, itself, appeared as all of that. Likewise are your present ideas of being someone in a body.

If, in deep dreamless sleep, you were not a body, how did you become a body yesterday? Now, you are not a body, again. Is your Existence changing its nature, or is something else happening?

Q.: Something else is happening.

N.: What is it?

Q.: As soon as I start to examine what it is, there is less of it.

N.: That is the nature of maya. It is seemingly beginningless, but when we find out its nature, it ceases to exist. The more we examine it, the less there is of it. It is like looking for darkness with a lamp in your hand.

Are you the body? Are you a pair of hands, right now?

Q.: No, not really.

N.: Then, could you have become a pair of hands yesterday?

Q.: The whole notion of yesterday seems a little far-fetched.

N.: It was also in the mind. Time, space, and everything are in the mind. Nothing external is the cause of your pseudo-bondage. Nothing causes ignorance. This is so for the example of gardening and holds true for any other activity or external situation. None of it causes your bondage.

Ignorance does not arise from circumstances, since circumstances are imagined based on ignorance.

Q.: They are an effect.

N.: The effect is not the cause of the cause, but the effect is the same nature as the cause.

Q.: The notion of forgetting is only so long as it is not examined.

N.: (Silence)

Another Q.: Sometimes, I am caught in a bad mood, in which I do not feel that I am happy. I don't like it, and I want to get out of it.

N.: The desire to get out of it is your first step out of it, for without the desire, no effort is made.

Q.: Yes.

N.: What makes up the bad mood?

Q.: When I plan on something, and it doesn't happen that way.

N.: Then, you become grumpy?

Q.: Yes.

N.: Do you know why you become grumpy? Becoming grumpy does not make the event happen the way you want it to do. It is not very effective.

Q.: Right.

N.: So, you do not become grumpy for practical reasons. (laughter)

Q.: It's not the goal of it.

N.: It is not practical or effective. So, why do you become grumpy?

Q.: I don't know.

N.: Examine it. If you can find out why you suffer in such circumstances, you can get to the very root of the suffering and pull the root out. Such is the "gardening advice."

Q.: I feel the bondage. I feel that I am trapped in all these senses.

N.: Trapped in the senses or trapped in your mind? Is the moodiness something that you see, hear, or touch, or is it in your mind?

Q.: In my mind.

N.: But you are moody about something that you sensorially perceive, that is, the circumstances.

Q.: Yes.

N.: Why do you want the event or circumstances to go a certain way?

Q.: I have an idea that it would probably make me happy.

N.: You want that event or situation to make you happy, and, when it does not go the way that you want it to go, you are unhappy or grumpy.

Q.: Yes.

N.: It is because you feel that your happiness or the potential to be happy has been stolen from you by circumstances going in a different direction. So, you have a very good reason to be grumpy, because your happiness has been stolen away. Now, the question is, who stole it?

Q.: (laughing)

N.: When you ask something else, be it an object, a situation, or another person, to give you what is innately yours, when you ask something to fill you up with happiness when you, yourself, are the source of happiness, you are going to wind up grumpy. If situations do not go your way, you are going to be grumpy, and, if they do go your way, it is just a matter of time until they eventually do not go your way, and you become grumpy again. Or, you become bored with the situation being the way you designed it, and then you are grumpy.

Q.: (laughing)

N.: It is not that grumpiness is the continuum, but as long as you think that happiness comes from something external, you are going to be unhappy. You look to a circumstance perceived through your senses to provide you with an experience that is non-sensory. Happiness is not something that you see, hear, feel, taste, or smell. Happiness is something more internal. It is not inside your body, but internal in the sense of who you are. Where your desire for happiness rises from is the same place as the source of happiness. It is the very same happiness. When you are happy, you are actually just experiencing yourself. Do you comprehend so far?

Q.: (nods in assent)

N.: You can know for certain that your unhappiness, or grumpiness, is due to some mistaken conception about yourself and about where happiness is. It is mistaking the Bliss of your own nature to be something else. It is mistaking yourself to be separate from the Bliss of your own nature. If a person knows where happiness is, what the source of happiness is, or what the nature of happiness is, she becomes serenely detached from everything else. Even if your senses and limbs are engaged, you are serenely detached. You do not look for something to give you your happiness, and nothing can rob you of it. You will not rob yourself. Then, if circumstances go as planned, you are happy, and if they do not go as planned, you are still happy. Is it clear for you?

Q.: Yes.

N.: Contemplate this deeply. Reflect on it and meditate, until you are absolutely certain of it. "Where is happiness?" is a very simple question. The Maharshi places this point concerning happiness as preliminary to the inquiry "Who am I?" in the book *Who am I?* He returns to a discussion about the nature of happiness later in the book. Like the question, "Who am I?", "Where is happiness?" is very simple, yet if we understand this one simple thing, it affects so much. A person who knows where happiness is is unaffected by circumstances, is detached from all of the world, her peace is steady, and she has a single-minded, one-pointed focus on knowing herself, because that is where the happiness is. She understands the motivation behind all other motives. She understands what impels the mind to motion. This is just by knowing where happiness is. One who knows where happiness is becomes utterly desireless, yet fulfills inwardly the essence of all those desires. Such is not the form of those desires, but the essence. Stay with this simple question until the answer saturates your experience.

Another Q.: What of a situation of extreme engagement of the senses in violence in a concentration camp? There may be torture, starvation, or extreme pain. Can one still connect with this Knowledge under such violent circumstances?

N.: The violence or injury is to the body only. The Knowledge is intrinsicly bodiless. The situation has no effect.

Q.: That is hard.

N.: Why do you say it is hard?

Q.: Even today, when I needed to put an extra cushion under me, it insistently needed to be addressed.

N.: Alright. So, there is constant discomfort, or constant pain, or unremitting acute pain.

Q.: Yes, and this is just mild.

N.: Yes, this is just mild, but it could continue to increase, depending on the evolution of the situation.

Q.: Yes.

N.: What has that got to do with your nature? Where are you in all of this? Are you the body?

Q.: I misunderstood. I misidentify freedom from sensory pain with Knowledge.

N.: If we want to eliminate sensory pain, an anesthetic will do, but giving someone an anesthetic does not endow her with wisdom. Nowhere has the Maharshi, Sankara, or, as in your case, the Buddha, recommended anesthetics as a practice. That is simply shutting down the nerves so that you do not have certain sensations. The Wisdom, which is Self-Knowledge, is not a sensory activity. It is not reached by the senses, and it is not disturbed by the senses. If you think of yourself as being wrapped up in the senses, either as a body or as some kind of sensing entity, you seem to be afflicted by them.

That your senses gravitate toward what is pleasant and away from that which is painful is just in the natural course of things, but you are not of the senses. The idea that you are a sensing entity or a nexus point of all the senses is only imagined in the mind. When you do not imagine such in the mind, you are unaffected, just as space is unaffected by whatever seems to be coursing through it.

Q.: Oh!

N.: The space contained within my hands now (his hands cupped together) is unaffected if the hands disintegrate (pulls hands away from each other). It is the same space. The space is analogous to your real Being, or pure Consciousness. It is not cooped up now, and it is not now outside. It is not put together, and it is not broken.

Q.: It is not fragmented by obstacles.

N.: There is no obstacle for the space. (Silence)

(Then followed a recitation in Sanskrit and English of verses from the *Ashtavakra Gita*.)

(Silence)

Om Shanti Shanti Shanti Om

True Silence

Satsang, May 8, 2005

(Silence)

Om Om Om

(Silence)

N.: The Self is forever nonobjective. It never becomes a known or unknown thing. Self-Realization is, therefore, nonobjective Knowledge of oneself. It is said to be most eloquently described and instruction about it is most eloquently given in silence.

The Maharshi is referred to as a silent sage. He was silent not only when quiet and when speaking, but silent forever. Likewise, the primordial Guru, Dakshinamurti is spoken of as being in a state of perpetual silence. What else is that but nonobjective Knowledge? Such is Being, free of the illusion of any attribute or characteristic or of any false definition.

The Maharshi says that silence is that state in which no "I" arises. "I" means the assumption of existing as an individual being rather than as pure, absolute Being. Absolute Being is nondual, eternal, infinite, and formless. Only that which is formless can be eternal. All forms have birth and death. The formless is alone perpetually existent. Silence is indicative of this perpetual Existence. It is the "I"-less, object-less real nature, which is the Unborn, the Uncreated. That which is ever existent is real. That which has a transitory existence is but a superficial appearance and is not real. In Truth, it never actually comes to be.

To know Reality as it is, you must know yourself. To know yourself, you must inquire. How else are you to know yourself except by deeply and constantly inquiring within yourself as to, "Who am I?" The Maharshi has said that the inquiry is necessary because it alone does not include the duality that one is attempting to transcend. What is this duality? "I and this." Stretching between the poles of "I" and "this" is all of maya, illusion, which is nothing more than delusion.

To be free of "I" and "this," to be free of duality, know yourself. Inquire within yourself. To inquire is to make your vision nonobjective. If you are spiritually searching, who is searching? If you are practicing, who is the practitioner? If you say that you know yourself or that you do not know yourself or that you do not know if you know or don't know yourself, who is the "I"?

Whatever is conceived as knowledge depends on the definition of this "I." However the "I," or individual, is defined, so does "this" appear. If we find out what truly is "I," we know Reality. That which knows and that which is known are identical. That is, in nondual Knowledge, which is Knowledge of one's own Self, there is neither an "I" nor a "this."

One's own Self cannot possibly be a body, for that is the known. One's own Self cannot possibly be a sensory thing or a mental thing. It cannot be the mind. What is it that truly deserves to be called yourself? Inquire.

If you so inquire, Reality comprehends itself. The Reality, of the nature of Being-Consciousness-Bliss, should alone be regarded as you. That which is truly you is illimitable. It is the Absolute. There is no other kind of you. The imagination of another you, a "second" or an individual, is the very root of all other delusion and delusion's consequent bondage and suffering. Knowledge of one's Self is, therefore, spoken of as the root of Bliss. Really, there is not the relation of a root and something else. The Knowledge, itself, is the Bliss. The Knowledge, being nonobjective, is of the nature of pure Consciousness and is not some perception or conception. A concept, a percept, a mental mode, a state, or a condition cannot possibly be eternal. The Maharshi says that what is not eternal is not worth seeking. Search for that in yourself that is nonobjective and, therefore, eternal, or timeless.

To so inquire and know, start with your existence. It is Consciousness. Where you start is where you end. Turn your mind inward and inquire, "Who am I?" Do not expect an answer to come to you. What comes goes. What appears disappears. That which has birth is perishable. Make your vision nonobjective. Neither seek to obtain something nor wait for something to happen. Make your vision nonobjective and know yourself. Cease to misidentify with whatever is objective, be it a subtle thought or the gross form of the body, or any of the attributes of those.

There is no beginning or end for your Being. It always is just as it is. (Silence) This is one's true Being, which has not a trace of individuality, which has not a trace of objectivity, and which is Existence pure. This alone is.

Imagine individuality and this which alone is real seems elusive. From that position, one is prepared to say that there is some distinction between God and the self. Turn within, inquire, and know yourself, and there are not two—one to elude and one to know or not know the other. The Self, Reality, is Absolute, and is silently self-evident.

Q.: I find that, by coming here, meditations are deeper than they are at other places. Coming here, I see what meditation can be.

N.: What actually happens? What is the difference? How do you mark off when you are here?

Q.: Somehow, it is different when we are meditating together than when I meditate alone.

N.: How do you know when we are together?

Q.: By all this sensory experience.

N.: When you dive deep within and find something of a space-like nature, is it sensory?

Q.: Of course not! (laughing)

N.: The senses cannot be the cause of a non-sensory state. So, what happens?

Q.: I can say only that something happens with my mind, but this is why I ask.

N.: Your existence is there always.

Q.: Yes.

N.: It is non-bodily in nature. So, here and there, which relate to the body and the senses, cannot possibly be relevant to turning within. When you intend to turn your focus within and actually inquire is when good experience shows. How you approach meditation has everything to do with meditation, doesn't it?

Q.: Yes.

N.: The real nature of meditation for Self-Knowledge must necessarily be nonobjective. The means and the end must be of the same nature. Otherwise, there is no guarantee of success with it.

I do not deny the validity, the importance, and the benefit of the temple and holy company. If we look to the essence, we find that it exists everywhere.

Q.: I have moments of not being the doer. It is more joyous.

N.: That is always the case. Peace and joy are innate. The moment false definition, or ignorance, is eliminated, proportionate to the amount the ignorance is eliminated, such bliss and peace shine. They belong to the substrate. Where Being is, where Consciousness is, there is Bliss. As Being is always existent, Bliss is always existent. Joy and peace are not things to be possessed. They belong to the substrate of your Being, which always is. Remove the superficial veil, and the substrate is already there without a moment's delay.

It is just as in the analogy of the rope and the snake. The moment the false, imagined idea of a snake is removed, the rope is there, for it was already there and now is seen clearly. The rope has not newly arrived. The rope is always there and was only mistaken to be a snake. So it is with ignorance and knowledge and bondage and liberation.

Q.: What is to be done regarding suffering?

N.: It is Knowledge and not a doing. *Atmabodha* by Sankara begins with the instruction that action cannot lead to Liberation, and Self-Knowledge is Liberation. This is very profound wisdom. Actions are performed with the body, speech, and mind. That which is performed with the body cannot result in bodiless Liberation. Likewise is it with the activities of the speech and the mind. The activity of the mind may be a thought, a state of thought content, or the activity of a state of no-thought content. These pertain entirely to the activities of the mind. Manipulation of these activities does not result in Self-Knowledge, or Liberation.

Liberation is knowing yourself. It is not a doing. Nevertheless, a practice of Knowledge is more intense than any practice of activity. Activities are performed sporadically. Knowledge is continuous. Activities are relatively exterior and gross. Knowledge is interior and subtle. That which is subtle is more potent.

The fact is that you are never the performer of action. The idea that you are the doer is just delusion. It is just a wrong idea. You never become the body. Bodiless you innately are. So, how could you do anything? You never become the mind, or thinking. No matter what the pattern of thinking is, there is still one who knows it. It is evident that one thought does not know another. The knower, apparently unknown, can never be confused and can never be a thought. If you have no relation to thought, how can you be a thinker?

When you have the image in mind that you are some performer of some activity of the mind, speech, or body, that image is objective to you. You know about it. You know about it to such an extent that you can speak about it. By whose light is that known? That never does anything.

Another Q.: The quiet is always followed by a mental storm, so how can I make the mind quiet as long as the ego is there?

N.: You have answered your own question. In Absolute Silence, there is no individuality. The quietude that belongs to the individual mind is just the calm before the storm. After the storm, there is more calm. Such quietude is nothing more than change of the content or forms of thoughts. Thought is inherently transient, isn't it? So, how can you make the mind quiet? This is not to say that there should be endless chatter in the mind, but that Silence is perpetual in which the false sense of individuality, which is the I-notion or ego, is dissolved. That peace is without destruction.

Put your efforts into dissolution of the false sense of "I." If you would disidentify from the forms of the individual, would you be plagued by mental storms? Your definitions shape the patterns of thinking. How you misidentify determines the content of the thoughts. Some of the thoughts appear more inward to you and some appear as if outward. If you look within yourself and question the very nature of the individual and disidentify from the various forms of the individual, so that you know yourself as you really are, not only will you find peace, which is more than quietude, you will find that thought is nonexistent. You are being tossed about by something that is merely a dream.

(Silence)

Another Q.: Clarity is very important. It becomes clearer as the meditations become deeper. What I believe in is very important.

N.: In what do you believe?

Q.: Are you referring to identifying with the concepts?

N.: Are you identifying with concepts?

Q.: (smiles)

N.: Is that your basic belief?

Q.: (laughs) They seem never ending. The ideas seem to be there.

N.: Where?

Q.: (laughs)

N.: What do you believe "there" to be?

Q.: This thing called "me," which is a conglomeration of thoughts.

N.: Do you believe yourself to be a conglomeration of thoughts?

Q.: No. My Self must definitely be much vaster than that, though those thoughts are there.

N.: Do they exist apart from you?

Q.: It seems as if identity becomes confused.

N.: You exist apart from them. None of your thoughts are continuous. You have only to fall into deep sleep to verify this. In that state, it is as if they have never happened. You can exist fine without them. Can they ever exist apart from you?

Q.: No.

N.: If they never exist apart from you, have they any existence at all? Even when you say to yourself that the thoughts exist, by what power do you say that? When you say that they are real or exist, the reality or existence refers to you.

Q.: The Existence is real, and that stamp of reality is from it..

N.: Even the apparent vividness of illusion owes its vividness to the Reality, which has no illusion.

Q.: Can you go back to why they don't even exist because it appears that they do? They are never there permanently. All of them come and go. They derive their reality from my saying that they are real. So, it must be that the reality is borrowed from the Self.

N.: They depend on you. They are never perceived apart from you. What is the nature of that "you"? Is it divisible? Is it mutable? If you are immutable and indivisible, how can the Self be a cause of thought arising in you? How can the changeless give rise to the changeful? How can the undivided give rise to the divided? If the changeless would change, it would be changeful, and only what is changeless is real. What is changeless is actually existent. What is changeful is either nonexistent or a misperception of what is existent. How can that misperception arise in that which is self-luminous by nature?

Q.: Can you state that again?

N.: How can ignorance appear in Consciousness, which is of the nature of Knowledge? Your nature is pure Consciousness. You said earlier that the thoughts occur only in you and they they do not exist apart from you. How can that which is undifferentiated give rise within itself to something that is different?

Q.: That is the start of the confusion.

N.: What causes it to start? What would cause the self-luminous to give rise to darkness? What would cause the unchanging to change itself? What would cause Reality to give rise to what is unreal? The *Gita* says that the Real ever is and the unreal has never come to be.

Q.: It appears that there is a thought.

N.: It must appear for someone.

Q.: Yes.

N.: Who is that someone? If he is one thing, there can be another thing, such as thought.

Q.: At the time, it seems that there are these other thoughts.

N.: What is this magic element called "time"? You need multiplicity of thought, at least two of them, in order to conceive of time. Are you a thought? Or two thoughts? Are you in time? Does your nature change at any time? Do you cease to exist at any time?

The one who exists when there is no thought whatsoever, as in deep sleep, or prior to your imagining such thoughts, is the same one who exists when thoughts occur and when thoughts have disappeared. That one is unchanging throughout. Is he bound by a thought?

(Silence)

Know yourself as you are. That is perpetual, illimitable, unconceived, pure Consciousness, pure Being. You cannot expect an adequate explanation of No-creation in terms of creation. You cannot expect a conceptual explanation as to why thought does not exist, even though it is completely unreasonable to assert that it does exist.

Q.: You said that Reality is undivided, so does thought exist by itself?

N.: It does not say, "I am real." You say that it is real.

Q.: The Reality is really myself?

N.: You are always just yourself. When all of your thoughts have come and gone, still nothing has come and gone.

Q.: Thought now feels very objective. That is always the case?

N.: How many thoughts have you thought during this lifetime?

Q.: Uncountable.

N.: You are the same now as before you thought all those thoughts. Existence remains the same. The Consciousness, which knows the thoughts, shines just as brightly as it was before you had all the thoughts. Nothing has happened. That unchanging Being-Consciousness is Brahman, the vast Absolute. All this is only Brahman, but Brahman never becomes all this. It just is, as it is. There is no second to act upon it. Although it is said to be the source of all, in truth, it is not the cause of a consequent effect. It just is.

That which just is, is alone you. The Upanishad says, "Tat tvam asi," That you are.

Is this clear?

Q.: Yes, very clear.

Another Q.: You have said that the beginning and the end are one and the same. I think that I have reached the start, but I have not. I think that I am inquiring, but I am not really inquiring.

N.: So, what is your intention? If your intention is to know yourself free from the illusions of bondage, don't bind yourself in the name of trying to be free. Don't suffer in the name of attaining happiness. Don't take what is not your Self to be your Self.

Q.: It makes me wonder what I am thinking. (laughter)

N.: Everyone looks for his own Self all the time. In the name of happiness, in the name of ascertaining what is real, in every idea, and in the attempt to know who we are. Of course, if you see this, you will not have an extroverted mind at all. (Silence)

Q.: I am happy.

(Silence)

(Then followed a recitation in Sanskrit and English from the *Ashtavakra Gita*.)

(Silence)

Om Shanti Shanti Shanti Om

One Self

Satsang, July 17, 2005

(Silence)

Om Om Om

(Silence)

N.: One Self alone exists, eternally. There is no other. There is no multiplicity of selves, outside of yourself or within yourself. The conception of multiplicity is only delusion based upon misidentification, which has for its root the false assumption of an ego-entity, an individual identity.

One Self exists, of the nature of pure Being-Consciousness-Bliss. It is unborn. It is unformed, uncreated, and imperishable. The idea of more than one self is only misidentification. If you mistake yourself to be a body, there appear to be multiple selves. Are you the body? This is what should be known.

(Silence)

In your spiritual practice, if your aim is to realize the Self, which is Brahman, you must ask yourself if there are two of you, one seeking to realize and one that is to be realized? Multiplicity of selves, such as "yourself" and "the Self," is born of misidentification, which is delusion.

Who is to realize what, when all that exists is this one Self? What, then, is Self-Realization? It is undoubtedly Knowledge of the Self, such Knowledge being not a perception or a conception, but utterly nonobjective. With nonobjective Knowledge, the knowing and one's own Being are identical.

Because there are not two selves, for Self-Realization, the Maharshi laid the greatest emphasis upon the inquiry, "Who am I?" It is an inquiry into the true nature of the inquirer and not an attempt to ascertain something objective to oneself. Whatever is objective to you is dependent upon you. Such is merely false appearance and completely unreal. It is an inquiry into who you are. If you wish to realize the Self, first know your own Self. If you know your own Self, the "your own" part will vanish, for the ego is not real. Individuality is not real. What remains is pure Being, which is, itself, the Knowledge.

If, in our minds, we treat Self-Realization, or the Self, as if it were apart from our own Self, our own Being, we seek it as if it were some mental mode, as if we were in one mode and would later be in another mode. Such is a state of ignorance and a state of knowledge, but the Knowledge of the Self that is infinite and eternal is not a mode of mind. It does not occur within a mode of a mind. It does not even occur within the waking, dreaming, and deep sleep states. It does not occur, for it is not an event. Not being in time, it is indestructible.

This Knowledge is one with your Being. Therefore, inquire within yourself as to what it is in you that neither wakes nor dreams, which does not sleep, and which has no objective attribute. What is it within you that is neither perceived nor conceived? If, within yourself, you determine this, you will have found the Self, and that which you have found you are. No new Self will have been produced, nor will you have been transformed from one thing into another, though all the bondage and suffering, which are a result of delusion, will have vanished.

(Silence)

Inquire within yourself and cease to misidentify with a body, a mind or the very idea of "I." You cannot be what is objective. So, who are you? Inquire. If you wish to merge with Brahman or be in union with God, who are you who seem to be broken off that you would merge or have union with That? Question this very identity.

If you inquire, in this nonobjective manner, the "I" and all else that depends on the "I" cease to be for you, because such has no real existence. It is the unreal alone that appears to cease. The Real ever is just as it is. Reality alone knows itself. Brahman alone knows Brahman. There is no other. The Self knows the Self. There is no second, no other.

It is for this reason that, in the *Karika,* Gaudapada says that there is no destruction, no origination, no one bound, no one who practices, no one who desires to be free, and certainly no one liberated.

(Silence)

Q.: I became deathly ill following a bee sting. I looked within to see what my Existence is and waited for the body to either have a cure or a heart attack. I watched everything going on. The question was, with death possible at any second, how else to take the meditation, the inquiry, deeper?

N.: Aren't you always at that moment of death?

Q.: Yes. I had been thinking that it is far off.

N.: You were very aware that you are not the body and the mind. You were also very aware of the urgency, or the importance, of remaining free from the body and the mind and realizing your real Existence.

The importance should not wane. If the sense of importance does not wane, the desire for Liberation will be strong. Since Liberation consists of Self-Knowledge, you need to know your Existence. If you are not the mind and not the body, nothing perceived and nothing conceived pertains to you.

What remains of your nature? There appear to be the Existence that you want to realize and you. What constitutes that "you"?

Q.: I do not know.

N.: That is where your inquiry should be directed.

Q.: Do you mean the ego "I"?

N.: Someone has the body and the mind. That is called "I." You divest that "I" of the body and mind. So, what remains of "I"? If you inquire in this way, the "I" will be consumed.

Q.: I had been doing meditation on the "I."

N.: Pull your mind inward into this inquiry, "Who am I?" fueled by the intense desire for Liberation. Feel that it is as important now as it was then.

Q.: At a point in the meditation, I feel the need to surrender. The inquiry seems to go just so far.

N.: What do you mean by "surrender"?

Q.: It is to let go and keep from being that "I."

N.: How will you let go of that?

Q.: I don't know.

N.: If you do let go of it, won't you still remain as "I"?

Q.: Yes. When I let go, I am here. I know where here is.

N.: Is "here" in this world?

Q.: No.

N.: Then, where is "here"? When you say, "I am here," what is this "here"? If your senses cease, and there is no vision or experience of the world, are you still here? If so, where is here? If your mind ceases to think, and, indeed, thinking alone constitutes the mind though it may be regarded as if it were an entity, are you still here?

Q.: Well, yes, surely.

N.: If you ask, "Who is here?" the forms of both the "I" and "here" vanish.

Either inquire so that the "I"-less true "I" alone remains, for that alone is real, or surrender. Then, God alone is, and nothing remains of you but God. In either case, the sense of "I" and "mine" vanish. "I," "my mind," "my body," "my life," "my death," etc. vanish.

Q.: During that event, it seemed that they were not mine.

N.: Can you repossess them? If you do, it is only imagination. The ideas of "I am the body" and "the body is mine" are only imagination. The ideas of "my thoughts" and that you are what you think are only imagination. How could you be a body? How could you be what you think?

Imagination ceases. So does creation. Since nothing that is imagined can go with you, you might as well be detached from all that is imagined even now. Since that with which you might misidentify really never has anything to do with your Existence, you might as well remain disidentified even now. Since, with freedom from attachment and misidentification, the innate bliss and peace shine, you might as well experience that even now.

Q.: I experienced peace, but it was surrounded by chaos.

N.: Yes, first it seems that, in the middle of the chaos, there is peace. Later, it is said that there is a drop of chaos in the midst of vast peace. Finally, there is only peace, and there isn't any chaos.

Do not let the experience fade in memory. The phenomenal portion of it will. The sensory portion will fade away in due course. The lesson, though, about the importance of Liberation and about what your nature is, should endure. Continue to inquire into the nature of your Existence.

Another Q.: The Maharshi said to inquire. He also spoke of the importance of pranayama and meditation. This is also mentioned in the scriptures. As an unrealized person, I have samskaras. I need to fry them through samadhi. I know techniques of controlling the prana. I am confused about what he meant by, "Inquire." One can intellectually understand that he is not the body, the prana, the mind, the buddhi, the ego, and the bliss sheath. So what, if it is intellectual? When he was first surrounded by people, they were very lucky and advanced souls. If one isn't that, because of many impressions, is it still right to inquire, even though there is really no need to do anything and there is no seeking? If one remembers something from childhood as an impression, my understanding from the scriptures is that the only way to get rid of that is samadhi. Does that make sense?

N.: Samadhi indicates utter absorption in the Self. That means that the separate individuality has vanished or dissolved. The inquiry should not be mistaken to be some activity of the vijnanamaya kosa, the sheath of the intellect. There is nothing intellectual about it at all. Why does the Maharshi recommend the inquiry? He said that it is the only method that does not include the duality that one is trying to transcend. It is not that other methods were ridiculed. If they are of assistance to you, use them. In the end, though, you must come around to knowing yourself, for the samadhi to be sahaja, innate, effortless, or natural.

There is no point in saying that there is nothing to seek. That is, generally, a misconception. The Maharshi advised inquiry and to know one's Self.

You do not require intellectual analysis to know that you exist. Start and end with the Existence. It is purely experiential and not theoretical. When you so inquire, even your comprehension of what the scriptures advise becomes very much clarified. You understand them from the very same position from which the Rishis uttered them.

Q.: What does "inquire" mean? What do I do? Is it just to be?

N.: How are you going to just be?

Q.: Between thoughts, all of us have the experience of just being. Is it that I just "groove" on that? Is that the inquiry? I could never figure it out, though I read all the books ten times. What do I really do? It is nothing intellectual. What is it?

N.: You exist. You know that you exist. What is the way that you know that you exist? It is inseparable from the Existence. You know that you are. This knowing should be turned in on itself rather than coursing through imagined objects. Now, the mind is accustomed to objective vision. Make your vision nonobjective. It is tracing the sense of existence within yourself. You may wish to have some detailed instruction about it, but how can detailed instruction be given for something that is nonobjective? There is precision in the Maharshi's instruction. In this sense, it is marvelously detailed, but such is entirely of a nonobjective, non-conceptual character, just as you are. You exist. You know that you exist. What else do you add to the Existence, in your mind's imagination? All that which is "I" or belongs to the "I." Relinquish the misidentification by Knowledge.

(Then followed a recitation in Sanskrit and English of verses from the *Ashtavakra Samhita.*)

(Silence)

Om Shanti Shanti Shanti Om

Nonobjective Realization

Satsang, October 23, 2005

(Silence)

Om Om Om

(Silence)

N.: The Reality of the Self ever alone is. The real cannot be made more so. This was clearly taught by Sri Bhagavan.

The Reality cannot be made more real, and, therefore, Self-Realization is not a new attainment. The Reality can no more be made to be more real than your existence can be made more existent. It is not possible.

If the misidentification, which is purely ignorance, with what is not the Self is abandoned, the Reality of the Self, which alone is, shines brilliantly in its own light. Therefore, efforts in sadhana, or spiritual practice, which is the inquiry to find out who you are, are directed at the dissolution of misidentification. If the misidentification with the body, the mind, and the sense of being an individual entity, or ego, is abandoned, everything is already accomplished.

Every limitation is only imagined. Every imagined limitation has as its root and for its very substance some misidentification, some conception of oneself as an individual or ego, endowed with some kind of form, which is usually the body. Ask yourself deeply if you are the body or if you can be a body. If you inquire in such a manner, all the limitations associated with being a body vanish, just as the misidentification does.

Similar is it with the mind. Can you possibly be what you think, whatever the thought is? It is imperative to be free from thought. Can you be a thought? Where is the connection between your Existence, which is of the nature of pure Consciousness, and some thought?

What is it that seems to define an individual that is carved out, as it were, from the space-like infinite Consciousness, our real Being? What is it that makes for individuality? It cannot be thought and the body, for these are appended to this so-called individual, as if they were clothing or sheaths wrapping it. What marks off the individual called "I"? Inquiring, "Who am I?", seeing where this "I" arises, or from what, is the inquiry according to Sri Bhagavan. Turning your mind inward, examine keenly what it is that is "I."

(Silence)

For Being, there is no appearance of ignorance and no disappearance of ignorance, For Being, which is the Reality, there is no birth of the unreality and no perishing or death of the unreality. With and for the individual is the illusion, the unreal. If you inquire and know yourself, at once and for all eternity, you see that which alone exists. Nothing has divided the forever-indivisible. The nondual is purely nondual. Nothing has broken off from it, to be outside of it or divided within it. It is not correct to think that you are separate from it in any degree. It is not correct to think even, "That is a part of me," as if it were the most interior part. Though it is proclaimed to be your inner Existence, you must realize the truth that you have no outer existence, that is, no other existence than pure Existence, which is Brahman. It is the only Self and the only thing that exists.

As it is the only thing that exists, in this is full peace. In this is perfect Bliss. This Being-Consciousness-Bliss is unborn and imperishable. It never changes. By inquiry, perceive this changeless Existence to be the only existence that you are. If you see what you are, you see what is. If you misperceive what you are and mistake yourself to be an individual, there is also something else that is. Where there is a self, there is something other. Where there is an individual, there is differentiation. In the Knowledge of yourself, realize that there is no individual, but just pure Being, and then there is nothing else, and there is no differentiation.

(Silence)

If you inquire into the nature of the one who seems as if a bound individual, you will find only bondage-free Being, and this is called "Liberation" or "Self-Realization."

So, then, know yourself.

Q.: You said that the Self is the only Being. That means that there is no other being. We need to know nothing else. Your wonderfully clear presentation of the teaching makes it hard to be mistaken about what is and about who we are.

N.: In general, it is very difficult to be mistaken about who we are. Anyone who seems to be mistaken is subject to difficulties.

Q.: One should ask who it is who makes the mistakes or some similar inner question.

N.: If that happens, the mistakes vanish, because all of the mistakes, the errors of delusion, are based on non-inquiry, non-knowledge.

Q.: Part of my practice now is to make all of the daily life activities items for inquiry. I am seeing the identification as the actor. Driving here, I ask myself, "Who is driving?" Driving goes on just fine, but the attention is within, and the identification as the driver seems to go away.

N.: That is right. You cannot simultaneously be the knower and the actor. This has been mentioned several times by Sankara. He says that one cannot have the action and the knowledge occur simultaneously. The understanding of what he is indicating is found in the inquiry. How can you be the doer and the knower simultaneously? If you are always the knower, you can never be the doer, or actor. Your body acts, but you know about it. Always, you are knowing. All the activities of your body, senses, and mind, and whatever else is involved, are entirely the known. All of them shine in the light of the original Knowledge, which is perpetual. You have never been an actor.

Q.: If I have a sense of breathing, I can ask, "Who is breathing?" If gardening, I can ask, "Who is gardening?" It seems different, though, if I ask, "Who is the inquirer?"

N.: If you ask who the inquirer is, everything is swallowed up. As for breathing, gardening, driving and such, all of these pertain to the actions of your limbs, your body, and your prana. With those that are considered mental or intellectual activities, they are activities of your mind or intellect. Like all activities, they appear and disappear. They have a beginning and an end. Like all activities, they are objective to you. They are something known. The known, which is transient, cannot possibly be you. Whatever is not you at one time cannot be you at some other time. What you are you always are. What is not the Self is never the Self. Your nature does not change.

So, did you really drive here this morning? (laughter) You are; you always are. Remain as That.

Another Q.: In a previous satsang you asked someone, "Who inquires?" You said that it cannot be the ego that inquires, because the ego does not exist and is only a concept, and that it cannot be the Self that inquires because the Self is solitary, undifferentiated Being that just is at it is. So, who does inquire?

N.: When you so inquire, what happens?

Q.: Nothing happens, but one realizes that which is transcendent of a nonexistent ego. It must be that which is and cannot be known but is what one is.

N.: Every spiritual practice, inclusive of inquiry, is, in one sense, based upon illusion. The purpose of them is the destruction of the illusion. What is unique about the inquiry to know yourself is that it does not include the dualism of the illusion that you are trying to destroy.

When the illusion is gone, there is no separate inquirer, and there is no separate activity of inquiry.

Q.: It is said here that effort is required to the extent that there is ignorance. When one inquires into the one who is making the effort, the result is that there is no one who makes efforts and that the effortless state is already present.

N.: So, in practice, we do not attempt to eliminate effort. We see who we are, and effort is taken care of by itself. If we simply attempted to eliminate effort, the ego would remain solidly intact, even though it's an illusion. Its effects would still be present. If only one's effort is fully put into realizing who we are, that which is natural, innate – sahaja, which is sometimes interpretted as "effortless" because it is natural—is realized.

Q.: It seems very simple.

N.: The Innate is very simple.

Q.: The instruction seems very simple. I just must do it.

N.: It is as simple as the nature of the one who receives it. If you find this nature to be supremely simple, not allowing even so much as a thought to crowd in, it is received. It is very simple.

Another Q.: When I inquire deeply, the experience is that there is no mind and no separation. There is a memory in the form of "What about that which seemed to have happened? What about the duality that seemed to have been there?" If I inquire more deeply, it is very clear that that never happened. Until it is clear that that never happened, there seems to be the potential for duality to rise again. When it becomes clear that it never arose, that has a finality to it.

N.: The Maharshi commented upon the distinction between yoga and jnana. One assumes that separation has occurred and brings about union, which is yoga. In jnana, or Knowledge, one examines to see if separation has even occurred to begin with. In That, which is final Knowledge, there is solidity. That is indestructible. Do not relinquish the inquiry until the very possibility of the imagination of difference has vanished. When the possibility of imagining differences has vanished, there is still no need to relinquish the inquiry. The inquiry is then revealed as ever-shining Knowledge. There is no giving up of the inquiry.

Q.: When one actually inquires, he has ended the duality the moment he starts to inquire, but it is not really a process, as if one were doing something.

N.: It is not an action. Knowledge is Liberation. Action does not lead to Liberation. Inquiry reveals Liberation.

Inquiry is not an activity. It is knowing, not doing. With the dissolution of the false belief in an individual, there is no one to continue the inquiry or to give it up. The entire question becomes moot. Moreover, what is it that is called "inquiry"? Since it is knowing and not doing, it is not an activity of body, speech, or mind, but something far subtler and more interior. If we examine its nature, it absorbs itself in pure Consciousness, which is the Reality. The Reality, itself, appears as the means in this practice, which is why there is such great certainty in it. It is asking God to reveal God to God. There is great certainty in that.

Another Q.: My being is more constant, and it has fewer breaks during daily activities.

N.: Is what you are referring to as "being" an activity or an experience?

Q.: No. It is just stillness.

N.: If you deeply examine what inquiry is and what stillness is, you will find them to be identical. There is not another practice of "being."

Being, or Existence, always is. It is neither a thing nor an activity. Inquiry is for the purpose of its revelation, when there is confusion. When there is no confusion, the very same thing that is the substance of inquiry shines as the Knowledge of one's Being.

Q.: When I am aware of the words, "Just stay there," it has the effect, in an instant, of a memory of who I am and stillness.

N.: The effect is due to understanding what is meant by "there" and who should stay. Consider the Maharshi's analogy of a man who is in the shade during a hot day, who goes into the sun, suffering, and then returns to the shade. The advice to him when he is in the shade is to just stay there. He already knows what the shade is. Since he is about to wander out into the sun again, the advice is to just stay there.

Another Q.: Consciousness plus a single thought is running out into the sun.

N.: Yes.

Q.: Just the thought of "I."

N.: From one "I," the entire multitude comes.

Q.: When hot, one inquires into "I," to discover that one has never left the shade.

N.: Yes, it was just a dream of going in and out of the sun.

Q.: It seems that one has a preference to be in illusion. What if one knows that all that is perceived and conceived is but a projection of an unreal mind and that it is unreal, but one wants to be in a nice dream?

N.: Then, he does not really know that it is unreal. Our nature being the Reality, which is also our Bliss, if we really know that what is otherwise is unreal, we will abandon the unreal. There is really no such state as knowing it is unreal but still wanting it or being attracted to it anyway or deciding to stay in the unreal. Similar is it with the idea that one has left the illusion but has now come back. Then, one really does not know that this is an illusion. It is like trying to now make use of the things in last night's dream.

Q.: Sometimes, I have a very nice dream. I dream that I am a young man.

N.: That is just a commentary on how unsatisfactory the waking state is. You are willing to switch it for another dream. (laughter) That does not prove the reality of the dream. It merely means that the dream of "the waking state" has become sufficiently unpleasant as to make you wish to go to another.

Q.: I should abandon both of them.

N.: When we know that an illusion is an illusion, it is over. There can be no question of entering it again. When we know ignorance as ignorance, we cannot entertain it anymore. We revert to ignorance only so long and as much as we think that it tells us something and that it is really knowledge. We revert to some misidentification with the ego and such because we think that that is possibly who we are. We go in search of who we are through those various thoughts. When we are truly convinced that this is not the Self and that this is only ignorance, it becomes quite impossible for us.

Q.: With the certainty of knowledge of the unreality of what is objective, it means ceasing.

N.: Dreaming, waking, and sleeping cease. One who knows the Self, while sleeping, does not sleep, waking, does not wake, and, dreaming, does not dream.

Q.: So, the Self, being transcendent of sleep, is not of the state of mind called sleep?

N.: The Truth is like sleep, inasmuch as it is formless and without anything else, but it is not to be thought that the Self is sleep. The Self is transcendent of any state of mind. Know that to be yourself that has never appeared in the entire waking state and that never appears in the dreaming state. Where there is such misidentification, there open up heaven and hell. I don't advise visits to either.

Q.: Neither would last. One would fall into the opposite polarity.

N.: None compare to the perfection of the fullness of real Being. The Existence that does not go anywhere and does not become anything, silently is. That alone is immortal. (Silence)

Another Q.: Vasanas cause suffering and need to be completely destroyed. Vasanas are who we think that we are. It is what we identify with. Is that correct?

N.: Yes. A vasana is a tendency. The tendencies are entirely based upon, or are composed of, what we regard as our identity.

Q.: Why does that cause such suffering? Is it the ambivalence in knowing who we are and seeing ourselves misidentify at the same time? It causes disruption, suffering, and unnecessary worry. We know that we are doing the wrong thing, but we think that that is who we are, and so we hold on to it.

N.: That shows how powerful the attraction to who we are is. One will even grasp something wrong in the attempt to find out who he is and hold a tenacious grip upon it because whatever is the Self, whatever is real, one loves. If one regards something wrongly as that, he loves that or craves that or desires that. This is because one intuits that whatever is real and oneself is bliss. Our nature is Sat-Chit-Ananda, Being-Consciousness-Bliss.

At the very same moment that there is misidentification, suffering starts. The moment the suffering starts, simultaneously there is the desire to return to one's natural state of happiness. Why is suffering associated with vasanas? Because they are not who you are. Who you are is alone Ananda, Bliss. What is not Bliss is not natural for you. You cannot tolerate that. For however long suffering may go on, there is, in truth, no becoming accustomed to it. Always, your nature is happiness. You are satisfied only when you abide in and as the Self, without interruption, so that your happiness is unbroken.

Q.: It is just a matter of letting go of any idea of who we are.

N.: If the false notions about who you are are abandoned, everything is accomplished. So, the Maharshi emphasized the destruction of vasanas for the purpose of Self-Realization.

Another Q.: I see clearly that the inquiry addresses not directly the revelation of the Self, but the destruction of egoity within the questioner.

N.: The inquiry is primarily a negation of the delusion, from the false notion of an ego to everything based upon it.

Then, the Self stands Self-revealed. No further effort is required.

Another Q.: When my mind is outward, there must be misidentification occurring. While at work, at times, I reflect on what is real. That reflection does not go on perpetually.

I have this computer problem. I was brave enough to load a new operating system. I thought I would try it. None of the drivers work anymore. Right in the middle of doing something, I see this blue screen that says, "You have this fatal problem in your computer."

N.: That is much like samsara. You have this fatal problem. (laughter)

Q.: Yes. It looks pretty for a few moments, but then there is the memory. I can examine what is in the memory.

N.: Again, it is like samsara, which is a play of memory. (laughter)

Q.: I started working on this to see which driver is causing the problem. While doing this, I reflected on if I need to be there as some one who needs to solve this and what is really happening. At those points, I feel meditative, but I cannot stay in that mode.

N.: Why not?

Q.: It seems that I have this belief that, when the body moves or I need to think of something, the Self goes away.

N.: Aren't you aware of the body's motions and the mind's motions?

Q.: Yes.

N.: How could you be aware of them if the Self went away?

Q.: (after a pause) So, it is always contained in the Self?

N.: Is there any place or any time outside of the Self?

Q.: Hmm.

N.: During the adventures with the computer, even before you meditated, did you cease to exist?

Q.: No. Even when I thought I solved the problem, voila, the blue screen appeared again.

N.: Still, you existed throughout all of it.

Q.: During the whole time.

N.: Existence is also Consciousness, shining with what we could call a small fraction of its light so that all of that can be perceived and, also, shining when none of that is perceived.

Q.: The content of what is perceived is a distraction. There is a difference when the blue screen appears and when it does not appear. (laughter)

N.: From what are you distracted?

Q.: Thinking that somehow I, as a mind and body, must solve this problem. I am distracted from realizing that really I am not that thought passing through my mind. That is objective.

N.: All the thinking put together is euphemistically referred to as "a mind." Are you the thinking? Have you ever become thought?

Q.: No. Have I ever become thought? Because there is a belief in it at times, it wouldn't necessarily be true. So, an occurrence never really happened.

N.: In truth, you never really become thought, do you? The entire world is only a figment within the mind. That includes blue screens.

Q.: Yes, exactly.

N.: You are never in that, are you?

Q. (after a pause): No. That would be jumping out into thought, which is not an option.

N.: What would jump out? You have said that it is not an option. You remain as you are.

Q.: It seems that my belief in my identity is what jumps.

N.: Belief is when you think something is so, that it is real. Whether apparently experienced or not, one believes it to be so. Where does belief have its root? From where does the sense, "This is so, this is real," derive?

Q.: From the place where it is real.

N.: Does the Reality ever change? Does it jump in and out of itself? Reflect on the experience that you described. Were there two of you, one the abiding Reality and one who was projected and engaged in the experience? Were there really two?

Q.: I am confused because it does not seem that thinking of something can occur. So, it is hard for me to place myself into that situation.

N.: Over what are you confused? Since neither thinking nor the world ever occurs, it is not possible for you to project yourself into that experience that never occurs. Over what are you confused?

Q. (laughing): The clarity of knowing that one can't imagine that, so it really can't occur.

N.: (Silence)

Q.: That is interesting. From my experience, in our discussion, it seems hard to put energy into imagination that would be "real" or objective. It would not apply.

N.: Return to the previous question. Are there two of you, one who can have or enter into some experience or be projected and another who is the abiding Reality? (Silence)

Q. (after a long period of silence): I was just absorbed in that wonderful experience. Was there something happening?

N.: Just what you experienced. (after a pause) The only thing that ever happens is yourself. (Silence) Even if you conceive of the Consciousness that is your Self as if in motion, it is still just yourself. Really, it is unmoving, the ever-still Self.

(Then followed a recitation in Sanskrit and English of verses from the *Annapurna Upanishad.*)

(Silence)

Om Shanti Shanti Shanti Om

The State of Identity

Satsang, January 1, 2006

(Silence)

Om Om Om

(Silence)

N.: You are the One that does not enter into any state, who has no mode or condition, who is never active, who is ever formless Being and unmodified, immutable Consciousness. If there is a state and if there is activity, you are all of that, but, in your essential nature, you have no state, no activity, no thought, no doing, and no form. Whatever be the state of mind, you, yourself, appear as all of that.

You appear as the experiencer of that state, you appear as the state itself, and then as if one in that state. This is true of waking, dreaming, and of deep sleep. When waking, dreaming, and deep asleep, you ever remain transcendent of all. You are not that which appears in such states, and you are not actually the experiencer of such states, but you ever remain as pure Being, as pure Consciousness, which does not wake, dream, or sleep.

If your nature is veiled to yourself, you sleep. If your nature is veiled plus you imagine, you dream and you wake. The waking one appears as the waking state. The dreaming one appears as the dream state. The sleeping one appears as the sleep state. Once we feel that we are in such states, and in any of the modes of those states, such as the various mental modes of which one is aware in the waking state, we naturally strive for Liberation and consider Liberation as a state beyond those modes, and, further, a state beyond these three states of waking, dreaming, and sleep. Actually, Liberation is the very nature of your Being. It is Being that is never really in any other state and has no state of its own, but just is existent, without change, condition, and certainly without any limitation.

When we inquire, "Who am I?", we cease to regard ourselves as having any of the attributes of those modes of mind. We cease to regard ourselves as a being who is with those states, such as waking and dream. We cease to regard ourselves as being an experiencer of those states, such as a waking experiencer, a dreaming experiencer, and a sleeping experiencer, for what you are in your real nature is not an experiencer of anything. You are not the individual, or ego, whether appearing as heavily defined with a body, attributes, personality, and such or more vaguely defined as one who passes through the states and experiences various modes of mind. All of that pertains to the individual, but Being is absolute. The Self is not an individual.

This Self, which is not an individual, is certainly not embodied and is what, in truth, you are. It is delusion to imagine otherwise. To inquire, "Who am I?" is to resolve, or dissolve, the delusion. As long as you consider yourself to be an individual, there is some kind of state and, within that state, innumerable experiences corresponding to the quality of that state. When, though, you inquire and know yourself and abandon the false sense of individuality, you find that you are never in any state. Inquiring for whom is this experience, for whom is this state of mind, we find that we are not the individual, not the experiencer, for whom the state supposedly pertains.

Though one may commence spiritual practice with the feeling that one is in a state of samsara and aims for the state of Liberation, or with the idea that one is in the three states of waking, dreaming, and sleeping and aims for the Fourth, Turiya, really, the nature of the Turiya, or the Fourth, is you, yourself. If you abandon the false supposition that you are an experiencer, an individualized being, who has any of these things, you find that Liberation is your own nature.

You are eternally free and have never been bound. You are always un-embodied, and you have never been born. You are always free from thought, and you have never been conceived. Cease to misidentify and, in Self-Knowledge, see which state is yours.

(Silence)

Q.: Sri Ramana's *Talks* and the *Gita* speak of the field and the knower of the field. From what you have said, I see that the experiencer is still the field. Ramana equates the knower of the field with the witness, and, deeper, the knower of the field is the Self.

N.: In relation to the field of experience, the Self is known as the knower of the field. Understanding its immovable, ever-shining nature, it is referred to as the witness. When all false notions of objectivity are cast aside, the Self is just as it is. If the Self is not known as it is, it appears as "I." As soon as there is "I," there is something for it, "this." Then, the attributes of "this" are superimposed on the "I," the knower of the field thus being defined by the field, by the known. Such is illusion. Then, with "I" and "this," more multiplicity sprouts. Though you are the knower of the field, you appear as if you were an entity within the field. It is just as in a dream. You are the knower of the dream, yet you appear as if someone in the dream. What happens? First, your own nature is veiled, so there is sleep. With sleep comes the potential to imagine. You imagine "I," "this," the dreamer and his dream. Then, the dreamer appears as if in the dream, endowed with the false attributes of the dream. All of it is you, but, really, you are none of that.

Another Q.: My job requires intention and focus for results. Recently, I have the grace of not worrying about results. There is also a relaxing of attention, but the job still requires the intention. How am I to have the intention without the identification as being a doer?

N.: How do you connect the two? If you have the thought that the work needs to be performed with a certain intensity, how, in your mind, does that connect with the assumption of the misidentification of being the performer of the action?

Q.: It is the habit of getting caught in the identification without being able to witness it. I am identifying with the "I am doing it, and I am accomplishing it."

N.: Are you?

Q.: The body-mind seems to be accomplishing it.

N.: Are you the body and the mind?

Q.: No.

N.: So, where does the doership come in? Where does the "I am the body" notion come in?

Q.: In the intensity of the act of performing that which accomplishes the result.

N.: The assumption is that work performed intensely leads to more misidentification than work performed in a more relaxed, or even lackadaisical, manner.

Q.: Or no action.

N.: Do outer circumstances, including the activities of the body, create one's bondage?

Q.: One's misidentification.

N.: Do they? Do activities produce such ignorance? Misidentification is just ignorance.

Misidentification is not a physical thing. Do physical things, such as activity or the rate of activity, or the mental attention that we must give to an activity, create the ignorance of misidentification? If we think that they do, we will be in search, perhaps endlessly so, of the right arrangement of objects, activities, people, and similar things, so that we can be free. If, though, ignorance is self-produced and is not produced by outer circumstances, and if we further recognize that the entire idea that outer circumstances exist is also part of that ignorance, we are quite free to be free. Do you understand the discrimination being shown?

Q.: Yes. Once I have the detachment and freedom from the bondage of needing to have results, the good feeling of freedom, I immediately begin to see that the activity is not who I am. Then, I am free to be involved in intense activity without identification. I just wanted more help and further clarification.

N.: Continue discerning. Be very clear that illusion is born of delusion. One's ignorance is self-conjured, and outer circumstances, including bodily activities, do not produce it. If you are quite clear about that, you have the opportunity to know yourself all of the time. You are the same one, whether your body is working intensely or slowly or is on vacation. You are the same Self, whether your mind must attend to some detail of work at hand or is able to roam about where it wishes. You are still the same Self. The Self ought to know itself and abide as itself, without any confusion of yourself with the instruments of the body and the mind, which are, relatively, inert.

Q.: When conditions are right, I have a tendency to not inquire as much but, instead, have a reliance on the outer, as if that is my provider and my sustenance. When difficulties come, I inquire more and turn within more. I am trying to alert myself when circumstances are well to maintain the same intensity of inquiry, because laziness occurs.

N.: It is like saying that one prays to God only when everything is in a state of calamity, or, when all else fails, pray to God.

Q.: Someone said, "You mean it has come to that so that we have to pray?" (laughter) That laziness comes, and the ignorance of outer dependency, too, so that I fall into a trap.

N.: When you depend on outer circumstances to provide you with your peace and happiness, you create your own bondage, don't you?

Q.: There is a re-commitment on my part to not allow myself to fall into the trap of identification when things are working as I think that they should or as the world says that they should work.

N.: Look closely. Does the thought, "Things are working out well, so now it is time to misidentify," actually come to you? (laughter)

Q.: It is subtler than that.

N.: The misidentification really has nothing to do with whether things are going well or not. It is unrelated to the mental cognition of things going well or not. It is possible to recognize that things are going well in your activities without misidentification and without considering those things to be the source of your happiness and becoming attached, just as it is easy for you to recognize that things are not going well and need attending to and still remain unidentified and unattached. If you are unidentified and unattached, you remain in the Bliss of your own nature whether things are going well or not, whether you are working quickly or slowly, intensely or taking it easy. If you are misidentified and attached, you suffer regardless of the circumstances. If you are disidentified and detached, you do not suffer, regardless of the circumstances.

Therefore, you do not need to watch out when things become smooth, afraid that you are going to fall into ignorance. Similarly, when things are going poorly, you do not need to watch out that you are going to fall into ignorance. Once you know where happiness is, and you know the direction to inquire, "Who am I?", there is nothing tricky. There is no balancing act.

Another Q.: In the last chapter of the *Gita,* Krishna speaks about action. Sankara very clearly points out the triad of the action, the agent of action, and the results of action. It is very useful for me to see that the results of action are not for me. A good day or a bad day has to do with the results of action and confusion regarding for whom those are.

N.: If you are the doer of action, you reap the results. If you are not the actor, the results are not for you. In the commentary, Sankara has very clearly pointed out how Knowledge is for you, for your own nature, and that Knowledge is the very substance of Liberation and of Reality. Action appertains to an illusory actor and the illusory objects or the fruits of his action. If we throw ourselves into the delusion of considering ourselves to be enmeshed in such, as the Maharshi declares in *Upadesa Sarah (Upadesa Saram),* the engagement in action throws one into an ocean of action, with no end in sight. But you are not the body, and you are not the actor. Your true concern should be about what you are. Always you are. If you just rest in what that "are" is, everything is fine.

As often as one misidentifies, overlooks the essential Being and imagines oneself to be something else, just so often he should inquire.

Another Q.: As I inquire, there is a mistake that I make. I think that I am something other than what I am. Just knowing that clears up the mess. The mess becomes smaller and recedes. My question is: did that ever really happen? Knowing that kills the ego. It requires me to continually know that. I have the idea that I must get it once, finally, and deeply enough.

N.: In as much as you know ignorance to be ignorance, it ceases to exist. It diminishes to the nil point. Both the approach that you need to know this continuously and the approach that you need to know this once and for all are correct. If you inquire into who it is that presently regards himself as not knowing this continuously, as if he were one thing and the Self to be continuously known were something else, or into the one who does not know this deeply enough, as if he stood outside his own nature and did not comprehend it, the illusion swallows itself.

To say that an illusion ever occurred is as illusory as the illusion itself.

Q.: One cannot make up an illusion and then say that it was real at some point.

N.: If you did, you would not regard it as an illusion.

Q.: If it appears to start, I can find the spot from which it started, but, when I find that spot, I see that it did not start.

N.: For every illusion of whatever kind, you can trace its starting point to "I," as Sri Bhagavan pointed. If you inquire as to what the "I" is, there is no individual. There is not so much as even a dot. Even the abstract conception is not there.

Another Q.: When there is veiling of my inner experience, the inquiry does not happen or is not as penetrating. How can I resolve that?

N.: In what state do you wish to be?

Q.: The state of happiness and freedom all the time.

N.: Is there anything that obstructs the freedom or happiness?

Q.: The "tenth man" is always there, but sometimes he does not recognize it.

N.: What prevents the recognition? What obstructs it? What composes the veil?

Q.: If I don't persist in finding out who experiences this or does this, I react rather than inquire for whom this is.

N.: So, lack of inquiry means a veil, and, from the veil, there is the projection of all kinds of divisions and problems. If you inquire, divisions are swallowed, or burnt up, and the veil, also, is incinerated. Is this your experience?

Q.: Yes.

N.: So, what do you need to know?

Q.: I don't need to know anything. What I need to know is who I am.

N.: You need to know who you are, and you need to inquire consistently and deeply.

Q.: Yes.

N.: If you know this much, apply yourself. Be diligent and persevering.

(Silence)

Another Q.: I read a quotation from the Maharshi recently that says with untroubled mind to realize the Self. The "untroubled mind" bypasses the idea of personality in the moment of meditation. It is any misidentification that one might have with the small self. There is also something of a faith and trust.

N.: The quotation is from the third verse of the *Five Stanzas to Sri Arunachala, Arunachala Pancaratnam.* It says, "He who turns inward with untroubled mind to search where the consciousness of 'I' arises realizes the Self and rests in Thee, Oh Arunachala, like a river when it joins the ocean."

Untroubled mind is important. What is an untroubled mind? A mind that is not caught up in egotism becomes untroubled. Egotism is not only when one is haughty and arrogant. Egotism can manifest with the opposite attributes, such as thinking poorly about oneself and being depressed.

Such is all about one's so-called "self." A troubled mind is one that whirls around this egotism. An untroubled mind is one that is turned inward. An untroubled mind is one that is based upon something much more solid than egotism. It is based upon something absolute. This does not necessarily mean that one has realized the Absolute, for, otherwise, the rest of the verse would not follow, and it would not account for all of the verses together.

"Turned inward with untroubled mind." Does it not signify that, in turning inward, one knows where one's peace and happiness really lay? Why does someone turn inward? It is only if he or she knows that in this way lies peace and in this way lies happiness.

"Inward" also has a deeper connotation. What is truly inward is nonobjective. What is nonobjective is not a product of our body, senses, and thinking. Your thinking about things may be subtle but not inward. Inward is when you go beyond thinking about things. It is certainly beyond yours senses and activities.

When you know where happiness is to be found, that it is to be found within, and you intend to take an inward direction, you become detached from outer things, and, therefore, you are untroubled by them. Because the life is based upon that which is absolute, rather than whirling around in the narrow confines of the small bubble of egotism, it is untroubled and not tossed around by wild cravings, fears, and such.

Turning inward and having an untroubled, not-worldly, non-egotistical mind means the attempt to find that which is the within-ness itself. What lies at the core is "I." So, he says "to search where the consciousness of 'I' arises." That is the notion of "I." From where does it rise? When we find that out, the Self is realized. The "I" rises no more, and the mind ceases to exist. Its troubles are long-gone by then.

You may find it useful to read the entire set of the five verses to Arunachala. They are very profound.

Another Q.: I am having a good time meditating on the source and finding the place of happiness. Anytime there is the outward-going mind, it leads to mischief, which leads to suffering fairly quickly. When my mind goes outward to the "good stuff," (laughter) it really isn't that good. It is very dry out there.

N.: With the idea of "good stuff," what makes it good?

Q.: Somehow, the ultimate gathers happiness externally. I am not sure how it gets there.

N.: The belief that it is good comes from you, doesn't it?

Q.: Yes.

N.: Likewise, the happiness. So, is there anything that is "good"?

Q.: No. It comes from me. That takes me back to the source.

N.: Where all the good is.

Q.: (laughing) If my mind is rattling with some outward-going tendency, it is good to take it back to the source. The source is where all the thoughts and desires spring from.

N.: The stuff and the desire for the stuff spring from your mind, don't they? According to your state of mind, there are the objects and the desires or other kinds of relations with those objects. Where is your desire when you are in deep sleep?

Q.: The desire is gone, and it is not outward.

N.: But you are not unhappy.

Q.: Right. There is no drive to go outward.

N.: Why is there no drive to go outward?

Q.: There is no belief in an external reality or happiness.

N.: There is no belief in an external reality, so there is no outward. The happiness of your own nature is already present, so there is no desire. You do not take up the position of being the waking state experiencer or of being some kind of embodied being. Since that definition is not there, the objective definition of the world is not there. Since neither the subject nor the object is there, the relation between them, be it desire or otherwise, is not there. Yet, you are there, and your happiness is there, without anything else. Knowing this, in what kind of rattling can you engage?

Q.: (laughing). There is no rattling in the Self. There is nothing to rattle against.

N.: So, no snake, no rattle. (laughter)

Q.: (laughing) The things that make the rattling sound are the thoughts.

N.: If the snake, himself, has not been born, his rattles are not there, either. (laughter) Remain firm in the Knowledge of what you are, which is not awake, not dreaming, and not sleeping, and not missing anything, but which is just formless, space-like Consciousness. That is perfect and full always.

Q.: If I take myself to be an ego-entity, I have some state or can be in a state. From a state, everything else springs.

N.: Once you have a state, you appear as if within it as some sort of body or form, and you also appear in it as the objects of the world of that state. Then, there are endless modes of interaction. Yet, none of that is true about you.

Q.: So, I should question the one who has that state. In Friday's reading of the Maharshi's teachings, he negated the body and thoughts.

N.: And the "I."

Q.: Yes. I should continue to look for the source of the "I."

N.: If we look for the source of "I," we find that which is truly "I." Then, it is no longer a source, because nothing has come out of it. (Silence)

As long as the real Self seems to have lent its identity to something else, you should search for the source of the "I" within you. The way is subjective and not objective.

Q.: Yes.

N.: In Reality, your Being is not a source. A source is where there are two.

Q.: This is important. It is more obvious, for the rattling is two. If the rattling vaporizes, the mind clears up.

N.: With the destruction of ignorance, the attributes of delusion also vanish. The attributes of delusion are any kind of suffering, any feeling of limitation, and any kind of bondage. If you eliminate the ignorance, the attributes of the ignorance are gone. All that is necessary is for you to remain very steady in this certain Knowledge of who you are, and, since there are not two of you, steadiness should not be difficult.

Q.: That is interesting. It should not be difficult?

N.: How can there be a difficulty when there are not two of you?

Q.: It definitely seems easier here.

N.: Then, remain here always.

Q.: It is just the outward projection that ever makes it seem difficult.

N.: With no conception of difficulty, abandon the outward projection and the veiling of your own nature. Remain in the certain Knowledge of who you are. Who would project what where? (Silence)

(Then verses of the *Annapurna Upanishad* were recited in Sanskrit and English.)

(Silence)

Om Shanti Shanti Shanti Om

The Silence of Dakshinamurti

Satsang, January 8, 2006

(Silence)

Om Om Om

(Silence)

N.: Dakshinamurti is silent, eternally silent. Sri Bhagavan is identified with Dakshinamurti, especially by those who seek his instruction. He is silent, with an eternal Silence. What is the nature of this Silence?

(Silence)

It is unutterable by any word and inconceivable by any thought, but its nature is realized by those who know themselves. Knowing themselves, they abide in a state of Absolute Silence. It is the absolute, formless, unborn, immutable, undecaying, imperishable Reality. To realize That for yourself, inquire within yourself to know who you are.

As long as you regard the Absolute, the Reality, God, your True Self, as "this," it remains unknown. When the objectifying outlook is abandoned, it is known, for then you no longer mistake the unreal for the Real or the Real for the unreal. Rather, by such inquiry, in such Knowledge, you know the Real as it ever is, and you know that the unreal has never come to be.

If you do not know the Reality of your Self, you imagine yourself as if limited or bound, even though you are the unlimited, and you, yourself, are the very quintessence, or nature, of Liberation. If you do not know your nature, if you do not know the Bliss of your own Self, attachment appears. If you do not know your Consciousness, your own Being, misidentification appears.

Know the source of happiness and realize that it is your own true Being, and there is no attachment. Then, there is never anything wrong, and the great, silent Perfection is self-evident. If you cease to misidentify, that is, if you abandon imagined, false definitions regarding your nature, there is no bondage, no limitation, and nothing wrong at any time, in life or death. If you simply give up the misidentification with the body, and, thereby, transcend the false belief in an existent world, is there ever anything wrong?

The Maharshi declares that Silence is the state in which no "I" arises. This means that the very seed of ignorance, the starting point of all misidentification, the "I" notion, the belief or assumption of existing as an individual entity, does not rise. That is, it is not imagined. That is the Perfect Fullness. That is your true state, which is a state that is not waking, not dreaming, and not even sleeping. That is your true Being, which is not a body, not a mind, and not some ego-notion or belief in a separated individuality.

The same Dakshinamurti, with whom the Maharshi is identified, is referred to by Sankara and others as "Adi-Guru," "the first, original, or primordial Guru." That is the source of spiritual instruction. What is that source? Can the source be found in duality? If so, how would Nondual Truth emanate from it? If it is not in duality, it cannot be external to you, and it cannot be something gross or subtle. That source is identical with that in you by which the Truth is known, and Truth alone knows itself. Brahman alone knows Brahman. The Self alone knows the Self. No other can do so, because of the transcendent nature of the Self, its utter nonduality, and because nothing else has ever come to be. How could something that has never come to be know that which always is? How can that which always is not know or be itself?

Question within yourself, "Who am I?" and discern your real nature, your actual Existence. How could your Existence ever be other than what it is? Just know yourself as you are, and everything is alright.

(Silence)

Q.: I need to remove my attachment or mistaken perspective in order to regain the jewel that is always hanging there. The Grace of the Maharshi supports me. This morning, I had the experience of casting my burden on Him, the Lord of the universe. I was trying to figure out how I was going to manage some situations. "I" was still in the picture. I was an actor, rather than getting off the stage.

N.: Casting off one's burden signifies the elimination of the attachment and the misidentification. If you are truly disidentified and detached, you can even be thinking about or planning an activity, yet there is no bondage and no suffering. The only suffering is when you feel bound. The only bondage is when you have become confused regarding your nature. If you really cast off the burden, you can't take it back. That would be stealing. (laughter) It's not good to steal from God. (laughter)

You may recall the Maharshi's analogy portraying feeling the weight and burden of such attachment and misidentification, with all the manifestations of such in life, as equivalent to one of the carved figures on a tower of a temple that is carved so as to appear as if it is holding up the entire temple tower. Perhaps you saw it at Adi-Annamalai Temple. There, the figure is made to look as if it is holding up the entire tower, but, really, it is just a bas-relief carving. The foundation holds all of it up. It is farcical that the figure is thought to be holding it up. Likewise, it is farcical to think that you, as an ego, are in charge of all this.

Emphasis should be placed on the actual attainment of freedom from misidentification. We should not make a shallow interpretation of surrender as if it meant that you just do not think about the situation or experience a momentary calm or relief from emotion, even if that momentary calm would last for days or weeks. What is indicated is an utter dissolution of the ego and no confusion regarding the source of happiness. There is, then, no misidentification with the body and, consequently, no false idea of being a performer of action, even when your body is engaged in an activity.

Q.: That is a lot of meditation: to remove one's sense of doership, to remove one's body misidentification, and to stay attuned to the source of happiness. I know it is possible. The clear responsibility is to remain inward, to remain disidentified, and to continue my spiritual practice.

N.: If you take care of that for which you are spiritually responsible, which is Self-Realization, all other responsibilities are already included in that. Then, whatever those responsibilities are, they feel as light as a feather.

Another Q.: Meditating on the source of the teaching, I start with the idea that it is separate. As I meditate, it changes from a concept, or a teaching, until I am not separate from it.

N.: Go the other direction. Do not be concerned with "this." Be concerned with "I." What you are describing is good, but what I am describing is foolproof.

Whether the source of the teaching appears to be the same as you, differentiated from you, or both, set aside that idea, whatever the idea is. First, find your nature and see if you are a distinct entity.

What actually is the teaching, or the Truth, of Nonduality? When we speak of a teaching of Self-Knowledge, what actually is the teaching? It cannot be the words that one associates with it or that are used for purposes of communication. It must be something deeper. (Silence)

Q.: There is something that is there as an object that, at the moment, doesn't seem to go away.

N.: What do you mean by "there"?

Q.: There seems to be some place where I am not.

N.: How do you know about it?

Q.: Because I am here. So, there must be a there.

N.: What is it that knows about here and there?

Q.: Someone who is neither of those places but both of those places.

N.: Alright. So, do the concepts of "here" and "there" have any existence apart from the one who knows them?

Q.: No. They are inert.

N.: If the one who knows them is misidentified with the body, "here" and "there" are physical spaces. If he is misidentified with the mind, "here" and "there" represent mental distances, mental differentiation, or even time. Are you the body? Are you the mind?

Q.: Looking at the body and the mind, I am not sure what those things are, but, actually, I know what they are.

N.: You may know what they are. You may be in doubt about what they are. Of one thing, though, you are sure. You are sure that you are. The fact of your Existence is undeniable. It is not possible for you to experience otherwise. Even if you conceive otherwise, you still exist to know that conception.

Does the body or the mind exist apart from you? Do here and there exist apart from you? If they do not, do they exist at all?

Q.: The only thing that I can find that is actually there is existence. It does not actually change into a body. It doesn't get mixed up with it, unless I start to say that that is what I am.

N.: Does the Existence change? What changes cannot be real. What truly is always is just as it is.

Q.: How do I forget that?

N.: Remembrance and forgetting are considered conditions of the mind. Do you ever actually forget your Existence? Are there two of you, one to forget or remember the other?

Q.: No. My Existence never goes outside of itself, forgets itself, and then comes back to itself to remember itself.

N.: Is it divisible within itself?

Q.: No, I cannot divide something that doesn't have any form. I don't know where I would go to not exist or to put it into pieces.

N.: The different kinds of differences are not true for your Existence: differences of the same kind, differences of different kinds, and homogeneous but divided within itself. Such are not true of your Existence. If the Existence steadily abides in the Knowledge of itself, you, yourself, are the source of the teaching. The teaching, the source, and the one who knows it are entirely the same. (Silence)

Can you see that it is better to even have the idea that the source of the teaching is something great, even outside of yourself, and abandon the ego notion than to retain the ego notion yet somehow think that the source is inside you? This is so because "inside" would be only within an ego context. It would not really be within.

Q.: It would be within a mistake. I don't want to be there.

N.: Clear?

Q.: It is clear, but thoughts start to rise.

N.: Who knows them?

Q.: I know them. They are mine.

N.: Inquire into who are you. (Silence) When thoughts appear to rise, do they rise outside of you or within you?

Q.: At first they seem to rise outside, but I know that they are inside. No, they are still outside.

N.: "Outside" is another idea inside.

Q.: (laughing) Yes.

N.: How many thoughts have arisen, in this lifetime alone? In this waking state alone?

Q.: A lot.

N.: Has the Consciousness that knows the thoughts been depleted even in the least degree by the rise and destruction of all of those thoughts?

Q.: No.

N.: Has the nature of Consciousness changed at all?

Q.: No, it is not affected at all.

N.: Do any of those thoughts actually define Consciousness?

Q.: No, not really.

N.: What does not define does not confine. Abide steadily in the Knowledge that your nature is Consciousness alone, and then say if there is such a thing as "thought."

(Silence)

Another Q.: Since nothing can be known except by the presence of Consciousness, the clear abidance as Consciousness, ever present, ever changeless, uncreated and undying, is the clear solution to what appears to be still going on. It is entirely due to Consciousness, and that is my real nature. It is formless. It lifts everything, wherever it seems to be, into the realm of Consciousness.

N.: If it is unchanging and uncreated, even "all" is no longer "all." Just one Self alone remains.

Q.: Indeed.

N.: That is Peace.

Q.: Yes.

N.: That is Shanti. (ed. note: "Shanti" means peace and is also the name of the questioner)

Q.: Yes, thank you.

Another Q.: I am contemplating what veils Reality. When I objectify, actually Reality is never diminished. Even the objectification really is just myself. I have just objectified it somehow. Even the energy and power are the same.

N.: Yes, even the apparent existence and the power behind the illusion are only the Reality. Really, illusion means that which is not.

To explain how superimposition of the unreal upon the Real occurs, how misidentification occurs, we loosely speak of having an objective outlook, seeing yourself as an object, although you are obviously nonobjective in nature. That is said just by way of instruction. Have you ever become an object?

Q.: (laughing) It's not that I become a rock or this cushion.

N.: Or a body. (laughter)

Q.: (laughing) Or a rotting body. If I think I am this object or that it has some reality, I need to notice from where the reality comes. Does it ever come from the object, as if the object is the life itself or the circumference of the reality is that of the cushion? When I see that the reality comes from myself, the experience expands.

N.: If the sense of reality comes from yourself, and if the objects keep changing, being subject to rising up and being destroyed, that tells you about Reality and its unchanging, nonobjective nature.

Q.: Do you mean that it is the substratum?

N.: By "object" is meant everything, from the notion of "I" to the states of mind, such as waking, dreaming, and deep sleep, to all of their content, which is everything experienced such as the various modes of the mind, the body, and the senses. When you dream, do you become any of the dream content?

Q.: Never.

N.: Does the dream content exist apart from you? Has the dream ever come to actually be?

Q.: Has it come to be as something existing by itself on its own?

N.: Even a dependent existence.

Q.: Dependent on the Reality.

N.: On the substrate. Such things have no independent reality. What does not have an independent reality but depends entirely on something else is only that something else misperceived. The substrate misperceived is all this. "I" not known appears as "it." Between the dual poles of "I" and "this" is spread all illusion. "This" depends on "I." So, know the "I." How could there be a veil between yourself and your Self? If you regard yourself as a "this," you pretend as if there were two. If a rope appears as a snake, does the snake have a dependent existence?

Q.: Obviously, it can't.

N.: It doesn't have any existence at all, does it?

Q.: No.

N.: We can say that the snake is nothing but the rope, but that means that the rope alone is. We can say that all of this is Brahman, but that means that Brahman alone is. You can say that all of this experience is really your Self, but, in truth, just the Self, which is unchanging, alone is. What is this talk of "experience"?

Q.: For example, I went to a restaurant last night at which they served different kinds of food. It was a new experience. Once I meditated on the Reality, the substratum, the essence, which was really, the whole time, that Existence, the existence of those objects decreased. Before, they seemed more objective, as "there is food, and there are different types of food."

N.: (smiling) After you consume them, they became less objective? (laughter)

Q.: (laughing) No, no.

N.: They then became part of you? (laughter) Until much later, when they were no longer part of you. (laughter)

Q.: (laughing) As soon as it sank into me that the entirety of what was going on was really just the substratum, it wasn't some object, such as the food. It may have had the appearance of food. (laughter)

N.: Just as you seem to have an appearance of a body. (laughter)

Q.: Yes, just like that. The body takes the food and drops it down the hatch.

N.: When, in last night's dream, you became hungry, you probably did the same thing.

Q.: Yes, dream food.

N.: Dream bodies eat dream food. It is just a matter of which dream you appear to be in.

Q.: What do you mean?

N.: Whether it is a dreaming dream or a waking dream. They both have the same false appearance of a subject and an object, a form in which the subject appears to be, and an object apart from himself. Within each, there are subtle thoughts, gross perceptions, and objects including food, bodies, and such.

Q.: Yes, but there are the assumptions.

N.: Whichever dream you are in, you are always prepared to deny the reality of the other dreams.

Q.: Yes. Because that substrate is not recognized, which is what goes through all those states.

N.: That which is the substrate is actually all-pervading, all-encompassing, but utterly transcendent. What has happened to last night's dream food and restaurant? We can say that they have gone away, but they never actually came to be. It is similar in this state.

Q.: Once the substratum is noticed, they become unimportant.

N.: What is important is to identify with the substrate, to know that what is referred to as the "substrate" is you. You are not what appears while awake, while dreaming, or while in deep dreamless sleep.

Q.: Yes, that is clear. So, it is a matter of being one-pointed.

N.: What do you mean?

Q.: To be one-pointed on who I am and not to stop short in meditation.

N.: The best, true meditation is when the meditation is one-pointedly upon the nature of the meditator.

Another Q.: Yesterday I heard someone singing. The beauty of it impacted me and brought tears to my eyes. It may have been a dream person singing a dream song, but it definitely was an experience of bliss. What I understand from you is that I should trace that beauty back to the real beauty, which is the Self. Is that what you are saying?

N.: Whether we speak of beauty, truth, bliss, or satyam-sivam-sundaram—the true, the good, and the beautiful—all of these have only one source. The source is entirely real. When we know the source and know ourselves as that, we abide as that, knowing ourselves as inseparable from it. It is from this vantage point that we can speak of dismissing everything else as unreal.

(Then followed a recitation in Sanskrit and English of verses from the *Annapurna Upanishad.*)

(Silence)

Om Shanti Shanti Shanti Om

Absolute Silence

Satsang, January 29, 2006

(Silence)

Om Om Om

(Silence)

N.: In a verse, the Maharshi explains that when, even in ancient times, Dakshinamurti could reveal the Truth only in eloquent Silence, who else could convey it by speech? He has also explained that Silence is that state in which no "I" arises.

The Reality of your Being, which is formless and eternal, reveals itself to itself when no "I" arises, that is, when there is no falsely assumed individuality, or ego. Therefore, when you attempt to know the Absolute by knowing the Reality of your own Self, who is in search of what? When you inquire to know the Self, "Who am I?", the very nature of the inquirer is the only answer. It is something that cannot be perceived and is utterly inconceivable.

If you know yourself, you abide in That as That, which is perfect peace and also perfect happiness. If you know yourself, you abide as that which is utterly indivisible and as that which is unborn and, also, undying. If you know yourself, Brahman knows Brahman, the Absolute knows the vast Absolute. There is no second one involved.

The Maharshi reveals that there is no one to say, "I have realized the Self," or "I have not realized the Self." Both statements are absurd. Why does he say that they are absurd? Inquire into your nature, and the reason will become self-evident.

There are not two of you. This everyone knows. Everyone's existence feels singular, "I." Perceptions may be multiple, as well as unreal. Your thoughts may be multiple, as well as unreal. Your existence is singular. So singular is it that you cannot stand apart from it to either know it or to be ignorant of it. The assumption that you can exist apart from your actual Being, which is the Absolute, is what the Maharshi refers to as "I." The "I" notion is a bare assumption with no fact to it. Based upon this one notion, made of this one notion, is the entirety of ignorance, which is just further misidentification. With such ignorance, or misidentification, comes the idea, "I am what I think," instead of being the nature of Consciousness. Or, the idea is, "I am some form, such as the body," rather than the nature of pure Being. Or the idea is that happiness is elsewhere, and, thereby, one becomes attached, rather than knowing Bliss is identical with Being.

To do away with all of the imagined bondage, to uproot the very cause of suffering, you have only to know yourself. That which is naturally sought as Liberation by beings who feel bound is found to be innate. It is the very nature of one's own Self. All that you need do is to deeply inquire within yourself, "Who am I?" to verify this in your experience.

Make the manner of your approach nonobjective. Do not treat the Self as if it were an object apart from you and yourself as if you were an individual, for that would be using ignorance to try to overcome ignorance. Rather, turn within, abandon the objective outlook, and know who you are. By "the objective outlook," I mean the confusion of thinking of yourself as something objective, as someone with some quality or attribute, as someone with a mind or a body, or as some kind of individual. Then, that which is unborn, for which there is no creation, reveals itself as itself. That is your Self. For That, all is perfect always.

If you think, or feel, that such is not your experience, or not always your experience, inquire, "For whom is this conception? Whose experience is otherwise? Who is it that stands apart from God and pretends to be something separate, independently acting and existing?"

(Silence)

Silence is truly Being, and Being alone knows itself. There is no other to do so. Know yourself as Being, as that which you really are, and that which was sought to be realized is complete.

(Silence)

A verse from the *Dakshinamurti Dhyanam* that is often included as preliminary to Sankara's *Dakshinamurti Ashtakam* begins with the words, "Mauna-vyakhya-prakatita-parabrahma-tattvam," revealing the Truth of the Supreme Brahman by silent speech. Silent instruction is the meaning. How can you comprehend Silence? Where "I" is not, but I still am, as the real Self, just there Silence comprehends itself, timelessly.

(Silence)

Q.: In meditation during my trip (to Tiruvannamalai), I examined the sheaths. I sense more strongly that the body is only awareness. The senses are only awareness. So it is with prana, the breath, and with thoughts. Even this idea of a separate person is only awareness. It was so strong that hearing the traffic and the taxis beeping their horns, it seemed that it was just Brahman going down the road. It seemed very much as the right direction. I want to become very solid in this Self-Knowledge.

N.: In what way for you is the Knowledge of the Self lacking?

Q.: There are still leftover ideas.

N.: What ideas?

Q.: Ideas of separation.

N.: What constitutes the separation?

Q.: (laughing) The ideas of separation.

N.: So, it is not a real separation, but only an idea of it.

Q.: That is the only thing that I can find.

N.: An idea exists only in your mind. It is not reality. It is merely imagined. Within the mind is imagined all that you have mentioned, whether seen as one or as multiple, inclusive of the so-called outer world, the body, the prana, and the cognitions. If a rope is mistaken to be a snake, which is illusion, whether we say that all the parts of the snake are really the rope or the snake is really a rope, the emphasis is on the rope. The rope alone is there, and the snake and its parts are not there at all. The individual and the objective sphere of his experience are not truly existent. You may regard such as the Self merely misperceived, whether seen as one or multiple.

If it is just the Self misperceived, trace the source of the misperception. Someone seems to be as if unstable in Self-Knowledge. Who is that someone? (Silence)

Descriptions of the five sheaths, panca-kosa, are made in the course of spiritual instruction only to refine the discernment regarding oneself. The sheaths are not real entities. If contemplation upon them causes you to inquire, "For whom are these?" it is very worthwhile. If it causes you to disidentify from all that is not the Self, it is good.

Q.: Some teachers say that, in order to receive God's grace, one needs to be in a place of no resistance. How can I overcome the resistance and become non-resistant?

N.: For your experience, what constitutes the resistance?

Q.: Fear of destruction.

N.: You do not wish to cease to exist.

Q.: Right.

N.: Have you even known a time when you ceased to exist?

Q.: Yes.

N.: What was that experience?

Q.: It is hard to remember.

N.: Yes. In one sense, you ceased to exist, but you still existed, only not as what you thought you were before, which is how you can recall the experience now. So, in the true sense, your existence never ceases to be. As for a second, which is the abode of fear and what you are calling resistance, you need to find out how he has not yet come to be. If you find out how he has not really any existence, you will find yourself perpetually in a state of Grace. Indeed, God and God's Grace are always there. If it were otherwise, God would not be God, and Grace would not be Grace.

We can only loosely speak of receiving grace, as if it came from somewhere else. When the idea of individual, or ego, existence is abandoned, God, Grace, is found to be everywhere. That alone is the Self, the Existence that can never cease.

You resist for the same reason for which you wish to be absorbed. You do not wish to go out of existence. It is an intuition of your real state. You, in your real nature, can never go out of existence. Birth and death have been superimposed upon your Self only by your imagination. Examine this imagination. When you find it to be imagination and no longer regard it as real, bondage ceases then and there. When you cease to regard as true what is presently regarded as true, the Reality shines of its own accord. Simply eliminate the ignorance, the belief in the unreal being real. That will suffice, and you will find that all your resistance has vanished. (Silence)

Q.: Enlightenment seems rather analogous to resonance of vibrational frequencies. When one is tuning a particular guitar string, there is a frequency to which one tunes it. One becomes aware of the string that is not in tune, and one changes it in such a way that it is in tune. I use that analogy in my self-discovery. I try to become attuned to a frequency. Once the frequency is met, I can feel it, if only for a moment. The other side of the spectrum comes back, and I am back in my old, bad frequency.

N.: Using the analogy, what causes you to go out of attunement? Once you have the resonance, or attunement, perfectly matched, what causes you to go out?

Q.: I was out of awareness. It is the awareness of awareness.

N.: If that to which you are trying to attune yourself is That, the one Absolute, what is the attunement or definition of the other string, that you are trying to make sound the same as the first string or frequency? If there is That, what makes up "you" that you come to the conclusion that you are not That, rather than you are That?

Q.: Illusion gets in the way.

N.: What is the source of the illusion? How does the illusion arise? Find that out. When you find that out, the dual string or frequency theory will vanish.

If there is That and there is you, and the spiritual instruction of the wise since the time of the Vedas is Tat tvam asi, That you are, make the connection obvious to yourself, that you are That, by examining what you regard as you. That, the One Absolute, the eternal and the infinite, will take care of itself. You have to attend only to the "you." See what constitutes "you," so that you feel that you are not That, or that you are That at sometimes and not That at other times. What makes up "you"? Whatever is regarded as a definition, that is, the identity of you, manifests as what you experience of the illusion. It gives you the idea that there are different frequencies. Continue to examine "you," and illusion, being unreal, will vanish. Then, there will not be two, one to be in or out of attunement with another. (Silence)

Another Q.: I am working on destroying the vasana of desire for food. By "desire" I do not mean the body's need to refuel itself. It is attaching my happiness. It starts usually with a bodily sensation, not necessarily of hunger, but discomfort. There is an unpleasant bodily sensation, and I think that I can fix that with some food, so that, if I eat the food, I will be happy.

N.: If you eat the food, you change the sensation. What has that to do with happiness?

Q.: It does change the sensation, though, sometimes, the second sensation is actually worse than the first one. (laughter) There is the idea of eating something else or more of the same, and the condition becomes worse.

N.: Does that make you happy? (laughter)

Q.: I need to ask that question in the midst of that.

N.: What do you mean by "in the midst of that"?

Q.: In the midst of the habit playing itself out.

N.: Do you need to wait for an opportune moment in order to be free? Is liberation determined by outer circumstances, time, or activity? Does time, or a particular time, create the attachment?

Q.: No. It doesn't, nor does the repetition of it.

N.: So, neither repetition nor particular time creates the attachment. Why would you need a particular time or occurrence in time to bring about liberation from the attachment?

Q.: I was thinking that I had to wait for the right moment to get rid of it.

N.: Is that true?

Q.: No. What, then, do I need to do to get rid of it?

N.: What exactly is it that you are trying to get rid of?

Q.: I am trying to get rid of that habit of thinking that I can be happy by eating food.

N.: Of what is the attachment composed?

Q.: A misunderstanding of what happiness is or where it is located.

N.: If the misunderstanding is cleared up, so that you abide in and as the happiness, all of the time, what care would you have about food?

Q.: I wouldn't have any. Food would no longer be confused with happiness. It would just be food for the body.

N.: As Ribhu says, it is just more mud to patch up the body's walls of mud. Since you would not be depending upon it for your happiness, your relation to it would not be binding.

Q.: It is very apparent now to me where the binding comes from.

N.: If only the question, "Where is happiness?" is internally answered, you remain free from all attachment. You are indifferent to everything in this world. One who knows that there is no happiness in this world then finds that there is no reality in this world. When he ceases to think in terms of the world being real, he no longer misidentifies. He no longer posits his identity in the world. When happiness, reality, and identity have been returned to their origin, the Real Self, there is nothing missing. Then, Reality comprehends itself; the Self knows itself.

At that point, as blessed food, prasadam, which means 'grace," you have consumed the entire universe, along with the body. So, that is what is on the menu. (laughter)

Q.: (laughing) You may take my order. (laughter)

N.: On Friday evening, during meditation, you spoke in a dialogue. Do you recall it?

Q.: Yes, toward the end of it, you spoke about the source of happiness. You said that once that is known without question… (questioner lapses into quiet)

N.: Go back to your original experience. I am not asking you to dwell in memory. Go back to your experience. The question that was asked of you was, "Is there any more doubt regarding what Bliss is or where it is to be found?"

(Silence) The doubtless answer is a matter of internal experience. Examine what happened immediately afterward in the same dialogue. (Silence) Can you see what happened?

Q.: What happened next was my identity was without question.

N.: Was it really?

Q.: (after a long pause) If it really was, I probably would not be having this conversation today.

N.: In the Vedanta texts, there is reference to "paroksa" and "aparoksa," meaning "indirect" and, literally, "not-indirect." These refer to knowledge or experience. When such is indirect, the intellect has a grasp of it. There is some idea of it. Or, it may be considered direct but not steady. When it is truly aparoksa, direct experience, there is no one to deviate from it. If one's identity is doubtless, there is no one to carry the seed of illusion ever again. There is, then, no one bound, no one seeking liberation, no one striving for liberation, no one practicing, and no one liberated. It is, the final and highest Truth. (Silence).

If you had stayed put in the experiential understanding of what bliss is and where it is, which are not really two different things but are spoken of separately only for purposes of spiritual discrimination, what would have been the result?

Q.: (after a long pause). Hmm.

N.: Who knows?

Q.: I don't think that there would be any questions. In that experience, there is no one left to make any statements about anything.

N.: Yes. When you experientially have Knowledge, you do not stand apart from it. Everything concerning Self-Knowledge, Advaita Vedanta, is to be known directly. It is not important to know about it. You must know it and know it as yourself. One drop of experiential, inner, true

Knowledge is worth more than an entire ocean of knowing about it as if you were studying it as a topic. The thought of it is never it. Hence, Silence.

The thought of "bliss" is obviously not Bliss. Bliss is, with or without the thought of it, just as Being is, with or without the thought of it. Likewise, Consciousness shines, with or without the thought of it. The "thought knowledge" is irrelevant. The thought-knowledge of the doubtless state is not the real Knowledge that is doubtless.

If it is really doubtless—nirvikalpa, without doubt—it is nirvikalpa, without differentiation. When the Knowledge of That is steady due to an absence of ego, it is Sahaja, innate, natural. It is not possible to separate yourself from that which is innate.

Do you see the manner of approach that is being pointed out? The same applies to meditation, spiritual instruction, satsang, reading holy texts, and anything else of a spiritual nature.

Q.: If I understand the importance of direct knowledge, to know it as myself is the only thing that is really important.

N.: Since you already know that the end manifests as the means, the Knowledge manifests as the inquiry, the approach to the inquiry should be of the identical quality or character as the end. The real should be all through, for, as the Maharshi says in *Saddarsanam*, "Duality in practice and Nonduality in the end is not good—not holy—advice."

Another Q.: To know directly, and not in the mind, is very important. You say that the Existence is rock-solid and is what is. You also mentioned that the world-illusion will not be present once one knows That firmly and as rock-solid. The meditation Friday night wasn't permanent, so the world-illusion crept in.

N.: Is the world-illusion permanent?

Q.: No, not at all. (laughing)

N.: Then, what is permanent?

Q.: The world-illusion does not really hold up that well.

N.: What is permanent?

Q.: The essence of the meditation is permanent. There is a certain intrinsic awareness of what is real and what is not real.

N.: Is the essence of meditation apart from the meditator?

Q.: What is apart from the meditator is the thought-form that says it will focus on here.

N.: Is that what meditation is?

Q.: Not really. (laughing)

N.: What is it really?

Q.: When I sit to meditate, there is a lot of stuff there.

N.: Where?

Q.: In the mind and connected with what is real as a combination. There are thoughts.

N.: There is Reality and what is in the mind?

Q.: Yes. There are hunks of thoughts. Some of them are "let's turn the mind inward and focus on the Awareness."

N.: What is your mind?

Q.: It is like a galaxy with these thoughts floating in it.

N.: If the thoughts float in your mind, what is the mind? If it is like a galaxy, what is the space?

Q.: If thoughts were like the stars in the galaxies, such would be such an infinitesimal part of it that the space in it would be overwhelming.

N.: What is the space?

Q.: (after a pause). The space is not a void, or empty. Maybe it is full. I don't know. Words don't describe that space.

N.: Something ineffable and formless that holds everything yet holds nothing. Is that the essence of meditation?

Q.: Yes.

N.: Is that apart from the nature of the meditator?

Q.: I think of myself as somebody who is sitting there and meditating.

N.: Is that what you are? Whatever you are, you permanently are. You do not change your nature. Is a sitting body what you are?

Q.: No. It is what I imagine myself to be.

N.: Who imagines?

Q.: There is no one and nothing to speak of. It is presumed that I am imagining.

N.: Do Reality and imagination mix? Or is the case as the *Gita* says: "The Real ever is and the unreal has never come to be"?

Q.: (after a long pause) Do they mix? No.

N.: Does the mirage water ever wet the ground?

Q.: No, it cannot touch that Existence. It does not have the ability to touch it.

N.: There is no association between the Real and the unreal. Not only is the Reality of your own Self immutable and utterly unaffected, but there is no second thing to affect it.

Examine what you were previously calling "the mind" or "thought" in the light of this.

Q.: I thought that it was definitely an entity and had individuality.

N.: Is there something called "thought"? Is there one who becomes entangled in it?

Q.: I don't know; maybe not. I don't know.

N.: (Silent for a while) Your not-knowing now is knowing much more than when you thought you knew.

Q.: Because it is not based upon something conceptual.

N.: An absence of false concepts of erroneous definitions is very much in keeping with the Truth.

(Then followed a recitation in Sanskrit and English of verses from the *Annapurna Upanishad.*)

(Silence)

Om Shanti Shanti Shanti Om

Determination of the Self

Satsang, February 5, 2006

(Silence)

Om Om Om

(Silence)

N.: Your true nature is determined only by your own nature. Nothing else determines the nature of your Self, Being-Consciousness-Bliss. Nothing other than your nature of Bliss determines your happiness. Nothing else other than this Consciousness determines real Knowledge. Nothing other than Being determines what is real. The senses do not determine this. Activities do not determine this. States and conditions of the body do not determine this. Your thoughts do not determine this. Mental attention, placed here or there, does not determine this. Mental states and modes of mind do not determine this. Time, place, and sensations of any kind do not determine this.

The Reality is not determined by the unreal, even to the slightest degree. Your Self, being the Reality, is not determined, in any way whatsoever, by any of the non-Self, the unreal. It is not determined by such in terms of definition and in terms of actual knowledge.

The identity of your Self remains forever unalterable. The only one who can know this unalterable nature is the unalterable nature itself. Only Consciousness knows Consciousness. That which is not Consciousness cannot do so.

Only Absolute Being, Brahman, which is your Self, knows itself. No one and nothing else can do so. When you inquire to know your Self, such is the Light of your own Consciousness illumining itself; it is self-luminous. Nothing else is involved. Because nothing else is involved, it is non-dual from start to finish. Because nothing else is involved, because there is no second, there cannot actually be any obstacle to the inquiry and its fruit of real Knowledge.

If, at any time, you seem as if bound, limited in any respect, or seem to have broken off from the absolute, perfectly peaceful Reality, and experience something else, know that the something else is dependent upon this definition of having broken off, of assumed individuality, and inquire as to who you are. Then, the ego, or individuality, being entirely unreal, will vanish. Thus, your Self knows your Self.

If the truth of just this much is traced within yourself, that nothing else defines yourself but yourself, that will suffice.

(Silence).

Q.: In the light of Friday's instruction and the mention of "trifling joy," I see that each vasana is only the attempt to be happy. I understand now that, to feel discontent or to seek happiness or to express the next vasana, I must first be not standing as who I am. I am not standing as the Bliss that is my Being. A thousand times you have instructed to look for the source of happiness, and I see that the bliss stimulates the vasanas. This makes it easier to look inside rather than outside for that which is real and doesn't need anything added to it.

N.: The motion of all the tendencies or vasanas is for the sake of your own Being, which is Bliss. Each time a tendency arises, you can inquire as to the real nature of Bliss, the real nature of Being, and, thereby, that which initially appeared to be some kind of obstacle or bondage merely points you to your real nature, which is Liberation. The vasana is dissolved.

In the midst of what is referred to in *Svatmanirupanam* as "fickle joy," and which you this morning called "trifling joy," there is actually one infinite, timeless joy that shines through that very experience. Through the limitations of misidentification, manifesting outwardly as attachment, it appears fickle and trifling, losing its infinity, its eternity, and its steadiness. Remove the limitations that adhere through delusion regarding your nature. Then, Bliss is no longer defined. We may say that then Bliss defines itself, which means that it is unconfined.

The intuitive search for your Self is the motivation of the vasanas, primarily through the form of seeking happiness. If you know the source of happiness and, inquiring, you know who you are, the very motivation to create such tendencies is cut.

The Maharshi teaches that the destruction of vasanas is imperative for Self-Realization. In the destruction of a vasana, be sure that it is destroyed from beginning to end, from top to bottom. Be very deep and be very thorough. The general rule for the examination of such should be that no vasana is too small to be overlooked in your inquiry, and no vasana is so big that you cannot get over it.

Another Q.: I have this feeling of, "What about me?" and that I need to keep this thing going. What follows is a body and a world that I now struggle in, trying to be happy. It appears to be an idea that I need to keep this going.

N.: What precisely are you keeping going?

Q.: I am not sure what it is that is going, because it doesn't have much to it if I examine what I am keeping going.

N.: What is your experience of the "it" that you are trying to keep going?

Q.: It is "I" that I am trying to keep going.

N.: Something can be kept going only if it started to begin with. See if you have been born. (Silence)
That a person perpetuates an ego because he wrongly identifies the ego-sense with himself and he intuitively desires continuous existence is sufficiently clear. Inquire directly into what it is that has started or if it has started. That is, what exactly is this "I"- sense?

Q.: If I try to hold the "I" that is separate, it keeps moving ahead until it is not there anymore. Is that "me" born? When the vasana starts to form, I think that it is I.

N.: How does it start to form? If the particular vasana or tendency being described is the sense of "I," or ego, how does it form?

Q.: If I look at the point where it starts, it's not there. I can remember the idea of an "I," or a personality. If I proceed to "Where did that start from?" it is like running up to a mirage. At a distance, it appears as if there.

N.: Alright. In this case, the mirage is both the subject and the object of the search. If you have seen that there is no such thing answering to the name of "I," how can there be any recurrence later? If you have not seen it deeply enough, who has not seen this deeply enough?

Q.: The one who has not seen it deeply enough is the one who is not really there.

N.: If he is not really there, then, as the Maharshi says in a verse, 'The thought 'I saw' did not arise, so how could the thought "I did not see'?"

Q.: Could you say that again, please?

N.: It means that both knowledge and ignorance, conceived as a duality, do not exist. "I see that I am not there." "I don't see that I am not there." Both statements are fallacious.

Who is there to see or not see when all that exists is the one Self? The inquiry reveals that.

Q.: One needs to ask who is not there. Who is it and where is there?

N.: That is why I asked you, "How did it start or what started?"

Q.: My experience is that nothing started.

N.: If nothing ever started, how can there be recurrence of that which never started?

Q.: (laughter) It clearly doesn't start. Is the question, "How could there be a memory that it started?"

N.: A memory of something that did not happen? If you say that it starts again, how can there be a recurrence of something that did not exist to begin with?

Q.: I need to ask what I think is actually occurring.

N.: Yes, and if all the occurrences are only the "I" in the guise of the occurrences, you, yourself, manifest as everything. Then, who are you?

Another Q.: To destroy tendencies from top to bottom, isn't that giving them too much attention and feeding them? Is it not enough to say, "I am not going there" and go within?

N.: If there is no reappearance of the vasana, or tendency, it is sufficient. The idea that we would strengthen ignorance by the examination of it is worthwhile to examine.

Q.: Yes. I see.

N.: If we bring light to illumine a dark corner or space, the light does not become darkened by the darkness. Rather, the darkness becomes illumined, or simply vanishes, for the darkness is merely the absence of light. Likewise, if we examine a tendency and find that it is not our happiness and that it is not who we are, we have not strengthened it. We have destroyed it. We destroyed it because it is destructible. Destructibility is the characteristic of the unreal. So, in one sense, we have destroyed nothing, but, in another sense, the destruction of the very causes, or seeds, of sorrow and bondage is brought about. They are dissolved.

If we do not examine and do not inquire thoroughly, we must be very sure that we do not continue living in that which we have not examined.

Q.: So, the examination does not strengthen ignorance.

N.: If it is thorough and deep, there is knowledge. Aside from knowledge, how to get rid of ignorance?

Q.: Yes, I see.

Another Q.: There is a feeling that arises when I say "I." It is a physical sensation, and I think that we are supposed to latch on to that physical sensation and feel that "I" thought. Then, everything goes away. Then, I become distracted when some thought comes. I return to the feeling of the "I" thought. There is quiet as long as I can hold to that "I" thought, but there is nothing purposeful about it. Random thoughts and emotions come up constantly. The idea that I could examine a vasana from top to bottom is just not clear for me. Either there is almost nothing or there is emotion or random thoughts. There is no purposeful or intentional examination of the vasanas occurring for me. Am I doing it incorrectly?

N.: Latching on to a physical sensation means directing your mental attention to that physical sensation. Whenever you give your mental attention in a concentrated fashion to one object, which could be a sensation or another gross or abstract object, other thoughts tend to recede or subside.

Q.: Yes.

N.: Consequently, because there is not the flurry of thoughts, you enjoy a certain degree of calmness. It is also observable that this state of calm does not endure. It is not eternal.

Q.: It is not.

N.: You know that what you search for, Self-Realization, cannot be an object, including this sensation. The purpose of one's inquiry should not be to latch on to any objective sensation, but to actually know oneself. You also know from your experience that, since attention flits about and can become concentrated, diffused, etc., whatever the substance of this Knowledge is, it should not be mistaken for mental attention. Mental attention is not an adequate instrument for knowing yourself. So, you will want to step entirely beyond that context if you desire real Knowledge.

You say that you have thoughts that seem, at first glance, to be random. Yet, you may also recognize that they are not so random. They do have patterns to them. Only the thought that they are random is random, (laughter) and even that idea may not be so random.

You say that emotions are constantly bubbling up. What is the cause of all those emotions? Trace the thoughts that constitute those emotions. Find out the misidentifications that are at the root of them. If we cut the vasana from top to bottom, such means that we cut the misidentification. We cease to take ourselves to be something that we are not. The entirety of everything that trails out from the misidentification, from the way of thinking to the particular modes of mind and thoughts, to what you call your "emotions"—which are thoughts given undue emphasis—and the repetitions of the same, collapses, dissolves, and does not return. That is freedom.

Q.: If I stay with the feeling of this "I" thought, there is an opening that happens. An expansion occurs inside.

N.: Is it a physical expansion or is it something else?

Q.: I think that it is my mind. It is a tight thing, like a sphincter, that opens. When reading *Self-Enquiry*, I got the impression that I am supposed to stay with the feeling of the "I."

N.: You are, but "the feeling of 'I'" refers to your sense of existence and not to a physical sensation. "Feeling" is said for lack of better words. It means that it is not a concept, mental form of any kind, or a thought. It is not a sense perception of any kind, such as seeing, hearing, touching, etc., whether such appear as manifestly gross to your senses or as some subtle sensation in the subtle body. You are to get beyond everything that is gross, subtle, and causal and really know yourself. To feel or hold on to the "I" means to inquire in relation to all that you are describing, "For whom are they?" There is a sense, not a sensation, of existing, of "I." Dwell upon that.

Q.: This is so confusing. When one reads enough of *Talks*, there are passages that deal with sensations on the right side. They are equivocal about it, but they say that it is an important experience because that is where the sense of the Self arises from, though they are incorrect.

N.: There are dialogues that describe the "I," "the Self," and "the Heart," that predominate in the book, *Talks with Sri Ramana Maharshi*, that speak of such as timeless, locationless, and absolutely bodiless.

Q.: Yes.

N.: There are other dialogues, which are relatively few in number, often in relation to *Ramana Gita* that deal with particular sensations that are subtle, and not physical or gross. They are very explicit about not referring to a physical heart, physical body, and such. They pertain to yogic lore pertinent to those who practice yoga and have subtle experiences. They endow those experiences with the wisdom that rightly belongs to Jnana, or Knowledge. Indeed, the entire *Ramana Gita* is fairly clearly divided between those verses that pertain to yoga and those verses that pertain to Jnana. For those with an interest in yoga, the Maharshi is the supreme yogi and can answer all their questions. For those who want to know the final culmination of yoga, he has said that yoga, or union, culminates in the Realization of the Self. For those who, then, want to know the Self, all the teachings of Jnana, which include Atma-vicara or Self-inquiry, Self-Knowledge, and the vast abundance of his spiritual instructions, were given.

If you have a sensation or an experience in any location, such is not the end. You must still further inquire, "For whom is this? Who am I?" If, in the experience of that sensation, you have been lifted entirely beyond the gross body and the world, it is very beneficial, but it is not the end point. If you find your mind feeling more expansive, by any means, it is beneficial, and there is no criticism of such, but you should not stop short with that. Similarly, you should not stop short with temporary calm, but find the permanent, eternal source of peace and find your Self to be That.

To accomplish this requires a deep inquiry, or examination, as to who you are, which is necessarily a negation of every false definition. When false definitions are repeated, they are called tendencies or vasanas. First there is the ignorance, and then there is the adherence to, or repetition of, it. Sankara has pointed out that the two constitute the denseness of maya, or illusion. So, we destroy the tendencies and we find out who we are in one motion of inquiry. We are thorough, and we are deep. Does this clarify the matter for you?

Q.: Yes, it does. There is something I need to do about being affected by upsurges of emotion, so that they are something about which I can inquire.

N.: If you abandon the attribution of your emotions to outer causes, such as circumstances and other people—the idea that they make you feel that way—and realize that the emotions are self-conjured, you will find yourself in a better position to examine and inquire. See which thoughts you think that, being repeated, are called "a feeling" or "an emotion." Once you have seen those thoughts, without attributing them to outer causes, focusing on what is the apparently inner thought, rather than the outer object of the thought, not justifying your thought, but with the recognition that you are responsible for your own state of mind, and are stable in that recognition, you will be able to see which of these repeating thoughts give the substance or "body" to this emotion. Then, inquire regarding what definitions of yourself are at play so that you think the way that you think.

Examine not only your thoughts, but why you think the way that you think. This always boils down to an inquiry as to who you are. Your sense of identity determines the entire pattern. Then, inquire within yourself, "Who am I?"

Q.: That is where a vasana could really meet its end?

N.: By examination in this manner, from top to bottom, from its gross manifestations to the repetitive thoughts or feelings, from the seed idea of the vasanas to the very misidentification that starts all of this, all of that dissolves.

Q.: That is tracing it out?

N.: That is tracing inward, more and more subjectively. It is not tracing in the body or subtle body. It is tracing subjectively and tracking down the "I."

Q.: I see that this state of identity is the fundamental foundation.

N.: When you destroy the vasana, your Existence, which is the residuum of real Being that is untouched by any of this, stands radiantly clear. The more radiantly clear this is for you, the easier it is to see these incongruous vasanas, or tendencies, as blatant cases of the shadows of delusion.

Another Q.: Earlier in life, my interest in love, my preoccupations, other interests, and such came from a recognition of my identity. My longing for the Truth has the same qualities, only more so. The real part of it does not have obstacles and is not supported by a sequence of thoughts. It is the recognition of what is worth caring about. I am looking at this to dispel the idea that there are any obstacles or that there is anything else so attractive that it would hold me back. It seems that it will wither with recognition.

N.: Yes, you adhere to something only because you want to do so.

Q.: So, I am confusing my identity.

N.: There is no glue to cause you to adhere to illusion against your will.

Q.: I can look at that both ways. The attraction to the Truth and the necessary lack of attraction to the false come from, not thought, but recognition.

N.: You naturally adhere to whatever you regard as true. What you regard as false, without any further effort to abandon it, is of no interest and of no consequence to you. So, in this deep sense, you have always sought what is true, during this entire life and before.

Q.: It is a shift to a new recognition in each case.

N.: You may be able to spot when the particular thought that put truth in that form for you began, but the yearning for Truth does not have a beginning point. It could be said that you have yearned for Truth since before there was time.

What is Truth? Since the Truth must be of the very nature of your existence, for, otherwise, it would be nonexistent truth, what is important is to know yourself. All of this, for however far back you can remember, has been an attempt to know yourself.

If you inquire to know yourself, you find that you are not the one who has been looking for the Truth as if you were apart from it or deficient in it, but you are the very space in which all of the search for Truth occurs. The search for Truth occurs nowhere but in the Truth itself. You cannot, in truth, step outside the Truth or separate yourself from it.

If you pretend to be an "I," a mind, and a body, it seems otherwise. Abandon misidentification by clear Knowledge, and you, yourself, are that for which you were seeking. All of the searching occurs only within yourself, which is never apart from the space of Truth, or the substrate. (Silence)

Q.: (with anjali, offering salutation with his hands) Thank you.

Another Q.: When I am busy, I do not like to be interrupted. It seems that this always happens. (laughter) It seems…

N.: Why don't you like to get interrupted? I don't mean to interrupt you right now. (laughter)

Q.: (laughing) I have a train of thought that is diverted.

N.: Alright. What is unpleasant about this?

Q.: The other person wants me to give time right then, and I am already on a telephone call.

N.: How does the bondage or unhappiness arise? If you become aggravated, such is because you feel that, in some way, it robs you of happiness. In what way does it rob your happiness? You may cite examples of this happening, but what is the reason for this loss of happiness?

Q.: I am so short because I think that my happiness depends upon whatever else is going on. It detracts from finishing what I am doing or prevents me from finishing it.

N.: Is there happiness only when you are done with the particular endeavor, or can you be happy all along?

Q.: I have a long list of "to do" things. The list does not seem to become any shorter.

N.: Yes, it is in the very character of manifest life that there is always something more to do. (laughter)

Q.: That I can't be happy until this is done is a ridiculous idea.

N.: After all, your Existence is still fully present and perfectly full. This is so the entire time, and it does not depend on a particular activity reaching its fruition.

Q.: I have this idea that I can't be happy until the action is done.

N.: Do you believe that?

Q.: (after a short pause) No, not really. (laughter) I pretend. (laughing)

N.: Become confirmed in your disbelief. (laughter)

Q.: Yes, it is foolish and a waste of energy.

N.: If you do not rob yourself of your own happiness, will the interruption, by whatever creature, be annoying?

Q.: (laughing) It could be any creature.

N.: This does not preclude you from telling someone that you cannot deal with him right now, for you need to attend to something, and that you will attend to him later. Thus, this does not necessarily determine your action, but it does determine your inner experience.

Q.: Yes, that is clear. I am no longer limiting the experience of myself to the completion of some task. If that is there during the activity, it doesn't matter if I am interrupted or not.

N.: All things, both those that are done and those that yet need to be done, depend on you. You don't depend on them.

Another Q.: In the destruction of a vasana, what is the acid test to prove that one is, in fact, thorough?

N.: Your own experience.

Q.: Sometimes, I feel that my inquiry may be shallow or superficial.

N.: If you have that perception, make your inquiry deeper.

Q.: Sometimes, I accept a mental image of release rather than the actual release, out of laziness or lack of concentration.

N.: Can you please explain more what you mean by "accept"?

Q.: I am too mechanical in the questioning and do not go deep enough.

N.: Do you find that satisfactory?

Q.: No.

N.: There, your natural discrimination is at work.

Q.: (laughs) So, don't accept anything except that.

N.: You can't accept it. There is only one thing that is agreeable for all. There is only one thing that is completely agreeable for you.

Q.: The true experience.

N.: You won't be satisfied with anything less.

Q.: As you have said, one should do whatever it takes to engender that deep experience.

N.: If you need to practice more deeply, practice more deeply. Practice is joy. If you need to practice more continuously, inquire more continuously. Continuous inquiry reveals blissful Knowledge. If you merely mechanically repeat some thought, you already know that does not work. It is not satisfactory. When you consider that the deeper approach is always available for you, there is no reason to resort to such mechanical thinking.

Another Q.: God, Self, or Guru reveals itself in a wondrous way. Consciousness is awakening to Consciousness. In some ways, it seems mysterious, yet, in other ways, it seems very natural. In my heart, I experience a rekindling of love for God, devotion to the Truth, and devotion to the Guru. Different spiritual activities hold a wonderful treasure that was unexpected. This unlocks and reveals that which is there.

N.: Did not Sri Bhagavan say that bhakti, devotion, is the mother of jnana, knowledge? (Silence)

Another Q.: When I mix knowledge with something else, it is harder to hold. When it is clear, my mind easily goes to it. I remember the teaching and see that there is no sense in letting my mind go toward any smaller thing. At other times, it seems more difficult.

N.: Why does it seem more difficult? What is the difficulty?

Q.: I need to eliminate the larger vasanas. The smaller ones are just distractions and do not carry much attachment. I was more physically exhausted, and it was more difficult.

N.: Because?

Q.: I don't know.

N.: How does physical exhaustion relate to blissful Being?

Q.: It doesn't. There is no relationship.

N.: Then, how does mental attention relate to blissful Being?

Q.: That doesn't either. I think that it is nice to be focused on what is real.

N.: When you focus on what is real, what actually occurs? Is it that you just think about what is real?

Q.: Oh no. That would be no good.

N.: So, what we are referring to as "focus" is much deeper and non-mental in character. It is something that shines even upon mental attention and is not dependent on it. Can you see this?

Q.: Yes.

N.: Whatever the state or condition of the body or mind, such does nothing in terms of determining your Being or your Bliss.

Q.: It is determined by whatever vasanas I hold on to at the time.

N.: Whose vasanas are they?

Q.: I am the vasana storage tank. (laughter) They come from me.

N.: Are you a vasana?

Q.: No. (laughing). I am definitely not a vasana.

N.: If you are not a vasana, are the vasanas your attributes?

Q.: I never thought of them in that way. They are attributed to me.

N.: Who is doing the attribution?

Q.: Not the Self! (laughter)

N.: If it is not you, if it is other than your nature, how could it be your attribute? If it is not your attribute, who are you?

Q.: I am a little confused. The trouble with vasanas is that one thinks that they are part of him.

N.: Do you?

Q.: Well, not now. (laughter) That's the difficulty with them.

N.: Are they difficult for you now?

Q.: No, not really.

N.: Yes, not really, because you are not that, and that is not your attribute. Are you planning to make them your attribute later? (laughter)

Q.: (laughing) I was preparing for that, but that is probably not a wise decision. When the Truth shines, it is clear. That is everything. That is so important.

N.: For how long is the Truth shining?

Q.: During the vasana, it seems as if it is not shining. Whenever I see through a vasana, I find that it is shining.

N.: Does it start to shine or is it shining all the time?

Q.: It did not just arrive.

N.: The shining Truth of the Self has always been and always will be. It does not start. It is. Abide in the continuous Knowledge of who you are. If you think that you have a tendency, or vasana, find out whose it is.

Q.: So, that is the first step. You said to take down the vasana from top to bottom.

N.: Yes, but I am showing you something that shines without top and without bottom. (Silence).

(Then followed a recitation in Sanskrit and English of verses from the *Annapurna Upanishad*.)

(Silence)

Om Shanti Shanti Shanti Om

Identity

Satsang, May 7, 2006

(Silence)

Om Om Om

(Silence)

N.: What we are, the Self, is Absolute Being. Being is Consciousness, and Being is Bliss. Its nature is Truth, its nature is Knowledge, and it is infinite. It is One only, invariable, and it is That which alone is.

Ignorance, which has no existence apart from the Self, for the Self is only One, appears to cast a veil over the single truth of the Self. When there is the veil, there is the projection of the unreal, which is characterized by multiplicity. To remove the delusion and, thereby, eliminate all duality and thus abide in the fullness and perfection of the Bliss of the Self, Sri Bhagavan gives the instruction to inquire, "Who am I?"

Why "Who am I?"? It is because what you regard as your identity is of paramount importance. Although the inquiry "Who am I?" can be used for a variety of goals, such as the submergence or removal of thought, the withdrawal of the senses from their objects, and such, the inquiry is of paramount importance because it deals with your identity.

What we regard as our identity goes into the composition of how we regard anything, even the view that there is anything to be regarded. The identity is the key, and the inquiry "Who am I?" is the introspective search to know your identity as it is. It is a nonobjective method because your identity, the Truth of the Self, is nonobjective. What you are can never be a known object or an unknown object. It cannot be an object, whether that object is gross or subtle, something sensed or something conceived.

Therefore, when you inquire to know the Self, you must actually inquire to know the Self and not be preoccupied with other nonexistent things. Plunge inward to know what your actual Being is. The negation of "not this, not this (neti, neti)," as stated in the Upanishads, is also for the purpose of revealing what your actual Existence, or identity, is. Loosely we speak of "becoming That" by virtue of such inquiry or meditation, but really this is not a becoming of anything. It is the Realization through Knowledge of that which is unborn, ever attained, and, when known in its own innate Knowledge, ever revealed.

It is the clarification of one's own identity, which is the essence of Knowledge, that is the real fruit of any spiritual practice. It is that with which Self-Knowledge and the path of inquiry deal exclusively. Let us consider the case of devotion. What happens? First, the identity in relation to objects is dissolved. The attachment to things is dissolved. Then, the fruits of one's actions, to the degree that they pertain to oneself, are lost or surrendered. Then, in such devotion, the idea of being the performer of action is lost. Clearly you can see the dissolution of false identity in this. Then, the very idea of life in the body, the senses, and being the enjoyer or the one who maneuvers the senses is dissolved or relinquished. Then, being the mind and the buddhi, which decides where the mind moves, is surrendered. Finally, the very notion of individuality, of existing distinct from God in any way, is abandoned. It is the same dissolution of false identity.

When we inquire "Who am I?", we dive directly into what is our identity and relinquish what is not our identity. This is the discrimination between the Self and the not-Self.

If you deeply consider whatever you regard as an obstruction, obstacle, chasm, or barrier between you and Self-Realization, you will see that it is not so much the thing, the thought, or the pattern of thought that seems to be between you and the Truth, but rather the identity, however formed and by whatever qualities characterized, of the "you" that is apart from the Self that has this wall or obstruction. Do you see what is being pointed out? To remove or hop over the wall or obstruction, you have only to inquire as to who is, what makes up the identity of, the one who is apparently bound, separated, or divided from the Truth.

The Realization of Truth is nondual. How can your experience be nondual, unless there is the utter elimination of the assumption, the false supposition, of existing as an individual entity? The Maharshi says in *Saddarsanam,* unless there is the elimination of that "I," how will the Truth be known?

The Truth alone can know the Truth. Consciousness alone can realize Consciousness. Another cannot do so. In nondual Truth, that which is realized and the realizer are identical. This means that they are one and the same thing and not two things of equal quality.

As long as the individual is taken to be real, how can there be this Realization? If one inquires, "Who is this that is styled as 'I'?", how could there be a state of non-Realization?

There are never two "I's." Instruction along the lines of a "higher Self and a lower self," "a self and the Supreme Self," "an ego self and the True Self," are for purposes of aiding the aspirant to Realization and are not statements of concrete fact. What is true is that the Existence, or real Being of the Self, is always One and can never be divided. Duality, even the slight idea of "I and That," is composed of mere illusion. It is delusion, only imagination. The cessation of such imagination is Knowledge.

(Silence)

Determine your identity. You will find yourself bodiless, without a mind, without senses, without prana, without beginning, without end, and without any thing or quality whatsoever, but perfectly full as ever-unchanging Existence.

Q.: Still, I hold the idea that the world is real. That means I still hold myself to be an individual. My discrimination as to what is real continues along with the inquiry. I am reading the commentary on Sankara's *Crest Jewel of Discrimination*. It is clear that the body, mind, and sense of identity depend on Consciousness. Consciousness does not depend on any of them. So, what is needed is not more discrimination but more inquiry.

N.: Let your discrimination and inquiry become identical. The Self is not a particular thing; it is the Existence. The existence of another is a notion based upon some attribute or characteristic regarded as your identity. When you discern your identity, you truly discriminate between what is real and what is not.

Rather than try to decide if the world is real or unreal, you can directly inquire, "Who is it that sees the world?" If the idea that there is a world still remains, you need to further inquire as to who sees the world. The seen is always the same as the seer. At the moments that you think that there is a world, what do you take yourself to be? You do not continuously think that there is a world. Consider deep sleep. Sometimes, in the waking state, you say that there is a world. What composes the so-called perception? Really, it is only a conception. What goes into the make of it? Something must be regarded as you before you say that it is. Discern this. Apply discrimination to this.

The determination as real or unreal of a world that is not is not of supreme significance. It is important to the extent that it involves your identity. Those who know the Self declare the Truth of no-creation. (Silence)

Those who do not know the Truth and declare that there is a creation are, themselves, not really created. Therefore, we should inquire to see if we are a created thing or if we have some objective attributes. Are we a perceiver, a conceiver, thinker, a sensor, a body, and so forth? Or, do these have nothing to do with us?

Another Q.: From your instruction today, I see more clearly the progression of misidentification, from the body to thinking that the world is real and from the senses to thinking that the body and world are real. I thank you. There is more to look at here, for sure.

N.: Perhaps, you see more clearly why the Maharshi has stated that all the thoughts are for "I." All of them trace to a root notion of "I." The "I" may seem to be endowed with a mind, senses, and a body. Those are the shapes that it takes. There must be some one, apparently, who takes those shapes or assumes those definitions. We should liberate ourselves from all those extraneous definitions and even the notion of "I." That is also extraneous to our nature. Then, we see the unchanging Existence, the pure Consciousness, that we have really been the entire time. That seen, bondage is over, and suffering can be no more. (Silence)

Another Q.: I just woke up before coming here. I usually wake up quite slowly. So, though usually I am awake by the time I get here, right now, my mind is barely awake.

N.: Half awake and half asleep?

Q.: (laughing) Yes.

N.: It must be the jagrat sushupti, the waking deep sleep, of which sages speak. (laughter)

Q.: It would be so good to know that I do not ever change states. My mind changes, and I believe that I change.

N.: What makes you say that you change states? You were the witness of the sleeping state, and you are now the witness of the waking state. What change has occurred for you?

There has been a change in the appearance of what is objective, which is merely imagined within the mind. What change has happened for you?

Q.: That is interesting. That gives more clarity. If I depend at all upon the mental faculty, that obviously disappears.

N.: Do you depend upon the mental faculty? What do you regard as you?

Q.: The mental faculty is not the commonality.

N.: The mental faculties are different in the three states of waking, dreaming, and deep sleep.

Q.: Even in the waking state, it is modified very easily.

N.: Very easily. Moreover, you can see these things change slowly or quickly, as you noticed this morning. The speed at which they change does not in any way alter the state, or nature, of your Existence. This is true for waking, dreaming, and sleep states, as well as for any kind of mental mode within those states. That which is changeful is not your Self. The rapidity of change has nothing to do with the Self.

Q.: If it did, I would oscillate back and forth.

N.: Yes. Fast or slow has no bearing on the Self. So, you did not arrive at the waking state this morning. I assume that that is what you meant when you said that you just got here. (laughter) You were not in sleep, and you are not now in a waking state. These states appear only within you. You cannot be anything that appears within them.

Q.: Yes. They change and are modified radically, and anything within those states is completely modified.

N.: Yes, and they are in those states, and you are not in the states. You cannot simultaneously be the ever-present Existence and something within those modifying, changeful states. You cannot simultaneously be the formless, real Being and some imagined form within a state of mind. It is not possible for you to abandon your own Existence. This is the experience of everyone. Since you cannot abandon your real Being, and since Being is undivided, utterly indivisible, how could you ever be anything that ever appears in any state of mind?

Q.: I had a very good experience of meditation last Friday. I see that the discrimination must be clear. I am still dependent on a state of mind. Yesterday, I meditated just before going to bed, but obviously it wasn't deep enough to go through any state, because it was modified.

N.: In what way did you undergo modification?

Q.: What I believe to be myself.

N.: That will always undergo modification, but does your Self undergo modification? If your meditation is upon the Self, it is of the Self, and it will not be modified. What actually is the substance of meditation?

Q.: The substance is always the same. One could not even meditate if he did not have that substance.

N.: That substance is pure Consciousness. It is the end or the fruit of meditation, the substance and essence of meditation, and it is what enables the illumination of meditation to happen. Does this Consciousness disappear when you are dreaming or when you are sleeping?

If you misidentify with the mind in the waking state, or with a particular part of it, such identity undergoes change or destruction when there is a change of the state of mind, such as dreaming or sleep. How meditation can be continuous then seems elusive. You grasp it, but it seems to slip away. It is all a matter of what you regard as your identity. Are you a traveler in the waking state, dreaming state, or sleep state? Or, are you the substrate or space on or in which these falsely appear? The substrate does not move. The space of Consciousness is not modified. Identify only with the space of Consciousness. Do not take yourself to be an illusory part.

Q.: This is very deep. What is occurring right now is due to inquiry. As you said, it is a matter of seeing clearly what I am not but was taking myself to be.

N.: Discarding what you are not but what you were taking yourself to be by discrimination, something remains that is solid and clear. It is the Knowledge. It is you, Being-Consciousness. The Self, or Brahman, is described as Saccidananda, Being-Consciousness-Bliss, as well as Satyam-Jnanam-Anantam, Truth-Knowledge-Infinity. You, who are Being-Consciousness, and also Bliss, are the infinite Knowledge, the infinite Truth.

Q.: To know this infinite Truth, I am accustomed to having a sattvic mind. My mind has now gone from tamasic to sattvic states during this conversation.

N.: That which knows the change from one guna to the other is beyond the gunas. You saw sleep; you see waking; you saw tamas, darkness or inertia, and you see sattva. Who is this you?

Q.: (quiet)

N.: The one who silently witnesses all this is not participating in it. To know the Truth, abandon the idea of being a distinct one who does not know. You will not remain as one who does know. We only loosely speak of a jnani. You are the Knowledge, itself. The Knowledge is the only knower. That is pure Consciousness. You cannot separate yourself from Consciousness in order to grasp it. If, though, you abandon the false assumption of individuality, you can be said to grasp the Truth fully, because you, yourself, are the Truth.

Q.: The understanding is of not being a separate knower of Truth but knowing Truth directly.

N.: Yes, because Truth is not inert but of the nature of pure Consciousness. It knows itself. It alone knows itself. A so-called "other" cannot know it. A so-called "other" does not actually exist. It is not who you are. With the identity as an "other," there can be no perfect Knowledge. Without that false identity and abiding as the Self, there can be no ignorance.

Another Q.: I wish to meditate on the world as unreal but not make that an obstacle, because what is essential is to know my identity. Your speaking of this reminded me of the Maharshi's statement that the seeker should be like the diver seeking air. One goes to where the light is and does not become entangled in anything because it is so urgent and important. If I were to meditate that the world is unreal and that would take me deeper, that would be great. If it did not, I would first have to find my identity. It feels very free to have this proper goal orientation.

N.: If one turns a statement of wisdom, such as, "The world is unreal," which is a statement of fact, of truth, into a mental opinion about which one argues, hopefully only in one's mind and not with other people, one needs to ask himself how that assists in Self-Realization. It does not assist in an understanding of what the wise mean when they say that the world is unreal. Realization is not a matter of convincing oneself to form the right opinion in one's mind. Rather, it is a matter of knowing who we are. Then, we see the truths of such statements as plainly self-evident.

You said that you did not want the meditation upon the world being unreal to become an obstacle. How could it ever be an obstacle? To arrive at the depth of its meaning, you must dive within to know yourself. You must look at the perceiver. Meditating on the unreality of the world cannot be an obstruction to one's spiritual practice. If, though, you did not do so in the light of inquiry, the approach would not go nearly deep enough.

Q.: The Maharshi seems to take up that theme in *Forty Verses,* in which he advises this rather than to argue "with form" or "without form," saying that all would delight in the bliss of the Self.

N.: We know from that instruction that the prime thing is to abide in the egoless state and know the Self directly. If we know the Self, we know what is real. The instructions do not mean that we should try to convince ourselves in our minds of an objective opinion, and it certainly does not mean that we should remain with the old opinion, such as that the world is real. The meaning is clear: we should inquire deeply and thereby find out what the wise have meant when they have stated the facts as they are.

Q.: The sages are giving a preview of what the scenery is from the vision of Truth, but this is not something for which one should hanker for its own sake. The seeker should not ask, "Where is my bliss?" but should ask, "Who am I?", having been guided by that preview without turning that into a diversion.

N.: It does not really represent a difficulty. There are not really these "dangers on the path."

The expounding of spiritual instruction has a greater purpose than a preview or "coming attractions." The purpose of spiritual instruction, as the Maharshi has said, is to restore the mind to its proper place. This refers to the mind that has wandered away and taken on an identity separate from the Self. The purpose of spiritual instruction, even as it is given, and, of course, when it is reflected upon and meditated upon deeply, is to cause the seeker to experience his own identity, to abide as the Self, even then and there.

Let us say that someone hears about eternal Bliss and starts to ask, "Where is my bliss? It does not seem to be there." This will lead to a deeper inquiry, "Where is bliss?" The seeker says, "Where, where?", and the wise say, "Here." The wise say, "It is." The one still in ignorance says, "I don't know. I don't see it." This questioning leads to a deeper inquiry as to where exactly this bliss is to be found. If it already exists, why is it not experienced? When that question is raised, it leads to a questioning of one's identity. Then, he sets about clarifying his own identity. There is no danger. Such has only helped.

When there is Knowledge of one's own Existence, Bliss is recovered. The desire for Bliss has led to such inquiry. So, you see that the path to Self-Realization is not tricky and fraught with pits and potholes. Yet it must be subjective, nonobjective.

Another Q.: I am understanding that it is irrelevant to consider whether or not the world is real. The path is the inner deepening.

N.: Yes, it is irrelevant, but the identity that is the basis of the belief that it is real or unreal is very relevant. In *Saddarsanam,* the Maharshi says that to discuss that the world is real or unreal, is happiness or not, and so forth and so on is vain, and that one needs to inquire into the Self. In *Who am I?,* he says that, as long as the world is regarded as real, there will not be Self-Realization. How do you combine the two statements? It must be with your own identity.

If you continue, in any degree, to think that the world is actually existent, or real, from what position do you think that the world is? From what unexamined misidentification do you take that view? If one does not abandon that view by Knowledge, but merely attempts to convince herself that the world is unreal, while the effort is noble, it will not bring about the desired fruit of practice. If, though, you do inquire and uproot the false definition, you will know what is meant by, "Brahman alone is real, and the world is not."

Whenever you think of these matters as objective topics removed from your own nature, they become quite irrelevant to Liberation. If they cause you to question your own definition and uproot the false identity, they become very relevant. Do you see?

Q.: Yes, I see.

Another Q.: What I understand is that, when we inquire "Who am I?", a process of dissolution of ignorance occurs. Whether I think that it does or does not, it actually occurs, for you have said that any inquiry is good. You have also said that it is not difficult, though we are required to be persistent in our practice. If the mind is lazy, it perceives it as a difficulty. Sometimes, I inquire "Who am I?" wanting to move into bliss, and I am in a thinking mode. It is a thinking complex, rather than surrender and moving into the depths.

N.: When you are in the thinking mode, how do you proceed?

Q.: Through thought.

N.: Yes, but it is not satisfactory. So, how do you proceed? To rise higher, what do you do?

Q.: Sometimes, I just give up, move out of it, and come back later. I move through it.

N.: Is that a dependable method?

Q.: No. I want to know how to move through it when I face it.

N.: If you just give up, even if you style that giving up with an elegant term, what, in effect, you are doing is allowing the mind to wander, and the mind, in its wandering, in the course of time, will abandon whatever it was thinking about. It is like a monkey in a tree, which abandons one limb as it grabs another. Of course, observing monkeys for a while, one sees that they do wind up in the same tree again. It is not a dependable method.

If it is truly surrendered, one's ownership of the mind is relinquished. If one truly inquires, one finds out for whom is all this thinking and finds his Existence to be thought-free. There is no such thing as a "bad inquiry," and there is really no failure in a spiritual practice, because the goal is not an objective thing to be obtained elsewhere. We could go further with this. Any aspect of spiritual practice is never in vain. Even the least effort applied bears fruit. Nothing wrong or bad can happen as a result of this.

Q.: When inquiring, should I have the conception that I am to identify with the true "I," or should I keep going deeper into the false "I," which is the ego? If I keep remembering what you teach about who we are, I will fall away from the false and into the Bliss.

N.: Bliss is where the multiplicity of "I"s is relinquished. Whether in the context of recalling instruction or otherwise, the inquiry should be carried on until the false idea of multiple "I"s is dissolved.

Q.: With persistence?

N.: Yes, be persistent. You can never persevere too intensely or too long. Perseverance overcomes the inertia of the ignorance.

Q.: Rather than being frustrated about wanting to move to bliss out of the thought complex, I should stay with the inquiry?

N.: If you wish to move into greater freedom and bliss, simply determine some misidentification or an attachment and destroy it. Your bliss and freedom are obscured only by the presence of misidentifications and attachments. Find a vasana and destroy it. Destroy it by knowing it as a tendency and knowing that it has nothing to do with your happiness or the reality of your Self.

Q.: See, in that moment, what vasanas are present? Then, move deeper into that?

N.: You won't need to move deeper. Just examine it and destroy it, and what remains spontaneously, naturally by itself, without further effort, will, itself, be blissful and shining of the nature of Truth.

Q.: Thank you.

N.: At present, it may appear that you navigate between states, higher and lower, but the essence of such navigation is to simply destroy the building blocks of that which constitutes the lower or bound state. The substrate, which was previously regarded as the higher state, alone remains.

Q.: What one truly lives by and has understood, whether a name be applied to it or not, is a direct experience?

N.: Yes, that matters much more. What one actually experiences is one's knowledge and one's advancement. The description and discussion of it with others are truly of no consequence.

Q.: So, one's experience is one's real standing. That is one's understanding.

N.: That is right.

Q.: One's life must be the same thing. When they are the same, the aspirant has actually reached a higher place than what was previously understood.

N.: In the course of such aspiration, if there is higher, or deeper, experience and also experience that is not as high or deep, it is incumbent upon the seeker to discern that occurrence, comparing and contrasting, and to examine what makes the difference. The difference is always what is taken falsely to be your identity in contrast to what you truly know to be your identity. Inquire, and the previous lower state dissolves. The honest examination of yourself, with the recognition of what you actually experience, what you experience at some times, and what you do not experience at all, is always worthwhile. This is not for evaluation purposes. The ideas of being a high being or a low being are egotistical. This is only for the purpose of discerning how and in what ways your experience can be elevated to and merge with the Absolute. Such honest self-appraisal is very beneficial.

Q.: So, clarity as to what is clear for me and what I actually understand and live enters into this.

N.: Yes. If you know that That is the truth for you always, yet what you are experiencing, or living as you say, does not match that one hundred per cent, you are prompted to examine your experience in more detail. What are the factors that cause your experience to be more limited than what you know to be the eternal Truth? Continue examining and inquiring until every last tendency, everything that separates the life experience from the Absolute, has been dissolved.

Q.: So, the practice is the recognition of the stability in all relative points?

N.: In practical application, that which is most beneficial for the aspirant is the perception of where it is not stable. Where it is already stable, you already know that by direct experience. That is self-evident. Merely to think about it again will not add to your experience. If you can discern where darkness still seems to be in the midst of light, it is eliminated.

Q.: In that context, the ongoing self-evaluation and self-examination are of great importance?

N.: Yes.

Q.: To gauge the path, one's progress, and one's own standing.

N.: How else to destroy the vasanas manifesting in the life unless one first honestly recognizes that these are occurring even though one knows better? Then, inquire.

Q.: Yes. Thank you. This is a wonderful satsang. This has felt very relieving. I have now the insight that deep knowing and deep clarity are equal to Realization.

N.: (Silence)

(Then followed a recitation in Sanskrit and English of verses from the *Annapurna Upanishad*.)

(Silence)

Om Shanti Shanti Shanti Om

Silent Truth

Satsang, May 14, 2006

(Silence)

Om Om Om

(Silence for a long period of time)

N: Thus the Truth. If you have a question this morning or if you would like to relate your experience or wish to speak about Self-Realization, which Sri Bhagavan has so graciously revealed, please feel free to speak or ask.

Q.: I am reading the *Crest Jewel of Discrimination*. I see now that, when discrimination is deep, the seeker starts to see the Reality within instead of the things in the world. He sees that the actions and the fruits of the actions pertain to some imagined individual. Then, detachment flows naturally. How can one be attached to something that he sees is not real? When there is detachment, then sama, peace of mind, etc. come. This makes me focus even more intensely upon the discrimination. Sankara says that, for the process to deepen, the discrimination must be complete. Inquiry cuts through so much and focuses on identity. What clarity and what a wonderful teaching! It is a focus beyond the mind.

N.: Whether we refer to this as discrimination, as inquiry to know the Self, as inquiry to destroy the illusion, inwardly focusing, or going beyond the mind, it amounts to the same. As for the fourfold sadhana, or requisites for Self-Realization, you may view them as sequential or as ingredients that, mingled together, are the qualities or attributes of successful, fruitful, spiritual practice. What is most essential is to know yourself.

You spoke of going beyond the mind. What is it that goes beyond the mind?

Q.: I see in inquiry that there is something that is always constant, and the mind is not always there.

N.: The mind is not always there, but that which is you is always there.

Q.: Yes.

N.: So, that which goes beyond the mind is already beyond the mind. I am sure that the same is mentioned by Sri Sankara in his *Vivekacudamani*. The Maharshi says that the mind is considered to be only a bundle of thoughts. It has a great variety of permutations. Are any of those thoughts you?

The mind is spoken of as manas, citta, and buddhi. Manas refers to those mental activities that deal with sensory cognition and association with the same. It is concerned with the registration of sensation, which is merely imagined in the mind and is not external, and the associations of good and bad, pleasant and unpleasant, painful and pleasurable, and such. Citta is memory. Since the thoughts of memory, with its sense of continuity through time, go into one's thoughts about the future, as well as the present thoughts, we can regard all such thoughts as the movement of citta. Buddhi is usually spoken of as "intellect." It may be understood as that which seems to direct the focus or attention of the mind, as well as that which deals with things that are not sensory in character, such as abstract thought and spiritual thought. The Self is beyond manas, citta, and buddhi.

How can that which is beyond the buddhi be reached by the buddhi? How can that which is beyond the reach of the intellect or mind be reached by the mind? The Maharshi states that the mind is inert. In the text, it is said to shine by reflected light. This means that it is inert by itself. Trace the light to its origin. The origin is Consciousness. Consciousness is neither an object of the mind nor a director of the mind. Consciousness, being innately transcendent of thought, is that in which the mind is nonexistent, for the real does not subsist in the unreal, and the unreal does not subsist in the real. Consciousness does not become a mind, and there is no mind arising in Consciousness. This Consciousness is your real Being. In Being, there is no non-being. In the Self, there is no non-Self.

Only the Self is capable of knowing itself. Brahman alone knows Brahman. No other can do so, because of the illusory limitations of that illusion and because it is illusion. That which never is cannot know that which ever is.

If you discriminate through inquiry as to what is your identity, you see that the Real alone is and that there is no second. That is the inquiry and discrimination referred to, and that is nondual.

Q.: In practice, seeing the limited adjuncts that I hold, I examine the senses. There is still, in me, an internal body sense. I do not know how to close my internal feeling.

N.: Do you refer to the sense of touch or to the sense of being alive?

Q.: It is internal body sensations. This feels like me.

N.: But you know it.

Q.: Yes, I know it.

N.: If it is the known, or objective, how can it be you?

Have you ever had an experience without that particular feeling being present?

Q.: Well, of course.

N.: But you did not cease to exist.

Q.: Of course.

N.: So, where is the connection? How can there be the identity of what you are with that sensation?

You are not the body, and you do not have any of the attributes of the body. The limitations of the body, including its birth and death, are not yours. Similarly, you are not the senses. Anything that has the attributes of the senses, on the objective side as something sensed or on the supposedly subjective side as a sensing entity, is not you.

Everything that you know of the senses is contained in your mind. How can you be the content of something that you are not?

You need not attempt to maintain the sensation. You need not attempt to cause the cessation of that sensation. Whether the sensation is there or not, you are. It cannot exist apart from you, but you exist just fine with or without it. If this much is grasped fully, you are not bound by it.

Will you be unhappy if the sensation disappears?

Q.: No.

N.: So, it has nothing to do with your Being, nothing to do with your Consciousness, and nothing to do with your Bliss.

Q.: I feel it as a sensation in the chest or the head.

N.: Everything with which you have misidentified at any time has supposedly felt like you. All you need do is to trace where the sense of identity derives. Just as you need only trace from where the sense of reality derives, so that you do not mix it up with objective, phenomenal illusions, so it is with identity.

If you continue to trace your identity, the one who traces is absorbed in that which he is trying to trace. That is pure Being-Consciousness-Bliss. It is entirely free of the body, senses, prana, or the sense of energy of being alive, and any aspect of the mind. It has no individuality, no ego sense. That can know itself. Indeed, that is the Knowledge.

(Silence)

Another Q.: Inquiry is a process of keeping the thoughts at bay. While inquiring, I daydream. Thoughts rise up, and I become a thought. What is it that causes veiling and appears to have changed my identity? It is a memory. It appears to be in the past. What is the substance of all that? It is like being able to remember a dream when one is awake.

N.: (Silence). What are you looking for?

Q.: I am looking for myself.

N.: Are you looking for confirmation of your idea or Realization of the Self?

Q.: It is confirmation of some idea.

N.: If that idea is confirmed, what then happens?

Q.: Not much. (laughter)

N.: You first spoke of keeping thoughts in abeyance. The Maharshi's words, "keeping off thoughts" actualy refer to being transcendent of and undefined by any thought. It has little to do with the increase and decrease in the number of thoughts.

Q.: That is so important. I have this idea that I must get rid of the thoughts. It is as if there is a hole in the ground with thoughts coming out of it, like water, and I need to put my foot on it.

N.: No, it is a mirage. Noting the number of thoughts is like counting the waves, few or greater, in the mirage, thinking that the desert sand is becoming wet and that you are drowning in it.

Q.: What you just said pointed out something that I consider real.

N.: When you consider something to be real and try to eliminate it at its own level, the most for which you can hope is a change of phenomena, in this case a subtle phenomenon called "thought." The Realization of the true Self comes about by discerning what is real. Implicit in that is the negation of all that is unreal. It does not come about by "monkeying" around with the unreal, with the plumbing in the mirage. (laughter) It is like thinking of turning on and off the valves of a mirage. (laughter)

Q.: That is exactly what I have been doing.

N.: In the description of your experience, you traced it to a kind of memory. The experience is good, but you will probably find it more fruitful to examine how you have put together the causality. Any description of illusion is necessarily as illusory as the illusion, itself. Your attempt to define it is purposeful only to the extent that it helps you to eliminate it. To that extent, any explanation of how duality, illusion, or ignorance comes to be is helpful but will have its limitations. The limitations are of the illusion.

If you say that there is memory and then veiling comes about, whose memory is it? Does the true Self have a memory? Does the space-like, timeless, location-less, unborn, uncreated Reality have a memory? It is not so.

Q.: It does not have a mirage.

N.: If you speak of multiplicity or projection, in this case, the mental projection in the form of memory, as having come prior to the veiling, the causality is somewhat inverted. It would be better to say that there is veiling, and, because of veiling, there is then a projection of the illusory multiplicity. You can see this in your everyday experience. In deep sleep, there is no projection of multiplicity. There is no body, no mind, no world, and no experience of any of that, but there is veiling of your real nature. Out of sleep comes dream, and one of those dreams you refer to as "waking." Out of veiling comes the projection of multiplicity, which is an illusion.

Q.: I can see that veiling occurs, and then there is a projection of a thought of some kind of memory.

N.: With the idea of time superimposed on it, you then think of it as the past and call it "memory."

Q.: What is this that veils? I do not understand that.

N.: It is the same as the one who has it. (Silence). We can call it "misidentification" or non-perception of your real identity, which is your real Existence. The Maharshi says that of all such vrttis, or modes, the root is the "I." It is the assumption of existing as an individual, prior to the idea of any attribute of that individual. There is one who appears to experience whatever the objective, or "this," aspect of the experience is, be such memory or anything else. It is he that appears as a veil for himself, while your real Being shines, self-luminous, without a veil and without division, always. Inquire into that one. If there is a veil, that veil is for a "me."

Who is that? If you inquire in this way, you find that there is no substance of which to create the veil. You cannot make darkness out of light. (Silence)

Q.: There is a tendency of mine to explain things and to think that the explanations are real, as if there were some value in them. It is a search in a dream world by a dream character.

N.: The search is right, but how will you complete it?

Q.: By finding out who is searching.

N.: If the desire for Liberation, the fourth of the requisites (of the four-fold sadhana), as a search, is turned in on the one who is as if bound, Liberation will be self-revealed. Toward the conclusion of the book *Who am I?*, the Maharshi says, explaining what is release, Mukti, Liberation, to inquire and know the nature of the one who is in bondage is release, or Liberation. Why did he say so?

Q.: Why did he say that? So that the guy could become free.

N.: (Smiling and chuckling) Yes, but also because there is only one Self, and there are not two of you. If there is a veil, there must be a veil between what is veiled and the one for whom there is a veil. This threefold division is not true. How can there be a veil for your Self? If it were another to be known, you might know or not know it, but in the case of yourself, how can you not know yourself? It is as absurd as saying that there could be a time when you did not exist.

Q.: Yes, it is truly absurd. Veiling is like saying, "I did not exist for a while."

N.: Yet you are there to report on it. However you wish to explain ignorance, or illusion, it is fine as long as it prompts you to inquire and thus uproot the very idea that such a thing exists. However you explain your bondage, though it is not really true, it is alright if it prompts you to inquire and find out that you have not really been bound, you have not become a separated, individual being, but you exist only as Being, which is unborn, undivided, and is with no form. (Silence).

Q.: It is all about inquiry.

N.: Yes, there is no substitute for knowing yourself.

Another Q.: What we see around us is an illusion, not because it is not real, but because we don't see it correctly. Isn't it true?

N.: If we were to see correctly, how would we see it?

Q.: As our Self. Seeing stops. It is identity.

N.: Alright. The Self is not multiple or divided.

Q.: Yet there is a truth to individuality.

N.: In what does that truth lie?

Q.: In pure Existence-Consciousness.

N.: Which transcends thoughts of individuality, division, or duality.

Q.: I have to use thoughts and words because I do not have vijnana now. When we get to the state of pure Being-Consciousness, that is not the end. We do not cease to exist, and this universe does not cease to exist. So, why?

N.: Why what?

Q.: Why is it? Why did it manifest? Why did we come into it?

N.: The idea of "us" who come into it is not being identified with pure Being-Consciousness, but as something else. If you would inquire into that something else, the root of your question, or doubt, would be eliminated. You would have the vijnana, the Awareness or Knowledge, for which you are searching. In That, there is just the Self, and to say it is all of this or that none of this is and only That alone is means the same thing. After all, when it is said that

Brahman is all this, it does not mean that there should be any emphasis on "all this." It means that just Brahman is.

Q.: The manifested is from Ananda. It couldn't be or express itself otherwise, if it didn't have a delight behind it.

N.: Delight is inherent in itself. One speaks of manifestation from some supposedly manifested point and not from the Self, itself. So, first, realize the Self, and then see if there is a universe or not. Otherwise, whatever is the definition of the viewer necessarily becomes involved in his view.

Q.: But, on the way, don't we have a responsibility, too? If we hurt ourselves, we usually stop it, unless there is something wrong. There is hurt going on and to not do something, well, evil succeeds when good does nothing.

N.: "Evil succeeds when good does nothing." Similarly, ignorance seems to prevail in one's own mind if one does not employ Knowledge, which is wholly good. Knowledge alone destroys ignorance. Nothing else can do so. Another part of ignorance cannot do so. This Knowledge is rooted in yourself. The Self, which is also Knowledge, is the very root of all that is true, good, and beautiful. When we find this root, we find that it alone is, and there is the utter destruction of the very cause of delusion, which, in its grossest form, manifests as what you call "evil."

Q.: Could you clarify that a little more?

N.: About what do you have a question?

Q.: What we call "evil" is not evil but a consequence of being in ignorance.

N.: The denser the ignorance, the cruder is its form. When its form is very grossly manifested in the crudest of actions, you call it "evil."

Q.: But isn't it our responsibility?

N.: There is a responsibility to attain true Knowledge, which is the very root of all that you call "good."

Q.: If someone comes to us and says he is going to kill us, just because he feels like it, what is our responsibility in that situation?

N.: To abide as immortal Being, whether you choose to stop his action or not. Continuing with the delusion that you are mortal, that you are the body and that you can be slain, won't help the situation.

Q.: But it is a choice to allow or not to allow. There is a loss of allowing if something can be done.

N.: You are not required to be indolent. Knowledge is transcendence and not indolence. We can look at the lives of those who have realized the highest Truth. Sankara and the Maharshi declare that the Self is and this entire universe is not. Yet, if you look at their manifested lives, how much good is there!

Q.: It is hard for us to see all the good that they did.

N.: We could go on for eons in the attempt to describe it, and it would not be adequate. That in itself is standing proof of how this Self, the Knowledge of which is what we are concerned with, is the very root of all that is true, good, and beautiful. It is all peace, but it is not indolent.

Another Q.: I have deep experience, but, then, I say to myself, "but." You have directed my mind inward and instructed me to inquire as to who has that "but." There is always a trail or trace of that one. I see that there is something to be eliminated.

N.: The Maharshi says that the ego is a ghost with no form of its own, that it feeds on forms, but, when sought, it runs away.

Q.: If it feeds on a form, it is good to eliminate that as a possibility.

N.: Yes, your inquiry should always be thorough. Both the ego notion and the apparent definition, the form that trails behind it, should be eliminated. How would the trail remain if there were no one who had it?

Q.: (laughing). It would not be possible.

N.: If there were no trails, how would a ghost with no form of its own survive?

Q.: The ability to inquire is determined by how little one's mind is going outward. If my mind is going outward, there is no way that I can look more deeply into myself.

N.: Isn't it the other way around? If you are looking at yourself, there is no way that your mind can go outward.

Q.: (laughing) Oh yes!

N.: Outward is the projection of illusion within the mind, which is then erroneously regarded as if external.

Q.: I want to find out who I am. The ability to do so becomes better as I eliminate what is objective. My mind becomes more focused and clearer. It could be more focused. It seems to be a matter of eliminating more and continuing to look.

N.: Is this focus a matter of thinking a particular way, or is it something deeper?

Q.: The essence is always deeper. Maybe it is a byproduct.

N.: The thoughts may coincide with or express the essence. Is the essence a thought or something else?

Q.: The essence is deeper than thought. If it were thought, that would be no good for that is part of what is being eliminated.

N.: There would be no freedom or real bliss in that.

Q.: It is a byproduct that seems to go hand-in-hand, but does not always. Sometimes, the Truth comes shining through, even when the mind is not focused.

N.: So, concentration, or focus, in as much as that is regarded as a particular line of thinking, is not the determining factor of Knowledge, is it? When you inquire, is it because you think along a particular line? Does that constitute the inquiry, or does something else occur?

Q.: I still believe that it is thinking along a certain line.

N.: What is your experience? Is that true?

Q.: No, it is not true.

N.: You just made quick work of your belief. (laughter)

Q.: That is part of the objectification that is being jettisoned. The mind's focusing is not necessarily a problem. It cannot obstruct what is real.

N.: Is there anything that obstructs Realization? The power of your belief is rooted in yourself. This is a reason why belief can be wonderful. What obstructs Realization? What makes you think that you are not realized? What makes you think that there is someone who is an unrealized entity, or a being?

Q.: Do you want the list? (laughter)

N.: All of it.

Q.: (laughing) It is a fictitious puff that does not last long. It does not hold up. It does not have much weight. It does not even look that interesting. (laughter).

N.: How can an uninteresting, fictitious, ephemeral "puff," as you put it, be an obstruction to the Realization of the Self?

Q.: That is the way all illusion is. It really is very boring. (laughter). There is certainly not anything juicy or great in it.

N.: There is no happiness in it.

Q.: No divine nectar there. (laughter)

N.: Juiceless, essenceless, tasteless. (laughter)

Q.: Unreal. Yet, for some reason, I believe that there is reality, myself, there.

N.: What is the basis of that belief?

Q.: The basis must be myself.

N.: How can you, yourself, be an obstruction to the Realization of your own Self? It appears as that, because there is nothing else, yet how can that occur? How can the unborn give birth to illusion?

Q.: I don't know. A bad habit?

N.: A habit has to be for someone. Whose habit?

Q.: It cannot be for anything grosser. It can't be for the body or for the mind, even though it seems that it partakes of the mind.

N.: All that is imagined. You do not become this thing or that thing. You cannot be this or be that. Just Being alone is. (Silence)

Another Q.: I try to take the hints of the words of the sages and follow where they are pointing to.

N.: To That.

Q.: I could take the words for granted, but I try not to and ask, "What is the nature of knowing?"

N.: When you so inquire, what is your experience?

Q.: At the very least, it is an inward direction.

N.: The words of the wise serve that purpose. In the inward direction lies silent Truth. The words of the wise shine with the power of silent Truth. Silent Truth is comprehended by the silent Truth. There is no distinction between the wise and their wisdom, or between the one who instructs and the one who receives instruction. The teacher, teaching, and the taught are all one and the same thing. The teaching is not a set of ideas. The one who instructs must necessarily be identified with That. Otherwise, how will it be clear instruction? The one who understands is, himself, That, which is the significance of the teaching. Thus, the Upanishad says, "Tat tvam asi, That you are." The aphorism is the instruction.

Q.: If an aspirant felt that there were partial understanding and partial non-understanding, the practice would be to inquire and eliminate the non-understanding?

N.: How would he do that? Does not his non-understanding have its basis in what he regards as himself? So, he would discern what he defines himself as and then inquire to discern whether the definition were true or false.

Q.: The partial understanding would serve as encouragement and intensity to continue inward.

N.: Yes, it may seem that way at the outset, but really what is true is self-evident. Even if we speak of what is known partially, that which is true is self-evident and does not really need strengthening. Your effort is primarily the destruction of ignorance. Knowledge, being the substrate, is already solid. If it seems that knowledge is unsteady, it is really the unsteadiness of ignorance prevailing that is the cause. We destroy the ignorance, and the Knowledge is said to become strong. Because of the longstanding habit of regarding oneself as an ego entity, or a bound individual, the wise and the scriptures say to you to make the Knowledge strong, because you are looking at it from the perspective of being a non-knower. How do you make the Knowledge strong? By inquiring to know who the knower is. In doing so, the ignorance is shattered. That which is changeful is that which is unreal. The unreal alone can be destroyed, and the changeful alone is changed. The unchanging Reality, which is the abode of Knowledge, seems to become steadier. Really, it is unmoving.

If you examine your experience, you will see that you are unsteady at those times of, and proportionately to, your misidentification. If the misidentification is regarding Being, you take an ego "I" to be real, or there are the ideas of "I am a body," or "I am in a body," and such. If the misidentification concerns Consciousness, you take a mind to be existent, though there is no such thing. Likewise is it with the senses. If misidentification involves Ananda, or Bliss, you become attached to something in an external world that is actually only imagined in your mind.

Such seems to create unsteadiness in the Truth, but the Truth does not become unsteady. To regain the innate steadiness, destroy the illusion. Is this partially understood? (laughter)

Q.: (laughing) I think I fully understood that partial understanding is to be removed. (laughter).

N.: Okay, that is good.

(Then followed a recitation in Sanskrit and English of verses from the *Annapurna Upanishad*.)

(Silence)

Om Shanti Shanti Shanti Om

No Other

Satsang, May 21, 2006

(Silence)

Om Om Om

(Silence)

N.: You are the Self, and that alone exists. There is no other. The conception of "other" is based purely on imagination and is composed entirely of imagination.

The conception that you have an alternative identity, other than the Self, is ignorance, imagination. The conception of "this," of a world and such, is only imagination. The conception of one who is caught up in imagination is only imagination. The conception of "I" is the root of all duality.

However dualism may manifest, whatever be the projection of multiplicity, it is always based on a veiling of the Truth of the Self. It is always based on the idea of "I."

If there is the individual, there is something other. The Absolute Self is viewed as other, and there are other "others," as well. If you determine by deep Knowledge born of inquiry what your real identity is, there is no "other" at any time.

If there is duality, if there is the notion of "other," there is the illusion of bondage, which seems as if real, and consequent unhappiness. If there is no other, there is no bondage, no one to be bound, and no unhappiness.

Examine your experience. Perceive how this idea of being other than the infinite Self, of being an individualized "I," is integral to the conception of any other kind of limitation, so-called experience, etc. Seeing that, determine who you really are. What is supposed as an individualized existence is, in truth, just pure Existence without the individual. The inquiry, "Who am I?" reveals this.

Whatever is born of imagination is also imagination. Whatever the ego "I" seems to undergo, seems to possess, the objective aspects of its activities such as of the body, speech, and mind, are entirely as imaginary, or unreal, as the ego itself. The knowing of oneself is the knowing of Reality, known by the Self, of itself. The purpose of spiritual practice is the elimination of the imagined. Since it is the elimination of imagination, and, therefore, the insubstantial and the nonexistent, truly speaking, there can be no obstruction to your spiritual practice, save that which is imaginary.

Knowledge is inherent in the Self. So, what could interpose and act as an obstruction between yourself and yourself? By deep Knowledge, which is not an activity of the body, speech, or mind, abandon the assumption, the false notion, of existing as an individual entity, an ego "I." If just that much is accomplished, the Self stands self-revealed. (Silence)

The ego cannot know the Self. The Self knows the Self. The ego cannot be ignorant of the Self, because it is not a knowing, sentient, separate being. Egoism, the individual with his limitations, is merely imagined. Likewise is everything based upon it, all that is other.

The Vedas and the Maharshi declare that the Self is One without a second, One without anything other. Comprehend the deep significance of that. (Silence)

Q.: I read that discrimination and inquiry are key to Self-Knowledge. Discrimination seems to be looking for the other to see if I can find one. This body stands as an "other." If that is real or not seems to be an appropriate subject for inquiry.

N.: Certainly, the one who perceives the body is not the body. So, bodiless is what you are.

Q.: And the senses, etc.

N.: Yes, likewise the senses and all else. You are without the body and without the senses. Any kind of definition that associates the body, its characteristics, its qualities, its activities, or its conditions with you is false. Likewise is it with the senses. Even if the definition be only that you are one who inhabits a body, or that you are the nexus point of all the senses, all such definition is simply false.

From here, comprehend that the body, not being the Self, still has no existence independent from the Self. This does not mean that the Self manifests as or transforms itself into a body. It means that the body, which is not who you are, has no substance apart from you, the bodiless.

Q.: Just like the ring has no substance apart from the gold.

N.: This entire universe is made of only you, the Unmanifested. The ring is not anything apart from the gold. Gold, itself, has no form or shape. The form of the ring is, in substance, only the gold. The form of all this is, in substance, only yourself. Inquiring even more deeply, we naturally ask, how does this gold become formed into a ring? Even if it is just gold, how does it take on the appearance of such a shape? You are left with two possibilities. Either the conjecture that there must be something that acts upon it, or direct inquiry, which is more advisable. Did the gold become formed into a ring? Did the rope become transformed into a snake that was only a rope? Or is that merely imagined?

Q.: In the inquiry, the experience is very much of One. I can see the confusion with this individual. The confusion confuses the individual. The experience is always One. We just become confused as to what that One is.

N.: The confusion does not actually create a transformation in your Existence.

Q.: No, it does not.

N.: Confusion confuses only itself. Existence, which is pure Consciousness, remains as it is. It is the very substance of Knowledge. Knowledge does not become ignorant. The ignorance seems to become ignorant. A false assumption falsely assumes its own and another's existence. This is one way of expressing it.

The experience of all is always of an unmodified, undivided Existence. Everything other than that is only a product of ignorance. Inquiry does not create the Reality. It simply reveals the fact. Deep inquiry is invariably the self-revelation of that singular, undivided Existence, which is never modified, even to the extent of water and its waves, in any way whatsoever.

When one thinks he is a body, in a body, or has a body, such are not conceived from wisdom. They are thought from the perspective of ignorance. We know all those ideas to be ridiculous as soon as we inquire and determine that our Existence is bodiless. Likewise is it with the senses. The idea that the body exists, at all, is conceived from what perspective? Is this from the Self, or does some kind of individual experiencer creep into this? As it is with the body, so it is with the senses, the mind, and the entire world. By the time you are considering "it," there is already an "I," and otherness is there.

Q.: From what you have said, the "I" is the first falsehood.

N.: If the first false notion of "other" is seen to be nonexistent, what happens to the rest of it? Then, there is no more question about a body, senses, mind, or any similar thing. The ideas rise as "I," "this," and "I am this." All of them are just notions. The only actual experience is perpetual Existence, which is without "I," "this," or any kind of differentiation. We should abide in that Being's Knowledge of itself. We should not put up with these false notions.

Another Q.: Inquiring, "Who am I?" prompts the question: are there two of me? Is there one looking for the other? Where is that question coming from? How does the idea of there being two of me start? Who is this me, and what is going on here? Is there something going on? When I start the sideshow, there is something going on, but when I stop the show, there is just nothing going on. It is much better when the show is over.

N.: (Silent for a while). How do you bring the show to a conclusion? The sideshow is over, and the circus is closed.

Q.: I have to inquire into who is the star of the show. Then, the star and the show are absorbed into Reality.

N.: In your experience, is this final, or are there alternating states, with or without the show, with or without an "I"?

Q.: There appears to be an alternation.

N.: What creates the alternation?

Q.: Something creates it that I cannot catch. I am not sure what is this alternation.

N.: You describe two states. One is with an "I," and one is without an "I." One is with a show, and one is when the show has ceased. If that alternation is not desirable, how are you going to put an end to it?

Q.: The easy answer is Self-inquiry. It is obvious that this is the only way that I know that can get rid of it. I actually know that, so why do I not do that all the time?

N.: Yes. Why?

Q.: (quiet for a while) There is really not a good answer for that.

N.: From what vantage point do you speak of two states?

Q.: From a vantage point of knowing both of those states. They are objects.

N.: Deal with the subject, not with an object. The objects fall within the context, or sphere, of the subject. Who is the subject? Who is the knower of both states?

Q.: The obvious answer is that I am the knower. I am unsure of who that is, at the moment.

N.: Become more unsure.

Q.: I was a little unsure. How do I become completely unsure?

N.: What do you know of this "I"? What do you know of this knower of all the states? There is the certitude of Existence. How can there be certainty regarding anything over and above that?

Q.: I don't know if there is anything. I don't know what else there is to really know. I must make something else up to know.

N.: Then, you have your alternating states.

Q.: Yes.

N.: Does Existence go in and out of a state? Does it not remain just as it is?

Q.: Yes, it is not in the realm of statehood.

N.: Existence just is as it is. It is always the knower. Does it ever become the known?

Q.: What is it that I call the "known"? If all that there is to know is Existence, that is the end of the show, right there.

N.: (Silence) The Knowledge of Existence is as invariable as the Existence, itself. If you assume that your identity is something other than Existence, there are these other options. Whatever the state is, with an "I" or without an "I," waking, dreaming, and sleeping, living and dying, is Existence in that? Inquire and know the Existence as perpetually transcendent of all. Know your identity as just the Existence and not as something other.

The Self has no alternation. Who goes into or comes out of a state? Like this should you inquire. If you inquire deeply, you will find that there is no one who enters into ignorance. You will also find that no one enters into Knowledge. If there is Knowledge, there is an absence of an ego. Knowledge knows itself. That is pure Consciousness, the Self. There is no one else involved.

When we speak of attaining or realizing Self-Knowledge, it is said loosely, by way of instruction, catering to the perspective that there is one who is in samsara or in ignorance. If there is one in ignorance, he is told to find Knowledge, Wisdom. If he is bound, he is told to seek Liberation. If, though, he liberates himself from his bound identity, so that there is Knowledge and not a trace of ignorance, he finds that there is only one Self and not a second self who has entered into the Self. We speak of merger. There are not two that become merged. There is just the indissoluble, undivided, homogeneous Existence, which is Consciousness and Bliss. That is the only Self.

Alternating states are as illusory as the one who seems to be caught in them.

From another angle of vision: cease to regard Self-Realization as a state to be attained. It is nonobjective.

Since it is nonobjective, Self-Realization, in its nature, is your Being. Therefore, be unconcerned with whatever states seem to come and go, and know what your Being is.

Q.: I try to get into a certain state, yet you say to find out who it is who thinks that he is in a state.

N.: If you are in one state and that state is bound, naturally you seek another state that is one of Liberation. It is alright as far as it goes, but this Liberation is attained by knowing your Self. If you know your Self, you see that you are stateless. The idea of being in a delusive state and attaining another realized state is said conceding the idea that there is an individual who has these states. Inquire into his nature. Self-Realization is Being. Being is not an activity. Being is not a state. Being is not an object. Being transcends all of those limitations and definitions.

Another Q.: There were those who determined with their minds that there must be an infinite God. The infinite God must be ever present and all-present. At the same time, they concluded with a complaint that there was a mystery here, for this God still seemed hidden. Their own existence was the standard by which they graded God's performance as a mystery.

N.: Was God's Existence a mystery to God or for somebody else?

Q.: Well, to them, of course.

N.: But not to God. If they would know their own Existence, God would no longer be a mystery. From the perspective just described, God is considered a mystery. The human being considers God a mystery; perhaps God considers the human being a mystery. (laughter)

Q.: The recognition of God is the development in human thought.

N.: Why would the recognition of God be a development in human thought?

Q.: Well, uh…

N.: Is there any proof that human thought is actually developing?

Q.: It is like the sense of happiness. Unhappiness is believed only due to the reference that complete happiness must be possible.

N.: So, it comes after the fact. The fact is the existence of happiness. The other is only in relation afterward.

Q.: Right.

N.: Likewise is it with the thought of God. God, or Knowledge of God, comes first. The thought of God merely trails after. That is why it is curious to call it a development.

Q.: (laughter) The unhappy person and the frustrated thinker both use a much more formless reference point from which to draw their conclusions. The reference point is the ideal of perfect happiness, in the one case, and the ever-presence of their own Existence, in the other case. The clue to their problem is in the reference that they are using.

N.: If, from the reference point of their own Existence, there would be the elimination of the false, limiting definitions superimposed on that Existence, God would know God without any mystery, without any conception of a human, and God is always happy. The unhappiness and the mystery, or perplexity, arise only from false definition. There may be the inclusion of the intuition that they also exist all the time to make the measurement, but they have superimposed the limitation upon that. They have identified the perpetual Existence with the limitation, which is how they can arrive at such inverted views. We can leave all of that aside, for that is for them. That is not for you.

Q.: I hope not. (laughter) It seems interesting to notice that even in the fallacy there is the clue to its undoing. It is in its basis.

N.: That is always so. The Maharshi said that maya carries the seeds of its own destruction.

Q.: In the mundane sense of identity, it is assumed that this is a voluntary choice; that someone can assume or create or take on an identity. It is an admission that it is an imaginary activity.

N.: It is an admission that one is there in order to do that, with or without the clear understanding that this is just an activity. The person who is engaged in ignorance may not recognize it as ignorance, for, if he would recognize it as ignorance, the activity would cease then and there. Always he exists. So, in that sense, everywhere and at all times, even all the illusion is pointing out the Reality, but we must know how to perceive it. Do you think that God has any of this confusion?

Q.: I did not mean to be disrespectful, and I was putting the words into the mouths of others.

N.: I am not implying that you were disrespectful. I am saying that it is better to be God than otherwise. If we want to know anything about God, we need to see such from God's perspective. We cannot look at God from the perspective of the limited individual and assume that we are going to see anything other than our own reflection. If we take up the standpoint of the individual, the individual, God, and the world are, all, equally imagined, just reflections of the same definition. If we know the perpetual, omnipresent Existence as it is, that alone is what we are, and there is no individual, or jiva. That, itself, is the nature of God. Some may regard that as mysterious, yet some may say that it is self-evident.

We should never assume that we will understand the Absolute in the context of human, mental conception. Just because it is never within the conception of the mind does not mean that it is hidden in any way or mysterious. That very same One is omnipresent. This means that there is no room for anything, even so much as a single particle, to be other than that.

Another Q.: When you asked what makes one swerve, in my mind was the answer: forgetfulness. The forgetfulness is part of the illusion. The Self cannot ever forget its true nature. So, if there is forgetfulness, it is a consequence of non-inquiry.

N.: That is right. Forgetfulness of the Self is a consequence of non-inquiry. It is a very peculiar kind of forgetfulness. Usually, we speak of forgetfulness as the inability to bring forth the thought about something. In this case, the forgetfulness consists of bringing forth thought about it.

The remembrance of the Self is similar. Usually, remembrance is getting the thought of something. Here, remembrance is remaining quite free of the thought of it.

Then, your Being knows itself.

Q.: It is not letting go.

N.: What do you mean?

Q.: Not letting go of the Self. Not imagining.

N.: Alright.

Q.: Not letting the "I" arise.

N.: When we hold on to the Self, we do not stand in any way separate, as if we were grasping something. It can be said that you simply desist from taking on false definition.

Q.: Yes. I just stop.

N.: With ignorance or the delusion of forgetfulness, by the time you are making an earnest inquiry to get to the root of it, it ceases to exist. Even in the very effort to put an end to it, it vanishes.

Q.: That is clear. It is not a big journey.

N.: It is the most important one, but it is not long.

Q.: A step in any direction is a misstep.

N.: Yes, but in knowing ourselves we see that there is no other place to which to wander.

Q.: Ah.

N.: It is not like balancing on the top of a pole.

Q.: It seems like that at times. Resting as the Self, there is not much edge anywhere off of which to fall.

N.: When you perceive it as if it were a state, you have an edge. When inquiry is deep and you have Knowledge of your Being, you can no more fall away from it than you can fall away from your Existence. It is absurd.

Q.: This is true.

N.: Keep making your vision nonobjective. (Silence)

Another Q.: You describe the state of abidance in the Self. In that state, there is nothing objective. If I believe in the ego, duality begins. So, there is effort to eliminate the duality. It seems as if I have these selves.

N.: But do you really? Whose is the duality?

Q.: I don't know. One is very flimsy, and one is always there.

N.: Can there be a duality between That which is ever real and that which is never real?

Q.: Duality in what sense?

N.: Can there be two such things, if the Real ever is and the unreal never is?

Q.: It seems that there are.

N.: Is Reality only at a point in time or is it always?

Q.: It is definitely always.

N.: Realization, to be nondual, must necessarily be of the identical nature as Reality, which is the Self. So, it is always and not at a point in time. A point in time is in reference to the individual who experiences it. The individual, being unreal, never is. The Self, which is Realization, always is. (Silence)

Q.: With that Knowledge, there is not going to be any ignorance.

N.: There is no ignorance or anyone in ignorance ever or anything else whatsoever. There has always been the one Self. This is the Knowledge-conclusion of the wise. That is both the Maharshi's instruction and His Grace. (Silence)

Q.: This is quite amazing. I feel that there is maintenance that needs to be done when I am practicing.

N.: In Self-Realization, how can we speak of maintenance? Who would do what?

Q.: Yes. Without the ignorant one, there is nothing to be done.

N.: Without the ignorant one, there is nothing to do to maintain the Self-Knowledge, nor is there any possibility of the recurrence of ignorance. Since there is no possibility of the recurrence of ignorance, there is, similarly, no possibility of the manifestations of ignorance.

Q.: (quiet for a while) This is not practice, right?

N.: What do you mean?

Q.: Practice implies duality and that there is separation.

N.: Maybe, but in practice, do you emphasize the duality or the nonduality? If you emphasize the duality, you might as well just be worldly. (laughter)

Q.: (laughing) That would be a big mistake.

N.: Practice is always the emphasis of the nondual. Even among the dualists, it is the emphasis of the nondual but unknowingly so.

Q.: In what way?

N.: There is some touch of devotion or of spiritual knowledge, all of which has its root and source in Nonduality, the Truth.

Q.: Then, continuous practice is the Realization and is maintenance-free.

N.: If practice is continuous, there is no scope for delusion. If there is no scope for delusion, yours is continuous Knowledge, which, being realized as identical with yourself, is maintenance-free.

Q.: On Friday, I had a very good meditation because the identity was more fused. That is just the way it is when one is realized. There is no loss of that identity. One knows that identity directly.

N.: Has the way it is changed since Friday?

Q.: (laughing) No. It is not like the sun coming out and then a cloudy day comes, so it is dimmed.

N.: That would be only for the perspective of being on the ground. For the sun, it is a sunny day all the time, with neither night nor day. If, since the time of the meditation, from then to now, something seems to have changed, what has changed?

Q.: Right at this moment, I do not know if anything has changed.

N.: Why relegate that which is high and true to the past? Why consider it as an experience? Actually, it is the direct, ongoing experience of Existence. It may be better to consider the entire samsara as a thing of the past.

Q.: Yes, it feels more and more like that.

N.: It is a thing of the past as in the sense that we can speak of a dream as a thing of the past. It is not that it really occurred, but it is behind us.

(Then followed a recitation in Sanskrit and English of verses from *Annapurna Upanishad*.)

(Silence)

Om Shanti Shanti Shanti Om

Space-like

Satsang, June 4, 2006

(Silence)

Om Om Om

(Silence)

N.: One Self alone exists eternally. Unborn, it admits of no creation ever. Nonobjective, there is no other for That, and That is what you are. It is considered to be all-pervading, yet it remains absolutely formless. It is considered eternal, yet it is timeless. The Realization of That is characterized by egolessness. This is the absence of the false assumption of existence as something separate from That, as an individual entity. The conception of existence as an individual entity, or ego, is ignorance. Abidance as the real Self, which actually alone exists, is termed "Wisdom" or "Knowledge."

All kinds of bondage and suffering have their root in ignorance. All freedom, peace, and happiness are founded upon Knowledge. Knowledge of the Self is not as if one self were knowing another self, for there is only one of you. The "you" that you really are, the Self, is the infinite, the eternal, the forever-unconditioned. Being changeless, the forever-unconditioned, is the sign of reality. If you know that within yourself, you know the Truth, you know Reality. The Reality comprehends itself, for there remains no individual "I" to claim, "I know it," or "I do not know it."

In your real nature, you are completely detached. You are all-permeating, but detached from all. Such supreme detachment is the abode of bliss. Where there is detachment, there is happiness, peace, and freedom. There is joy without condition or limit. Where there is attachment, there seems to be a limitation superimposed upon the innate happiness, or a condition set upon joy, love, and so forth and so on. When, in your spiritual practice, you become detached, you are simply knowing the truth about happiness, the truth about your nature.

Misidentification is delusion. With the delusion of misidentification, Being seems as if an object. It starts with the notion of "I" and proceeds to be endowed with a mind, senses, a body, and such. With misidentification, the Consciousness that you are, which is entirely unformed and homogeneous, without subject and object, appears as if thought, as if sensing, and appears as if that which is thought and sensed. With misidentification, or delusion, the Reality of the Self—Being-Consciousness-Bliss—seems to be something that it can never be, and that which really never is seems to be as if something existent. What actually never is? All differentiation, all duality, and everything from birth to death that seems to come from it.

The Maharshi states quite clearly that the egoless state is our real state, the only real state that there is. That state is worldless, bodiless, mind-transcendent, and utterly "I"-less. That which is referred to as a "state" is the very nature of your Existence. So, in realizing Self-Knowledge, it is not so much that one obtains a new state for oneself, but, rather, there is the recognition within oneself of what has always been the case. That is the unborn, imperishable Existence, the homogeneous Consciousness, and the uncaused Bliss. (Silence)

For Self-Realization, the Realization of the Absolute Brahman, what is required is a very profound inquiry into one's own nature. Such discriminating inquiry yields natural detachment. It yields natural transcendence. It reveals the fact regarding your Being. Inquire deeply within yourself as to what you really are. Thereby, pass beyond everything embodied, everything perceived, everything conceived, everything associated as a limitation with the assumption of existence as an individual being. You are not the individual, which is but an imagined, false assumption. It is imagined as in the example of rope seen falsely as a snake just due to lack of good light. See the rope for what it is; know your Self for what you truly are. As declared in the Vedas and many other scriptures, you will find it to be space-like. That is, it is without any form. You will find that there is no place where it is not, so it is space-like. You will find that it has no interior or exterior, so it is said to be space-like. You will find that, though it is in all things, it is not in anything, so it is called "space-like." You will find that, though everything is in it, yet nothing is in it, so it is said to be like space. You will find it to be without limitation, without change, without division, and without motion, so they have called it "space-like." (Silence)

Now and always, this space-like Consciousness, the Reality of pure Being, is what you are. Being is neither a thing nor an activity. Know it for yourself by inquiring within, "Who am I?" (Silence)

The Upanishads declare, "Aham Brahmasmi, I am Brahman." Find the Truth of it within yourself.

Q.: I asked the universe to protect anyone from any stabbing last night. I feel that the request I made earlier to the universe about protection led me to protect a man from possibly stabbing himself.

N.: (Silence)

Q.: How does this relate to the teachings of spirituality? How did a meditation asking for help lead me to be of help?

N.: When you say that you prayed to the universe, you were not praying merely to the inert matter in it, were you?

Q.: No.

N.: So, what is it that you referred to as "the universe"?

Q.: It is what I call the "protector," and the universe, both of them. The universe is the collection of all.

N.: It is something that protects, something that is all, and something that is not inert or unintelligent, for, otherwise, you would not expect an answer. Inasmuch as you refer to the universe, it is something very vast. Prayer is recognition, and you recognize the existence of some conscious power or principle that is quite vast, which is even evident in your own activities, which is given credit for all life and death, and which can protect but also dissolves all things. With the recognition, there is the diminution of what you regard as you. Out of the recognition of something that is absolute and the diminishing of the ego comes everything that is true, good, and beautiful. Consequently, your later interaction.

We don't need to wait for something so dramatic to abide in that which dissolves the false sense of ego. When we no longer wait, we find that that which we call upon in a time of need is actually present all the time. When we see that it is there all the time, prayer changes from solicitation to reflection upon its omnipresence. When contemplation upon its omnipresence and the like passes beyond attributes and even beyond the thinking of the mind, it becomes meditation. When meditation becomes quintessential in its introspection, it becomes atma-vicara, or Self-inquiry. When the inquiry penetrates deeply to the core of one's Being, so that one's Being is found to be that to which one originally prayed, the Absolute, the statements such as "Aham brahmasmi, I am Brahman," strike home.

Another Q.: For certainty, the seeker needs to inquire as to what is lasting within himself. Knowledge comes from dispassion. This seems to be the crux of the matter.

N.: If we know what the source of happiness is, if we know what the source of our desire for happiness is, if we know what the substance of the experience of happiness is, and if we find all of these to be the same within, which is the nature of the experiencer, to what would we be attached? Happiness is not complete unless it is lasting. Everyone desires happiness. They do not desire only a brief moment of it. They desire for it to be always. Such is an intuition that bliss and immortality are our nature.

Whenever you are attached to something, from a subtle thought to an activity, circumstance, object, or another person, what is your view of happiness?

Q.: Strongly attached to the thought that happiness is these ideas.

N.: The more the attachment, the less happiness is experienced, that is, the more there is limitation imposed upon it. When we are detached, it is because we know the causeless nature of happiness. We do not expect anything to give it to us. Nor are we in need of it from anywhere else. Your within-ness itself, your own Existence, is the happiness desired.

Q.: So, I don't have to seek externally.

N.: One who knows the source of happiness is detached. His detachment guarantees the solidity and unwavering character of his happiness. When the confusion regarding identity is with thought or the body, we say that such is misidentification. When the same misidentification is in the form of mixing up one's happiness with objects in the world, such is called "attachment." It is the same silliness at work. What yields detachment also yields disidentification.

Detachment can be said to be of two kinds. One is the kind of which we are speaking now. It is attained by the discernment of where happiness is. The other kind of detachment is supreme detachment. It is abidance in That, as That, in which nothing else has ever come to be. That is the Self. It is not attached to anything at any time, for there is nothing besides it. Therefore, this detachment is not attained, and the attachment was never attained. The first leads to the second. (Silence)

Another Q.: There has been much confusion for me. I became very drowsy, and I let that slip by as if it were alright, because I do not want to do self-examination of my action. I was troubled by the feeling that it is incorrect to fall asleep when so much knowledge is presented. I read a book about Ramana Maharshi by Kunju Swami. It said that he (Ramana) would disguise himself and go to a temple to worship. He felt bad about what he had done. I wondered why he would feel bad if he is identified with the Self, which is perfect. It is as if he were identified with a mind-body having done something wrong. If he is the Self, why is he upset about what he did? I don't address things that don't feel right to me. Is it the ego that wants to be perfect in everything that it does or is that coming from the Self, which is all good in everything and expresses that?

N.: Your question assumes that to be constantly engaged in the examination of oneself or the manifestations in the mind would be ego-forming and that ignoring such and not engaging in self-examination would be ego-dissolution. You may wish to examine that concept to see if it is borne out in experience.

The second aspect of your question concerns your paraphrasing of a story about the Maharshi that is probably lacking in certain respects. Perhaps, what you are quoting from Kunju Swami is out of context, or, perhaps, the book in which you read this is not clear. You suppose that the Maharshi felt bad about himself or depressed in some manner. The story of how he went in disguise is bit humorous. Tell me how someone who wore only a loin cloth went in disguise. (laughter) It would be difficult, except for perhaps changing the Siva marks. That would not be much of a disguise. In any event, you may wish to review the passage and understand its context rather than assume that the Maharshi was subject to emotional moods, which is not the case at all. One who has transcended thought does not even have the stuff from which to make moods.

Consider deeply whether or not you wish to maintain the supposition that to examine yourself through critical discrimination and inquiry builds up the ego while being oblivious to such takes down the ego. You may find that such is an inverted view.

Q.: Not to be oblivious? Would you say that again?

N.: Your question assumes that examination of the workings of your mind builds up the ego. The ego is, after all, only a false supposition. Your question assumes that to not inquire and examine maintains the ego in a dissolved state or in a state of abeyance. You may wish to seriously reconsider that proposition. You can do so in the light of the Maharshi's instructions about the destruction of vasanas, or mental tendencies, in the light of any Vedanta work, or in the light of many other spiritual texts. You may wish to also examine your experience. See how that proposition works or if it works at all. That this view might be entirely inverted is what was suggested.

You may find that self-examination never does any harm. The worse thing that could possibly happen when you examine yourself is that you find that you were already right, so you would not learn anything. Other than that, you could find some tendency, vasana, or misidentification and, being aware of it, inquire and thus liberate yourself from it.

As for your falling asleep or not, that is of no concern here.

Q.: I should not have.

N.: You are that which transcends all three states of waking, dreaming, and deep sleep and the thoughts, mental waves, and emotions that appear within those states. You are that which is the silent witness of those three states and which, in truth, never enters those three states. You are that which is undefined by what appears in your waking state and dreaming state, and even the emptiness of deep sleep you are not.

Q.: I feel inadequate and ask for grace to always be able to see if there is a deviance from Truth and correct it. I can see that there is danger in falling away from that and saying that I am fine, and everything is fine, when that is not really representative of Self-abidance.

N.: That is clear.

Q.: I must always have the fluidity to be able to see and correct.

N.: You see all the time anyway. There is nothing mysterious about ignorance or about Knowledge. When, in imagination, you concoct some ignorant concept and then act upon it, don't you know about it? If you did not know about it, how could you bind yourself with it? How could you act upon it? You do know. The so-called ignorance is only formally so. We actually always know. Self-examination and Self-inquiry simply reveal what we already know.

Q.: To have the power to know that rather than fall into a tendency as if one were out of control is just to stay still.

N.: Depth of inquiry is what is required. If it is fueled by the intensity of purpose, that is, the intense desire for Liberation, obstacles are not really found. What higher state of grace could you desire than to have your inquiry be constant? If your inquiry is constant, your Knowledge is constant. Then, it becomes self-evident that the Knowledge, which is innate, appears as the form of the inquiry.

Q.: That is what I am asking for and not how I stated it.

N.: That for which you ask you are already endowed with. Use it.

Q.: The other night I had a dream. A policeman came to give me a ticket because I was parked in the wrong spot. Is this the Self correcting itself? Is it coming from ego sense of having done something wrong?

N.: There are more direct ways to realize the Truth than attempting to analyze the echoes and images of your dreams. The Consciousness that knows all the happenings of the dreams never itself appears as a thing in the dreams. The same is so now in the waking state, which can be regarded as another dream. Find out the truth of this Consciousness and identify with it.

Another Q.: It is said that there is no need to repeat as a mental assertion the mahavakyas. An ordinary human being does not have to say, "I am a human being," because it is an unquestioned experience for him. If someone dreamed he or she was a cow and woke up in a fevered delirium with that thought, that person would need only to know that that was crazy, "I am just not a cow," and would be done.

N.: As well as wiping away whatever remaining hay was in the mouth. (laughter)

Q.: And stop eating grass and running with the herd (laughter) to take care of the things that lead to that assumption.

N.: (laughing) I am just kidding.

Q.: To cease taking the objective to be the subjective, the known to be the knower, even on a mental level, can help. It is not inquiry yet, but is that a helpful form of Self-remembrance, and then proceed to inquire? The cow and human difference is the sharp separation from identification with the objective known and the remembrance of the teaching of sages that the real can be only the subjective knower. I try to fathom what that means.

N.: It is from the knowledge of the subjective knower that the mahavakyas were declared. The great sayings, such as "Thou art That," "Supreme Consciousness is Brahman," "I am Brahman," and "This Self is Brahman" are statements of direct Realization, which is direct experience. We do not repeat them, but we realize the truth of them. The truth of them is your nature. In the statement, "I am Brahman," what is the "I"? In the statement, "Tat tvam asi," "That you are," what is the "tvam," what is the "you"?

There is the knower, and there is the known. The latter includes cows and the human body. Eliminate the known from your sense of identity, from the knower. What remains?

Q.: You used the term "space-like." It seems appropriate.

N.: The mental activities, your thoughts, which have innumerable permutations, are entirely the known, aren't they? For whom are the thoughts? Who knows them?"

Q.: They are not known by another thought upon which I put my name.

N.: One thought does not know another thought, and thoughts are not self-known. They are not self-luminous; nor do they light each other. Nor do they exist apart from the one who knows them, though the one who knows them exists quite distinct from them. Who is the knower? This inquiry cannot be mental, can it?

Q.: No, that would be more thoughts. That would be a cow again.

N.: It would be a herd passing by. (laughter) It would be a bunch of thoughts grazing, but they are not you. None of your thoughts—not one of them—have ever been you. None of them are a definition for your nature. You can be quite sure that whatever you think of yourself, that you are not. What remains?

(Silence)

Another Q.: Nome, at times, I catch myself telling myself a story. It seems to dissolve into space, but only for awhile. I do not see much bliss in it, but there is peace. Is it just another thought?

N.: Does your experience seem to be just another thought?

Q.: It seems to be dissolving into a cosmic space, when I am able to catch it.

N.: How much is just a story?

Q.: Hmm.

N.: Just your daydreams?

Q.: No.

N.: Your entire personality?

Q.: (laughing) I wish.

N.: The idea that you have a bodily life?

Q.: Yes, the idea that I have a bodily life.

N.: The dream commences with the idea that you have been born.

Q.: Yes, it all comes from that.

N.: Everything based upon that, including the personality that you wish were a dream, is just as much a story as that idea that you were born. Regard a story as just a story. Be thorough. Only that which is not dependent on the conceptions of the mind is not a story. Only that which is a nondependent self-existence is not a story.

If you proceed deeply into your nature, which alone is not a story, you will find that which the mind, at times, calls "bliss," and, at times, calls "peace," and, at times, calls something else, but which really is quite beyond description.

Q.: Can I use the dissolving to go deeper?

N.: What else is depth but dissolution?

Q.: I need to seek to dissolve.

N.: We do not really use dissolution, do we? The "we" dissolves. The way is always nonobjective. Dissolve whatever you regard as "you." That which is truly you is unborn and indestructible.

Q.: And beautiful and good.

N.: Yes, and quite beyond the story.

Another Q.: The Maharshi says that, in deep sleep, one exists as he is, so we should find out what is different in this state. When I come here, there is a fullness. I do not feel defined. There is this fullness that I do not know how to describe. There is more of my identity that I need to question and dissolve.

N.: Sri Bhagavan reveals that you exist always, in deep sleep as you do now. In deep sleep, there is no experience of the manifestations of an ego, the mind, the body, the world, and so forth and so on. Now, these things appear, but your Existence remains the same. Those things come and go according to the state of mind. Existence remains the same. We know from this that Existence cannot be anything defined within those states. Therefore, it cannot be anything confined within those states.

The Existence is immutable. Changelessness is the sign of reality. If something appears to change its nature, it is an illusion. Illusion is that which is not.

Q.: In deep sleep, there is no mind. Everything in the mind is gone.

N.: But you still exist.

Q.: Yes.

N.: Your Existence does not change. What is otherwise is not your Existence. That Existence would go out of existence is absurd. It is impossible for you to imagine a state of nonexistence. Existence always is and always knows itself. That which always knows itself and exists by itself and is referred to in the instruction about deep sleep is the only thing that you are all the time. That, itself, is the Purnam, the perfect fullness. Variations in states are according to the mind. What is the mind?

Q.: The mind is contingent upon my belief. If there is a belief in something, there is a mind.

N.: The mind depends on you.

Q.: Yes.

N.: But you do not depend on it.

Q.: I do not, for the mind can be totally gone in deep sleep.

N.: Yet, you still are. Does the mind have any existence at all apart from you?

Q.: That is an important question.

N.: Does the mind ever declare that it is, or do you say that it is?

Q.: It does not say, "I have now found the mind."

N.: What has only a dependent existence actually has no existence at all. It is something else that is misperceived as or erroneously called that thing. What is the real nature of your mind?

Q.: (quiet for awhile) The mind is not just the thoughts, but also the one who has the thoughts. Is that true?

N.: You can look at it that way. What you call your "mind" is a combination of the thoughts and the one who has, or knows, the thoughts.

Q.: What the thoughts pertain to?

N.: They do not pertain to other thoughts. Or, if they do, they have nothing to do with you.

Q.: (laughing) Yes, that is true. They definitely don't pertain to me.

N.: You can either see that thoughts pertain only to other thoughts and have nothing to do with you, and you can go happily on your way without thought from then on, abiding as the Self, and the mind won't trouble you ever again, or you can see that your mind is a combination of the one who knows it, appears to have it, and the form of the thought. The one who knows it is of the nature of pure Consciousness. The form of thought depends utterly on the Consciousness, in order for it even to appear. It is only Consciousness that appears in the guise of that. The nature of your mind is Consciousness. What form or wave does Consciousness have? Thus, you find that there is no such thing as a mind.

Q.: It seems that a lot of it is just assumptions.

N.: All of samsara is like that.

Q.: There is nothing tangible. I had this assumption. It was unquestioned.

N.: All of samsara, the repetitive cycle of birth, death, and all the experience pertaining thereto, is only false assumption. It is imagination. The scriptures refer to it as maya, illusion. The Maharshi says that maya is that which is not. It has no existence whatsoever, not even a temporary existence. If we know the nature of maya, it ceases to exist for us. There is no such thing as existent maya.

Q.: Maya is any assumption?

N.: Is there one that you wanted to retain?

Q.: No, actually. That leads to suffering.

N.: Suffering has its root in delusion only, not in reality. Therefore, if you know yourself, Reality comprehends itself, and suffering is abolished. Such elimination of the imagined bondage is called "Liberation."

Q.: The Self is Bliss. When it is not seen, I may believe that the bliss is outside or objective.

N.: Who is the "I"? Who is the one who does not see?

Explanations of maya or ignorance are just expedient teaching for the Truth to be self-revealed within you. In truth, there can be nothing real about a description of that which has never come to be. (Silence)

(Then followed a recitation in Sanskrit and English of verses from the *Annapurna Upanishad.*)

(Silence)

Om Shanti Shanti Shanti Om

You Are

Satsang, June 11, 2006

(Silence)

Om Om Om

(Silence)

Nome: You are not the body. You are not the mind. You are not the ego. Of all that appears to arise or manifest, you are the source. Of the unmainfested, you are the Existence. Of all that is known, you are the Consciousness, which is Knowledge, itself. Of all joys, you are the Bliss.

In all perceiving, you are the knowing, which is Consciousness, Knowledge. Of all experiencing, you are that which is most immediate. Among all things, you are that which is all-pervading yet utterly transcendent.

You are that which is timeless and location-less. You are that which is never born and which never perishes, for you are not the body, you are not the mind, and you are not the illusory ego.

You cannot be perceived, and you can never be conceived, yet there is never anything of such that is other than you. You are, simply, the indivisible Reality. In the abandonment of the misidentification with the body and the mind, and in the abandonment of the false assumption of being a separate, individual entity, or ego, all of this is self-evident.

Of all that is said and thought, of all that is taught and learned, you are the Silence. (Silence)

Inquiring within, "Who am I?", you know yourself. When you know yourself, the essence revealed even by the Vedas is you. Knowing yourself in your real Existence, your real identity, you find that there is no alternative identity and no other existence. The Self is the Nondual.

Knowing yourself is knowing Reality. Reality knows itself. Not knowing yourself is the unreal imagining the unreal. If the unreal imagines the unreal, it does not amount to much.

Knowledge of the sole-existent Self is Liberation from the imagined bondage. Ignorance, which has no support and no actual substance, is the only apparent bondage. Therefore, the way to eliminate the imagined, or apparent, bondage is Knowledge of yourself, for you are not the body, not the mind, and, most certainly, not the ego.

Q.: In much of Sri Ramana's teachings, he says that the mind and the ego are the same thing. What I want to understand is that this mind or ego never existed to begin with, that is, that they are the same nonexistent thing.

N.: Do you consider them as existing now?

Q.: (laughing) Yes and no. When you spoke of who we are as the Silence, there was the presence of the Silence. Still, they recur as the identification. I want to be clear that I can't identify with them because they don't exist. Identification with something that does not exist is remarkably stupid.

N.: For the clarity you seek, inquire into the "me" to whom these reappear. The "me" may be referred to as a mind, because these things are conceived, or as an ego, for the notion "I" is integral to every other thought or idea. It may be regarded as something subtle or as a thought or as a vague supposition. However it is regarded, see what the nature of that is. If there is a thing corresponding to the name "I," there is differentiation, delusion, bondage, and the rest of samsara. If, upon inquiry, you find that it is rootless, that there is nothing there, that there is one who exists, but there is not a trace of an ego or mind, all the instruction about the unborn, the uncreated, and the undifferentiated is self-evident.

Q.: Though they are subtle, there is still something finer and subtler.

N.: You see the mind. You see this misidentification as an ego. The nature of the seer is far subtler than them. It is also far more enduring. It is much more your identity than they are.

From the Maharshi's instruction, you know that the mind is nothing more than a bundle of thoughts. If we regard them as a bundle, such is called "a mind." If not, there is a multiplicity of thoughts. He also refers to the ego as a ghost with no form of its own and also as a knot that seems to tie together pure Consciousness and the insentient body. It is neither, but it seems to appear as a knot between them that ties them together. When we combine the two that cannot really be combined, that is, the body and pure Consciousness, bundled together such is called an "ego." Examine these bundles.

Q.: Can Consciousness turn into a thing?

N.: Without knowing about it?

Another Q.: Why without knowing about it?

N.: If he knows about it, he cannot be that thing, for it is objective. The knower always precedes and succeeds the thing known, existing before, during, and after. You need to see that your nature is only pure Consciousness. That is your only identity. Consciousness does not change its nature but always remains just Consciousness. That which is real is immutable and always remains such. Consciousness is real and cannot change its nature. Examine closely what appears to have happened so that Consciousness seems to be something that it is not. The more we search for ignorance to examine it, the more it dissolves before us. (Silence)

Another Q.: This instruction is similar to, yet far vaster than, letting go of ignorance in the waking state dream of life, such as relative ignorance about a relative thing. I recognize that it is unnecessary, pointless, and undesirable, and I have cast up a magic barrier—magic because there is no conceivable mechanism for the barrier to work or make it a barrier—and that it is just thoughts. These thoughts need to give way to direct experience that is far deeper.

N.: It is as you describe. Why do you think that you are in a waking state?

Q.: I have memories of some success of relative ignorance passing into a better understanding. It went through that process.

N.: Alright.

Q.: In the dream, the character goes through that process.

N.: In that case, there is the process of getting rid of some limited thought for a clearer thought. The similarity of that to going beyond thought entirely is so. Why did you refer to yourself as being in a waking state?

Q.: That is one of those magic barriers that are unnecessarily constructed.

N.: Are there two sides to this imaginary barrier?

Q.: (quiet)

N.: If a wall is made of space, are there two sides to it? Even now, and always, what is your state? Are you one who appears in a waking state, or are you the one who knows of the coming and going of the waking state? What is your experience?

Q.: What amazes me is the appearance of the Maharshi's teaching in this relative life, the meeting with a disciple of the Maharshi, and the grace of getting living instruction. I am blown away by the bliss that I sense in the sage. If this is the waking state and this is the appearance of the Reality in that state, or the reflection of it, where is that bliss by which I am so blown away? Certainly, it is not in a body. It is still there. How can it be known? How is it that it is known?

N.: Is it known with your senses or by something deeper?

Q.: It is not known by the senses.

N.: Is it known by mere intellectual thought or by something deeper?

Q.: It is known in the way one knows love or that someone is loving.

N.: So, it is known in the depths.

Q.: Yes.

N.: Here, the bliss does not have an object as its cause. It does not have conditions. It is known in the depths of your Consciousness. Consciousness, Bliss, and Being are one and the same.

You say that the Maharshi appears in the waking state.

Q.: The teachings appear in the waking state for this character.

N.: Yes, but what are those teachings?

Q.: That there is no waking state. (laughter)

N.: You may say that the Maharshi's teachings appear in your waking state to wake you out of your waking state. They appear in the manifested world to wake us from the manifested world to realize the worldless, transcendent Reality. They appear as if in samsara to destroy the samsara, the cycle of birth and death. Yet, is the Maharshi, himself, one who is ever born? Does he ever die? That which is without beginning or end is Grace.

The instruction is apparently heard in the waking state. So, you might erroneously say that the instruction comes from the waking state, but it does not come from the waking state. Nor do you actually listen to it in the waking state or any other state of mind. It appears to be so. There is the face, there are the words, etc. What actually occurs with upadesa, spiritual instruction? What actually is the experience?

Q.: The very first time that I went into a satsang hall in San Bruno, I walked into a fairly crowded, little place. Two waves went through my mind. I looked at the teacher in front, and I felt that that is the happiest being that I ever met. The second thought was that this strangely reminded me of myself. I did not know what the second one meant. How could that be? Those were the first two thought waves. The essence of that has never changed.

N.: Were they just thought waves?

Q.: They could have been. I never had thought waves like that. (laughter)

N.: There is a deeper knowledge shining.

Q.: It was instantaneous, and it was not based on testimony of the senses or analysis by the mind.

N.: Nor is it restricted to the waking state. We must always understand and proceed on the basis of our direct experience. It we do so, we find that it matches identically that which composes the teachings of the wise sages. Your experience was a deeper knowledge and not of a thought wave. Your experience of your Self and of the Maharshi is something transcendent of the waking, dream, and deep sleep states. It is not necessary to take up the mental perspective that it is coming through your waking state thoughts. The experience is no barrier. There is no reason to construct, through conceptual thinking alone, the idea that there is a barrier and that you are on one side and the

Truth or transcendent state, the Maharshi, the sages, and such are on the other side. There are not two sides.

It is important to be humble and egoless. It is also important to dive deep and to not deny one's own experience. Do not postpone truth and bliss. You see as an analogy what, in the world, are called ignorance and knowledge and can apply it to a certain extent to true Knowledge and the destruction of delusion. Then, do not put off the destruction of delusion and the realization of true Knowledge, as if that were ahead of you to be theoretically conceived of now and to be experienced later. Plunge in. Do not be in the "planning stages" in regard to this inquiry, saying that you will inquire "Who am I?" later. Here and now, one should inquire.

Another Q.: I tend to deny the depth of my experience and believe in something else for a while. There is an apparent movement to something away from myself. I think that I need to return to something, but it is clear that it is the wrong thing to which to return.

N.: Do you, yourself, go anywhere or return anywhere? If your Being is steady, what possible relation could all this coming and going have to you? What relation can you have to that which comes and goes?

You say that sometimes you deny your experience. Do you deny your existence?

Q.: No, that is impossible.

N.: Of all experiencing, you are that which is most immediate. (Silence) You are of the very nature of Existence, which is inseparable from itself.

Q.: The most immediate experience is That, and there is not anything beyond That. If there would be, it would be something that I was making up.

N.: If you make up something, inquire as to what actually is your identity. What is your nature? You will find it to be always pure Existence, which is pure Consciousness. (Silence)

Another Q.: So, that means that nothing ever happened and that there is nothing physical. It means that there is never any body.

N.: (Silence) It is only from the "I am the body" misconception that one speaks of physical things occurring. It is only from the "I am the mind" misconception that one thinks of possessing a personal life with events, experiences, occurrences, and such. All of that occurs within the mind but seem, by the mind's own power, to be projected outside. Without misidentification with the body or the mind, and free of the idea of being an ego-entity, the possessor of the body and the possessor of the mind, who can say what happens? (Silence)

Another Q.: The knot assumed to be between the body and Consciousness, the Cit-jada-granthi, is where we assume the ego to be. It is identification with some process of perception. Investigating the ego, asking "Who am I?", is really asking what this assumed perception is. The more I look into it, the more I find that we have absolutely no idea of it. It is just pure assumption, just like the ego or the Cit-jada-granthi. This investigation into "Who am I?" is investigation into some perception process that we assume exists but that does not exist at all. That should clear up the knot. Everyone holds on to his assumption by not investigating.

N.: How is it that you speak of the "everybody"?

Q.: In the phenomenal world, when I try to talk with somebody about it.

N.: By what means do you know the "phenomenal world" and the "everybody"?

Q.: That is the same thing that I am trying to investigate. It seems to disappear as soon as I look at it. As soon as I look away from it, I assume it is there.

N.: If the misperception, or perceiving process, comes and goes, according to whether you look at it or not, who is it that has these two states?

Q.: Yes, that is the question.

N.: The emphasis is placed on identity. Who am I?

Q.: As long as I assume that I am such and such, that I am a connection between something that presents itself and something to which it is presented...

N.: Who supposes that assumption?

Q.: That is the "Who am I?" question, yes?

N.: The assumption, that is, the assuming, and what is assumed are identical. They are identical with the one who assumes. Thus, again, the emphasis is upon identity. The Maharshi very succinctly stated it thus as, "Who am I?"

A process occurs for someone. For whom would the process appear?

Q.: That is the assumption. That is the essence of "Who am I?" and not what I am trying to describe.

N.: Abide in the essence, and then see what happens to the world, everybody, and all else.

Q.: Jaya Bhagavan.

N.: (Silence)

Another Q.: I have a good experience. Then, choosing a wrong identity makes it dissipate. This goes unquestioned. When I come here and listen to a discourse or you dialogue with others, it always boils down to "Who you are." If I do not believe in an existent entity, there are no sprouts. If I believe in an entity, I paint the entity with different colors.

N.: Let's start with the belief. What happens? Does the real Self, of the nature of Being-Consciousness-Bliss, which is described as Satyam-Jnanam-Anantam, Truth-

Knowledge-Infinity, have the problem? Does that assume anything?

Q.: (laughing) No. That which the scriptures describe as the highest doesn't have any problems.

N.: Brahman did not decide to become deluded, but Brahman is always just Brahman. So, when you say that your experience fades, what occurs?

Q.: My identity...I...it seems that I am never rooted in...no, I cannot say that either. When I meditate on what is real, it seems solid.

N.: You are absorbed in that.

Q.: Yes, it seems solid. What happens from that to ignorance? What is real is rock-solid. It is always there.

N.: It is unmoving.

Q.: It is unmoving. This other state is moving all the time.

N.: What is the cause and substance of the other state?

Q.: It is a chunk that breaks off from the Absolute.

N.: How does the Absolute become chunky (laughing) and break off?

Q.: (quiet for awhile) I don't know. When I look from what is deep, that does not explain it. There is nothing there to explain it. I do not find pieces or even an entity to break.

N.: It is infinite, so there is nothing to break off, as if there were an edge. It is absolute, so it is without modification. It is you; it is the Self. So, there is no separate identity.

Q.: That is the beauty of it. If I just notice what I take myself to be and who I am directly, it is not very complicated. If I directly inquire as to what is really going on here, I see that I made a mistake. I just had a type of belief in something, and that belief really had no substance. It was really my Self imagined as something else.

N.: Only your Self exists always. A mistaken belief: the seed of the belief is the one who has it, and he, himself, is that belief. Is it a false assumption assumed by the false assumption itself?

Q.: (laughing) We have that problem in engineering at times. They say that here is the source and here is the destination.

N.: The engineering team of Brahma-Vishnu-Siva had the same engineering problem. (laughter)

Q.: They call me and say that they have this disastrous problem. They say that the source is going to be somewhere else, but they do not realize that there is no source. They need to make a source. It then runs out of control, because (laughing) there is no source.

N.: Maya's engineers are just like that. (laughter) There was no source. This does not have a place at which it begins.

It seems to draw its power from Cit-sakti, the power of Consciousness. So, it is borrowed power, but it has no power source of its own.

Q.: And it is between two imaginary things.

N.: So, ignorance and samsara are said to be rootless. Maya is said to be beginningless.

Q.: Even though there is a belief in something being real?

N.: The belief is the same rootless thing. The one who assumes, the assuming, and the assumption, that is, the ignorant one, the ignorance, and that about which he is ignorant, are the same thing.

Q.: The solution is to find out its rootlessness.

N.: Since ignorance pertains to oneself, the answer is to find out the nature of oneself.

Q.: In the state of ignorance, though, it is hazy. Even the clarity of noticing what is real requires some focus to recognize that this state has transpired and there is a deeper state.

N.: From where does that focus, or discrimination, viveka, come?

Q.: Ultimately, it comes from the Self.

N.: It comes from the Light of the Self, but, in the Light of the Self, there is nothing else that remains. Such is called destruction by Knowledge.

Q.: What will remain?

N.: You discriminate between what is real and what is unreal, between who you are and what you are not. In this discrimination, you find that who you are is the Reality and that the unreal has not come to be at all. Nothing exists corresponding to the unreal. Thus, Knowledge is said to "destroy" illusion. It is in this way that bondage is eliminated.

Q.: When you just said that, it struck me: I should note how unreal illusion is. This is what we have been speaking about all along. Once it loses weight, it doesn't have substance, so that there is not much to investigate. (laughing) It would be good to see if it ever could have any substance.

N.: That is a necessity. We must be so certain of our Knowledge of the Self, the Reality, that there is no alternative possible at any time. With that, the very possibility or potential to be ignorant, and, therefore, to be bound and to suffer, becomes impossible. Where another, be it another state or another identity, is utterly impossible, for all eternity, that is Nonduality.

Q.: It is upon this that all discrimination and all practice are based. What does not live up to that should be destroyed.

N.: (Silence)

Another Q.: Why is it that bliss is associated with the Self and not other experiences that we undergo, such as fear?

N.: Because Bliss is our very Being, our very nature. That which is called "fear" is only a veiling, an obscuring, of Bliss. It is a covering of our Being. Where Being, the Self, is perceived, there is no duality and no fear. When the Self is not known as it is, there can be fear because there is duality. Likewise is it with other emotions. Fear, anger, frustration, envy, jealousy, desire, and such emotions are constructed of thoughts. Bliss is of the nature of pure Being-Consciousness and is not constructed of thought. Indeed, it is when erroneous thoughts are destroyed that Bliss shines, and, when erroneous thoughts are destroyed, the other emotions become impossible. One needs to think of something in order to be afraid of it. Bliss is not like that.

Q.: At one time, I took the route of saying that I am not the body, thought, etc., but did not attempt to find out who I am. There is nothing else to do there. No inquiry goes on there, but it does not continue and does not give bliss. It gives some kind of tranquility. When I do a japa meditation, I get a physical experience in my forehead. I have another experience when the focus is on the heart. Sometimes the two are mixed.

N.: Whether there is experience in the heart, forehead, or at any other location, there is one who is aware of these. The one who is aware has no location. The one who is aware has no definition. When tranquility, or peace, is experienced in meditation, it is his own peace, or tranquility, that is experienced.

Inquiry should not be regarded as merely asking the question, "Who am I?" The Maharshi says that one should ask the question once and dive in. That diving in, or inquiry, is more than asking the question. "Who am I?" refers to the searching for one's Existence, which transcends the words and thoughts used to describe such search. If one remains truly without definition, one is stateless. For the truly undefined, or for the true definition of one's own Self, there is no beginning or end. If the state is temporary, or if inquiry seems impossible there, you may need to examine what other definitions still lurk therein. When the spirit of inquiry and the remaining undefined, that is not defining yourself as a body, as a mind, or as anything else, are fused, the experience is direct. When the experience is direct, peace and bliss become the same, and they become the same as one's own Self.

The mind makes various interpretations. It is like looking at the various facets of a gem and describing such as different gems. It is like looking at the various waves and disregarding the one water. Though the mind makes various interpretations, the nature of the meditator remains the same. Who is he? Once the rope is mistaken to be a snake, one can then describe the snake as with various colors and parts. When the notion of the snake is discarded and the rope is seen, it is quite singular and without variety. If we consider meditation in objective terms, there are various parts and different kinds. When the meditator is purely the source and substance of the meditation, that is, when the meditation is entirely upon the nature of the meditator, such inquiry, which yields a truly undefined, unconfined state, is absolutely one and partless. Meditate on the nature of the meditator. (Silence)

(Then followed a recitation in Sanskrit and English of verses from the *Katha Upanishad.*)

(Silence)

Om Shanti Shanti Shanti Om

Sahaja Samadhi

Satsang, June 18, 2006

(Silence)

Om Om Om

(Silence)

N.: In revealing the nature of Self-Realization, Sri Bhagavan called such, "Sahaja." The term means "natural" or "innate." He spoke of Sahaja Samadhi, the absorption in the innate, the absorption in that which is natural. He and other great sages have spoken of Sahaja-sthiti, abidance as the innate or the natural abidance.

What is innate, or truly natural, has no coming or going. If something is innate, it is one with your Being and inseparable from your own nature. Absorption in that which is inseparable from your own nature must be something without a beginning and without an end, without a coming to you and without a going away from you.

What kind of absorption is this? If we are absorbed in something else, we may then come forth from that something else again. If there is absorption in the Innate, there is no coming and no going. Therefore, in your quest for Self-Realization, you inquire to know the very nature of your Being.

You should not wait for something to happen to you, for what happens to you is not the Innate. What happens to you is just an appearance. An appearance, which is subject to disappearance, is, ultimately, unreal.

What appears and disappears is the assumption of individuality, or the "I" notion, as well as all that is appended to it. All that appears and disappears is truly unreal. When the unreal is known as unreal, it ceases to be experienced, and there is absorption in the Innate. This is not an absorption, or samadhi, of one thing into another; rather it is yourself in yourself, remaining as yourself.

Regard only that which is innate as your identity. What comes goes and cannot be part of you. The body comes and goes and cannot be you. The mind comes and goes and cannot be you. Every perception comes and goes.

Every conception comes and goes. None of this can be you. The assumed experiencer and all that he experiences come and go. This cannot be you. What is it in you that can neither be obtained nor lost? To know that, and to know that as yourself, is to abide in the Innate, Sahaja.

If you think that Self-Realization has not yet come, you must discover what is meant by "the Innate." If you expect it to come, you must know what is meant by "Innate." The Maharshi said that to say, "I have realized the Self," or, "I have not realized the Self," are both equally absurd. Such is so because there is only one Self and not two. The Self is the very substance of Realization, being of the nature of illimitable, unformed, unborn Being-Consciousness-Bliss.

(Silence)

What is necessary is to abide in the Knowledge of who you are. Similarly, if we say that God is within, what is the "within"? This must be known.

If you establish yourself, in illusion only, as if you were an individual entity, if you pretend, or assume, from pure imagination, that this is the case, by inquiry, find the root of this individuality. Where the false individuality, or ego-sense, ceases, there is the samadhi that is Sahaja. It is the absorption that is natural.

In the description of Self-Realization, sometimes, the Maharshi said that it is Sahaja Nirvikalpa Samadhi. Nirvikalpa means doubtless or undifferentiated. Where the ego subsides, there are no doubts about what is real or about the Self. Where the ego subsides, there is absolutely steady Knowledge. How can the Knowledge be absolutely steady? It is because it is identical with Being. It is the innate Knowledge and not something that comes and goes.

Do you see how the Realization must always be of the nature of the Self that is realized? Thus it is truly nondual. If it were of another nature, the knowledge would not be steady, and neither would the happiness and peace that one desires.

Nirvikalpa also means undifferentiated. In truth, there is only undifferentiated Existence, which is undifferentiated Consciousness. With the delusive rise of the notion of "I," division starts. If you examine your experience in your mind, you will see that all the ideas of differences are based upon the fundamental idea of "I." Once there is "I," there is difference, such as the difference between you and the universe and the difference between you and God; thus, jagat-jiva-para, the world, the individual, and the Supreme. All seem differentiated. Where the notion of "I," of a separate individuality as one's identity, is no more, there is no differentiation. Then, what is realized and who realizes are identical.

Such is the natural state, the Innate. It is not a state of the body. It is not a state of the senses. It is not a state or condition of the prana. It is not a state or condition of the mind. It is not anything experienced by anyone, but when the idea of "anyone" whatsoever is abandoned, this Self alone is found to exist. This alone is truly direct experience.

If you seek by deep inquiry, within yourself, that which is innate, this absorption in the Innate, the natural state, will be found to be yours. If you deeply inquire, "Who am I?", you are absorbed in That; you abide in That as That itself. (Silence)

Q.: The appearance of red in a clear crystal is unreal. (ed. note: reference is to an analogy in Sankara's *Vivekacudamani.*) I know mentally that the crystal never becomes red.

N.: Your very nature is extremely clear, like a transparent crystal. What colors do you imagine in it? If something completely clear, because of the proximity of something red, blue, etc., appears as if red, blue, etc., what are these colors? Your Being is entirely clear, having no definition whatsoever. What colors do you superimpose on it?

Q.: The color of the misidentification.

N.: What is the misidentification? With what do you confound yourself? What do you mix up with yourself? If you continue to so examine, guided by the Knowledge of what you truly are, you will find your experience to be exceedingly clear.

Q.: The crystal does not have any adjuncts.

N.: Nothing adheres to it. The colors that are apparently added to it are so only by reflection or illusion. Nothing has happened to the substance of the crystal, and, similarly, nothing has happened to your Being. Your Being has not become something else and has not become embodied. It has not become something caught in the mind, in the waking, dreaming, and sleeping states.

Q.: It is clear that whatever is my identity is always my identity. The thought-confusion that occurs when looking outside in imagination, makes it seem as if many, but, inside, that is also absurd.

N.: So, the looking outward and the imagination of multiplicity are actually one and the same thing.

Q.: Yes.

N.: Continue discriminating, comparing and contrasting, your actual experience and the imagined diversity. Every time you see some aspect of ignorance as absurd, it is no longer yours. (Silence)

Another Q.: My nature is bliss. Sometimes, this is so direct that there is nothing else other than that. At other times, it seems that there is someone experiencing that, and it has a quality of two. There is one who is removed from it, thinking about it. The duality exists when I don't look at it and stop looking at what my nature is.

N.: What do you want?

Q.: If I look, I already have it.

N.: Are there alternative states for you?

Q.: There appear to be.

N.: So, then, what do you want?

Q.: I don't want to change states.

N.: Based on what seed does a change of state occur? What starts the change of state?

Q.: It is that somebody is not in that state anymore.

N.: What composes the "somebody"?

Q.: (after a pause) I make up the "somebody."

N.: What goes into that "I"? You should discern this. Whatever makes up the "I" becomes the "somebody." The moment that there is somebody, Bliss-Being-Consciousness seems as if removed from you. Then, they are viewed as objective, even though the Reality of Being-Consciousness-Bliss is nonobjective. The "somebody," which is, in the relative scheme of things, objective, is mistaken to be the subject. That which is the Self is assumed to not be the Self, and that which is not the Self is assumed to be the Self.

When you say that you have it when you look implies that you do not have it when you do not look. Who is the "I" in that statement?

Q.: It seems to be made only of "I." That is the only part that is real. I cannot see anything more to it than that. What appears to be a second "I" is the same.

N.: The same primary "I."

Q.: I would need to make something else up that is not "I."

N.: Who is the maker?

Q.: There is either no maker or it is "I." When it is clearly "I," there is no maker.

N.: It means the same.

Q.: If I examine it closely, it is inescapable.

N.: There is only you experiencing yourself at all times. Even ignorance is such, but, if we know this, there is no more ignorance. Thus, Sahaja is said to be the Knowledge that is beyond ignorance and knowledge. Everything is absorbed in and actually is only the single, undifferentiated Being. This Being is Consciousness. The idea of consciousness is delusive. It is illusory and completely false.

Q.: This is a great relief.

N.: If bliss appears to be reduced at any point, you have only to know what your Being is. The tendency to develop an idea about Being, or to treat Being as if it were an objective state, into which you enter and from which you depart, which you see at some times and at other times do not, should be abandoned.

In addition, whatever attributes that "somebody" possesses should be thoroughly examined. His tendencies, whatever they are, should be destroyed. The same inquiry that determines what is real and who you are will accomplish this. If you can question the validity of the basic assumption of "I" and find the substrate of real Being, certainly you can so with every manifested tendency. They are all the forms or guises that the "I" takes on.

Another Q.: I have lived a very long time in the city of illusion. In this arising, I ask, "Who is this 'I' that has lived there that long?" This inquiry swiftly reveals the absence of this "I" that has lived there very long. Instantly, there is the true Self, the true "I," for which there is neither liberation nor bondage. It happens quickly. It is a shift from imagination to abidance.

N.: The Reality is always there.

Q.: Yes, it is.

N.: So, you say that the shift from the illusion to the Reality happens so quickly, because it is already there.

Q.: The movement that seems to enter into the idea of "I" seems to be instant in time. The arising of the illusion seems to be the realm of time. Imagination seems to be in the realm of time.

N.: Yes, and the time is also imagined.

Q.: Yes, yes.

N.: So, it is not possible to say whether the "I" arises slowly and gradually or quickly and suddenly.

Q.: That is true.

N.: Nor is it possible, or even reasonable, to say that it disappears slowly or quickly.

Q.: So, I cannot say that I have been in illusion for a long time.

N.: We may say that to begin with, and that recognition impresses upon us the urgency of knowing the Truth of the Self, the Reality. Yet, a man who sees illusion as illusion is no longer in it. He finds that he was never actually in it. It was an illusion, after all. Otherwise, we would say that it is a reality.

Within the context of time, we could describe it like this. One moment in Truth has more weight, more substance, than ages spent in illusion.

Q.: Yes.

N.: Similarly, one drop of Bliss is worth more than eons of suffering. One Knowledge of Liberation is worth far more than all the delusive notions of being bound. Of course, That is not really limited to a drop or a moment.

Another Q.: Gandhi spoke of the foolishness of consistency. The consistency is always present within. If I try to search outside for it, there is unsteadiness, and I cannot find a foundation for any kind of consistency. I think that this is that to which he was alluding. It is looking for it in a dream.

N.: To look for consistency, or permanence, in a world that is changeful by its very nature, is an impossible task. That which is absolutely steady and perfectly consistent is your nature. Nothing else is your nature. The repetition of mental tendencies, delusive conception in which, just because one has thought something previously, one continues to think the same way, is foolishness.

Consider what you regard in the context of "I know." Thus you will determine what you really know and what is merely repetition, the thinking that you know it because you thought it previously. It is an attempt to make something solid that is intrinsically vaporous.

Q.: It is looking for security in some other form.

N.: What kind of security can one find in repeating thoughts or in outer, changing, transient form?

Q.: It is foolish.

N.: (Silence)

Another Q.: To see what keeps me bound, it is helpful to know where my freedom is. From the perspective that I am the mind, there is no way that I can get past the mind, though, when my intention is sincere, that is what really matters. I had felt myself to be something grosser, but, during the discourse, it struck me that there is something far subtler. Meditation on Friday was described as merger with Being. I felt that must be the case. As my vision expands, my ability to absorb this or to dive deeper also does. Yet, I keep "hitting my head against a wall."

N.: What is the wall, and what is the head?

Q.: The wall is trying an approach that does not work. The head is holding on to these stupid ideas, to a string or pattern of ideas about happiness being found externally.

N.: How do you hold? Obviously, if we can hold ideas, there will be walls and pseudo-bondage. The bondage will feel as if real. So, how do you hold? Obviously, it is not with your hands.

Q.: It can't be in the mind.

N.: The mind is the ideas.

Q.: Yes. What would be the space that would contain such? Who knows where the boundary would be? It is not like a room, the world, the galaxies, or the universe. It is just an idea of "me," as existing somewhere.

N.: Yes, but how do you hold that idea?

Q.: Of that one? (laughing)

N.: If that idea holds the others, how do you hold that one?

Q.: (quiet for awhile) I am unsure. That one is different. It is an assumption that does not hold up very well.

N.: Yes. It is like a thought with no form to it.

Q.: The form is myself. It is filling imagination. So, if I imagine it to be a body, it fills that. If I imagine it to be a mind, it fills that.

N.: Alright. If you don't imagine it to be something, it has no form of its own.

Q.: Yes, but it has substance. It is substance, but not like a pillow. (gesturing toward a meditation cushion)

N.: What is the substance? If it is Existence itself, where is the holding of the idea of "I"?

Q.: (laughing) That is unfair. If it is Existence, nothing can stand.

N.: Does something exist other than Existence? Inquire deeply: is there something existing other than pure Existence?

Q.: I do not see that other. That seems to be important. That other is postulated in all of my illusion.

N.: Indeed, the illusion is nothing but the conception of a second, of an other.

Q.: (quiet for a while). The meditation, then, is, if there is anything pertaining to the other, to try to find out where it is.

N.: How would "other" come to be? How would such imagination be held? By whom?

Q.: (quiet for awhile) It seems that just movement of the mind assumes it to be. The mind moves.

N.: If the mind does not move, is it a mind?

Q.: At that point, it is not a mind.

N.: The mind is like the wind, made of air plus motion.

Q.: Yes. There is not a mind, but if there is a movement, it seems as if there is a movement in the mind, or in the Self.

N.: How does the Unmoving move? The motion and the mind are the same thing.

Q.: Yes.

N.: When you say that the mind moves, where does it actually go? How does the moving arise in the Unmoving? (Silence)

If it arises, the Unmoving remains as the substrate, the all-encompassing space, the illumination, and the only substance present. It is like the air with the wind.

Q.: So, it is not other. It is the same.

N.: Deeply discerning the Reality, which can be comprehended only by itself, where is the birth of motion?

Q.: In the same place. It could not be outside of it.

N.: There is no outside for the infinite. There is no inside for the homogeneous. (Silence)

(Then verses from the *Katha Upanishad*, in Sanskrit and English, were recited.)

(Silence)

Om Shanti Shanti Shanti Om

The Self Alone Is

Satsang, June 25, 2006

(Silence)

Om Om Om

(Silence)

N.: The Self alone is. Nothing else ever is. This is the simple Truth. For the Maharshi's Grace and the continuous revelation of the Truth, we can never be too thankful. If you have doubts regarding the Reality, which ever is, or, if, through imagination, you assume the unreal to be real, inquire within, "Who am I?" and thus know the Truth. When you know Reality, or the Truth, it is Reality that comprehends Reality, for there is no second.

There is only one Self. It is the Ever-existent. There is no other. Therefore, in truth, there is no one in bondage and no bondage, no one aspiring to liberation and no separate state of liberation; nor is there a liberated individual.

Just the Self, of the nature of illimitable Being-Consciousness-Bliss, alone is. For His Grace and the continuous revelation of the silent Truth, we can never be too thankful.

Q.: I was berating myself for trying to objectify the Self. Thinking it over, I reflected that there could be no alternative. The Self cannot be objectified, and nothing can be objectified. The other night, when you were joking with Advait (a young child), it seemed clear to me that, if something appears objectified, it only appears that way. That is what we can call "maya." As you just indicated, there can be no alternative. I want to be sure that I am going in the right direction.

N.: Nonduality does not have an alternative. It is not one among many. It is that which alone exists. It can never be a known or unknown object. If you imagine objectivity, the objectivity is still only That—That misperceived through delusion. Yet the delusion, itself, does not have a separate existence. To resolve the nonexistent maya, and that is what maya is, that which is not, find out for whom it is.

It is evident that your Being is nonobjective. If "I" arises, the notion of existing as some kind of individual, an object is imagined. The imagined object always corresponds to the definitions superimposed upon the individual who does not actually exist. Follow the Maharshi's advice by inquiring, "For whom is this?" "Who am I?"

Q.: Your advice was the direction to inquire, "Who would be limited by it?"

N.: If we inquire, "Who is bound?", we find no bound individual at all. We find just Brahman, just the Self. It is One Self (oneself). You don't have another kind of Self.

Q.: We can never be too thankful.

N.: Sri Bhagavan has indicated that our gratitude consists in our steady abidance in That as That, itself. (Silence)

Another Q.: Can you define abidance.

N.: It signifies an absence of misidentification. It means that the entire sense of your identity is the Self and not with what is not the Self, such as your mind, the body, or any object of the world.

Where identity is posited, so are reality and happiness. When your knowledge of happiness, its source and what it is, is steadily inward, when your knowledge of what is real is not cast out on what is unreal, and when your sense of your identity is that which the "I" truly is, and not what one assumes it to be, such is said to be abidance.

Q.: So, it is to keep the knowledge of that.

N.: A steady, continuous, deep inquiry becomes steady abidance. The same Knowledge that is the abidance is in motion, so to speak, in inquiry. The end appears as the means.

Q.: I should consider it as that always.

N.: It is one Knowledge.

Q.: So, I should not go into delusion.

N.: If you inquire, within yourself to know who you are, you cut the very root of delusion, or illusion.

Q.: Yes.

N.: Simultaneous with the disappearance of ignorance is the revelation of true Knowledge. If a piece of cloth covers this piece of wood (ed. note: Nome covers a portion of the wooden dais with his shawl), the removal of the cloth and the revelation of the wood are simultaneous. There is no delay, because the wood was always there as the substrate, merely covered. In a similar way, your nature, the Self, is eternal. The sign of Reality is that it is without beginning or end, and, therefore, unchanging. It is always perfectly there. The inquiry removes the illusion, the imagination, which is represented by the cloth in this analogy.

Q.: Ok. Yes, it is a magic show. (laughter)

N.: Who is the magician?

Q.: What if I find out I am the rabbit, the all?

N.: If you find that you are the rabbit, it is your duty to disappear. (laughter)

Another Q.: The ego gave itself a form that was obnoxious. My mistake is that I still hold on to form. What a relief it is to penetrate and see that. What a blessing! Some are open, and some are dull. I was not open for a long time. Grace had a way of making itself known. My cup of thoughts became emptier, and the Heart shone. Our stories of our problems are just not true and are not who we are. How wonderful!

N.: (silent for a while) Observe what it is that actually brings about depth of Knowledge. Is it the lapse of time?

Q.: No.

N.: What are the factors that cause you to dive deep?

Q.: Self-inquiry. Everything becomes quiet. Self-inquiry has a way of erasing everything the mind, the ego, may think that it is. The body goes away. The ego goes away. The daily life goes away. There is nothing left, and, in the beginning of that, I was scared.

N.: Something is left.

Q.: There is not even a happy feeling left. Even that is not there is the present state.

N.: If it no longer scares you, there must be a "you" that is left.

Q.: I got it. (laughing)

N.: The discrimination involved in inquiry is propelled by the intensity of one's desire for Liberation. The purpose that one has, the earnestness with which one pursues, naturally manifests as the perseverance and intensity with which one practices.

Discrimination manifests as detachment from the unreal. You are no longer drawn out.

Q.: By practice.

N.: All of these fuse together in practice.

Q.: The desire for Liberation, to know who I am, is of such importance. I become upset over not remembering to practice Self-inquiry.

N.: It would be better to just inquire. The measurements, the distinctions, and the adventures of the person have the same degree of reality, of unreality, as the person herself. The adventures of a dream character have the same degree of reality as the dream character. When you wake up, how do you regard the dream character that you thought that you were, the dream activities, and the dream time? All of it becomes insignificant because it has no reality. The one thing that was invisible in the dream is the one thing that composed the entire dream, but it was not involved in that. That is Consciousness. It is the same now.

Q.: I listen to the recordings of satsangs over and over again. I always find that there is a point that I thought that I understood but which I really did not.

N.: The traditional advice is to engage in ongoing listening, reflection, and to deeply meditate and thus be absorbed.

Another Q.: I am thinking about my attachment to work at my job. A body has a job. Identifying with that is on a much grosser level than the higher, bodiless and worldless level at which we were speaking on Friday night.

N.: How do you identify with the body? It is not you, so how do you identify with it?

Q.: Through imagination.

N.: Then, the association with its characteristics and activities is, likewise, just imagination.

Q.: Yes.

N.: When you do something through imagination, is it real?

Q.: (laughing) No. It does not create a mark.

N.: So, in what way can you say that you are attached?

Q.: Even during the entire time that I was driving around in circles, trying to get to…(ed. note: refers to a previous conversation in which he described how, due to road construction, he drove through detours in an attempt to get to a job appointment)

N.: The fate of everyone in samsara. (laughter)

Q.: (laughing) Yes, it was sort of like that! (laughter) I was not that frustrated. It was somewhat hilarious, I thought, while I was driving around in circles and thinking, "O' my God!"

N.: At least you gave credit to where it is due. (laughter)

Q.: Yes, my God. (laughter) I guess it was my prarabdha karma.

N.: Were you going in circles?

Q.: No.

N.: Did your happiness depend on it?

Q.: It was not really dependent, but there is a preference.

N.: Your ability to discern what is preferable and what not is not necessarily an attachment. Confounding happiness causes suffering. Did you suffer?

Q.: I was driving down a different street than the street that I thought I was driving on and wondering how in the heck did they change the buildings! It was so confusing.

Another Q.: Did you really think that they changed the buildings?

Q.: No, not really, but I was really puzzled because all the roads were changed.

N.: Either you were confused about the directions or they changed all the roads and buildings. (laughter) Did you suffer as a consequence? Did you lose your happiness?

Q.: It was the third wrong turn, with each wrong turn resulting in ten more minutes of traffic, which ends up on a freeway jam-packed with cars. Even then, it wasn't so bad, yet I thought, "O my God, not on this freeway again!"

N.: Did you suffer? Did you believe yourself to be a body in a car going around in circles?

Q.: I was just trying to get there. I was not concerned with anything else.

N.: There were thoughts about that. Where were you during the entire experience?

Q.: I was not aware of where I was.

N.: Do you mean that you were not thinking about it?

Q.: Yes, that is what I mean.

N.: Is thinking Knowledge?

Q.: No.

N.: Whether you thought about it or not is rather insignificant. You might prefer to think about it, but absence of that thought does not mean absence of Knowledge. You may have preferred to arrive at the destination of your intention, instead of touring the same few blocks again and again, but that does not necessarily mean attachment. You must be free of attachment and ignorance. To be free of ignorance and attachment, you should discern what constitutes such. Then, inquire.

Q.: Without ignorance, things are very clear and space-like.

N.: Is the state of Self-Knowledge really a state? Is it a condition of the mind? Is it like waking, dreaming, or deep sleep?

Q.: I shouldn't say that it is, but, because I invest reality in my thoughts, that idea occurs.

N.: You lend the reality to your thoughts, and, without doing so, they do not have even a semblance or appearance of reality. This tells you something.

Q.: Yes. Not even a semblance.

N.: In Truth, there are no such things as thoughts. They have never been born. So, also, is it with this world.

Q.: I do not understand the connection. The thoughts have no semblance of reality.

N.: If they have no reality except that which is imagined, if they have no existence except that which is lent to them, they are, in themselves, nonexistent. They have not been born, been created, or come to be.

Q.: Oh.

N.: If thought has not come to be, the world, also, is likewise. The experience of the world is utterly dependent upon the state of the mind. You, though, of the nature of Being-Consciousness, are not in or of a state of mind. (Silence)

Q.: Looking at my state now, it is different.

N.: In what way is it different?

Q.: It is more difficult to comprehend illusion or to think that it exists. It is clearer.

N.: Did your Existence become clearer? Did your Existence become clouded?

Q.: This is interesting, because I believe that.

N.: What is the nature of the one who believes it?

If the Self is real, it ever is just as it is. Clearer and clouded, closer or further away, is for someone. Who is this other one? When you say that you believe, what is the "I," the source of your belief?

Q.: In that state, that is unquestioned. It is assumed to be something.

N.: Question it now. You say that it is assumed to be something, while it, itself, is the one who assumes. It is absurd.

Q.: Questioning it, I can't see any location. Investigating what is the essence of me, it seems very space-like. I cannot define it as someone to have something, as I did in my statement.

N.: Like space, it does not actually become enclosed by anything else, does it? It pervades that something else, being inside and outside of it. It has no form of its own. There are no corners in space. If you imagine that there is a corner, you have only to dive into the corner to see what actually makes up the corner. The more you dive into it, the smaller the corner becomes.

Q.: That is clear. It is nothing more than…

N.: Imagination. It is just like that with the ego and the Self. If you imagine the Self to be individualized as an ego, inquire as to what that "I" is. Its "I-ness" or egoity vanishes. The space-like, the abiding Reality, remains. It is of the nature of utmost clarity always. It never went around in a circle, whether that be on the highway or in the samsara. For that which was never bound, the Reality of Liberation is certain.

Another Q.: Suffering is just as imagined as the one who dreams that he is suffering.

N.: (Silent for long time) All kinds of suffering are needless, aren't they?

Q.: There is no kind of suffering that is necessary.

Another Q.: What about suffering due to illness or injury?

N.: The body is subject to pleasures and pains. If we think that we are the body, we suffer in those pleasures and pains. Our experience becomes limited, and our own Bliss is veiled. If we know that we are not the body, we do not suffer even if there is pain. If we know that we are not the body and are detached from its pleasures and pains, we don't have suffering, grief, and sorrow.

Q.: These are conditional on thinking of myself as a body?

N.: Thinking of oneself as the body and, therefore, contained or imprisoned within the experiences of the body. Then, you think that what happens to the body happens to you, but that is not true. When we see that it is not true, we realize that the sufferings have been needless. We were free the entire time.

Another Q.: In discriminating, I find myself leaving one corner exempt. I still feel disappointed if the body is unwell or if the job does not go well. Janaka was disappointed that the teaching from Ashtavakra did not take explicit verbal form as he had expected. It is grace when the inquiry address that, too. If I have given all to the Guru, the Self, and want only the Self, that goes, too. Nothing is exempt.

N.: What would you want to exempt?

Q.: (laughing) I would not want to exempt anything, but I find myself exempting things.

N.: Why? If you choose not to examine and negate something as being unreal, when you have some intuition or knowledge that Truth is otherwise, why?

Q.: In some strange way, I must still think that I enjoy some sense of identity, reality, or happiness in the exempted area.

N.: Will you negate something as being unreal if you think that your happiness is connected with it?

Q.: That would cause some kind of conflict.

N.: You would have a conflict of interests. (laughter)

Q.: Yes, my interest would be in the happiness.

N.: So, there is not much mystery to this exemption.

Q.: The inquiry can put it all before the Absolute to see what stands the test of reality.

N.: Whatever you say that you are bound by, that is what you appear to be bound by. That of which you wish to become free, of that you, indeed, become free. See with whom the determination rests. There is nothing obstructing the Realization of the Absolute. Obstacles or delays appear according to what you hold fast as being your happiness, being real, and being your identity.

If you are convinced, due to some bizarre idea, that your happiness depends on a certain idea or object, you won't examine it, will you?

Q.: I will protect it from that examination.

N.: Because you know how fragile it is. You know that, by merely looking at it, it will be destroyed. Who is it that by his mere glance can destroy things? (laughter) That Siva is indwelling. That indwelling Siva is the highest Bliss. It is the Good.

Q.: As in the story about Ashtavakra, whenever it works correctly, the shift in knowledge is as quick as placing the other foot in the stirrup. It takes no time.

N.: It requires no time because the Knowledge, just as Existence, is already existent. The Maharshi says that what is not eternal is not worth seeking. You are not looking for an existence or knowledge that is not yet or which needs to ripen or such. What you seek to know or to realize, as if it were now unreal to be made more real, is actually the Reality, itself.

You know how fragile the false is. If you see the false as false, the ignorance as ignorance, it is destroyed then and there. Only the destructible is destroyed. The indestructible, which is the immutable, is never destroyed. In the indestructible lies your immortality. In the immutable lies your peace. Within lies your happiness. What is within is your Self. There is your happiness, the peace of the unchanging Absolute.

If you really know this, "neti, neti" applies to everything else. You don't hesitate to examine and inquire, because you know that, in doing so, you always realize that which is happiest. There are no exceptions.

Q.: Noticing the transience of things helps by taking some of the attractiveness out of it.

N.: It is an intuition of your nature. You yearn for that which endures because of your everlasting nature. You attach yourself to something in the name of happiness because you know that happiness is your nature, but that happiness is realized by nonattachment and by the absence of ignorance.

(Silence)

(Then followed a recitation in Sanskrit and English of verses from *Katha Upanishad*.)

(Silence)

Om Shanti Shanti Shanti Om

Real Identity

Satsang, July 2, 2006

(Silence)

Om Om Om

(Silence)

N.: The Self is Being. It does not become other than what it is, and it is invariable. Knowledge of itself is inherent in it. The Knowledge is of the nature of pure, unalloyed Consciousness. It is not a mere perception or conception. It is absolutely nondual.

If ignorance regarding the nature of the Self prevails, there is the assumption of individuality. One takes oneself to be an ego. The "I" is the birthplace of all duality. From it, by it, and within it is imagined all the misidentification with the mind, with the body, and so forth and so on. The birthplace of duality is the notion "I." That is the starting point of all the imagined bondage. It is the point of commencement of illusion.

Ask yourself, "What is this 'I'?" If it is the birthplace of duality, has it, itself, been born? If it is the starting point of illusion, is it, itself, real? If it proves to be illusory, an illusory beginning for illusion is completely nonexistent.

What do you consider "I" to be? Inquire within regarding your own nature. Who am I? If you would have Liberation from all of the imagined bondage, and, therefore, freedom from all suffering, you must know yourself as you are.

If you regard yourself as an individual entity, you undergo limited experience, which is, consequently, suffering, and the bondage and limitation correspond precisely to the definition of the "I." If the "I" is regarded as the body, one experiences and becomes bound in a world that corresponds to that body. If, though, you inquire to know yourself and realize that you are not the body, you are unaffected by the world, you are not in the world, and you even ask yourself, "Is there a world?"

Similar is it with the mind. If there is misidentification with the mind, you regard states of mind and individual thoughts as existent. From what perspective do you say that these things and these thoughts exist? It is entirely according to the definition of "I," of what you regard as yourself. If you deeply inquire, "Who am I?", you know yourself and identify with what is really yourself. There are not, though, really two of you, so that one identifies with another. It is not that kind of union. Therefore, the Maharshi stated that to say, "I have realized the Self," or "I have not realized the Self," is absurd. Why has he said so? It is because the Self is Absolute Being and not in relation to anything else. It is indivisible Existence, which is unformed and for which there is no creation.

The Realization with nonobjective Knowledge that there has never been the bound individual is the destruction, as it is called, of all the bondage. The Realization that there is no one to be deluded is the dissolution of all ignorance. What remains? That which has always been the case:

undifferentiated Being, forever-unmodified Consciousness, and invariable Bliss.

It is not that you see the Self or that the Self occurs to you; rather, you are the Self, and there is no other kind of "you." Realizing this is Brahman knowing Brahman, God seeing God. So, for whom does Realization belong? For whom does the state of non-realization belong? Continue to inquire as to who you are and discern what pertains to you and what does not, who you are, that is, the Self, and what you are not. You will find that what you are is ineffable and inconceivable, yet immediately, directly known with the Knowledge that is of the nature of pure Consciousness, unmixed with anything else. (Silence)

Whatever you experience, you are there. However you practice spiritually, you are there. Who is this "you"? When you say of anything, gross or subtle, "I know it," who is this "I"? If you think, "I experience it," who is the "I"? If just this much is realized, then, as Sri Bhagavan said in verse, "The notion, 'I see,' did not arise; how could the notion, 'I did not see.'" (Silence)

If only you know yourself as you truly are, that to which you aspire is realized to be present, perfectly full, forever. If only you realize what, in truth, you are, the very root of ignorance, suffering, and bondage is destroyed and never returns. If only you realize who you really are, the blissful immortality of which the Vedas speak, the immaculate Brahman, is realized as your very identity and as your continuous experience. If only you realize who you are, you know with absolute certitude that there is no unrealized state.

Q.: When in practice, there is only one. The state of out-of-practice seems to come back. I notice the fluttering of the sense of the individual, which comes with quite a stack of stuff. I would like to catch it in the act, so that I can examine it to see if there is any reality to it.

N.: The fact that these ideas are not present continuously is ample proof that they are not you, for whatever is you is you always. That which is you or yours does not cease even for a moment while waking, dreaming, in deep sleep, in life, or in death. It is not that this comes back to you, but, rather, you create it. The ideas forming the tendencies constituting ignorance are not lurking somewhere waiting to hop on you when they get the advantage. You conjure them, and their only solidity is the reality or identity that you lend to them.

You said that when it comes back, there is a stack of stuff. The ideas branch out. Examine those branches. Trace them to the root. Perceive the ways the tendencies manifest, and trace back the vasanas, or tendencies, to the false definitions that give rise to them. If you can see that they are truly not who you are and, therefore, are not real, they cease. They can return only if you conjure them up again, and you will do that only if you still regard them as part of your identity, as having to do with reality, or, in a more extroverted case, having to do with your happiness.

You are liberated from whatever you examine in the course of inquiry. You want to know how to catch them then and there. When you catch them does not really make a difference, since time, itself, is not real. It is enough to know yourself and to remain free, disidentified from such delusion. If, though, you wish to catch them as they occur, you can do that easily, for it is not as if you were unaware of them. Where your awareness is, so is your discrimination.

Q.: I have been reading *Timeless Presence*. In relation to thinking of being the performer of actions, I notice the importance of surrender and devotion in practice. The idea that this is our doing is a piece of fundamental ignorance. To understand that whatever occurs is God's doing or Ramana's doing or the universe's doing is one of the doors to freedom from that imagined identity. This idea that I am doing it is a source of trouble.

N.: Yes, but it is only an idea and not reality. If you know that it is only an idea, what is your question?

Q.: How to know that none of those ideas have any substance?

N.: If you know that they have no substance, how will they adhere to you? Whether through knowledge or devotion, the idea of being the performer of action, of "I do," must be abandoned. Are you the body?

Q.: So far, I have found no proof.

N.: If you are not the body, how can the activities and attributes of the body be claimed as yours?

Q.: They can't. How can the organs of action be associated with me?

N.: Stay with that. (Silence)

Another Q.: What was that which was destroyed and came back?

N.: That to which reference was made is illusion or ignorance.

Q.: When I ask the question, "Who am I?" it is not the voice of Silence that comes back. I find differentiation.

N.: When, turning the mind inward, questing within "Who am I?", the mind may produce various answers. These can be various thoughts, modes, or states of mind. One should not halt with any of them but should continue to inquire until the mind dissolves. When the mind dissolves, there is no interpretation. There is direct experience. To have the mind dissolve, seek the very source of the mind.

Q.: It is a process. Before I ask the question, I must go through the sequence to be really sure that I am in touch with the Self.

N.: The Self is already there. You can be very certain of that.

Q.: Yes.

N.: You have only to ask the question. Turn the mind inward, which is what the question signifies. Turn the mind deeply inward to question within, "Who am I?" Self-Knowledge is essential. The Self is already there. We need only inquire deeply enough. Then, there is no misinterpretation.

Q.: To turn the mind inward is a new realization for me. I do not have a good grasp of it.

N.: In the path of final Knowledge, of Vedanta, the mind's belief in its own conceptions is regarded as an outward-turned mind. You believe something is so because you thought it, whether that something be an externalized desire for something in the world or an abstract idea in the mind. An inward-turned mind is when the mind ceases to believe in its own notions. Then, the sense of identity and the sense of reality, as well as happiness, entirely return to their origin. The very source is their rightful place.

Q.: Thank you.

Another Q.: Any belief in a thought, even abstract, prevents that Reality from shining. Grosser thoughts, such as desires, are very outward and are obvious. The subtler ones are…

N.: Gross or subtle, which idea is not objective to you?

Q.: They are all objective.

N.: By what light do they shine?

Q.: By my light.

N.: That Light is not extinguished.

Q.: No.

N.: Reality does not cease to shine at any time.

Q.: You just described this inward turning to the Self. Part of delusion is that this is forgotten. It is assumed that this object is I. It becomes cyclic and sprouts.

N.: Illusion is described variously by different sages. One such description is veiling and projection. The latter implies differentiation. There is the veiling of the Reality and the projection of the multiplicity of the unreal.

Q.: If it is an object, it is already so wrong.

N.: What is an object?

Q.: My Self would be an object.

N.: How does your Self become an object?

Q.: It does not become one, but it is believed to be.

N.: Who has the belief? (Silence). Does the Self have delusion?

Q.: Those questions definitely introvert the mind. Inside the circular thinking, though, those questions may not arise. The mind is not introverted.

N.: Why is it not introverted? Obviously, in a state of delusion, the questions do not arise, because, if a question such as "Who am I?" would arise, the delusion would be nonexistent. The Self is always shining. It never ceases to shine. It is Knowledge, itself. That is pure Consciousness, pure Being. The Upanishads (*Katha* 2:2:15, *Mundaka* 2:2:10, and *Svetasvatara* 6:14) say, "Not there the sun shines, not the moon and the stars, not these flashes of lightning shine; whence is this fire? That alone shines; accordingly all shines. Of the light of That, all this shines brightly." It indicates that its nature is self-luminous Consciousness, known only to itself, existing only for and as itself without another, and, in consideration of all else, it is the light, or the knowing, in all else.

The Knowledge is the Self. The Knowledge is not possessed by the Self. So, it cannot be lost. Prajnanam Brahma, Supreme Knowledge is Brahman.

Who becomes deluded? Is there some other? If there would be another, he would need to pre-exist the delusion. Otherwise, there would be no causality. If delusion is the effect, there must be a cause. That cause is the one who is deluded. Outside of delusion, can there be a deluded one?

Q.: Puncturing that framework is the key. I need to see that this could not have occurred.

N.: Of what substance is the framework of delusion constituted?

Q.: The framework is a mixture of me, the Self, which is the Reality, and a notion of individuality. It is "me" plus the grand "me."

N.: The Self plus the notion of "I" becomes all this illusion. Without that "I," there is no ignorance. Just the Self alone exists, and that is Truth and Bliss. From where did this other "I" come? Did the Supreme Self, Brahman, give birth to some ego-"I"?

Q.: Ah, that does not make any sense. That would imply that even Realization would not hold up because the realized could have illusion.

N.: If the ego existed ever, even for a moment, it would mean an interruption in the Reality, and there would be no liberation, which is absurd. Liberation from all the imagined bondage is in the Knowledge that the ego-entity has never come to be. Inquire within yourself. If you are the Self, is there another, an ego, an individual, the one who becomes ignorant? Can your existence be two?

Q.: The only time that it feels as if two is within those circular patterns. There is just the belief that there could be an inside of it.

N.: Where is the "it" in which all this occurs?

Q.: It is not the body. As for the mind, who knows where the mind is? (laughing) It is totally ridiculous to conceive of the mind being in the body.

N.: It is probably better to say that the body is in the mind, but where is the mind?

Q.: The mind is definitely in the Self. There is no question about that.

N.: So, there is nothing outside of the Self. Does the Self have parts within it? Is there an inner space and a greater space?

Q.: No. It is not like looking through a telescope in the attempt to see the end of the universe, though that would be useful, if one could see the end of the Self.

N.: (laughing) The end of the Self?

Q.: They do not think that there is any end to space.

N.: Perhaps, because there is no end to the knower of it.

Q.: It is just a reflection of the Self.

N.: If there appear to be two states, you must inquire for whom they are. If they are for you, you must inquire to see if there are two existences, a real Self and a secondary self, Siva and jiva. You must inquire. If you do so, you will not find any individual there at all.

Q.: It is exactly as you are saying. With the existence of a secondary state, there is the mind and everything else following that.

N.: Such is said to be illusion or ignorance. Ignorance is something that is not true. Illusion is something that does not exist. If you seem to go in and out of the Self, inquire as to who it is that goes in and out. The unreal "I" will be consumed, precisely because he is unreal. When he has been destroyed, it is not as if there were something existing that has been destroyed. We only loosely speak of the "destruction of ignorance."

Q.: But, in another sense, it is destroyed.

N.: It must be thorough and complete.

Q.: Yes, because it returns, it must be destroyed.

N.: It returns only so long as one believes it to be real.

When we know it to be unreal, that it has never come to be, we find that what has never come to be does not return. There is beginning and end, birth and death. For that which has birth, death is certain, and for that which has death, birth is certain, but, for the unborn, there is no death.

We can say that there are two things that are unborn: the Reality, which is without beginning or end, and the unreal, which never began. Of course, between the Real and the unreal, there are not really two things. (laughter)

Q.: One always posits the reality of happiness somewhere. All of that amounts to confusion regarding myself. With individualization, it sprouts. Yet, what is real, the Self, is always. Reality is there.

N.: The Self is the only Reality. It alone exists. The Self is the identity, the only identity. You cannot be another. The Self is, also, happiness. In it, there is perfection. Nothing is lacking. With the misidentification of "I," identity seems to belong to an individual, that which is objective is mistaken to be real, and happiness is pursued as if it were external to oneself. The external pursuit becomes attachment. The rest is misidentification. The misidentifications and attachments constitute the ignorance. It is the same as the veiling and the projection of multiplicity spoken of earlier.

Q.: The veiling is a notion of an "I." From there, all projection takes place.

N.: The real Self, though, is without cause and effect, without "I" and without "this." (Silence)

Another Q.: I have understood from you that the Truth from the Sadguru, Sri Ramana, does not occur in the waking state. You have also told me that anything that can appreciate it, recognize it, or feel the depth of it could be only the Reality. An inert mechanism of the mind never knows any of that. With faith in the word of the sage, I can anticipate that the clarity of Reality can discriminate. What is lacking that clarity is just another thing to discriminate.

Only the Real knows. I can inquire and watch as the Real continues to know.

N.: Faith and discrimination have the same root.

Q.: It can be turned on the mechanism that was formerly given credibility, namely, the mind.

N.: It is inert and has no knowing of its own.

Q.: So, who could continue to conjure ignorance? If some would appear, there could be only a trusting confidence that its days are numbered.

N.: Ignorance prevails only so long as we believe it to be true. The moment that we see ignorance as ignorance, it ceases to be for us.

Q.: Anything that would even partially believe it would itself be ignorance.

N.: Ignorance is inert and does not have the power of belief. Its apparent power is entirely borrowed. We may say that it is a testimony to the power of belief, or faith, that it makes even ignorance appear as if real, something insubstantial appear as if real.

Q.: It is a projection of reality onto ignorance.

N.: It is a testimony to the strength of the root of faith.

Q.: Oh, I see. So, even the apparent persistence of ignorance is that.

N.: Yes, a testimony to Truth.

Q.: I often think of Sri Sankara's statement, "By the word of my Guru, Sivo'ham." I try to get into the state from which he said this.

N.: For Sankara, the Knowledge, the Truth known, Siva, himself, the Guru, and the word and the Silence are identical. (Silence)

Another Q.: I have an idea that something outside of reality determines reality. I think that this is wrong, for where would that thing get its power to do so?

N.: Examine your experience. All the time, you seem to be saying, "This is real. That is real." The "this" and the "that" are interchangeable. The quality, if we can call it such, of being real is consistent. It does not diminish, no matter how many times different things are thought of as being real. Trace that quality of being real to its source. Does anything declare its own existence? Sri Bhagavan said, "Does the world say that it exists, or do you say that it exists?" The idea, "It is," comes from you. The perception that "it is" comes from you. You are the knowledge. Trace the knowledge to its real nature.

Q.: I have the experience of something continuous that is unquestionably real. Being real, it is not a thing that can be described, but it is unmistakably known. That seems to be the only thing that I really know. Right now, it is very difficult to say that there is something else.

N.: Did that which you now recognize just begin, or has it always been the case?

Q.: (after a pause) It is not something that has a beginning.

N.: Then, it is not an occurrence.

Q.: It does not come and go.

N.: Thus, spiritual experience is not an event. It does not come and go or occur. That of which we speak as a spiritual experience is That which is, but usually subsumed under the idea of a personal entity who has it. Yet it is precisely in the dissolution of the personal entity that the experience shines. It always shines, but the cloud has been removed. Therefore, emphasis is placed on knowing yourself, rather than the attempt to measure what happens to you.

Q.: In the instruction to know myself, I think that there is the assumption that there are times when I don't know myself.

N.: If you would know yourself, what would happen to time? If you would know yourself, what would happen to the one who does not know himself? (Silence)

Do you recall Sri Ramana saying that there is no one who does not experience the Self at any time? Why did he say that?

Q.: The Reality is inescapable. The ideas that I ever escape it and that there is one to escape it are absurd.

N.: The recognition of the absurdity of that is the escape from samsara. (Silence)

(Then followed a recitation in Sanskrit and English of verses from the *Katha Upanishad.*)

(Silence)

Om Shanti Shanti Shanti Om

Knowledge and Devotion

Satsang, July 9, 2006

(Silence)

Om Om Om

(Silence)

N.: A knower of the Self is the Self. In Truth, there is nothing but the one, nondual Self. Nothing else exists. So, it is not possible for another one, which is unreal, to know the Self.

What happens in the Realization of the Self? The Self is ever real and never becomes more or less real. It neither appears nor disappears, but always exists. We can say that the unreal is unrealized, and this is said to be Self-Realization. That which was imagined to be real ceases to be so.

Numerous scriptures declare that the knower of Brahman is Brahman and that the knower of Brahman becomes Brahman. What does it mean? Does it mean that someone else becomes Brahman, that is, something that is not the Absolute Self becomes the Absolute Self? Brahman is just Brahman; the Self is just the Self. It never becomes something other, and, being all-transcendent, nothing becomes it. It is formless, and, for that which is formless, there can be no other. No unreal form, gross or subtle, can become the transcendent Truth.

The unreal is unrealized. This is what is so essential in spiritual practice that yields the fruit of Self-Realization.

The knower of the Self is the Self. Is there another knower in you? Can the senses and their activities be knowers? Is it not that something else knows them, yet is unseen, is un-sensed, by them? Can thinking, that is, the mind, know the Self? Is it not that thinking shines by the reflected light of some unconceived knower?

If, in the spiritual practice of inquiry to realize the Truth of the Self, you consider yourself as one thing and the Self as another, direct your inquiry to the consideration of that first thing. Who is it that stands apart from the Self to think, "I know it; I don't know it; I am trying to know it"? Who is that one? If we inquire in this manner, we realize conclusively that the Self is only one, without a second. For that which is without a second, ignorance and delusion are impossible. Where there is the assumption of a second, of another one, there can be the play of ignorance and illusion. Upon inquiry, we realize that the second one has never been born. He has never come to be, and, likewise, his illusion. When we realize this, ignorance is conclusively destroyed and does not return.

Therefore, the knowledge of identity is essential. Realization is identification with That, the Self. To identify with the Self, we need not stand apart and then create a union of our so-called self and the Self. We have only to unrealize the unreal, that is, cease to regard as real what we previously assumed to be real and as who we are. That suffices. All differentiation or duality has its root, its seed, in the assumed individuality. Clarity of knowledge regarding who we are eliminates this false assumption of individuality and, with it, all duality is erased. What is erasable is unreal. The Real can never be removed, nor has it been.

Q.: I am examining to see if this assumption of "me" is there all the time. I have heard that, if it comes and goes, that is a hint of its unreality. The assumption is not there in all of the three states. In deep sleep, there is no assumption. In the spaces of meditation, the assumption is not there.

N.: How does this flimsy phantom arise? There are states in which the "I" assumption does not manifest or rise up. On other occasions, it seems to arise. How does that happen? How does it start?

Q.: It is not put there by any external experience.

N.: Yes, that is true, for the idea of something external comes only after the "I" rises.

Q.: I don't know which comes first. Instead of remembering the Truth, I remember the illusion.

N.: Who is it that has the remembrance? Who gives the resurgence to that conception? The "why" or "how" resolves itself into "What actually is this ego?" If you have the conviction that this is not the truth but only an assumption, you need to determine how unreal the unreal really is. What is the significance of "only an assumption," and "only imagination"?

The Maharshi said that there is no false "I." What is its significance? Have faith, or conviction, in his word that the true Self is and the ego-self is not, and experientially verify the plain fact, which is the ultimate Truth, of his statement. The true Self is the only Self, and a false self simply is not.

Whether it is referred to as imagination, a false assumption, or as something nonexistent, continue to inquire into the depths of such. In your own experience, in the most interior, direct manner, what does this mean? This is what is to be known.

Another Q.: When I am in the state in which there is no memory, no experience, and no one, if I question that state, I feel that I am going to lose that state. Is that correct?

N.: The mind acts like a veil to cover that state so that your Self seems to disappear. Why not put an end to the mind?

Q.: I do not understand. When I am in that state, how can I manage to bring in a question?

N.: Where there is no questioner, no question need arise. If your mind later draws you out, why not destroy the mind?

Q.: The mind does not draw me out, but the bell at the end of meditation does.

N.: How does the bell bring you out?

Q.: The sound of it ringing.

N.: How does the sound become so powerful?

Q.: Because it is a signal to come out. Isn't that the purpose of the bell?

N.: Why should it be a signal to go out? Perhaps, it is a reminder to stay in. (laughter)

Q.: I supposed that everybody came out when they heard the bell. Isn't that it?

N.: Came out of where?

Q.: Out of that state of nowhere, no one, and no consciousness.

N.: Maybe they should stay in.

Q.: It would be better.

N.: Who made the rule that the bell ringing means that you must come out? Here, when the bell is rung, Om follows thereafter. Om cannot possibly have the significance of going without.

Q.: So, I am supposed to stay in that state when you are speaking?

N.: You should remain in the state of the Self at all times.

Q.: Oh!

N.: Whether hearing bells, Om, listening or talking, whether you are seated here in satsang in the temple or your body is elsewhere or engaged in activity, at all times, and irrespective of the conditions of the body and the senses, you should remain steady in the Self. Everything has that purpose. Most assuredly, those things that are of a spiritual nature have that purpose. So, conversation in satsang is intended to keep you within and not without.

Q.: I try to open my eyes in meditation, but I keep going back within. To look around, I must open my eyes.

N.: There is no rule here that you must open your eyes. The opening and the closing of the eyes should not determine one's inner state.

Q.: It is easier.

N.: It may appear that way, but, once you conclusively realize that you are not determined by the senses or their activities, the opening and closing of the eyes, the movement of the limbs, and the activating of your ears and such make no difference whatsoever. In the Maharshi's teachings, so much emphasis is placed on the Knowledge of oneself, what your identity is. That is remaining within. Otherwise, one is ruled by the little eyelids, eardrums, and such. They should not govern your experience.

Another Q.: When I start to search for where the ego arises, there is the assumption that it is actually there. As I trace from where it comes, the reality attributed to it starts to break up. It appears to me that it is only the lack of examination that allows it to continue. There is no place from where it comes.

N.: Can it come from nothing?

Q.: (quiet for awhile) No. That would assume that nothing is something, so that something could come out of it.

N.: Yes. It is not reasonable that something apparently existent could come from something nonexistent.

Q.: Yes, illusion could not come from nothing.

N.: What is the source?

Q.: (quiet for awhile) When I look at it, it is no longer there. I must conclude that I make it up. When I look to where it came from, it dissolves and leaves me with the question, "Who made it up?" It did not make itself up. This leaves one free to free himself.

N.: There is no second entity. The Reality of the Self is what is. If ignorance is imagined in conjunction with it, the same real Self appears as the source, lending its reality to all illusion. If, through Self-inquiry, the illusion is traced inward to its source, the source ceases to be regarded as a source and is known as it really is. No trace of illusion remains.

Q.: You say that the source is seen. I do not understand that.

N.: All illusions have their source in oneself. If that source, oneself, is seen, it is not a source. It is the forever-undifferentiated Absolute, and illusion is simply not.

Q.: Isn't seeing it as a source based on some notion of "two"? It is the idea that that something is coming from a source to somebody.

N.: The Reality of the Self appears as the source and lends its reality to all else when all else is imagined. By the conjunction of imagination and the Self, the singular Reality appears as if a source for all of the unreal. Thus, one says, "This is I, and that is real." If, in the midst of such, you inquire, "Who says that is real? Who says this is I?" the Reality of the Self shines entirely by itself. (Silence)

We cannot actually discuss the Self, as if we could stand apart from it, as if it were an objective topic. We cannot accurately analyze the ego without inquiring into its nature. If we inquire into its nature, it is absorbed. (Silence)

Another Q.: Does this have to do with Self-remembrance?

N.: You could call it such.

Q.: What is the difference between Self-Realization and Self-forgetfulness?

N.: When Self-forgetfulness becomes impossible, since there are not two selves so that one may forget the other, such is called Self-Realization. In Truth, the Self is beyond memory and forgetfulness. They are thinking. When you think of something, you say that you remember it, and, when you do not think of it, you say that you forgot it. The Self can never be thought of, for it is never a known object, and it is never an unknown object. It stands beyond such. We can loosely speak of forgetting oneself and remembering oneself, but, in this case, unlike other kinds of memory, once known, it is never lost.

Q.: Can it come to me as a wish for Self-Realization?

N.: You could, but your prayer would be more efficacious if it were for the dissolution of the "me." If one wishes, "Let it come to me," the distance between that and the "me" is constituted of the definitions concerning the "me." If, by any means, the "me," or ego, is dissolved, what one wishes to come is already the case. Thus, in spiritual practice of whatever form, the emphasis is always upon ego-dissolution. Ego-dissolution is the essential Knowledge. Knowledge, in the deep spiritual sense, is always the active key in any fruitful practice.

Q.: The seed of ignorance is to create a separate entity?

N.: Yes, to create a separate entity is the seed of ignorance, and it is the ignorance. That entity experiences the ignorance. It is wrapped up in itself, in ignorance about itself.

Another Q.: I have been taking the unreal to be real, but, from the instruction today, it can be seen that all this has not come to be. When I inquire and when I come here, I have a certain focus. My mind dissolves more quickly, and I see what you are pointing at in a deeper way.

N.: That is why one goes to temples and holy places and keeps holy company.

Q.: Yes, it is definitely a big benefit. I wish I could see this more, because this is the way it truly is and should not be dependent upon a body sitting in a holy place.

N.: Are you the body?

Q.: (laughing) I guess so in this particular case. The body sits in a holy place.

N.: Is that your experience?

Q.: No.

N.: When, anywhere, you have a deep experience, are you the body?

Q.: No. The body is always out of the picture. If it's in the picture, there is no experience.

N.: So, what do you mean by "being dependent upon holy places and holy company"?

Q.: The ability to drop off what is unreal and to have a feeling for what is real becomes clearer.

N.: Aren't these abilities described by you inherent in you?

Q.: Yes, and they are definitely not dependent upon bodies. So, it is not one body giving to another body.

N.: Bodies do not enter into this at all.

Q.: Yes.

N.: So, what could possibly be the meaning of "dependent on holy company and holy temples"? If the Truth is entirely bodiless, and if that which is bodiless is necessarily worldless, and if it is only from the position of being a body that one can think of being in a world and of going to different places in the world and being in various situations in the world, and if you are bodiless, what is this talk of dependence?

Q.: It has nothing to do with the bodies but with the clarity and inward direction of this teaching. There is this focused energy entirely pointing toward this one thing. Not a moment goes by when it is not directly showing where one can find freedom. It has continuity.

N.: It seems that it would be good to depend on such.

Q.: (laughing) Yes. The continuity about the existence of the Self is here, with every questioner getting the same inward drive to realize the Self. It is incredibly helpful. The guru represents what is and is standing in and abiding as That. It is like the gravity of the sun, bringing everything in because that gravity is so strong. Satsang is like that. So, it is not bodies, but it is the gravity of the Self.

N.: You say that it is a very strong gravity.

Q.: Yes.

N.: How far does it reach? Is it like celestial things, such as the sun, away from which the force that is referred to as gravity seems to lose its effect according to the factor of distance?

Q.: The distance is created by my mind. That alone matters, and it is only a belief in the distance. When the belief is clear that what is real is present right now, it does not matter if it is in satsang or wherever. It is direct.

N.: So, nearness and farness are determined only by the mind.

Q.: Or, by the lack of the mind.

N.: The lack of the mind is locationless and spaceless. As the Maharshi stated in *Saddarsanam*, "We, the timeless and spaceless, alone are." The mind can measure near and far, but, where there is no mind, there can be no such talk. (Silence)

Q.: The drive to know the Self seems to come naturally from the realized. Yet the realized say that the unrealized essentially does not exist at all in the ever-present realized state.

N.: This means that the unrealized one in you does not exist. There is only one of you, which is the Self. The unrealized jiva does not exist. So, who can stand apart to say that he does not know this?

Q.: (quiet for awhile) I project something, assuming a self, but, as that starts to happen, I inquire to determine if that is real.

N.: So, the intensity to abide in and as the Real is there.

Q.: It is always there, even when my mind is cloudy. It notices the cloudiness and recognizes that it is not satisfactory.

N.: Is there any cloudiness regarding the Knowledge of your own nature? Can you any longer seriously take yourself to be an individual entity? (Silence)

Q.: I had a very good experience Friday night. During our discussion, I became clear, but I could not hold on to that state.

N.: What happened?

Q.: Doubts arose.

N.: What doubts?

Q.: That it would not be possible to hold on to that state. (laughing)

N.: What was the reason for the doubt? What was going to make it impossible?

Q.: It was that my nature is fundamentally different from That.

N.: Steadily inquire into this: what is actually your fundamental nature? As long as you treat your nature as if it were a state that could come and go, you will be absorbed and then will seem to re-emerge. The Self is not a state.

Q.: How does one know that it is not a state?

N.: How do you know that you exist? Isn't your knowledge of Existence quite independent of any kind of state?

Q.: Yes. The sense of Existence is very, very subtle. It goes through the mind.

N.: Being's Knowledge of itself cannot possibly be a state and cannot be bound by the mind. One of the verses of the *Kathopanishad* says that, first, there is knowledge of existence, and, then, that knowledge-existence is revealed for what it really is. First, there is knowledge of existence, and, then there is the revelation of what that existence truly is.

Q.: That is deep.

N.: No mental state enters into this.

Q.: What is the difference between the first and the second?

N.: It is a description of inquiry that results in Self-Knowledge. You exist, and you know that you exist. When the Knowledge of Existence shines of its own, without any imagined obscuration superimposed upon it, such is the latter Knowledge of what it truly is. Do not treat your Self as if it were a state or your identity as if it were apart from the Self. If you treat yourself as if you were apart from it and thus as one who can lose it, immediately inquire as to who that is.

Q.: Or, as dependent?

N.: That arises later. Without the ego, what is the temple, what is satsang, what is holy company, who is the guru, and who is the Self?

Q.: All that depends on someone for whom it can be.

N.: Yes, or all of those are of the identical Existence and nature. In that case, you are utterly dependent, in as much as you cannot be separate from your own Existence. After all, we do not liberate the individual from the Absolute; we are liberated and abide in the Absolute by being free from the individual. If we would take the other, dualistic approach, we would then say that we need to navigate very cautiously as to when we may use that which is sacred and when we may not, lest we would become dependent even though good is coming of it. That is flatly absurd. Hence, the *Gita* says that no harm ever comes from this dharma. Likewise, no harm ever comes from satsang, temples, spiritual teachings, the guru, etc. There is no such thing as having too much of such. There is thus no question of being dependent on that. The absurd question of that is based on dualism. Even if one would accept such dualism and be dependent upon that, such would be fine as long as one was independent of everything else.

Q.: Yes, one is totally dependent on that and on the realized.

N.: It is like saying that you are dependent on your own Consciousness.

Q.: So, to get rid of that dependence would be a complete mistake. That is everything.

N.: The idea was only a misapplication of terms within a dualistic context.

Another Q. There is a decided change. There is much less mental activity of the needless type. I am also much more prone to be forgetful. I do not know if this means I have surrendered and am done with it. I would appreciate your advice in the matter.

N.: The two should be distinguished. The first thing is surrender, and the second thing is the frailty of the mind and its mental activities. In this regard, the mind and its activities are not unlike the other senses and their activities. It is a subtle sense. Just as the eye, ear, etc. are not immortal, but are subject to change and decay, likewise is it with the brain. Just as the activities of the senses are subject to decay and change, likewise the activities of the mind, such as memory, etc.

When surrender of the mind occurs, it means the abandonment of misidentification with the mind. Everything is given over to the Supreme, to God.

Q.: Ah!

N.: God bears the responsibility for it. One's sense of identity is no longer entangled in it. The sign of surrender is not necessarily reduced memory or reduced mental activity, no more than sign of deep devotion, or surrender, or inquiry, would be reduced acuity of vision or hearing. These are lost, as well, eventually. This is so for all the bodies here and their senses.

Q.: I did not hear that. Can you repeat the end of this instruction?

N.: Loss of hearing is for the ears, and the sign of surrender, or devotion, or inquiry is not the reduction of the hearing, but rather the ceasing to be bound by the states of hearing, etc. Likewise is it with the relation to the mind. The sign of surrender or of deep meditation is not the reduction of the abilities of the intellect or memory.

Q.: There is no connection?

N.: There is no connection whatsoever. It is freedom from the mind, memory, etc., and not reduction of memory. Decay of the nervous system and many other factors, mental or physical, can bring about various forms of mental changes and mental decay. These have nothing to do with surrender.

Q.: Yes.

N.: Surrender and inquiry leave one in a transcendent state. Loss of memory, mental attention, mental acuity, etc. may have other causes, including phenomenal ones, such as infirmity, disease, the use of them, and other factors.

Q.: So, you say that there is not necessarily a direct connection with my interpretation and the fact that I have intended to surrender the mind.

N.: Surrender of the mind is wonderful and good, indeed. There is no connection between surrender and loss of memory, just as there is no connection between surrender and deafness, blindness, or the loss of taste sensations.

Q.: Yes, there are factors occurring, such as my advancing age.

N.: You can clearly discern that if your tongue lost the sensation of taste, such would not be caused by the surrender of the desire for food. The transcendence of desire would not necessarily mean that the taste buds would become inert. That would simply be a function of the tongue.

Q.: That is a difference I notice. That was my question. Thank you.

Another Q.: These things are temporal and part of the finite. Are these temporal things part of the infinite? Are they separate from the infinite?

N.: They have no independent existence, but the infinite remains beyond them. Thus the verses in the *Gita*: I am in all these things, yet I am not in all these things. All these things are in me, yet none of these are in me. This is my sovereign mystery.

Q.: Does the finite mean that identification with the ego, the impediment to reaching the Absolute, is there? It is because of the shortcoming of the finite.

N.: As long as there is attachment to the ego, there is clinging to the finite, which forms the boundaries of one's bondage.

Q.: All actions mislead one into deception, from the finite point of view, as ears, eyes, and sense.

N.: A spiritual person does not depend on the senses to determine identity or to determine reality.

Q.: That is the revelation of the infinite, which is always.

N.: Yes. When we cease to regard the senses as the determinants of reality and identity, we, ourselves, stand as the un-sensed, and the Reality is known purely as the Existence, which is said to be unformed and un-sensed.

Q.: The infinite Absolute has a relation with the finite.

N.: If there is the finite, the finite is only That. It appears in That, disappears in That, is supported by That, is illumined by That, and is absorbed in That. In Knowledge, we see that the Infinite alone is, and the finite has never disturbed it. There is only the infinite. Thus the Vedic verse,

om pūrṇamadaḥ pūrṇamidaṁ pūrṇāt
pūrṇamudacyate |

pūrṇasya pūrṇamādāya pūrṇamevāviśiṣyate ||
om śāntiḥ śāntiḥ śāntiḥ ||

Om. That is the perfectly full. This is the perfectly full. From the perfectly full, the perfectly full springs (issues forth).

Of the perfectly full, having taken the perfectly full, the perfectly full alone remains.

Om. Peace, Peace, Peace.

(Then verses from the *Kathopanishad* were recited in Sanskrit and English.)

(Silence)

Om Shanti Shanti Shanti Om

Sri Ramana Maharshi's Self-Realization

Satsang, July 16, 2006

In celebration of July 17th

(Silence)

Om Om Om

(Silence)

N.: "If one can only realize at heart what one's true nature is, one then will find that it is infinite wisdom, truth and bliss, without beginning and without an end." What is Sri Ramana's Self-Realization? (Silence)

When even Dakshinamurti could express this only by Silence, what else can be said about it? (Silence)

Where all words and thoughts turn back, unable to grasp or comprehend, that is this Realization. The Realization is nondual, so it is the very nature of the Reality, itself, which is without a beginning and without an end.

The Unborn, the Imperishable, is the Self, and the one who has realized the Self is only the Self and nothing else. Realization entails not having even a trace, even a possibility of a trace, of anything other, whether such be the notion of "I," which is the false assumption of individuality, or any kind of "this," which is the notion of an objective thing.

The Realization is nondual, yet beyond the conception of "nondual." It is infinite, yet beyond any conception of "infinite." It is the Self, yet beyond any conception of a self. It is utterly transcendent, yet it is without the idea of anything else existing over which to be transcendent.

Listen to what the Maharshi has said. "This is Liberation or Enlightenment or Self-Realization. The individual being, which identifies its existence with that of the life in the physical body, as 'I,' is called the 'ego.' The Self, which is pure Consciousness, has no ego sense about it. Neither can the physical body, which is inert, in itself, have this ego-sense. Between the two, that is, between the Self, or pure Consciousness, and the inert, physical body, there arises mysteriously the ego-sense, or 'I' notion, the hybrid, which is neither of them, and this flourishes as an individual being. The ego, or individual being, is at the root of all that is futile and undesirable in life. Therefore, it is to be destroyed by any possible means. Then, that which ever is alone remains resplendent. This is Liberation or Enlightenment or Self-Realization."

When that which alone is and is ever shining remains, without a trace of the imagined ego, such is Self-Realization. Inquire as to what it is that is called "I." When you think "I," to what do you refer? Is it to the body? He has already declared that the body does not have an ego. To what does "I" refer? Is it to something connecting the pure Consciousness with the body? Is it to an individual being who seems to inhabit the body? That is just the mysterious hybrid. It rises and disappears based upon its own imagination. It is not that which ever is and which alone is. So, to what does "I" really refer? Know this. If this is known, the knower, what is known, and the knowledge are identical. This leaves no trace of the possibility of ignorance or the illusions imagined within that ignorance.

The Realization is of the nature of the Reality, so it neither comes nor goes. It is the "I"-less true "I." That which does not come or go is the Reality, and, thus, the Realization, which is egoless, is not something that occurs to the individual. The individual is nonexistent. When this is known and the innate Being shines without delusive obscuration, such is called "Self-Realization." It is not an event or occurrence. It does not happen. It is not in time. That which is beyond time, space, and the individual is what is real. That is the unborn and the imperishable. That is the abode of infinite wisdom and bliss, for that is the Truth.

Having realized the Truth and abiding perpetually as the Truth, the Maharshi, out of compassion for those devotees who approached him seeking the Truth, recounted the Realization in terms of something that happened only to show them that which is transcendent of all time, occurrences, space, and the "I." Listen to what he recounts. It appears as if an event, but really it is about eternal Truth. It appears as if something happening, but really it is about that which is. It has no arising and disappearance.

"It was about six weeks before I left Madurai for good that the great change in my life took place. It was quite sudden. I was sitting alone in a room on the first floor of my uncle's house. I seldom had any sickness, and, on that day, there was nothing wrong with my health, but a sudden, violent fear of death overtook me. There was nothing in my state of health to account for it, and I did not try to account for it or to find out if there was any reason for the fear. I just felt that I am going to die and began thinking what to do about it. It did not occur to me to consult a doctor or my elders or friends. I felt that I had to solve the problem myself there and then.

"The shock of the fear of death drove my mind inward, and I said to myself mentally, without actually framing the words, 'Now, death has come. What does it mean? What is it that is dying? The body dies.' And, at once, I dramatized the occurrence of death. I lay with my limbs stretched out, stiff, as though rigor mortis had set in and imitated a corpse so as to give greater reality to the inquiry. I held my breath and kept my lips tightly closed, so that no sound could escape, so that neither the word 'I' nor any other word could be uttered. 'Well, then,' I said to myself, 'this body is dead. It will be carried stiff to the burning ground and there burnt and reduced to ashes, but, with the death of this body, am I dead? Is the body 'I'? It is silent and inert, but I feel the force of my personality and even the voice of the 'I' within me apart from it. So, I am Spirit, transcending the body. The body dies, but the Spirit that transcends it cannot be touched by death. That means that I am the deathless Spirit.'

"All this was not dull thought. It flashed through me vividly as living Truth, which I perceived directly, almost without thought-process. 'I' was something very real, the only real thing about my present state, and all the conscious activity connected with my body was centered on that 'I.' From that moment onward, the 'I,' or Self, focused attention on itself by a powerful fascination. Fear of death had vanished once and for all. Absorption in the Self continued unbroken from that time on."

"Absorption in the Self continued unbroken from that time on." For one who has realized, there is no second, no other state, and no possibility of another state. There is no "I" but the one true Self. Being unconnected with the body, this Self-abidance is forever, without birth and without destruction.

In this recounting, it seems as if an event occurred, but what actually happened? It is Knowledge, but not mere thought-process. Though the story begins with someone inquiring, it concludes with just the one "I" that is Being and no individuality. Nothing happened to the individual; the individual vanished.

Similarly, turn your mind inward. The transitoriness of the body that was then perceived is common to all. Perceive this for yourself. With the birth of the body, did you begin? With the changes of the body, did you change? With the actions of the body, do you act? With the perishing of the body, do you die? In this way, question within yourself. What pertains to the body, and what is truly your identity?

If you recognize your thoughts behind, that is to say, more subjective than, the body, continue to inquire to determine what is the "I" behind all those thoughts.

In the inquiry, the inquirer dissolves. His identity is absorbed. What remains is that which alone exists for all of eternity.

"The Self alone exists, and the Self alone is real." If that is realized, it is perfection. "The Self alone exists, and the Self alone is real. Verily, the Self alone is the world, the "I," and God. All that exists is but the manifestation of the Supreme Being." The emphasis here is not so much that the Supreme Being changes into all of this, but all that exists, whether cognized as the individual, as the world, or as God—anything—is only that Being, which is Supreme. One Existence is, at all times, everywhere. Always, everywhere, you are. Timeless, spaceless, and location-less you are.

Bhagavan says, "There are only two ways to conquer destiny or to be independent of it. One is to inquire whose this destiny is and discover that only the ego is bound by it, and not the Self, and that the ego is nonexistent. The other way is to kill the ego by completely surrendering to the Lord, realizing one's helplessness, and saying all the time, 'Not I, but Thou, O Lord,' giving up all sense of 'I' and 'mine,' and leaving it to the Lord to do whatever He likes with you. Surrender can never be regarded as complete, so long as the devotee wants this or that from the Lord. True surrender is the love of God for the sake of love and nothing else, not even for the sake of salvation. In other words, complete effacement of the ego is necessary to conquer destiny, whether you achieve this effacement through Self-inquiry or through bhakti marga."

Egoless abidance is the natural, true state. Dissolution of the ego is spiritual practice, and this takes the form of inquiry or surrender. It is not inquiry so that I can be something. It is not surrender so that I can obtain something. Such would be merely a larger, imagined ego. Surrender is effacement, or dissolution, of the ego. The inquiry is a destruction, or dissolution, of the ego. Without such dissolution, some unknown destiny, the effects of the previous ignorance of the ego, manifesting as karma, seems to roll the ego about. The individual who identifies with the ego is perplexed accordingly. The only thing that can be done for Liberation from that delusion is, as the Maharshi reveals, the bringing about of the destruction of this ego-sense, which is only imagination. Inquire and see that the ego and its experiences are not real, or recognize the supreme power of God and abandon all care for the ego, without claiming anything as "I" or as "mine." Then, all attachment is gone. So, unhappiness has been removed, and peace is preserved, because, without the ego, you abide as the changeless, absorbed in That.

Bhagavan says, "Our real nature is Liberation, but we imagine that we are bound and make strenuous efforts to get free, although, all the while, we are free. This is understood only when we reach that state. Then, we shall be surprised to find that we were frantically trying to attain something that we always were and are. An illustration will make this clear. A man goes to sleep in this hall. He dreams that he has gone on a world tour and is traveling over hill and dale, forest and plain, desert and sea, across various continents, and, after many years of weary and strenuous travel, returns to this country, reaches Tiruvannamalai, enters the Asramam, walks into the hall. Just at that moment, he wakes up and finds that he has not moved at all but has been sleeping where he lied down. He has not returned after great efforts to this hall but was here all the time. It is exactly like that. If it is asked, 'Why, being free, we imagine ourselves bound?' I answer, 'Why, being in the hall, did you imagine that you were on a world tour, crossing hill and dale, desert and sea?' It is all in the mind, or maya."

The ego and the samsara, the dream character and his dream adventures, are entirely in the mind. It is maya, illusion, which is the stuff of imagination. You are not now other than the Self, and you are not at a distance from the Self. You are always the Self, abiding in the Self. Put an end to imagination. That is all that is required. There is no obstruction to Self-Realization, for there is no other thing to obstruct. There is no distance to Self-Realization, for there is no separate self that ever broke apart from the one real Self. You have no second identity. Just put an end to imagination, and such is called "true Knowledge." In Knowledge, there is no bondage and no suffering, because of the absence of ignorance.

Bhagavan says, "In a sense, speaking of Self-Realization is a delusion. It is only because people have been under the delusion that the non-Self is the Self, and the unreal the Real, that they have to be weaned out of it by the other delusion called 'Self-Realization.' Actually, the Self always is the Self, and there is no such thing as 'realizing' it. Who is to realize what and how, when all that exists is the Self and nothing but the Self?"

"Self is only Being; not being this or that. It is simple Being. Be, and there is the end of ignorance."

(Silence)

Such Wisdom, such Grace, such Truth truly taught, such Silence.

(Silence)

Q.: Listening to the Maharshi's Realization, I can see that it involves the ultimate discrimination of the body's transience. I hold on to trivial things. I have been very busy with a number of things.

N.: The entire universe is like that. (laughter) It is for a relatively short time.

Q.: It does not matter what job I get, for it will not determine my happiness. Some of the less challenging jobs would allow me time for meditation, while the more challenging ones would allow for less time for seated meditation.

N.: Whatever would be the situation, would you be in it? Are you the one that acts? Either see that there is a greater power that does everything, and your body is but an instrument in it yet with which you have no connection, or realize that there is never anything really going on, for there is neither the experiencer nor the object of experience, neither "I" nor this world.

Q.: I ask myself how deep is this state, and it becomes more absorbing. It is very deep! Nothing is going on, and then I think that I must act.

N.: Is that the same "I"?

Q.: Definitely not.

N.: Are there two "I"s in the one of you?

Q.: There are not two. There seems as if there are two when there is that belief.

N.: Does that seeming to be two occur to another, a third, one? Does the idea of two occur only to the second?

Q.: It occurs only to the second and not to the first.

N.: So, the notion of an ego occurs only to the ego and not to the real Self. If, to begin with, the ego is not there, how does the notion arise at all? If we say that the real, eternal Self is abiding and another one appears to arise, but the appearance of arising appears only to it and not to the real Self, that is to say that it is its own delusion, how can it start? Such would require it to pre-exist itself, which is absurd.

Q.: I can see that it does not exist much of the time.

N.: Does it, then, exist any of the time? Can it exist at one time and not at another? If the Self is the Self, it is always the Self, and the Self is its own Liberation, which is its own natural state. If the Self would be an ego, even if but for a moment, it would always be the ego, or always be endowed with an ego if it were its characteristic, but such runs contrary to your experience.

Q.: That would be a continuous ego.

N.: A continuous ego or samsara is not your experience. How can something that is discontinuous actually be existent? How can that which is existent ever be discontinuous? How can it be diminished in any manner or at a distance or separate from you?

Only the one Self is everything, but the one Self does not actually become anything. Only the one Self is misperceived as the ego and its samsaric cycle of thinking of birth and death. This is the explanation. Who perceives it as such? This is the inquiry.

Does the misperception have the misperception? Is that possible? The True Self is pure Jnana, Knowledge. It cannot have ignorance. The Maharshi said it "is pure Consciousness and has no ego-sense about it."

Q.: This, as always, is said from the depth, because anything real must be experienced from the real?

N.: That is true. The unreal can actually neither experience nor be experienced.

Q.: In the Maharshi's case, there was instant depth. He went from wondering about the body to Realization quickly in the same meditation. Even inside the circular thinking, it can be dissolved like that (snaps fingers) because it has no substance. Is this what you are saying?

N.: It is because one is never inside any circle. The snake can disappear because there is no snake; there is only a rope.

Even the idea of "instant," to which you alluded, pertains only to the individual caught in that cycle. Only such a one can think in terms of here and there, now and then, and instant or gradual, but the Self has nothing to do with such.

The fact is that the Real alone can know the Real. The Self alone knows the Self. The non-Self never knows the Self, because the non-Self does not exist and has no knowing capacity. So, the non-Self does not quickly or slowly come to a Knowledge of the Self. There is Knowledge, which entails absorption of identity, or the restoring of it to its right place. The bondage and the one who is bound are not real.

There is nothing inherent in the maya to retard one's spiritual practice, for depth and intensity of inquiry are what determine it.

Q.: That depth is there always?

N.: It is where you are.

Q.: There is the need to eliminate the belief in the unreality. It is amazing that one could lie down and have such a deep, complete meditation, yet, in a certain sense, this must happen all of the time.

N.: In the sense that whoever realizes ultimately realizes in the same essential manner. It does not mean necessarily lying down on your uncle's floor. What is realized and the realizing are always the same. In the context of the story, that this occurred in this manner is incredibly wondrous. That the Realization should be with this one inquiry and that there be steady absorption, or abidance, from that time onward are very wondrous.

Q.: There was such clarity. He did not have any idea of difficulty in realizing. That is sure.

N.: He was concerned with death, turning the mind inward, and "Who am I?" and not anything else.

Q.: There was an immediacy, too.

N.: There was urgency and immediacy. There was utmost directness in the inquiry. The absorption, or abidance, was absolute and complete.

It is not likely that many, if any, will duplicate the manifest experience of Sri Bhagavan, yet what was realized, the actual, interior Knowledge, which was inquired into, is essential for all.

Another Q.: I make up somebody who is unrealized. There is not really somebody who is in that state. It is just a habit to make that up and keep the momentum of it going. There is really nothing that keeps me from stopping that imagination.

N.: How will you cause it to cease?

Q.: (quiet for a while) The only way is to figure out who it occurs for, who seems to be doing, and who seems to be thinking.

N.: Yes, find out who you are and examine finely, with precision, the ways in which you misidentify, that is, the forms in which the "I" seems to appear.

Q.: Doing that now, there are flickers of forms starting to arise. I think that I am already too late at this point. I missed for whom they are arising.

N.: You never miss. It is not a race in time, except in the sense that all things are transient, and you should realize before the transience culminates in expiration, before the transient expires. If the transience expires, it is fine, but you will not want to be identified with the transitory things.

It is never too late. In whatever form it appears, it is the "I" notion that manifests as such. It is not that it came and went and has left a trail behind it. It is there as the trail. If you find that there is some form of a definition as a mind, as a body, as the conglomerate of these things, as some attribute, as with some activity, or as with some quality of these things, inquire then and there. Ask yourself if you can be these things and why do you take yourself to be these things. Who takes himself to be these things?

Q.: That is very direct.

N.: The same true Self constantly exists. There is no such thing as catching it too late.

Q.: To say that it is too late is saying that, for some moment, the Self is not there. It is a mysterious blank.

N.: It is equivalent to saying that the Self ceases to exist and the ego takes over, and then the ego ceases to exist, yet the ego's habits continue. How can the tendencies continue without the ego-notion? How can the ego stand up on its own without the existence of the Self?

The idea of "too late" is as ridiculous as the idea of "too soon."

Q.: This takes away the idea of time.

N.: (Silence)

Another Q.: In Ramana's awakening story, the idea of cause and the idea of time seem to be totally absent. From the outside perspective, it seems like an accident with no previous cause. Elsewhere, he has said that his sadhana must have gone on in some other form. The story, though, seems so accidental.

N.: Divine, but not accidental.

Q.: Nothing appears to have led up to it for Venkataraman. Time and cause seem to play no part. I remain puzzled about it.

N.: The story of his Self-Realization is really a timeless one, isn't it? It is not a mere accident. It would be better to say that the entire world was an accident or a mistake.

Q.: That could be said about anything, couldn't it?

N.: Hmm, hmm. From another perspective (laughing), an accident is what an atheist believes in. (laughter) He still has belief; he just calls it an accident.

Q.: We can, though, dispense with time and cause in the consideration of what Realization is, can't we?

N.: Perhaps, that is why the Maharshi has not stated a cause, but he has spelled out the process of Self-Realization and the inquiry that yields such Self-Knowledge. Because it is Truth and does not pertain to the individual, but transcends the individual, it is timeless. Because it deals with Reality, it has no other cause.

So, the story is actually a universal one and an eternal one.

Q.: So, looking for any sequence in time or cause is simply an illusion?

N.: It is better to look to what he imparted and revealed, which is the truth of it.

Q.: That is to be free of imagination.

N.: If one is free of imagination, the story becomes one's own, but then one has abandoned all other stories about oneself.

Thus, we see a similar story with Naciketa, in the *Kathopanishad*, with his interview with death and in the case of Markendeya when, for him, Siva gives death a kick in the chest. It is always the same old story.

Another Q.: The new Knowledge is a matter of straightforwardness. This is what the recipient supposedly moves to. This is instead of being self-deceiving.

N.: Because he intensely desires it. Thus, the desire for Liberation, which becomes the desire for Self-Realization, or Self-Knowledge, once one knows that Liberation lies within. So, straightforwardness, or honest inquiry, is in the light of knowing the secret of Bliss, where happiness lies. Knowing that Bliss lies in That, one makes every effort for it, quite naturally. The effort consists of the destruction of the previous delusion. Faith in the Truth, faith in the Sadguru, and faith in his instruction and in his example are of tremendous assistance. In light of that, effort is applied to the dissolution of one's own delusion. When delusion is gone, the individual and his bondage prove to be unreal.

(Then followed a recitation in Tamil and English of Bhagavan Sri Ramana Maharshi's *Five Verses on the One Self*.)

(Silence)

Om Shanti Shanti Shanti Om

Purnam

Satsang, January 7, 2007

(Silence)

Om Om Om

(Silence)

N.: Undifferentiated Being is who you are. That alone exists, and that alone is real. All spiritual practice is for the purpose of this nondual Realization.

Know this undifferentiated Being alone to be your nature, and all is perfect. (Silence)

There is a verse associated with the Upanishads:

ॐ पूर्णमदः पूर्णमिदं पूर्णात् पूर्णमुदच्यते ।
पूर्णस्य पूर्णमादाय पूर्णमेवावशिष्यते ॥
ॐ शान्तिः शान्तिः शान्तिः ॥

om pūrṇamadaḥ pūrṇamidaṁ pūrṇāt
    pūrṇamudacyate |

pūrṇasya pūrṇamādāya pūrṇamevāviśiṣyate ||
om śāntiḥ śāntiḥ śāntiḥ ||

Om. That is the perfectly full. This is the perfectly full.
  From the perfectly full, the perfectly full springs
  (issues forth).
Of the perfectly full, having taken the perfectly full, the
  perfectly full alone remains.
Om. Peace, Peace, Peace.

Purnamadah purnamidam means That is perfectly full, this is perfectly full. The emphasis is not on "this" as differentiated from "that," the manifest from the unmanifest; the emphasis is on the perfect fullness, purnam. That is the perfect fullness, and what may be referred to as "this" is the same perfect fullness. The singular, perfectly full Brahman, which is our real Self, is invariable. It is immutable.

Because That alone exists, the verse could conclude with just the one phrase, "That is perfectly full." The rest follows as an explanation, so that the fullness of that perfect fullness is fully realized.

What is known as "this" is only That. That which seems to be one's experience is only the Self, which is the perfect fullness. It is Being, which can neither be born nor be destroyed, which does not increase or decrease, but ever remains its undifferentiated self.

"From the perfect fullness, perfect fullness arises, or comes forth." The emphasis is not on the idea that something has come forth, but it is on the ever-existent perfect fullness. Nothing else constitutes anyone or anything anywhere. What is this perfect fullness? It is the unborn, imperishable Existence.

If, or when, "the perfect fullness comes from the perfect fullness, the perfect fullness alone remains." Before anything is created, there is the perfect fullness. When anything is created, or imagined, there is the perfect fullness. After the dissolution of such, there is the perfect fullness. Before the beginning, after the end, and all throughout, you are that perfect fullness, the infinite, eternal Brahman. That is the Reality of undifferentiated Being. You are not a being, a "this" that has come forth, but if you imagine yourself to be such, inquire as the Maharshi instructs, "Who am I?" Thereby, the "this-ness," the limitation or objectivity, will be negated as a mere illusion, for it is entirely unreal. All that remains is the ever-existent perfect fullness of undifferentiated Being.

We conclude the verse with Om shanti shanti shanti to indicate the superlative peace of this utterly nondual Realization. It is the perfect fullness that is indestructible. It is the innate, undifferentiated Existence of your Self. Inquire to know yourself and thus realize what the sages have proclaimed to be the Truth. Then, you, yourself, are the peace that you experience.

Q.: I am confused about happiness. My experience is that happiness is an emotion. Looking for the source of happiness, I must ask what the difference between that and other emotions is, such as the source of anger and sorrow.

N.: When you are in sorrow, you are suffering due to the lack of happiness.

Q.: Yes.

N.: Then, such can be regarded as a form of the desire for happiness.

Q.: Ok.

N.: When angry, you are annoyed that your happiness has been stolen from you. At the moment of anger, you do not recognize who has robbed whom. You are angry about the lack of your happiness. So, it also is a form of the desire for happiness. When angry, you do not wish to remain in an angry state. It is not an end in itself, but it serves another purpose. Likewise, in sorrow, you are not sorrowing just to remain in grief, but rather your grief is due to the removal, obscuration, or veiling of your happiness.

You may experience various emotions that you regard as forms of happiness. The common element is happiness. You also experience happiness in the absence of emotions, perhaps more powerfully than with the emotions. Sri Bhagavan often mentions deep dreamless sleep, in which there is a profound peace, or happiness, but in which, evidently, there are no emotions, for there are no thoughts to create the emotions. Emotions are particular patterns of thinking to which undue emphasis is given.

You experience happiness with and without things. What is this happiness? You experience happiness with and without emotions, but, when the emotions are removed, you are happier than you are with them. At any time, does the happiness come to you from external sources? Do objects provide happiness?

Q.: No, no. I am clear about that.

N.: So, when happiness wells up, it must come from something that is not an object. Is happiness a sensation?

Q.: It seems to be.

N.: What kind of sensation is it?

Q.: Bodily.

N.: Is it seeing, hearing, tasting, touching, or smelling?

Q.: If I am in a state of happiness, I feel it is the chakras. The body feels good.

N.: Do you regard the chakras as bodily?

Q.: Yes.

N.: Have you ever experienced happiness without the sensation that you associate with the chakras?

Q.: I have never discriminated to that extent.

N.: Look into this. When you are happy in deep sleep, do you experience chakras?

Q.: No, but I would not call that happiness. There is peace, but I do not know about the happiness.

N.: When you are at peace, are you happy or do you feel that something is lacking?

Q.: Nothing is lacking.

N.: If you are in a pleasurable moment or if you are thrilled by some sensation, but you do not have peace because you are agitated, are you really happy?

Q.: By your definition, no.

N.: How is it for you? One of the signs of happiness is that desire subsides. Since, in your desires, you wish for a state of happiness, however defined, when that happiness shines in your experience, desires should subside. If the desires persist, can you be said to be happy?

Q.: Certainly not completely.

N.: Incompletely means that it is mixed. To the degree that the desires have subsided, to the degree that you have found the source of the happiness, to that degree the happiness shines unobscured. To the degree such discrimination has not occurred, to that degree the innate happiness is obscured.

How many desires have you had?

Q.: Many.

N.: Have the desires arisen from outer things, been caused by the external things, or have the desires arisen from within you?

Q.: Unlike happiness, which comes from within, in the mind, I can desire things that are outside the mind, such as objects and states.

N.: Is the desire produced by the object or by your own mind?

Q.: Well, my mind.

N.: When it thinks of the object.

Q.: Yes.

N.: You have had a great many different kinds of desires.

Q.: Yes.

N.: In all those desires, were you searching for a bodily sensation?

Q.: No.

N.: For what were you searching?

Q.: Happiness! (laughter)

N.: If you would experience bodily sensations or the sensations that you said that you associate with chakras all of the time, would that be happiness? Would you grow weary of the sensation?

Q.: If I had it all of the time? It would be different from not having it.

N.: The discrimination between the sensation and the subtler happiness is being pointed out. You may wish to examine your experience to determine if there has ever been a time when you were happy, to any degree, when that sensation has not been present. If happiness is dependent upon bodily sensations, it is very precarious. Many things can cause the bodily sensations to change. If you examine more deeply within your experience, you are sure to find that happiness is one thing and sensory sensations are another. Even subtler sensations are passing phenomena. The pleasurable ones you associate with happiness, and the painful ones you don't. If you dive within, you will find that happiness shines when you know yourself to be transcendent of sensations and the body and that happiness is not a bodily state. It is a state of you, but you are not the body.

Another Q.: I am happier, but the desire is still there. The desire is for happiness. I feel that it is like a tug-o'-war.

What the desire really wants is in here.

N.: What the outward mind desires is really within. It is a search in objects, circumstances, and events for that which is not an object, circumstance, or event but is the Self. The power in the motion of the desires may be regarded as a testimony to the innate wisdom that knows that happiness is our natural state. We are not satisfied until we find it completely. We find it completely by knowing that it is within and what the "within-ness" is. Because the "within-ness" is our own Self, it cannot be known in an objective manner. Hence, the purpose of Self-inquiry, which is nonobjective Knowledge.

When you find your Self, you find happiness that does not come to an end, because your Existence does not come to an end. Desires are said to be extinguished, because, for the entire time, the search by desire was an intuitive search for your own Self. Knowing your Self and being unable to part from your own Self, your very Existence, you are the happiness. This Self is not a body, mind, or ego. There is nothing contradictory in it.

Another Q.: This clarifies for me that happiness is beyond the ego. I have good experience of Being, though it is incomplete, and so ideas enter.

N.: Who has had the good experience? For whom do the ideas arise?

Q.: To be more accurate, no one has the experience. The claimant comes in after the fact. My own Being is the Truth. That is where my happiness lies.

N.: If you know this, does illusion recur?

Q.: Yes, that is why I am speaking.

N.: The inquiry regarding for whom the illusion appears was indicated. What is the definition of "you"? Ideas arise for someone or are based upon some identity. What is that identity? Inquire into this.

Q.: Someone is already there prior to the arising of those ideas or things.

N.: Find out if there is someone there.

Q.: Without questioning, there will be an appearance.

N.: In lack of inquiry, all kinds of nonsense appear.

Q.: This lack of inquiry is a lack of questioning or examination.

N.: Yes. If you do not inquire into the Self, you will look for the same thing in that which is non-Self. As the Self is not the ego, the body, or the senses, the Self may be said to be non-sense, but it is really the non-Self that is utter nonsense. (laughter)

Q.: That is my experience.

N.: (Silence)

Another Q.: These dialogues about happiness are great.

N.: Are you happier?

Q.: Yes! Definitely. (laughter). Discrimination between sense impressions and the source of happiness is so important. A sense impression is neutral. Repeated, they become dull.

N.: The attempt to satiate the senses by repetition of the sensory experiences will not, in any way, provide happiness. If you associate a sensation with happiness and repeat the sensation ten thousand times, you are not ten thousand times happier.

The senses, as you say, are neutral. They are not real. If we attribute our happiness to them, we will attribute our suffering to them, as well. Thus, one becomes caught in the midst of pleasure and pain, which is not a happy state.

Q.: The mind goes outward. One way to bring it inward is to notice from where happiness comes. It does not come from the object. This helps me to focus inward.

N.: This is the reason why knowledge of the source of happiness figures so predominantly in the preamble to *Who am I?* by the Maharshi, and appears later in the text, as well. If you know the source of happiness, you become detached from everything else and develop a naturally one-pointed desire for Liberation. Your mind is turned inward, and your peace is no longer disturbed by the various vicissitudes and other changes of life. You are not dependent on external things, and you experience within the welling up of the bliss of the perfect fullness. Desires are extinguished, because you know the source of them. The source of happiness, the source of the desire for happiness, that which is capable of experiencing happiness, and the very "substance" of happiness are completely identical.

Q.: What is capable of experiencing happiness is deep.

N.: Is it the eyes, ears, or nose? Is it the body or intellect? It is none of these.

Q.: The senses try to gather impressions of the objects. In my mind there is the accumulation of the attempts to find external happiness. My mind tries to establish reality, to determine what is real. There is not much juice in the thoughts.

N.: The only way the mind can establish what is real is by finding its own source. If it turns inward to know what knows it, its form dissolves.

Q.: All this starts with the "I." Then, the mind starts to churn. Then, something seems fouled up.

N.: If you lose track of your identity, something seems out of place. Then, the seeking to get it back in place begins. If we lose something, we should search for it where we lost it and not elsewhere.

If the senses are fine, the external world does not matter much. If the mind is afflicted, the same senses do not matter much. If the mind is happy and at peace, the aches, pains, and such do not matter much, and still one feels fine, because the identity is not mixed with the senses. If the inner is content, the outer loses its significance. If the inner is not content, the outer seems to be more significant. The more that one searches in the outer for the inner, in the non-Self for the Self, the less happiness there is. It is an inverted view.

Q.: It is based on non-investigation.

N.: Exactly so.

Q.: Whatever is not investigated goes on automatic pilot, which does not usually do a good job of finding it.

N.: Such is the repetitive cycle of illusion.

Q.: The automatic pilot does not take one where he wants to go. (laughter)

N.: And there is no estimated time of arrival. (laughter) Investigate the nature of happiness, what is real, and, most importantly, "Who am I?" If you inquire, you find happiness and peace to be innate. Thoughts, sensations, and the world no longer disturb. That which is the innate Bliss is also Existence and Consciousness, apart from which there is no other existence or separate mind.

Q.: Complete detachment is equivalent to Realization, you have mentioned. This pertains to the body, senses, mind, and the individual.

N.: Yes. The Maharshi says that vairagya (dispassion or detachment) and jnana (knowledge) are the same. One is regarded as not adhering to what is not the Self, and one is regarded as adhering to the Self. They amount to the same.

Q.: How is the sense of individuality eliminated?

N.: By inquiring to see if it exists.

Q.: There must be attachment to some external reality.

N.: Why must there be that?

Q.: I am thinking about the detachment.

N.: To what do you feel attached?

Q.: If I don't inquire, it could be whatever. It is not permanent.

N.: Is it real?

Q.: No, because it is so flimsy.

N.: It is impermanent and unreal.

Q.: Yes. Yes.

N.: We speak of detachment to further your experience of what is true. Your nature is utterly detached. It is the perfect fullness, which alone exists everywhere yet which is not attached to any particular thing.

Q.: That is everything. Without that, one does not have anything.

N.: When there is attachment, there is confusion regarding happiness, reality, and identity. It is mixing up the Self with the non-Self. When there is detachment, there is no such confusion. If you inquire, "Whose is the attachment?", it is similar to the inquiry, "Whose is the misidentification?" That false assumption is, itself, misidentification, attachment, and ignorance. That very ego has no existence, and this is realized as soon as you inquire into its nature. You find that there are not two states, one with the ego and one without. Sri Bhagavan says, "The egoless state is the only real state that there is."

In truth, your Being is ever detached. It is not connected to anything else, for its nature is nondual, infinite, and homogeneous. There is nothing to which it could become attached. There is nothing in its nature connected to anything else. So, the practice of becoming detached is really the recognition of the fact regarding the Innate. The same holds true with happiness.

Q.: So, Realization is not mental or sensory. All these things disappear. I should notice the qualities of the Realization, that it is the source of happiness and peace.

N.: It is Sat-Cit-Ananda, Being-Consciousness-Bliss. It is satyam, jnanam, anantam, the true, the knowledge, the infinite (limitless).

We can be quite sure that that of which the Rishis have spoken since the time of the Vedas is not a sense experience; nor did they speak of some mere intellectual recognition. No mere sense experience could earn the appellation of "blissful immortality." No mere mental conception could be called, "Brahman" or "Atman, the Self." (Silence)

This is wondrous. You are not a mere sense perception. You are not a mere intellectual conception. What they realized is what you are. Self-Knowledge is the essence.

(Then followed a recitation in Sanskrit and English of verses from the *Bhagavad Gita.)*

(Silence)

Om Shanti Shanti Shanti Om

Nirguna Brahman

Satsang, September 30, 2007

(Silence)

Om Om Om

(Silence)

N: Nirguna Brahman, the quality-less, attributeless Brahman, is the solitary reality. That Brahman alone exists is the meaning of nonduality. It is said that all of this, the entirety of one's experience, ranging from subtlest thought to the forms of objects of the world, is saguna Brahman, Brahman with attributes, Brahman with qualities. There are not two types of Brahman. The meaning is clear. It is that all this is only Brahman, and Brahman alone exists.

The notion of differentiation of any kind arises entirely dependent upon the previous, purely imagined assumption of an individual "I." All the differences appear in the midst of that which is undifferentiated, starting with the notion of "I." All disturbance appears in the midst of that which is only peace, starting with the notion of "I," which is the supposition that there is some existent individual. It is an assumed misidentification. Likewise, all suffering, worry, fear, etc. in the midst of great Bliss appear starting with the notion of "I." All bondage starts in the midst of immense freedom only with the notion of "I." How is it that this notion is imagined? For whom is it imagined?

The Maharshi taught that we should inquire, "Who am I?" in order to realize conclusively the Self as being the solitary Reality. Who am I? If only this profound inquiry is made, the very root, or source, of all the illusions and of all differentiation, proves to be nonexistent. With the root, or cause, absent, the effect is also absent. The individual and his lifetimes-long story both disappear because they are unreal. Brahman remains as Brahman and alone has existed always. What is it that is real? Only the indefinable Brahman. What is all that which disappears? Nothing but Brahman. Brahman is invariable in its nature. Inquire, know the true nature of yourself, and thus abide in That as That.

This being realized, there is nothing further to be obtained. In this, all questions are answered, all doubts are resolved, and all illusions are gone. Abandon the misidentification, if there be any, with the differentiated body, mind, and ego, and know the Self, the solitary Existence, just as it is.

Q.: When I daydream and I ask who is in this situation, the situation dissolves, yet I am still present. How do I deal with it when the experience first comes into my senses? The memory of the experience I can dissolve, but, when the experience first occurs, how can I separate myself from that?

N: The same principle will work. The same delusion is also at work. If you cease to regard it as real and cease to misidentify as the individual character who is wrapped up in it, it will dissolve.

Q.: It is easier to do that when sitting here in the meditation hall and the experience is happening just in my thought.

N.: Perhaps, you are in mediation all the time.

Q.: That is what I need to practice.

N.: You may not be bodily sitting, but, in a profound sense, you are in meditation all the time. The apparently vivid sense experience is not different from a dream. Before inquiring to rid yourself of the difficulties of a memory or a daydream, you could register the complaint that it seems so vivid and so real, though, upon a little inquiry, it is not so real. The same is true with sense experience. It is imperative that the misidentification with the body be relinquished in order to reach such freedom. If the "I am the body" conception is retained, you feel as if in the experience, and it is seemingly difficult to extricate yourself from the limitation of it. If the "I am the body" conception is destroyed, you are not in the situation.

Q.: Now or then.

N.: At either time, the limited experiences are just images appearing in you. If you further inquire as to who you are, the images cease, for they are not real. What remains is the actual Existence. Is this clear for you?

Q.: It may be after I listen to it a few more times on the CD.

N.: When you find yourself in some circumstance that seems limiting, overwhelming, overpowering, or in some way binding, first and foremost, know where your bliss is. Secondly, abandon the "I am the body" misconception. You can inquire further from there, but, even with that much, see what you experience.

Another Q.: While reading the *Karika* of Gaudapada, people complained in the text, when there is no complaint. I skim quickly because it is not of interest, but such must be in there for some reason. When there are doubts and explanations, should I read thoroughly through that also or just dismiss it?

N.: The commentaries are only for the purpose of elucidating the nature of the truth. There can be no hard and fast rule as to whether or not you should read a commentary. In the fourth chapter of Gaudapada's *Karika*, he describes certain doubts or different viewpoints that could arise, and, in Sankara's bhasya, or commentary, throughout the text, he brings up various questions or doubts that could arise for someone who is trying to meditate on the very truth that Gaudapada and the Upanishad declare. Then, he gives an appropriate answer, showing the way to meditate or the knowledge that should shine in one in order to eliminate the doubts. If you find it useful, read it. If you are already beyond the doubt, it is optional.

Ultimately, all the doubts and their answers are for one purpose, and that is the revelation of the Self, which is beyond doubt for anyone. Therefore, the answers, whether provided by Gaudapada or Sankara in his commentary, are really for the purpose of bringing about a cessation of misidentification and a clarity of knowledge regarding one's true identity. In that case, the doubt is resolved and the question is answered at the deepest possible level. If commentaries upon a text are read as a form of guidance for meditation, they are generally of more use to the seeker of Truth than if they are read as a logical discussion about some topic.

Another Q.: In my Existence, there is clearly no mind. It just does not occur in what I know is my essence. I was meditating: if it is not there, where is it? That is the only thing that is clearly real, and the mind is not part of that.

N.: It is not part of That, but it is not apart from That.

Q.: This is the part I need to straighten out, because it does appear to be part of it, or it appears to be so different in its nature that it does not affect Existence at all.

N.: It does not affect Existence because it is so different in quality and in character, but does it exist on its own?

Q.: It is like a cloud that does not exist without the sky.

N.: It is in the sky and of the sky, but you would not call the cloud the sky.

Q.: What is this that I think? How can I come up with something that truly does not exist on its own? I cannot get hold of the thing that I think is not real.

N.: Are you attempting to define the mind using the mind? If so, how will you get an accurate definition?

Q.: I think that is what I am doing. It is trying to use the mind to understand itself, when it has no real capacity to do that.

N.: Yes, that is, the Maharshi says, the thief dressing as a policeman to catch the thief, which is himself. He is not apprehended. We could say that Consciousness plus thought, that is, Consciousness plus objectivity, appears as a mind, which then says "I know." This that it knows could be anything. Can we then make an objective study of the mind that contains all the objectivity? If the inquiry is nonobjective in nature, what is left to the mind?

Q.: It is just sky.

N.: Vasishta says that the mind is like the movement of wind in air. The air, or the sky, is representative of Consciousness. Is the wind made of anything but air? Does it have an existence separate from the air? No matter how fast it is, does it go anywhere outside of the air?

Q.: No, it does not become separate or have its own reality. Reality is always there.

N.: Consciousness, unmoving, vast, and infinite, is the real Self. The same Consciousness, regarded as moving, appears as a mind. In highest truth, the immovable does not move. Brahman is invariable. If you want to know the nature of the mind, you must actually inquire and not attempt to use the same mental processes that are said to constitute the mind to try to determine what it is. So, actually inquiring as to your nature, what can you say about your mind?

Q.: I do not have one.

N.: If you do not have one, is it elsewhere? Is there another space in which it can be?

Q.: No, there is not.

N.: So, to say that you are the witness of the mind and still regard the mind as existent is a first step, yet an important one. When the nature of the witness is realized to be infinite, undifferentiated Consciousness, that alone is found to exist, and there is no more any question of a mind.

Another Q.: I had a very deep meditation on Friday. From that experience, I think that deeper knowledge, or lack of ignorance, is closer to Enlightenment. That I do not identify with an ignorant one is important. All comes from that with which one identifies. If the root is an ego, from there, a body and a world, or a mind and a world, spring. I know in my heart that I really have to know this. About a week ago, you were reading from *Talks with Sri Ramana Maharshi*, in which it was said that meditation should go on always, even when the body is not seated.

N.: Yes.

Q.: I can see that, the less ignorance I have, the more that is possible. If there is ignorance, I need to figure out the cause.

N.: You must trace its root, which is the false definition. All the ignorance is subsumed under the definition of ego—of "I." Tracing it is part of meditation. When the ignorance vanishes, that is also meditation, is it not?

Q.: Yes, that is definitely meditation. No ignorance is automatic meditation.

N.: Then, meditation is the natural, interior Knowledge.

Q.: Yes, with the lack of ignorance, meditation goes on. Even though the mind may be occupied, all of a sudden, I discover that what is really happening is not the occupation of the mind, but something much deeper.

N.: The mind's occupation with its own thoughts is never a concern for you, is it? You are always beyond the content, the presence, and even the absence of thought.

Q.: I was describing two different states. One is a recognition of something deeper.

N.: When you recognize what is deeper, does that which is deeper start just then? Does it commence with the recognition, or is it the recognition of what is already the case? Now, are there two of you—the one who has recognized the real Self and the other who becomes preoccupied and wakes up again?

Q.: The idea is that there are two selves.

N.: Is there really an individual who becomes caught in the mind's occupation and then frees himself from it? If he is caught, he must free himself of it. That is axiomatic, but is there really a second one? Is there anything that constitutes your identity except the immaculate, ever-free Existence?

Q.: When, with effort, it is investigated, it seems not to be there. When it is not investigated, it is just assumed that there is a box, wherever that imagined box is. You are saying that the box really is just total imagination and that the box is made of myself.

N.: Yes, you are right. If the individual is assumed, there is also everything that follows. If it is not assumed, the

Reality shines. Is there a place for the assumption to occur in the Reality? Can there be a box, as you call it, in the infinite space-like Consciousness?

Q.: That box is composed of ignorance, as some sort of boundary.

N.: It is ignorance, it is the potential for ignorance, and it is the one who is ignorant, without whom there cannot be any ignorance, all in one.

Q.: How could there be two? In one second, it appears to be there, and, in the next second, it is gone.

N.: For whom does it appear to be?

Q.: It does not seem that it appears to be for the ego.

N.: Yet, when the one for whom it is is gone, that one is always gone. Is that not so?

Q.: Yes, that is true.

N.: For the ever-liberated one, there has been no bondage. The ego, which is but a false assumption, cannot, in reality, assume itself.

Q.: Yes, that is clear from what you were just asking.

N.: Being-Consciousness is invariable and has no ignorance. It is what remains when everything is said to be gone. The real does not imagine the unreal. The unreal cannot truthfully imagine itself. There is not a third alternative. There cannot be something partially real and partially unreal, for that would be subject to discrimination that would divide the unreal from the real. Ignorance cannot be supposed by the real Self, and it cannot suppose itself. When, in your experience, you see that the ignorance is gone, what remains is actually what was always there all by itself. Nothing actually was created. So, in the highest sense, nothing is destroyed. The holy texts say that, because there is no non-enlightenment, there is no enlightenment.

Q.: I was thinking about these holy texts. The sages can really enjoy them because they understand from where they come, and for the aspirants, like myself, they push one in a direction where one must lose ignorance. That is where one really understands them.

N.: They thrust you in a direction in which you are called upon to abandon whatever misidentification that makes the truth revealed therein appear as not self-evident. Once the misidentification is eradicated, the Truth is self-evident.

Q.: One must be very introverted when he reads a holy book, because he must see how it applies and be able to identify his ignorance.

N.: There are many ways of reading sacred texts. The best is to do so in a state of profound meditation in which the inquiry regarding what your identity is is the focus while you are reading. Then, the descriptions of Reality, or Liberation, are entirely about you, and the elimination of some delusion is not so much about elimination of delusion for some other person at some other time, but it is the elimination of your own.

Q.: The holy books and talking with sages, including satsang here, is so absolute. There is no partial ignorance, no gradual steps to enlightenment, and no such thing as "enlightenment." It comes from such a high place. I notice that, with every answer you give, just as in the holy books, even the smallest step is very deep. Just noticing that one is not the body is a very deep step.

N.: It is very deep. Consider all the consequences of this. As for association with the wise, whether in written form or verbal form or in silence, the Maharshi said that you catch the samadhi habit from them. Here, samadhi means sahaja, natural absorption.

Q.: They do not allow one to hold to ignorance. They cannot take it away, for one must himself eliminate it, but they are the guiding light to that, and I think that is invaluable. If I take my mind to be myself, it is hard to notice anything beyond it, and I believe that to be my master. The sage says that I am not the body and not the mind.

N.: It is not a mere topic that two parties are thinking about. It is something far deeper. It is of the nature of direct, immediate experience. In the end, having discarded the body, mind, and such definitions, there is only one Light shining for itself.

Q.: Yes, the sage, who is not the body and not the mind, stands as that.

N.: Likewise the one who questions him. There is neither a bound one nor a liberated one, neither a disciple nor a guru, neither an instructed nor an instructor; just one Light, shining for itself, exists. You answer your own question, and you yourself are the answer. That "you" is what I am.

Another Q.: Each illusion is mutually supporting other illusions, somewhat like a structure of cards. There is nothing really holding it together. Bewilderment is an unnecessary focus on what this card is, how this card works, and how these cards come into being. The bottom card is the assumption of an individual ego. The foundation is Being. If that is the direction, the cards collapse. The bewilderment is swept aside, and what is left is the truth, pointing to the core of Being.

N.: That is right.

Q.: There is no reason to wait. It is never too early to do that. Nothing else has to happen first.

N.: There is never a reason to delay one's spirituality. You never have to do something first, before you commence an inquiry to know your nature. Your Existence, the Self, is already there. If preparation were needed, it is the preparation. You can always inquire.

(Then followed a recitation in Sanskrit and English of verses from the *Avadhuta Gita*.)

(Silence)

Om Shanti Shanti Shanti Om

Mandukya Karika 2:32

Satsang, March 30, 2008

(Silence)

Om Om Om

(Silence)

N.: The Self alone exists. This Knowledge, which is not for any other, but only for the Self, by the Self, in the Self, of the Self, is realized conclusively in a self-evident manner, by all who, following Sri Bhagavan's direction to inquire "Who am I?", realize the ever-nonexistence of an individual entity. (Silence)

In the unreality of the individual, shines the Reality of the Self, in which there is no ignorance, no bondage, no potential for suffering, and no duality of any kind. To realize the nondual Truth, inquire, determining the nature of your Being. That which knows Being is Being. Brahman knows Brahman.

The individual, or ego, never really came to be. Knowledge of this is spoken of as its end. Really, it is only the Self, which is perfectly full at all times, that exists. (Silence)

The essence is always egoless, and the means of spiritual practice is egoless-ness. That which adheres to egoless-ness is devotion to Truth. That which reveals that the ego was never born is Knoweldge. If the ego is not, there is no doubt about anything else, and the perfect fullness of the real Self is found to exist uninterruptedly forever.

Q.: Why does Ramana have me ask the question, "Who am I?" It must imply that I do not know who I am. If there is someone who doesn't know who he is, how is that one going to figure out who he is? Who is this one who does not know about himself? How am I to know myself? What allows me to know who I am? This brings me to my existence, which is the only thing that I know directly.

N.: That contradicts the presumption with which you started.

Q.: Where did I start?

N.: The supposition that there must be someone who does not know who he is.

Q.: It was the supposition. It is a place to start.

N.: The inquiry does not assume anything. It starts with the basic Existence, which is beyond doubt by all. That is why Sri Bhagavan said that inquiry is the only means that does not include the dualities that one is trying to transcend. "I am one who knows, and that is something to be known" is a duality.

Experience shows directly the efficacy of inquiring, "Who am I?" Your vision becomes nonobjective. The entire conception of a "this," the objective portion of one's experience, is to be abandoned, consuming the "I" for whom "this" would be.

Sri Bhagavan said that the "I" that seems to be integral to the inquiry burns up, like the stick used to stir the funeral pyre, in the course of the inquiry.

Q.: The experience is that of being swallowed up by oneself.

N.: Yes, very much so.

Q.: Until there is no other self.

N.: (Silence). If one assumes that the individual exists, then, as the Maharshi has said in the "Five Verses on the One Self" (Ekatma Pancakam), that is like a drunken man forgetting who he is and, giving a performance in the midst of a crowd, asking "Where am I? Who am I?" while, all along, he is himself.

Where there is no other, where Being and Knowing are one and the same, is the place of the inquiry and Self-Knowledge. (Silence)

Q.: The idea that I could pretend to be something else is really quite pointless.

N.: The idea also is consumed in the inquiry. Who would harbor pointless ideas? The "I" that supposes that "I am separate from the Self" is already considered separate from the Self. Who is he?

Q.: (laughing) He is an imposter and out of control at times.

N.: The Maharshi said that he is like the uninvited wedding guest who was not invited by the groom or the bride. He took all that he wanted until he was wanted on some important matter; in other words, his identity was questioned, whereupon, he quickly disappeared from the scene.

Q.: When I inquire…

N.: He vanishes. So, the inquiry does not really suppose anything, does it? It is based in Reality.

Q.: If I suppose something, it is not inquiry but something else.

N.: Such would lose its liberating power.

Q.: It would veer off into some objective pursuit.

N.: Or, it would take one only thus far but no further.

Q.: It is becoming difficult to wander because to do so I must imagine an entire story. To maintain that, and with all the suffering that goes along with it, I feel, "No!"

N.: It runs contrary to your nature.

Q.: It consists of a few habits that can be easily broken by inquiry.

N.: The habits, or tendencies (vasanas), are broken. We could say that they are pulled out by their roots, but they turn out to be rootless. The potential for them, the one who engages in them, the one who imagines them, and the starting point, the "I" mode or aham-vrtti, prove to be utterly unreal. There is no one to create the tendencies. There is not actually anyone in them.

Q.: If now I try to imagine tendencies, they are very hollow. There is no one actually in those dreams.

N.: Inquiry enables you to discover how true that is. Then, a dream that did not really begin is said to be over. (Silence)

Another Q.: As long as the ego subsides, progress goes wonderfully well. The story goes badly at the point that the character says, "I have come thus far, so it's okay to let the ego have free rein." The best intentions, even reflected in a dream, parallel the subsidence of the ego. Confusion and bad outcomes parallel the release of ego. If there is confusion, I can ask if that is an ego expression or is it a humble openness to the teachings of the sages, and it will always be the first. Whether it is a dramatic story or the subtle inward turning of the mind, as long as the ego is not given free rein, things will tend to go well.

N.: The ego is at the root of everything that is of the nature of suffering, bondage, unhappiness, discord, desire, doubt, anger, and all that is better to be without. Egolessness, and all that proceeds in this direction, is at the root of everything that is of a divine nature, all happiness, peace, fearlessness, joy, and such. Not only is this true of the story and the intentions, but how else is the story to be brought to a conclusion, which is the most blessed state, except by abidance in egolessness?

Q.: This applies even to the subtler obstructions.

N.: Whether the definitions encrusting the ego are apparently gross or subtle, even the notions that the ego is and is important—no matter how they appear—all of them are equally false and useless. Anything that is inclined toward egolessness shines, to the degree of its egolessness, with the Truth. Truth is always beneficial. If there would be any kind of obstruction for one's spiritual aspiration, if the aspirant would simply remove the ego-notion or the manifestation of the ego-notion, the obstruction would dissolve before him. What else constitutes an obstruction toward Liberation except the ideas regarding the "I"? Even the idea that you are obstructed is based on the idea of "I." All kinds of suffering are very self-centered, aren't they?

Q.: It is easy to see that it is the ego that gloats, but I must remember that it is also that which wallows.

N.: It wallows in its own imagination.

Q.: There is a perverse satisfaction in self-imposed suffering.

N.: What kind of satisfaction is it?

Q.: It is incomprehensible.

N.: Not satisfactory. (laughter)

Q.: This seems like such simple instruction but so powerful: just take the ego out of everything.

N.: The most direct way to remove the ego from everything is to find out if it exists. (Silence). If the ego proves nonexistent, there is no starting place for the rest of the delusion. There is nothing to which delusion can adhere. If there is no ego, there are no differences anywhere. If there is no ego, there is no one to imagine the bondage and then become caught in what he has imagined. Where there is no ego, there alone is satisfaction. There can never be any satisfaction in suffering.

So, inquire within yourself. Determine what the "I" is. If it seems as if individualized, an ego, discern what it is.

Penetrate through the seeming, and discern what it actually is. If you so inquire, only the Self will be found. There will not be a trace of ego anywhere, and no one will be able to say where it went.

Another Q.: I don't see any center for whom I imagine myself to be. It becomes its own barrier. It re-emerges. How do I go deeper?

N.: From where does it emerge?

Q.: Thought.

N.: Where does thought emerge?

Q.: It seems to be here.

N.: By "here," do you mean the body?

Q.: From the body. The Maharshi said to look for the "I" in the heart. It is a physical center.

N.: Do you ever have thoughts that are not connected with the body?

Q.: I think that I do.

N.: Where do those thoughts emerge?

Q.: Beats me! I have seen written answers, so I go to those answers.

N.: The scriptural answers point you toward knowing yourself. If we make them a topic of study and learn the answer, we must proceed from there to experientially verify the truth of them.

The body, itself, is a thought. Thought cannot arise from it. From where does thought come?

Q.: Thoughts come from the mind and body, from the physical structure in the body.

N.: But, as you mentioned before, there are thoughts that are not connected to what is physical.

Q.: Yes, surely. Well, no I don't. I ask myself who is suffering and who is doing, and it goes to another center. There is no thought there. Then, it immediately comes out.

N.: It must come out from somewhere. There must be some root. There must be someone for whom all this is experienced.

Q.: The only answer is to keep inquiring.

N.: Yes. If one would continue inquiring, there would be no differentiation ever. Inquiry, though, is not an activity. If it is conducted as an activity of the mind, there will be breaks in it and going in and out.

In a dream, you are apparently endowed with a dream body. Would you say that your dream thoughts come from your dream body? Such would not make any sense, would it? The waking state is similar to the dream. The subject-and-object relation is similar. The body is merely a thought. It is a kind of thought regarded as sensation that determines the experience of the body, apart from which you have no experience of a body. You experience, though, your own existence always, whether thought is present or not, whether the body is present or not. What is the nature of the existence?

The existence is the same, regardless of whether you think that you are withdrawing or going outward or bound or free and such. What is the nature of the existence?

You know that you exist, even without thinking about it. For this knowledge, you do not require a body or a bodily sensation. Even in deep sleep, you know that you exist, though there is not a thought "I exist." Existence should know itself as it is, at the same depth that you know that you are. That is the inquiry. It is not a mere mental process.

Q.: So, it is beyond thought. It is just the presence. It is just my existence knowing my existence, without any additive.

N.: Add the "I" notion to Existence, and you treat Existence as if it were something objective and the individual as if it were your identity. The Maharshi declared that the individual is a ghost with no form of its own. So, it takes a form. Further misidentification with thought occurs. One pattern of thinking is sensation in the body. Then, you feel that you are the body, in the body, the body is the start of your existence, the body is the source of thought, etc. Nothing could be further from the truth.

Q.: This is exactly what has happened.

N.: If you find yourself tumbling along in that way, go back the way you came. Trace your existence.

Another Q.: It is obvious that with Self-inquiry, without ideas, what is real and what is not real would be completely apparent. Self-inquiry is totally nonobjective. Anything to do with the world and the mind is gone. Now, I am just looking for myself. This is somewhat hampered by ideas to the contrary, such as I am a mind with sprouts of other things.

N.: Whether they are of the mind or the universe, those ideas are yours. They do not speak of themselves. They are known by you. Apart from your knowing of them, they do not exist. They do not declare their own reality. You say, "I know; I know this; it is." All of this depends on you. Inquiry to know the Self is discernment of what is real. Knowledge of Reality is actually only Knowledge of the Self.

Q.: Knowledge of the Self as opposed to anything else?

N.: Anything opposed would still be dependent on the "I" that knows it. Self-Knowledge is not opposed to anything but does transcend all.

Q.: In actual inquiry, the real knower is not connected to the objects.

N.: If the known is subtracted from the knower, it suffices.

Q.: Similar is it with any idea that appears in the mind?

N.: If the known, or objective portion of the idea, is removed, what remains?

Q.: (quiet for awhile) Definitely, whatever was believed is gone.

N.: The known dissolves in the knowing, and the knowing dissolves in the knower. Without the known and not in relation to anything else, by himself, what is the nature of the knower? (Silence)

Q.: This is different. (quiet) It is not describable.

N.: (Silence) The ineffable, the inconceivable, and the immutable are you. You cannot be anything else. (Silence) The one knower, of the nature of just pure Consciousness, is you. How can you say that you have ideas?

Q.: They pertain to someone.

N.: That someone is nonexistent. That which exists, of the nature of pure Consciousness, is solitary Being. In Being, there are no means by which the differentiation of ideas could arise. There is not a stoppage of that which did not begin.

Q.: Because?

N.: It must first be there in order to stop. It does not continue, and it does not stop.

Q.: I see that that is something in which I believe. If something stops, it begins.

N.: Reality does not begin and stop; and, truthfully, the unreal cannot be said to begin and to stop.

Q.: The experience is never that the Reality stops. Only thought appears to stop.

N.: If there is thought, it appears to stop and begin, and to again stop and to again begin, but you do not. You are without beginning and without end. If this beginningless, endless Being is known, as you really are, there is nothing else to begin and to end.

The Reality is only One. It is not true to say that there is the Self plus ideas. You must first imagine yourself to be some kind of individual conceiver, some individualized awareness, for you to speak of the ideas. Otherwise, there is just the indivisible, real Self. That is unmixed, undivided Consciousness, indivisible Being.

Sasvati, would you please bring the copy of the Upanishads that you are carrying? (She brings it forward and hands it to Nome) Thanks.

This is from the *Karika* by Gaudapada on the *Mandukya Upanishad*. It says:

māṇḍūkya kārikā 2:32

न निरोधो न चोत्पत्तिर्न बद्धो न च साधकः ।
न मुमुक्षुर्न वै मुक्त इत्येषा परमार्थता ॥

na nirodho na cotpattir-na baddho na ca sādhakaḥ |
na mumukṣur-na vai mukta ityeṣā paramārthatā ||

It means: There is no control, or no stoppage, there is no rising up, origination, there is no one bound, and no one practicing, or one who engages in sadhana—sadhana means spiritual practice or the requisite means—there is no one who is desirous of liberation, no liberated one, thus. This is the Supreme Truth.

What is in common with all of the negations? There is no individual. There is no dissolution and no origination. The Reality does not dissolve. The Reality does not originate. The unreal does not originate, and the unreal does not dissolve. Because this is the truth, there is no one bound. There is no individual to be bound. If there is no individual to be bound, who practices? The practice is the dissolution of the idea of a bound individual. There is actually no one who practices. There is no one who is desirous of liberation. There is no one who is liberated. Being unreal, the individual cannot desire liberation. The Self is Liberation. It cannot desire itself. It just is itself. There is no one liberated. The individual is not bound, and the individual does not become liberated. The individual simply does not exist. The Self is not bound, and the Self does not become liberated. The Self just is. From the perspective of bondage, we call the Self "liberation," as if it were a state to be attained by the individual. The truth, though, is that the individual is not. This realization is said to be liberation from all of the imagined bondage. Yet no change has occurred. The Reality of the Self just is. No one realizes it. The Self, itself, is the Realization. "This is the highest, or the supreme, Truth." "Artha" can also mean purpose, but, here, paramartha must mean the Supreme Truth, for, where there is no bondage, no aspiration, no practice, and such, one can no longer be said to have a purpose.

Q.: Because a purpose would pertain to someone?

N.: It refers to going from one place, condition, or state to another. The Supreme Truth is the Reality. The Reality is nonobjective, so it is indicated by a process of negation. There is nothing more to be said. (Silence)

(Then followed a recitation in Sanskrit and English of verse 31 of chapter two through verse seven of chapter three of the *Karika* of the *Mandukya Upanishad.*)

(Silence)

Om Shanti Shanti Shanti Om

Undifferentiated

Satsang, April 6, 2008

(Silence)

Om Om Om

(Silence)

N: Undifferentiated and, thus, doubtless is Being, which is the real Self. Every doubt, every notion of illusion, is based upon some false supposition of differentiation, as if that which alone is could become two or other than what it is. A doubt is always of differentiation, and the resolution of the doubt is always the relinquishment of the supposed differentiation.

Thus it is with questions and answers. The explanations in the teaching are, in one sense, based on the differentiation, yet the purpose of them is the dissolution of that very differentiation.

The primary differentiation is the assumed identity as an individual "I." This assumed differentiation is integral to every other differentiation, such as a conception of a mind, a conception of a world, or the conception of anything else. The dissolution of the world and the subsidence of the mind are the abandonment of this false differentiation. It cannot be negated in an objective fashion because such presupposes the differentiation as existent, and that is the very thing that one wishes to abandon.

Abandonment of differentiation is the Realization of the Truth. The direct approach is the inquiry into your own nature: Who am I? This inquiry does not presuppose differentiation and then attempt to explain or transform such. The inquiry asks if there is any such differentiation, and, since the way is subjective and not objective, the inquiry is, "Who am I to perceive some difference? Who is it that perceives a mind, and who is it that supposedly perceives a world?"

The undifferentiated state is the state of Reality. It is innate. (Silence).

The natural, or innate, Self does not transform itself into anything else. There is nothing else to act upon it to transform it into something that it is not. (Silence)

If your desire is to realize the Supreme Truth, to know Reality as it is, find within that which has no birth, no death, no change at any time, which does not undergo any kind of modification or transformation, and which does not enter or exit anywhere. The one who finds that is himself that. It is not that you become Brahman, but, rather, Brahman is what you are. Such is the immutable Self.

If differentiation appears to persist for you, inquire for whom it is. Who am I? Upon inquiry, there is Self-Knowledge. In Self-Knowledge, you realize that, not only does differentiation not persist, but it did not start. That which truly is always is just as it is. (Silence)

Q.: Any obstacle can be said to be a doorway. Any suffering tells me where not to go. Many qualified-nondual teachings describe the path in terms of becoming. The image is that of a caterpillar becoming a butterfly. If a butterfly tries to comprehend its nature from the premise of being a caterpillar, it can never do so. The inability to comprehend causes me to drop the image of becoming altogether. The futility reached by the mind's attempt to comprehend prompts a more subjective inquiry.

N.: The idea of becoming is that of arriving at a state in which you are That. That is the Self. The Self is already existent. So, it amounts to saying that you become what you are.

Perhaps, the supposition is that there is someone apart from the Self who will be transformed in some way into That. What you are, the Self, though, always is the case. Knowledge reveals it. It does not transform you into it.

The purpose of analogies such as that of the caterpillar and the butterfly is to point out one's real identity. The same one which is a butterfly later appears as a caterpillar earlier. The identity does not change; only the form does. Take that much and dive inward. Do not suppose a transformation of Existence.

Q.: So, the butterfly was always a butterfly.

N.: What is it that appears as both caterpillar and butterfly? What is it that appears as the aspirant and the realized being?

Q.: The knower who says, "I am limited," and the knower who could say, "I am unlimited." The commonality is the knower.

N.: Is the nature of the knower limited or not?

Q.: If the second is ever possible, it could not be limited in the first. Otherwise, all the spiritual teachings would be a cruel hoax.

N.: So, does the limited become the unlimited, or is it that the unlimited really is and the limited is only an illusion?

Q.: It must have always been unlimited if it should ever become unlimited.

N.: Then, there is no limited one. Limitation is only an illusion. If you inquire to know who you are, the unlimited knows itself as it is, free of the imagined limitations.

At a point in practice, it may seem as if a limited being reaches for an unlimited Being, but the very nature of Being is to be without limitation. It is formless and imperishable. It is changeless. Inquire into the very nature of the one who is supposedly limited, and you find only the unlimited. (Silence)

Another Q.: Where can I start the inquiry. Can it start outside of myself? That assumes something has broken off from me, and I cannot start from there.

N.: You must start with the nature of the starter.

Q.: The inquiry cannot really start from some place else. Do I actually start? When I really inquire, it does not actually start. It is as if it is over before it starts.

N.: (Silence)

Q.: Inquiry is great because it does not have a beginning or end. It requires nothing outside. It does not depend on anything else to kick it off or to know how to do it. It does not require understanding, and it has the best reward.

N.: (Silence)

Another Q.: Considering the Maharshi's analogy of the movie and the screen, do I look into the projector? It seems to be a painful thing to do. Should I bend the projector so that it shines back? From childhood, I remember a way of tricking the body so that one thing feels like two. Without looking at it, when I place a thin pencil between my crossed fingers, it is perceived as two objects. Now, it seems to apply.

N.: In what way does it apply?

Q.: I am misinterpreting one thing to be many things.

N.: Such as the misinterpretation of the senses determining reality?

Q.: Yes.

N.: By your senses alone do you know of the body and the world, yet you have given an example in which clearly the senses give the wrong information. Knowing this, how could you continue with the assumption that whatever you sense is in any way real?

What was painful about the movie analogy?

Q.: The painfulness of the light if I looked into a projector.

N.: The movie is only an analogy given by the Maharshi to indicate the insubstantiality of both the subject and the object in your experience. A movie is projected upon a screen. A picture of a king is projected and, before the king, is enacted some drama. The drama and the king are both illusory. They have no substance, and only the screen is there. The king is the equivalent of the subject or experiencer. The drama he sees is equivalent to the entire objective experience, from subtle thought to the forms of the world. All the differentiated imagery has no substance. The screen alone is there. It does not become wet when the image of water is projected on it, and it does not burn when fire is projected. It is not affected by anything that is projected. The screen is analogous to your Being. Just as the screen does not become the images, so Being does not become an individual with a mind, a body, and the senses. Just as the screen is unmoved and unaffected by whatever is projected on it, so your Being is unaffected by the events of the world, the birth, life and death of the body, the movement of the senses, and the movements and shapes of your thoughts. As the screen is there prior to the movie, during the movie, and after the movie is long gone, so Being exists before, during, and after this universe. To realize the truth of this is not painful for anyone.

To discover your real Being as it is, inquire into the very nature of Being, which is also Consciousness and Bliss. Abandon the misidentification with the body, the mind, the ego and such. No longer mix up the screen with the images.

Another Q.: You have taught that Self-inquiry is nonobjective. Even if objective, the intent would be right, but the depth comes from the nonobjective.

N.: That's right.

Q.: If fully nonobjective?

N.: Then, the intention is fully fulfilled. Even if objective conceptions are initially mixed in with the inquiry, the intention will set everything right. If the intention is to know oneself, one does not stop.

Q.: I am thinking in terms of mental and physical attempts. Any attempt to inquire and to know myself must be completely internal and not outward-turned.

N.: Yes, the inquiry is entirely internal. It is more internal than even the mind. Nevertheless, any spiritual effort put forth, whether the effort be physical or mental, is worthwhile and bears fruit. For complete Self-Realization, it must be entirely internal and entirely nonobjective.

Q.: It is a removal of ignorance. I can give an example of my own ignorance. I take Sudafed to try to keep the sneezing down. Because I believe in thought and the mind, when it alters my mind, I feel that my state has changed.

N.: Does it do anything for the sneezing, or does it leave the sneezing as it is, and you think about it differently? (laughter)

Q.: Before the Sudafed, it was out of control sneezing, but, afterward, it definitely improved, so at least I can sit here without making a big noise every minute. (laughter)

N.: I thought someone was blowing a conch shell. (laughter)

Q.: I associate myself with the physical and mental alterations.

N.: In what way does it have to do with yourself? You existed before the sneeze, you exist after the sneeze. You existed before the Sudafed and after the Sudafed.

Q.: It seems that there is a certain clarity associated with the Knowledge of Existence.

N.: Yes. Is that affected by a sneeze or some medicine?

Q.: No. The ignorance seems to be the trouble in this. It is the identification.

N.: How can you identify with a sneeze? (laughter) How could you possibly be a body? Or, considering the mind in its various modes, how could you possibly be that when your Existence is continuously the same?

Q.: Yes, that makes sense.

N.: Your Being did not commence at birth and will not cease with the perishing of the body. Your Being did not begin with a particular mental mode or state. It does not end when a state changes.

Q.: Yes, that is so true. It is so important.

N.: Is the clarity of Self-Knowledge to be equated with the acuteness or dullness of the intellect? The sun shines, and the light falls upon a small piece of mirror. According to the condition of the mirror, the reflection will be bright or dull. Does that affect the original sunlight? The mind, or the intellect, shines by reflected light. Its form is like the mirror. The original sunlight is your Self. That which so shines so that you can see the clarity or the un-clarity of the intellect is the real Knowledge. That is pure Consciousness. That is what you are. This is truly nonobjective. As the body is objective to the intellect, so the intellect is objective to the inner Consciousness.

Q.: Yes, this helps. Thank you. I take up any state, any change of state, or depend on the clarity of my mind in a sattvic state, and then I associate that clarity of the Self, of Consciousness, with the sattvic state, which may be less cluttered than a tamasic or rajasic state of mind.

N.: That is so. Still, you are beyond the gunas, beyond those qualities. That which shines so those qualities can be recognized is beyond the qualities. That is pure Consciousness. That is what you are. The mind has qualities, the senses have qualities, and the body has qualities, yet you are without qualities. You are just Consciousness. So, if you are afflicted with the illness of illusion and transmigration, this is recommended. Ten out of ten jnanis who cross the stream and count themselves on the other side recommend this "medicine." (laughter)

Q.: It should be instantaneous medicine. There is no waiting because this is the Self.

N.: This is your Self, so it is timelessly true. What do you think? Should one give up clarity for the sake of the sinuses? (laughter)

Q.: That does not make any sense.

N.: No, it does not.

(Then followed a recitation in Sanskrit and English of verses from Gaudapada's *Karika* on the *Mandukya*

Upanishad and verses from the *Kaivalya Navaneeta.)*

(Silence)

Om Shanti Shanti Shanti Om

The Mind

Satsang, May 24, 2009

(Silence)

Om Om Om

(Silence)

N.: The Self is non-individualized, indivisible, Being-Consciousness-Bliss that is forever without misidentification and without modification. It is the Reality, which is one without anything else whatsoever. If individuality is assumed, and so long as it is assumed, there appears to be a mind, yet what is the mind?

Sri Bhagavan said that the mind is only a collection or bundle of thoughts. He also said that the primary thought upon which all other thoughts depend is the notion "I." So, the form of the mind is the various thoughts; the various thoughts form the mind or are the substance, as it were, of the mind's form. If the thought forms were removed, what would remain of the mind?

None of the thoughts are capable of knowing themselves. They are known by something else that is not a thought. If we remain without inquiring into the "I," assuming the thought-forms to be real and to be us, we appear to be bound. If we become aware of that which knows the thoughts, but is not a thought, here lies the doorway to Liberation, which is freedom from the imagined bondage. The forms of thought are known by something. That something is Consciousness. Apart from Consciousness, the thoughts cannot even appear, just as the images in a movie do not appear independent of the screen upon which they are projected. Thoughts have no existence of their own but depend utterly on the Consciousness that knows them. The Consciousness, which knows them, does not correspond to, or is not defined by, any of the forms of thought. Yet, not one thought can stand independent of the Consciousness. So, the only existence imagined as thought is the Consciousness, which is innately transcendent of thought. If we understand in this manner, we find ourselves free from thought.

The Knowledge of the Self is of the nature of pure Consciousness. It is not a thought-form. It is not a mode of mind. It is quite beyond all of that. Similarly, it is not a state of mind, and it does not occur within the contexts of the states of minds, such as waking, dreaming, and deep sleep. Consciousness, which is really the Self, transcends the three states of waking, dreaming, and deep sleep and is not contained within them, though it is the only substance of which they are made. Since it is the only substance of which they are made, of which the entirety of the mind is made, and because it is forever without modification, is there a mind? Do these states actually exist? What exists is the Consciousness of the real Self. To be eternal, Knowledge of the Self, which is Self-Realization, must be of the very same nature as the Self that is realized. So, if the Self is beyond any mode of mind and any state of mind, the Knowledge that is to be realized is also beyond any state of mind and beyond any mode of mind.

It is axiomatic that the end and the means must be of the same nature. Often, you have heard me say that the end itself appears as the means. That which is pure, absolute Knowledge appears as Self-inquiry, and this Self-inquiry is not a mode of mind. A mode of mind, however refined, can take one only so far. For Self-Realization, there must be this absolute Knowledge, which is invariable and utterly mind-transcendent. It is often described as that in which the mind is absorbed or that in which the mind is utterly destroyed without a trace. Such traceless destruction lies in the Realization of the perpetual Existence of the indivisible Consciousness, which also signifies the perpetual nonexistence of the "I" or the mind. The Knowledge, therefore, which constitutes the inquiry and the Realization of the Self, is not a form of thought, is not a particular thought, and is beyond a train of thought. It is quite beyond a mode of mind or any state of mind.

Similarly, it is beyond the scope of mental attention. If one assumes the mind exists, then, in the context of that assumption, one is told to turn the mind inward. Turning the mind inward, one comes to the real nature of the mind, which is pure Consciousness that is free of the mind. Within the context of the mind, one is told to focus and to pay attention to the Self, but how could the Self, which is always the Knower and never the known, be an object of attention or an object of concentration? Turning one's focus, one's attention, or one's concentration inward bears some results. The fruit is due to the Knowledge-essence and not to any form of the illusory mind.

Sometimes, the mind is spoken of in terms of its various parts or aspects, such as manas, which means "mind," and in this context, that aspect of the mind that contains all kinds of cognitions, buddhi, intellect, which seems to be endowed with the ability to discern, and chitta, which also means "mind," but, in this context, may be taken to be memory, that which can not only remember or recall thoughts from the past, but also possesses the ability of the mind to be able to compare one state from the past with the present state now. The appearance of continuity of memory is called chitta, while buddhi manifests the actual discernment that discriminates as to which is better and which is not. Because of the light of Knowledge shining as discrimination, Adi Sankara said in *Atma Bodha, Self-Knowledge,* that the Self, or pure Consciousness, shines, but it is reflected especially, or shines especially, in the buddhi, in the intellect, for it is that which has the ability to discriminate.

If we trace this ability to discriminate, we find that it is of the Knowledge-essence and does not belong to the mind, or buddhi, however described, at all. If we assume that the mind has some knowing ability, this is the false combination of pure Consciousness with the forms of thought that constitute the mind. Those very thoughts have no existence independent of the Consciousness and so, in truth, do not exist at all. That which has no actual existence does not have the capacity for Self-Knowledge. The Self has the capacity of Self-Knowledge. The Knowledge is innate. It is of the perpetual shining of the Being-Consciousness-Bliss that all truly are.

If you misidentify with the mind or take the mind to be an existent entity, it will either appear to give you trouble in the form of it being an obstruction or it will seem as if you are situated within the mind and attempting to know the Self or Brahman. As long as that duality prevails, the Knowledge will not be realized, or, though it may shine sporadically, it will seem to fade as soon as the dualism reasserts itself. Self-Realization is said to be the destruction of the mind, which includes the complete abandonment of the misidentification as being a mind or being a mental entity, the core of which, as the Maharshi stated, is the notion "I." Nonexistence of "I" is the nature of the Self. Destruction of mind is the nature of Liberation. Turn the mind outward, and it becomes engrossed in its own imagination. Turn the mind inward, and its form dissolves. What remains is the pure Consciousness of the real Self.

Now, what is this "turning the mind inward"? It is the profound inquiry to know the Existence of the Self as it truly is. Such succeeds by the abandonment of the supposed identity of the one who so searches. The mind will never know the Self. As for the Self, it never has a mind. Thought passes, mental modes pass, states of mind pass, the attention given to any object passes, the attention given to anything else also passes, concentration and diffusion both pass—all pass—and the Consciousness remains unborn, undivided, and undying. What is your mind? Who seeks to know this? The mind, being unreal, knows nothing. The Self, alone being real, knows itself only.

Q.: I would like to discriminate between the grace of being in the presence of the sage who transmits the truth in the way that it was and still goes on and two other scenarios. One is that in which the mind is busy attending to something but in a minimal, nearly egoless way, and the other one is that in which there is entanglement of egoistic tendencies. I would like to see how the first two need not be any different at all.

N.: In what way do you perceive difference?

Q.: I do not see why they would have to be different.

N.: In what way are they different?

Q.: The Self is not defined by the functioning of the mind in the second case. It is as innocent as the coursing of blood in the body. It is completely harmless to receiving the transmission from the sage. The coursing of the blood is not getting in the way at all. I can envision that the function of the mind in a low-ego mode could be just like that.

N.: Why just low? Why not no?

Q.: No is better.

N.: Where do you see the distinction?

Q.: I never felt as solidly supported in the second scenario as I felt and still feel in your presence and during this discourse.

N.: How do you determine what is presence? When are you in it, and when are you out of it?

Q.: The shining of Consciousness felt very solid as the discourse was transmitted and still feels solid thanks to that.

N.: Alright. Can you anticipate a time when it will no longer feel solid?

Q.: No, but if I wanted to play the game of personal history, I could recount times.

N.: In what is the personal history contained?

Q.: You said the chitta played a role there. It is another function that could either be invested in or allowed to remain harmless.

N.: Do you have functions?

Q.: I do not have to identify myself with that function any more than the blood.

N.: Do you possess functions? Do you have functions? Are you a functioning entity?

Q.: It now seems to be an illusion of function because these are inanimate structures, thoughts, even if subtle. They have no function. They are illumined by Consciousness, and imagination ascribes function to them.

N.: If inert things do not function, and if Consciousness, which is ever still and self-luminous, is quite beyond the very idea of function, what are you talking about when you refer to "function"?

Q.: It is an imaginary realm of being that does not exist.

N.: The idea that "I am the performer of action, subtle or gross," is the characteristic of delusion. Describing it in eloquent terms does not make it any wiser. It is still action, and the confusion regarding oneself as the performer of action, with body, speech, or mind, should be done away with.

Q.: The horrible third scenario is when egoistic tendencies are at play, even attending to the same matter, instead of being egoless.

N.: In that context of egotism, is the idea of being a performer of action bigger or smaller?

Q.: Oh, it is rampant!

N.: So, your experience tells you the direction in which to head.

Q.: Yes, I am set on the direction, but I am just curious as to what is going on there.

N.: Misidentification. Ignorance.

Q.: So, it is an appraisal of what is real that is way off the mark.

N.: When you are caught up in egotistical thoughts, can that be called on the mark?

Q.: Is it an incorrect conclusion in which what has been taken to be real is what is not real?

N.: That is the characteristic of all ignorance. What is not the Self is taken to be the Self, what is utterly unreal is taken to be real, and, in its outer, grossest manifestation, what is not happiness is taken to be happiness. If the idea of being the performer of action is part and parcel of the delusion, you would not wish to carry that with you, in any form, into wisdom.

Q.: I would not want to take credit for it?

N.: Yes, you would not want to carry the idea of being the actor, even if you call it "functioning" rather than acting, because it would be a new, eloquent term for the same old tendency, which is a form of blatantly manifested egotism.

Q.: To claim to be the actor seems similar to claiming that thoughts have some power. Both require a thought to state that.

N.: Both require a thought, and both are based upon absurdity. To claim that thought has power, when it is obviously you who emphasize the thought and give power to it or say that it is real, or to conceive the idea of "it stands on its own, it is real, and it has power," is plainly absurd and flies against all experience. Likewise is the idea of being the doer of action. As you are not the body, how can you possibly be the doer of action? As the infinite Consciousness, God, does everything, how could your actions alone be done by you? It is absurd.

Q.: Those have to be thoughts, too. That thoughts do anything has to be a thought.

N.: Yes, it is only a thought and not Reality.

Q.: Consciousness could not shine with the conclusion that thoughts have power. Only a thought could say that.

N.: In this context, conclusions are arrived at by the mind. Consciousness is beyond all of that. It is conclusive in its Existence as itself. It does not think, it does not draw conclusions, and it does not draw erroneous conclusions. That which knows the correct and the incorrect, the knowledge and the ignorance, is the true Knowledge, and that is pure Consciousness.

Another Q.: I have insight into this, but I have not burned up the ignorance. I repeat the ignorance over and over again. I am reminded of the depth of Reality and experience it, but I do not burn up the ignorance.

N.: Only because you do not see it fully as ignorance. Should ignorance be seen completely as ignorance, you cannot retain it. Only if, and to the degree that, it seems to possess some kind of validity do you retain it. You are Reality. You are the Truth, and you always want to know the truth. When something is utterly false and you know it thoroughly to be false, you do not adhere to it.

Q.: I consider the ignorance to be some sort of reality.

N.: You regard it as true—such as it is what is, it is the way you are, it is the way life is—but that ignorance is easily revealed as ignorance and ceases to exist simply by the deep examination, the inquiry, "Is this so?" "Who am I?"

Q.: When you say that I should see ignorance as ignorance, and I inquire, there is no half step, and there is no partial seeing.

N.: There may be, but Reality just is. It is not more real at one time and less real at another. You are not more the Self at one time and less the Self at another. In terms of insight, we can speak of full and partial and so forth and so on, but as for true Knowledge, or pure Consciousness, how could that be partial or full? It is fullness beyond all measurement of fullness. Do you exist partially?

Q.: That does not make any sense.

N.: You do not exist more at one time and less at another.

Q.: There is no opposite.

N.: No opposite and no division.

Q.: So, there are no such things as ability and inability. There is the recognition of what drives, motivates, and helps one to destroy ignorance. I have not burned up the ignorance. So, there is a mistake.

N.: Because you do not see the ignorance as ignorance but regard it as true or valid in some way or another, you retain it or adhere to it. If you can perceive that it is ignorance and only ignorance, it ceases to exist from that moment on.

Q.: It is as simple as that?

N.: If ignorance, which, in reality, has no existence whatsoever but is like imagination, is destroyed, the innate Knowledge of the Self shines. It is never partial and is never unsteady, just as your Existence is never unsteady and never partial.

Q.: That entire ignorance is not steady because it cannot hold up. It seems to hold up when it is imagined, but even that imagination does not hold up.

N.: Does it hold up, or do you hold it up?

Q.: I am the one supporting it, because it is all generated from my belief in it. I say happiness is there or some sort of reality is there.

N.: It is a testimony to the power of the belief that it can even make the unreal appear as if real. The belief must have some very powerful source.

Q.: It seems that the source pervades everything, but it does not assert itself. If I lay something on top of it, it will not assert itself over it.

N.: Alright, who is the one who does that? How does he come forth distinct from the source, that is, the Reality of the Self?

Q.: By non-investigation. Because there is a belief in something other, it seems that it is there. Perhaps, that is believing in ignorance after the fact.

N.: Who is it that comes forth or appears to be born and to grasp, to adhere to, to uphold, etc., the ignorance? Who generates the ignorance and then becomes confused and trapped within it? Who is that?

Q.: It is obviously not the real Self, as you keep saying. How can the Self have ignorance because it does not generate ignorance?

N.: Is there a second to the One without a second? (laughter) Is your existence divided, so that there is a true Self, of the nature of infinite Being-Consciousness-Bliss, and a second self, an individualized one? Is your existence divided?

Q.: It is never experienced as divided. It is only thought to be divided.

N.: Ignorance appears only in the forms of thought and imagination and is never the actual experience. It is never the actual Existence. If you can perceive that it is only the forms of thought and nothing but that, apply the instruction with which the satsang commenced about the mind and its destruction or dissolution.

Q.: Once I enter into thought, there is a belief in a world and a body, if it is not investigated.

N.: Non-inquiry leads to all kinds of imagined differentiation, from which come all kinds of bondage and suffering. Inquiry dissolves all of that.

Q.: I have tried this many times and, in a sense, have been unsuccessful, but, in a certain sense, there is less belief in ignorance. Some ignorance is destroyed in the process.

N.: It is because of the Knowledge-essence, which is what makes any practice successful. Moreover, how are you measuring success or the lack of it? Again, are there two selves that one has to reach across a chasm to another? What is the distance you are trying to traverse? Is the Existence of the Self missing so that it needs to be obtained anew? Or is it not always existing?

Q.: Because it is our Self, it is never really missing.

N.: Consequently, not a drop of practice ever goes in vain. Even the least bit of practice has its benefit.

Q.: That is why they said intense, fiery practice, tapas, in what we were reading Friday.

N.: The Maharshi quoted a passage that said tapas is Brahman, because what appears as the means is, itself, the end. That is the mind-transcendent Knowledge. Practice is not performed by the ego, for the ego does not really exist. It is simply an illusion to be abandoned. It is a false assumption. Practice cannot be by the ego. What was described at the commencement of this satsang is why, in essence, the practice is that of pure Knowledge and is not within the context of the mind, though we casually say, "Turn the mind within." What actually happens when you inquire, when you turn the mind within? Is the experience and the result a mode of mind or a state of mind or something else? If you were the mind, you could speak in terms of success or failure, partial or whole, but are you the mind? That which knows the innate freedom from the mind cannot be the mind.

Q.: Truly deep spirituality, then, does not assert one way or the other because there would be no need to assert something that is innate or to assert something that is totally not innate. That must be why they say the best recourse is silence. The mind is just not present in that case.

N.: What is the mind?

Q.: It is the individual, the concoction of the individual thought.

N.: Then, what is the individual? For the "I"-less true "I," the Real ever is and the unreal never is. This singular truth is indicated in silence. (Silence)

(Then followed a recitation in Sanskrit and English of verses from the *Tejobindu Upanishad.*)

(Silence)

Om Shanti Shanti Shanti Om

Meditation

June 19, 2009

(Silence)

Om Om Om

(Silence)

N.: The Supreme Brahman is the Self, the only Self that actually exists. The nature of this is Being-Consciousness-Bliss, unlimited, undifferentiated, and free of beginning and end. To realize the truth of this, inquire so as to know yourself.

The knowledge of yourself is nonobjective. The inquiry to know yourself is nonobjective in nature. It consists of the essential Knowledge. Inquire, determining your real Being with this nonobjective Knowledge.

If this does not seem immediately possible or complete, within the inquiry, negate the various misidentifications with the body, with the senses, with the prana, with the mind, including the intellect, and with even the notion of individuality. What remains, the Knowledge remaining after the abandonment of such misidentification, is naturally, innately, nonobjective. In the nonobjective, egoless Knowledge of yourself is found the infinite and the eternal.

Meditate by inquiring, one-pointedly, nonobjectively, "Who am I?" If it appears that there is anything else experienced other than the one Self, the Supreme Brahman, inquire, "For whom is the experience?" Whether it be of the senses and the body or something subtle or thought, for whom is this? Who am I? Inwardly remove the false definitions, the conceiving of the eternal in terms of the non-eternal, the infinite in terms of the finite, the Self in terms of what is actually not the Self. Inwardly inquire "Who am I?" and know Brahman by the light of Brahman. If there is thought of anything else inquire, "For whom is this? Who am I?"

(Silent meditation)

Q.: The only place where I know to start to do it nonobjectively is with "I," and I have to figure out who I am in order to do that. That becomes the inquiry. It is so direct that it does not start looking anywhere. It stays focused on "I." I do not think I have ever figured out how to inquire this way until you said that instruction tonight. It is much closer than I thought it was.

N.: The inquiry entirely consumes you, yet it is not something done. It is not a mental mode. Of course, we often speak of turning the mind inward—inquiring—but, in essence, it is not a mental mode at all.

Q.: What I have been mistaking as inquiry for a long time is trying to produce some sort of mode. It is so far downstream from the inquiry.

N.: I would not say that it is harmful, but it will not bring about the final fruit. The final fruit is found in the actual inquiry, "Who am I?" It is not, "What am I in relation to such-and-such within the mind?" but, "Who am I?"

Q.: The instruction is so simple. If followed, it is the easiest thing to do. I need to question why I want to do anything other than that.

N.: Whatever else would be done, it would at best be ancillary, a limb of the inquiry but not the inquiry itself. In the inquiry, that is to say, in the essential Knowledge of the Self, is where there is direct experience of Reality. It is immeasurably vast, ungraspable by any concept, and incomprehensible to an intellect. It is supremely simple because it is of an undifferentiated nature, and the practice, or path, consists of the very same substance as the end. All of the mental modes combined do not amount to even a speck of the actual vast Knowledge. The vast Knowledge is indeed simple—simple as Being is—unalloyed, undivided, with nothing between it and itself.

Another Q.: I perceive an object, and it is there. I am right up against it. It is deceptive because of the proximity, but it is still an object.

N.: What is the object?

Q.: One of the mental concepts. I confuse the inside of the body and think that my consciousness is inside of it. If that were true, I would be surrounded by this stuff. It is that close and that deceptive.

N.: The deception is in the delusion of misidentifying. Your nature is really something completely transcendent of the body and not limited to a bodily location, but, through delusion, it seems as if the two are close, and, not only close, but the same. It is like holding a piece of colored cloth near a clear crystal so that you think that the clear crystal is the same color as whatever the cloth is—red, blue, etc. The crystal does not really become red or blue. It still remains transparent.

Held in close proximity, only through delusion, they seem as if the same, so that the attributes of the body are superimposed on your Existence. When you meditate, when you inquire, discern and distinguish between what is merely the body and what is your Self. Sri Ramana often points out that the "I am the body conception" is the crux of ignorance. Indeed, the elimination of the misconception of "I am the body," "I am in the body," and "I have the attributes of the body," tends to bring about the dissolution of the ego, because the ego is left with no form to call its own.

You know about the outside of the body and the inside of the body. Are you mixing up the knower and the known?

Q.: Often.

N.: Then, practice discrimination. Distinguish between the body, which is known, and the Consciousness, which is the knower. Practice this discrimination experientially. It will not do that much good if it remains something about which you think. What is being spoken of is your own Being, your very Consciousness. That which is aware of the body right now is not the body. That which knows the inside of the body or the sensation of being within a body is not inside a body.

Ignorance tends to make for an inverted view, so that that which is very close to you, indeed identical with you, seems as if at a distance. This is the infinite and eternal Absolute, called "Brahman" or "God" or the "Self." Similarly, ignorance makes that which is very far from you seem as if you are right up against such. Those are the thoughts, the body, and the sensations. Spiritual practice puts everything in perspective. Is it clearer for you now?

Q.: Yes.

N.: Practice.

Another Q.: I mistake myself to be a body in a world. It is just thoughts that create that. Without belief in it, it is gone. I still have too many misidentifications. Once the meditation seems to be over, though there is something that goes deeper than the thought and the body, I still become confused.

N.: What determines when the meditation is over?

Q.: When I am no longer able to focus, or when I am focused on illusion.

N.: Why does the focus change?

Q.: It is the belief in a body in the world.

N.: Alright. When you are absorbed in profound meditation, is this merely a matter of a change in focus, or is it a deeper knowledge? Is it just that you are not thinking about ignorance, or would the ignorance, even if conjured up in thought, then and there, seem blatantly absurd?

Q.: I have that belief, though. I thought, "This is just contrived by the mind."

N.: Which is contrived by the mind?

Q.: It makes up all this stuff and seems to be in control, but it is not always there.

N.: It comes and goes, so it does not truly exist. You who exist do not come and go. Where is the connection?

Q.: Only this belief in it. In this belief that happened during meditation, it seemed so justified, yet it crumbles when it is questioned.

N.: Yes, within imagination, it seems as if solidified, though it is held up only by your belief in it, like a dream. When you say, "I have so many misidentifications," what is the nature of the "I" who says that?

Q.: That I do not know. It is assumed to be something. My meditation broke it apart, but it seems entirely justified inside itself.

N.: Of course. You are lending reality to each idea. So, this seems so, this seems so, this seems so. The "seems so" comes from you. It can be projected on any amount of ideas or imagination without the source of it being altered in the least.

Q.: That is amazing. Is it true that noticing the source right then is part of meditation?

N.: Yes. The return of reality and identity to their source is meditation.

Q.: I need to be more fervent in discrimination. If the mind moves, it does not mean that I move. When I identify with the mind, I think that I move. Often in meditation, a thought seems cohesive, and then, all of a sudden, it is gone. It does not even exist.

N.: Yes, when ignorance vanishes in the light of Knowledge, the thought forms it takes disappear, the belief in it disappears, and the very power or any reality of illusion also disappears. Its cause is gone.

Stay with that which is nonobjective. This is "I," the one who lends reality, the one who seems as if individualized, but, when inquired into, is utterly non-individualized, not an entity at all, but just the infinite Consciousness. Shift, through the inadvertent ignorance, to the notion of being an individual or a mind, and you seem to move. Sankara compares this to sitting in a boat looking at the trees on a river bank and saying that the trees are moving. You, in your real nature, do not move. You cannot become other than the Existence that you are, which is unborn, formless, unembodied, and attributeless. When meditation ceases, what else is that but the resuming of misidentification starting with this assumption of "I"? Distinguish it and inquire.

Q.: There is all of this creation in the mind, but the inquiry is not asserting anything.

N.: Yes, it is not asserting any kind of conception at all, but remaining in true Knowledge. It is not asserting "this is so," "that is so." It is not asserting "I am like this," "I am like that." It is not asserting "I am an 'I,'" "I am a mind," "I am a body," "the world is real," and so forth and so on. The innate Consciousness, which is the real Self, has no such conception.

Q.: That is why inquiry can be done at any time.

N.: Yes, time and place are not factors. Inquire like this and know for certain that there is only one of you. There is no second self; just one Self.

Another Q.: What is the nature of a body?

N.: What did you want to know?

Q.: What are all these bodies? Are they part of the Self?

N.: In as much as everything is only of the Self and there is no second existence, all the bodies are the Self. In as much as, in delusion, one thinks, "I am the body," and limits his existence to a particular body, the body is said to be not the Self. On the one hand, it is the abode of birth, decay, death, and things that are transient, etc., that manufacture all kinds of suffering. On the other hand, it is a holy temple. You need to know the indweller. Though called the "indweller," the Self is really beyond the scope of the body. So, on the one hand, the body is a fragile thing to which one should have no attachment whatsoever. On the other hand, it is a divine gift or vehicle, and one should consider deeply the purpose of its life before it is over. On the one hand, the body is not the Self at all, but, in truth, the Self alone exists, and all bodies everywhere are yours.

Q.: You come to this through Self-inquiry?

N.: All kinds of wisdom come by turning within and inquiring to know who you are. If you turn within, inquiring "Who am I?" consistently, ardently, knowing that, in doing so, you will find the very source of happiness, you will also find that you will open the treasure of endless wisdom.

Q.: So many of my thoughts are superficial, and it really hurts me, yet I conjure that up in the mind to guard against going totally crazy.

N.: Why not use your mind in a different way?

Q.: Suggestion please?

N.: You just described your thoughts and the futility of the kind of thinking in which you engage. No one forces you to think the way you think except you. You can undo the thinking. You can unlearn it very easily. Just find out why you think the way you think. If you deeply seek the reason for it, the search will lead you to definitions about yourself, which shape your thinking. Then, if you inquire, you will liberate yourself from those definitions, and your mind will be free to go back to its original state.

Q.: So, when one asks "Who am I?" he does not start thinking with the mind what that is. I just allow something to come up, or maybe nothing will come up?

N.: You need not plan it beforehand. Just actually inquire. There is no harm in thinking about these things. Filling your mind with spiritual thoughts can be helpful; it is just not the actual inquiry. It will not give the height or depth that is imparted in the teaching, but, if you are going to think, you might as well think about good things.

Q.: I am searching for a framework in which to operate.

N.: Do you know the source of happiness?

Q.: I search for sensations.

N.: What about the source of happiness? Do you really think that happiness will come to you, let alone permanently, through bodily sensations?

Q.: That has not been my experience, but I have postulated that many times.

N.: You have experimented all these years, with an uncountable number of sensations, and they have not made you happy. You can use the collection of your experience to point you in the better direction. Do you know the purpose of life? Your life is not purposeless.

Q.: What comes closest is justice.

N.: What do you mean by justice?

Q.: Fairness, opportunity, no starvation, people have a place to sleep, some kind of security.

N.: These are noble ideals. From where does their nobility stem?

Q.: I read them in a book.

N.: From where did the book writer get them? (laughter)

Q.: Dr. Martin Luther King.

N.: From where did he get them?

Q.: He said he got them from God, but I do not know that to be the truth.

N.: You like the fruit, but you are not sure of the root; is that it?

Q.: Yes. I do not know that to be the truth.

N.: What is true?

Q.: Real. It is an impact of what is happening. I cannot explain it.

N.: Perhaps, you should find out more about that. What is real? What is true?

Q.: Sensations have been my measurement.

N.: Your senses perceive such a small amount. How could you find what is true and real that way?

Q.: Very little. I have not always known that. I was brought up in a very narrow thinking mode, with strong suppression of emotions.

N.: All that is ancient history. You cannot use that as an excuse for the present state of mind.

Q.: I do not want to do that. I am just telling you where I came from.

N.: Finding out what is true, what is real, is essential and has a lot to do with the ultimate or highest purpose of life. It has a lot to do with the source of all the things that are good, beautiful, and virtuous, some of which you described. They have a source. Some call that source "God," some call it the "Self," and some call it "Brahman." There are many other terms for it, as well. If you find deep within yourself, in full experience, what that source is, you fulfill the purpose of life, and you find a happiness that never comes to an end.

The first consideration regarding what is true, what is real, is that it is always, eternal, ever-existent. If something comes and goes, it is to be considered as unreal. Only that which endures, without a moment's interruption—and is consequently beginningless and endless—is real. The only thing that is to be regarded as true about you is, likewise, that which is all the time, without a beginning or birth, and without an end or death. What comes and goes is just accidental and not true about you at all.

Not one of your sensations endures forever. They are very short-lived. What you have known through them is not at all the truth. If you want to know the truth, find that which is existent always, never interrupted, and not sporadic. How can you find that which exists always? Start with your own existence.

Q.: Is that the body?

N.: No. The body comes and goes. It has a birth and a death, and you are aware of it only in the waking state. It is not constant. You need to look for that which is constant, uninterrupted, and ever-existent. What has a beginning and an end is not true even in the middle; it is just a false appearance. What is truly real exists always and never becomes unreal, even for a moment. Search your experience, outwardly, inwardly, and in any direction you like, and see if you can find that which always exists. Once you have found that, you will also have found the source of happiness that is perpetual, and this inquiry, this Knowledge, this Vedanta, will become very important to you. Then, you will dive in to know that Existence first hand, permanently, and you will be at the very root of all that is true, good, and beautiful.

Q.: Thank you.

(Silence)

Om Shanti Shanti Shanti Om

Meditation

April 30, 2010

(Silence)

Om Om Om

N: One absolute Being forever is. It manifests itself as the Existence of all things and of all beings. It manifests itself as the Consciousness that knows in all beings. It manifests as the perfect, omnipresent Grace that shines as happiness in the hearts of all beings. To know oneself as completely this absolute Being is the purpose, the essence, and the very substance of meditation.

Meditate in a manner of dissolution so that there remains the Grace that is present everywhere, yet no recipient of it. Meditate in a manner of dissolution so that the mind is absorbed in the real Knowledge, which is Consciousness, like a piece of salt dissolves in water. Meditate in a manner of dissolution of the false individuality so that the identity, once imagined to be located in the reflection in the mirror, returns to the original Existence, which is this absolute Being.

Dissolve. Be absorbed. True Knowledge is the way to accomplish this completely. With the dissolution of the false identity, absorption of the "I" in the Self, all perplexity disappears, all confusions are resolved, and all bondage vanishes. For this true Knowledge of your Being, the Self of all, inquire, "Who am I?" Inquire and thus dissolve and be absorbed.

The ever-shining Existence, the perpetually-existing Consciousness, and the perfection of Grace are what remain. (Silence)

Q.: Usually, my approach is to listen to the instructions and afterward meditate. This time, I meditated along with the instructions. They are a description of what meditation is. Is there an "I" that I claim as I? Is there just that which remains when I ask, "Who am I?"

N.: If you truly ask the question, "Who am I?" there is no particularized thing called "I," yet all that there is is thoroughly I. There is nothing other than the one Self. Dissolution, or absorption, is only in Knowledge. In truth, there is no distinct, separate thing, with its own form, to dissolve, but the Knowledge that recognizes this is called "dissolution."

Nothing prevents you from meditation from the beginning with the same intensity to which you are accustomed at the end. The ability and the source are there all the time.

Q.: What is other than that? I make up something, but I really can't make up something that veils it.

N.: Even if something were to be made up that appeared as a veil, still, it would not depart from being within the Consciousness that knows it.

Q.: The Consciousness knows it, but it does not see it. The viewpoint of Reality dissolves the idea that it is outside. It also dissolves the idea that it is inside, too.

N.: (Silence)

Q.: A daydream about some occurrence earlier in the day arose. The belief in a world and a body and such crystallized into something that seemed real. I wonder what made it appear real. It is just a dream. In it, it seems as if real.

N.: Then, the next perceptions or ideas arise, and they seem as if real. The reality is equal thought after thought, experience after experience, and state of mind after state of mind. The reality does not diminish. It is constant. That which is constant is you.

All of the forms that are illumined or taken to be real are not constant. Not only does the sense of reality derive from you, but the reality, just the existence, is you. If there is a thought, the existence in that thought is you, though you are not a thought. If there is a daydream, or if the daydream appears as if solidified or crystallized, the existence of all that is you. There is no state in which the Existence ever becomes other than what it is. It cannot go out of itself. The thought and the crystallized daydream never depart from being within that. The Existence, itself, though, is entirely without differentiation.

Q.: That seems clear to me when the illusion is not taken to be real. The mind loses its power, but I return power to it, in the form of whatever I give importance to.

N.: The very existence of illusion is your Existence. Once illusion is imagined, it is your reality that is lent to it. When you lend reality to illusion, Reality as it is is not seen. So, dissolve illusion. Since illusion consists entirely of imagination and your belief in it, there is no difficulty in its destruction, or liberation from it.

Q.: I wonder about my belief in it. I think that there is something real or my happiness is there. It is so merged that I become confused. I see it as something objective.

N.: When in illusion, the Reality is still so close that it seems as if the illusion cannot be separated from the

Reality. The wise know that this is only indicative of the immediacy of the Reality and its homogeneous nature. Even though it appears as such, you can still easily discern what is true and what is not, what is reality and what is only a mere illusion. Discern what is self-existent and what is entirely dependent on your belief in it.

Q.: Is it a matter of extracting my belief? For example, considering friendship, I connect my happiness with the world. I should notice from where that comes.

N.: If you profoundly notice from where that comes, you remain peacefully detached from all of the illusion. You identifiy as the undivided Oneness that pervades all forms, but you are not attached to any of them.

Q.: The attachment is a mistake. It is confusion regarding happiness. Happiness should be known to be nonobjective.

N.: That is clear.

Q.: The thought is that it will make it more real, but it doesn't. It makes it less real.

N.: The thought makes that seem less real and veils it. Knowing the source of happiness yields detachment from all of the unreal appearances. You remain as their undivided Existence but unentangled with the appearances.

Q.: That is the way it should be. I get glimpses of that, but I need to make it firm.

N.: There is a great, unmatched fullness in this.

(Silence)

Om Shanti Shanti Shanti Om

Self-existent, Self-luminous

Satsang, May 2, 2010

(Silence)

Om Om Om

(Silence)

N.: The self-existent is the self-luminous. It is eternal. It reveals itself to itself in all of its undifferentiated Existence, as soon as misidentification, even the least trace of such, in the form of "I," the assumed individual, vanishes. For this Realization of the Truth, by the Truth, which is utterly non-dual and absolute, inquire. Inquire so as to cease to misidentify with the body and with any thought. In this, all is accomplished. The self-luminous is the self-existent. The truth of the Self remains ever a mystery for the ego and ever self-evident for that which alone is capable of knowing itself. Know yourself.

Q.: When you say don't misidentify with the body and with any thought, and, when that is accomplished, all is accomplished, it is not quite an instruction. It is a description of Reality.

N.: That is because it is instruction in Knowledge, which transcends activity of the body, speech, and mind.

Q.: It is the Self instructing itself about itself.

N.: That is true. No one else is allowed here. (laughter)

Q.: When I read *Ribhu Gita*, the description of the Self becomes very clear. Reading for a while, I think that it is Ribhu describing Ribhu. As I keep reading, I realize that this is not a description of somebody to somebody else. This is a description of myself. But I cannot even claim that it is myself as though it is a portion of the Self. That is where my practice teeters. It is misidentification with which I say, "I can't believe I am the Self. That just cannot really be my nature."

N.: The practice is directed toward an inquiry into that very "I." The Guru, in this case, is Ribhu. The Guru's ability to reveal the Truth rests precisely that he does not conceive of another—a teacher and the one who is taught. He sees no such difference. The disciple who also sees no such difference, by destroying the sense of his separate "I"-ness, realizes what the teaching is. Moreover, if such holy texts were only about the experience of someone else, though they would have some value, such would not be of supreme value. In that they are about your real nature lies their supreme value. Ribhu's description, whether given in the first or second person in the verses, or even in the third person, is more about you than any thought you have ever had.

Q.: Following what you said, thoughts have so little value compared to one's direct experience. For anything other than that, I need to ask, "Who is paying attention to that thought?"

N.: If he who pays attention to, or entangles himself with, that thought is just another thought, is one thought binding another? Thoughts never show anything about the Reality, but they cannot possibly stand apart from the Reality. Thoughts have no existence apart from you, but you are most certainly not a thought. In truth, there is no such existent thing as a thought.

Q.: You said that any reality that may be experienced in any form or thought, whether gross or subtle, the existence in the thought, is one's Existence. I am most interested in myself, because that is where freedom lies.

N.: Since the Self is not particularized or individualized and most certainly not a form, your interest lies in Existence. Existence is infinite and eternal.

Q.: It is no small wonder that this is really the only thing that I am interested in.

N.: To abide as the infinite and the eternal is to be blissful, which is in accord with your natural state. The Existence that is everywhere at all times is you. It is without difference. No duality and no form apply to it. You are the

Existence. There is not a second existence or another existence. Difference is unreal. The thought of difference is also unreal. The Existence that appears as that thought and the difference is only the undifferentiated Existence, which is real. Similarly, the knowing in all knowing is only of one kind. It is Consciousness. Consciousness is the undifferentiated Existence. To think, "I am like this, I am like that," is only imagination. To think, "I know this," is only imagination. There is only one Existence, one Consciousness, even in the imagination. To abide in it, as it, free from imagination, is what is true.

Another Q.: It intrigues me that, from the earliest teachings of the Maharshi and thereafter, the simplicity of not identifying with the body is put forth by him as a major stepping stone into deeper inquiry and Realization of Truth. An evolution has occurred in my understanding. First, my emphasis was on enduring the suffering of the body, not being attached to the pleasures of the body, pride in the body, and change in the body. It is the limited, anchoring point to which the individuality attempts to hold. Without that identification, none of the rest is complicated. It is not just the gross qualities of body identification, but also the reference of it. If the reference is gone, there is no place to hold on to something limited. The earlier impressions were carried over from a religious training. It never, in my earlier education, got to the point where I was asked to let go of individuality and to see what it can hold on to if there is no imagination of the body.

N.: If you are bodiless and, of course, then, unaffected by birth and death, pain and pleasure, activity and inactivity, and so forth and so on, what remains of you?

Q.: A sense of existing as a knower, and the vision of that knower expands through the Grace of the Guru from what it was when it was anchored to individuality. It naturally expands and is to be celebrated, hastened, and surrendered to.

N.: Is this the present experience?

Q.: I feel that the direction is right. I aspire to expansion without limits.

N.: Is the "I" who aspires an embodied individual?

Q.: Sporadically.

N.: If, at times, he is and, sometimes, he is not, he cannot be your nature. Whatever is actually your nature—your Existence—must always be without interruption and without modification. A body is subject to modification and, obviously, is objective to you, so it cannot be you. Likewise is this supposition of an individual. Who are you? The inquiry is into the very nature of the inquirer. If you know that what you seek to realize is bodiless and egoless, why continue to set it apart as an objective thing, whether as a goal or something to study? Making your vision nonobjective, determine who you really are. The essence of the aspirant is that to which he aspires.

Another Q.: Thoughts demand attention from me.

N.: How can you say that thoughts demand your attention, when you conjure them up, and they have no separate existence? Whether you regard thoughts as somehow retained inside you or as expressed, still, all the thoughts are in your mind. Indeed, apart from the thoughts, what mind do you have? If you cease to misidentify with any thought, what remains is of the nature of Being-Consciousness. In this lies absolute freedom.

The character who seems to be entangled in his own thoughts is just another thought. That is not you. You can easily look behind thought because you are already there. The one who knows all the thoughts is himself not a thought. What is his nature? It cannot be conceived, but it is realizable. The realization consists of true Knowledge. True Knowledge, or Self-Knowledge, is not a thought form.

Everyone already has a sense of this. You exist, and you know that you exist. This knowledge of existence is regardless of thought. When you have ever so many thoughts, still, there is the existence, and you know that you exist. When you have few thoughts, still, you exist, and you know that you exist. When there is no thought, as when there is the state of deep, dreamless sleep, still, you exist, and there is the knowledge of existence, but not a thought-form. Starting with this existence, attempt to inquire to know it as it is.

All of your thoughts are fleeting, even the repetitious ones. You do not move. The apparently unknown knower of all the thoughts that are known does not move. He does not become one thought and then another thought and then another thought. He is not on one side of thoughts and then on the other side of thoughts. He is not in the thoughts at all. If you would find him, the experience would be comparable to waking up from a dream.

Your thinking is determined by what you regard as your definition. With whatever you misidentify, thus is determined the way you think. Become very curious about why you think the way you think. Trace your ideas to the identifications that are their basis, such as the "I am the body" conception. When you discern the identifications merely as misidentifications, the very cause of those previous thought-forms is absent, and the forms of those ideas constituting the bondage and the anxiety, etc., also subside. In the end, you find that all the misidentifications have their root in one. The Maharshi referred to it as the "I"-thought or "I"-notion, "ahamvritti," or "I"-mode. If you enquire into the "I," only one "I"-less true "I"—the absolute Self—is realized to exist, and you find that all of your anxiety, all the suffering of samsara, was needless. You must, though, actually practice and inquire to experience this for yourself.

Another Q.: I did a lot of physical activity yesterday, and maybe I did not get enough sleep. Something has been modified, and I call that myself. I think that I have to go back to that state before I can do some meditation.

N.: Back to which state?

Q.: A clearer state.

N.: Has that which knows the modification been modified?

Q.: No.

N.: Since that is the knower, that is certainly of your nature, while the mind, the body, the prana, and such cannot be you.

Q.: Yes. Meditation frees one of all the changes in prana, etc.

N.: The inquiry that liberates you from such is not dependent on such.

Q.: It does not depend on anything.

N.: Yes. So, just as it would be absurd to say that the body must be in such and such a condition in order to realize that you are not the body, similarly, it would be ridiculous to say that the prana must be in such and such a state in order to transcend it. Similarly, it would be absurd to think that the mind must have a certain arrangement of thoughts in order for you to realize that you are never a thought but the pure Consciousness.

Reality, which is only the absolute Self—pure Being-Consciousness-Bliss—does not depend on anything else. It is self-existent and self-luminous. It does not depend on anything else to know itself. The real ever is; the unreal never is. The real cannot possibly depend on the unreal.

Q.: There is a certain freedom in the real that gives a detachment from the unreal. The detachment makes it totally independent of the unreal. I don't know it that way, so I feel that I am bound by those things.

N.: By what are you bound? To what are you attached?

Q.: To all these objective things that I think myself to be.

N.: In what way do these things bind you?

Q.: Getting older, dying, change, etc.

N.: All of that refers to the body. Are you a body? When you think or say, "I take myself to be the body," is that "I" the body?

Q.: No.

N.: If you want to say the sense of reality and belief come entirely from him, agreed. Then, what is his nature? How can you lend reality to ever so many thoughts and experiences? When they fade away, he remains, immutable and not depleted at all.

Q.: That is amazing. It cannot be touched at all. There is not even an iota of depletion.

N.: It is not touched because it is entirely transcendent. It is not touched because it is the solitary Existence—one without a second. So, your so-called attachment is only figurative; it is not real.

Q.: That is really important. I give credence to that belief that I have taken to be real.

N.: Then, the unreal appears as if real. It is merely further proof of how omnipotent Reality is. Even an infinitesimal speck of it, as it were, can make the entire unreality appear as if real and the non-Self appear as if the Self. It is a testimony to the Existence, not to the delusion.

Q.: Yes. This is extremely helpful. Thank you.

N.: No matter what the change of state—of body, mind, senses, prana, etc.—you exist. The Existence is simultaneously Consciousness. It does not ever change. It does not rely on changes in that which is not the Self in order to reveal itself. Self-Knowledge shows this.

Q.: I think that it is attachment to a sattvic state of mind.

N.: Yes, but sattva derives its sattvic quality from Sat. Sat is Being, Truth. Therefore, the sattvic state of mind depends on you, but you not on it. You can inquire, no matter what the state of the body or mind may appear as. When you inquire, you see that your freedom is absolute, that you are the Self and not the mind. The form that the mind was taking before is also destroyed. If the mind does not exist and if the one who is entangled in the mind does not exist, but only pure Sat exists, certainly any mode or condition of the mind does not exist. With no arising of "I," there is no arising of the mind. With no arising of the mind, there is no arising of modes within the mind.

(Then followed a recitation in Sanskrit and English of selected verses of *Brihadaranyaka Upanishad*.)

(Silence)

Om Shanti Shanti Shanti Om

Only One Self

Satsang, May 9, 2010

(Silence)

Om Om Om

(Silence)

N.: The Self, which alone truly exists, and which is absolutely one, is yourself. There is no other kind of "yourself." The Self is absolute Being, without beginning, without end, free of form, embodiment, and individuality. There is no other kind of Being. This is your Being.

The Self is Consciousness—self-luminous, infinite, and homogeneous. This is your Consciousness, and there is not a second or third type of Consciousness.

The Self is of the very nature of Bliss, and there exists no happiness apart from that.

The appearance of a self other than the Self, a reality other than the one Reality—Brahman—is merely an illusion. The power of illusion is just one's own knowing, or believing in, it. Illusion is not inherent in Brahman or the Self, but is merely delusion. It is delusion to regard what is not the Self as the Self, what is unreal as real. The elimination of the illusion so that Reality comprehends itself is what we call "Self-Realization."

The Maharshi teaches that one should inquire, "For whom is the illusion?" The inquiry is entirely nonobjective in nature, for the idea of an objective sphere of experience is also illusion. Inquiring within yourself, "Who am I?", ascertain your true nature—bodiless, unborn, with no creation, limitless, and without rising or setting. It is not a body, and is not embodied. It is completely formless, yet entirely real.

Ascertain the nature of your very Existence by enquiring into what it is that appears as the individual. If the inquiry is nonobjective, as it ought to be, there is the self-revelation of perpetually egoless Being-Consciousness-Bliss—your true Self.

For whom is the illusion, the illusion of a separate Self or of differentiation of any kind? The illusion cannot be for the real Self. The real Self, as the Maharshi explains, is true Knowledge, which transcends the usual conceptions of ignorance and knowledge. True Knowledge, to be true, must be innate, for the innate alone does not rise and set. What, then, is ignorance and for whom is it? Difference is imagined from the standpoint of an "I," the individual, yet the individual "I," itself, is a form of ignorance. Can difference imagine itself? Does ignorance delude itself?

The scriptures declare that it is impossible to define maya—illusion, for how could that which has no existence be defined? Though it has no existence, one appears to dwell in it and be bound accordingly until he inquires, "Who am I?" Then, the very root of illusion, the very root of delusion, vanishes because it is unreal. What remains, knowing itself, is eternal.

Question the assumption that you are a body or have any of the characteristics, activities, or qualities of a body, such as being in space, in time, in a world, and so forth and so on. Inquire, and determine if you are the body or not, and the birthless, imperishable Truth becomes self-evident. Inquire into what you regard as "I." Discern what is objective, for you cannot be an object of any kind, gross or subtle, and abandon that definition. Eliminate this misidentification. What remains as "I"? (Silence)

True silence is that in which there is no "I-notion." To abide in silence, therefore, truly means to abide free of the notion or assumption of an individual. There exists one immeasurable mass of imperturbable silence—never-ending Being, limitless Consciousness—which is the perfect fullness. The illusion that dreams otherwise is rootless. If it seems otherwise to you, trace the seeming to your knowing of it, your believing in it. Trace the believing or knowing of it to the reality of your own Being—to the knowing of your own Consciousness. Know the Being-Consciousness as it is.

Brahman knows Brahman. There is no second. No matter how you practice, in the end, you must come to this—Self-Knowledge.

Q.: In many of Sankara's works, he concludes a section with, "And having inquired and realized the Self, one knows what is to be known and has accomplished what is to be accomplished." That seems complete in itself, but I wonder if there is anything beyond the direct face-value of it?

N.: What is there to be known?

Q.: The real identity of the one who wonders what there is to be known.

N.: Alright. Without his identity being known, all that he supposedly knows is only ignorance—various forms of delusion. Only if he knows himself does he know what is real. Knowledge of something unreal is also unreal. Knowledge of Reality alone is real Knowledge.

In addition, because the Reality alone exists and the unreal never comes to be, the Reality alone is what is to be known. It is the only thing capable of true Knowledge, and it is the only thing capable of truly knowing. In the Knowledge to which Adi Sankara refers, there is no triadic division of knower, knowing, and known. If one knows That, the Reality rests in itself, and there is complete peace. If that is not known as it is, seeking will go on until one does find.

What is there to be accomplished? Everyone seeks for happiness all of the time, yet it is only when one realizes the Self that this happiness shines unveiled in all of its fullness. This is what is to be accomplished.

One always wishes to know all the time. You attempt to know; you attempt to know what is real. Even in all kinds of ignorance, in all kinds of permutations of thinking, sensing, etc., always you want to know. The Knowledge of Reality as it is ought to be accomplished. If not, one is only living and dying in an unreal dream.

What needs to be accomplished is something that is perpetual and eternal. If something is gained, it will be lost; if something appears, it disappears. The supreme accomplishment must be something that neither arises nor sets, neither appears nor disappears. Where else can that be found except in one's own identity—the Knowledge of one's Existence—for you cannot separate from your own Existence. The one who accomplishes such is the Existence. No other can do so. The Existence is simultaneously Consciousness. Consciousness is the very substance of true Knowledge, which is the non-triadic, transcendent Knowledge.

Therefore, it is only through Realization of the Self that one has known what needs to be known and accomplished what needs to be accomplished. If you do anything else but do not accomplish that, of what avail is it? If you know everything else but do not know yourself who knows, what kind of knowledge is that?

Q.: I have a question about what could be called qualified experiences in the direction of knowing Reality. It is that which is qualified as a partial or incomplete vision of the Real. Why assume a stable, ongoing reality to the incomplete part? Why not take that apart and keep seeking for the Real that is behind instead of dismissing it as a passing experience and hoping for better next time?

N.: Yes. That is wise. The one who would dismiss it is what is passing.

Q.: Even incomplete inklings of the Real are good. If only the incomplete part would be taken away!

N.: If you inquire into the individual who yearns for the complete to dissolve the incomplete, that very "I," there will be no incompleteness.

Another Q.: The idea that I am an individual is totally rootless. It is hard to imagine how one would actually imagine himself as something else.

N.: That would suppose you were there to begin with.

Q.: What exists is there already, and there is no reason to make anything more. It would be a silly, fruitless exercise to add to what you have described as an infinite, imperturbable mass of Bliss.

N.: We can say that illusion is pointless; we can know it as nonexistent. We can also say that illusion is the attempt to know oneself, but in an inverted or fruitless manner. In whatever manner it is described, there actually is no getting away from the Self. Nameless and formless, it is the ever-existent. It is not that it becomes one-without-a-second upon Realization of the Absolute, for it is always one without a second. By this, along with other means, one transcends the idea that Realization is an event. The Realization must necessarily be of the same nature as that which is realized; otherwise it will not be nondual. If it is not nondual, it is only illusion. If it is nondual, the realizer, the Realization, and that which is realized are identical—one and the very same thing. If it is ever-existent or eternal, it is not an event. An event occurs to someone, but who is there?

Q.: I understand that my Existence is never an event. It never stops. It never changes. It is just pure Being, as it is always, and I am never anything other than that.

N.: Sri Ramana's Grace is marvelous, isn't it?

Q.: Yes, the Grace and the devotion are as unbroken as the Existence.

Another Q.: It makes sense that ignorance can not come out of ignorance, but it seems that it does for me. It appears as though ignorance spawns more ignorance.

N.: Ignorance may appear to spawn more ignorance, but where does it actually start?

Q.: It does not start. The ultimate starting point is not there.

N.: The ignorance is just the story of the adventures of a man who never existed.

Q.: So, the missing link remains missing. That seems to be the ultimate fulcrum that needs to be understood. The whole illusion hinges upon that assumption.

N.: The starting point of illusion or ignorance is said to be the "I" or ego-notion. Has anyone ever actually seen the "I"?

Q.: I could imagine something, but that could not be myself. That is already objectified. So, I always have to be before that.

N.: The effect of imagination is of the same nature as its cause—imagination. You exist. Existence is not imagined. Indeed, there can be no imagination apart from the Existence. Where in Existence does ignorance rise? Where within the Self does "I" spring up?

Q.: Yes, that does not make any sense.

N.: It cannot spring up outside it, because That is infinite. How can it spring up within it, if it is undifferentiated?

Q.: There is no corner or a place or a starting point. It is only some differentiation in the mind.

N.: What is the root of the mind?

Q.: (laughter) I was going to say that differentiation, but, hmm...

N.: So, the differentiated "I" is the root of the mind and in the mind the "I" appears?

Q.: Yes, it seems as if the "I" is assumed to already be there.

N.: Assumed by whom? Can the real Self assume an "I"? Can another that comes after the "I" assume it? It is not possible.

Q.: There is something solid that everything is based upon, as you were saying. That is always the real part.

N.: Yes, what appears as the substrate is alone real. Just as we casually say that the rope is the substrate of the snake, but the snake is not actually there at all, for there is only the rope; so it is with delusion and the Reality—the differentiated and the undifferentiated. If the Self does not give rise to "I" and if anything other comes after the "I" so such cannot give rise to it, can "I" give rise to itself without it first existing? It cannot be.

Q.: So, there is the Existence...

N.: If you would just stop there, it would be fine. (laughter)

Q.: I should not imagine anything else?

N.: "There is Existence" is true. "There is Existence, and, but, and also," is not true. "I am" is true. "I am this, I am that," is not true.

Q.: It is a combination of something that is real mixed with something that is totally unreal, and the unreal becomes.

N.: Yes. Is it not the very definition of ignorance or the ego? The real mixed with the unreal. Because the unreal cannot stand apart from the real, it is always a mixture. You cannot have just the unreal. But the unreal is, after all, unreal. So, the Real alone actually exists.

Q.: So, discrimination is not leaving what is real. It is not just discriminating the unreal from the real.

N.: By keen discrimination, perceive that there is no one to leave the Self—no one to leave Reality—no other reality to go to and no other kind of self to become. Tying together, as it were, with an illusory knot, the Reality, which is pure Consciousness, with the idea of "I," and a body, and so forth and so on, illusion is displayed. Turning inward, inquiring into your bodiless, "I"-less real nature, illusion vanishes. When the snake is imagined it is not that something has actually been added to the rope, not even in the least degree.

Q.: That is why, in a certain sense, Enlightenment is instantaneous because it never did not occur.

N.: It is timeless. It does not come slowly, and it does not come quickly to any individual. The liberation from the individual is, in itself, timeless. The individual, or jiva, does not become enlightened. Consciousness is already self-luminous. In that Light, no shadow can be. The idea of jiva-hood, or individuality, is abandoned. From the supposed position of bondage, such abandonment is known as liberation. The real substance of liberation, though, is just the Existence of the Self that always is. Because it always is, Liberation is declared to be eternal. Because it always is, it is not a new attainment. Because it is not a new attainment, it will not perish.

(Then followed a recitation in Sanskrit and English of verses of the *Brihadaranyaka Upanishad.)*

(Silence)

Om Shanti Shanti Shanti Om

Can and Are

Satsang, May 16, 2010

(Silence)

Om Om Om

(Silence)

N.: One Self alone exists, eternally. It is purnam, the perfect fullness, of the nature of Brahman, the vast Absolute. It is Sat-Chit-Ananda, Being-Consciousness-Bliss, unborn, endless, indestructible, completely formless, and undifferentiated. That ever is, just as it is, and this one Self, infinite and eternal, is your very Existence. There is no other kind of Self.

It cannot be lost, and it cannot be attained. It is, and there is no one who exists separate from it to miss it or to grasp it. It is said to be realizable, not in the sense of making it more real, for it is already real,—as Sri Bhagavan has stated, "How to make more real that which is already real? How to realize?"—but it can be realized in the sense of Self-Knowledge, in unrealizing the unreal. It is not mistaking to be real that which is unreal, not imagining the Self to be that which it is not. To realize the Self is to abide in That, as That itself, with no differentiation. The immensity and depth of this are ineffable, and, in revealing the truth of it, silence is most eloquent, as in the case of the Maharshi and, in ancient days, Dakshinamurti.

There may be said to be two approaches in the attempt to realize this. One approach is to try to bring this vastness within the context of the present conceiving mind. This is not recommended because this is the way samsara is caused. The other approach is the dissolution of this very mind and absorption of the truth by being absorbed in it.

The Maharshi said that that which he realized, what he attained, is certainly possible for all. The *Gita* declares that the same Self dwells in the hearts of all. There is not a multiplicity of selves. A multiplicity of selves is an illusion born of imagination. It is possible for you to realize, and that which seeks to realize is, itself, that which is to be realized. That is Sat-Chit-Ananda, Being-Consciousness-Bliss. It is possible for you to abide as Being, for Being is your very Existence, apart from which there is no other existence. All that is required is a profound inquiry to know your Existence as it is. Chit is Consciousness. It is possible to abide as the infinite, space-like Consciousness always, for that, indeed, is the only Consciousness that actually is. Ananda is bliss. It is possible to abide in the fullness of Bliss, for happiness is undoubtedly within, and within is the Self, which is truly yourself.

What is required is an inquiry to know that which is within, to know yourself. What is actually your very Existence? It cannot be that which appears and disappears, gross or subtle. What actually is your very Consciousness? It cannot be anything perceived or conceived. Relinquishing such from your sense of identity, what remains? Certainly not a body, certainly nothing of the senses, and not anything conceived in thought—the mind. What remains?

Unrealize the unreal. That is, cease to regard as yourself that which your Self cannot possibly actually be. Who is the individual who misidentifies, who can be apparently capable of being a bound one? Who is the individual? If the individual is sought through the profound inquiry, "Who am I?" there is found to be no individual at all answering to the name of "I." All that is found to exist is vast Being-Consciousness-Bliss, without beginning and without end.

There being, in truth, no one bound, there is, in reality, no bondage. Realizing this conclusively without doubt and without differentiation is referred to as "Liberation." It is Liberation from the imagined bondage. Certainly, this is possible; certainly you can accomplish this. By your own light, discriminate as to what is real and what is not, who you are and what you are not. Discriminate, inquire, fueled by the desire to know yourself, because to know yourself is to abide in lasting, indestructible happiness.

You cannot be simultaneously the eternal, which is the immortal, and the transient. You cannot be simultaneously the non-objective and the objective, the motionless and that which is subject to activity, the undifferentiated and the individualized. Inquire. The nature of your Existence is always the same. The Self never changes its nature. What is the unchanging nature in you?

Brahman is beyond description, yet the Vedas have declared, "Tat Tvam Asi, That you are." That is Brahman, the real Self. Who is the "you" that is That? Only the real Self. As for the "are" part in "You are That," it is self-evident.

Indeed, you can know the Self and repose in the innate state. There comes a time when you laugh and recognize that it is not possible not to know yourself. Is there one self who does not know another? Bodiless, mind-transcendent, and egoless you are. Realize this at heart, and you will remain naturally happy and at peace. By your own light, inquire within yourself.

Q.: The deeper I seek, the clearer it becomes that what I seek is my own nature. I am the bliss that I seek. The seeking and the sought become absorbed, so that there is just the one abiding Reality that is not divided at all.

N.: (Silence)

Another Q: What are thoughts?

N: Not different from that which knows them. How do you know that you have thoughts?

Q: Because I'm aware.

N: That which is aware cannot be a thought. Do the thoughts stand up on their own and declare their own existence, or is your only experience of thoughts your awareness of them? The awareness has no form and is always the same, no matter how many thoughts appear. Even if no thoughts appear, it is the same. It is without modification.

If the significance of this is truly realized, you will know that thought is utterly nonexistent.

Q: Why does it sometimes appear that a certain thought can hold so much weight and another thought can seem just as noise?

N: It is because of the identity behind each of them. Thoughts, or the form of thoughts, proceed from the identification you suppose for yourself. To whatever you lend your identity—your Existence, your Reality, or, more externally, your happiness—that seems vivid and seems to have more weight.

Q: So, is it just a belief?

N: What is the root of belief? From where does it come?

Q: It is like a thought.

N: Yes, but even if there is no thought, there is still belief, only it is not belief in something. It comes from your Reality.

Q: Is Consciousness the same as awareness?

N: Commonly, people say, "I am aware of something." It is Consciousness plus the notion of an object. If we remove the objective notion, which is merely illusory, Consciousness remains, or is revealed, just as it is. Then, we can say that there is no awareness other than pure Consciousness, but pure Consciousness never actually becomes modified into awareness of something else. When you are aware of something, does the something exist outside of the awareness? It has no independent existence. That which has a dependent existence really cannot be said to exist in its own right at all, but is only the substrate upon which it depends appearing as that thing. Trace the substrate in your experience. You will find that there is only pure, homogeneous Consciousness, and, in this, lies great bliss.

Another Q: If there were any other stuff, it rests on this knowing of it, but the knowing is exactly what the sage talks about. It is pure knowing. This helps me to give myself to what has been put forth in the scripture.

N: That of which all the sages speak is the nature of the knower. There is only one knower. Multiplicity is only in the known. All the scriptures are written about you. Even if you have contrary ideas or doubts, they shine in the same light. They are known by the same knower. So, while you may doubt what may be said, you never doubt the knower in yourself. The knower is constant and is beyond doubt. It is the same as your Existence. No one ever has a doubt regarding Existence. You exist. You know that you exist. The Knowledge of existing and the Existence are indistinguishable. They are one and the same thing. The Knowledge is Consciousness. The Existence is true Being. Being-Consciousness is what you are. You cannot stand apart from it to not know it.

Q: This tempts me to share this memory. It's something I saw and remembered throughout my childhood. There was a plastic, inflatable swimming pool with water and a new, little toy sailboat. I'm in the back of a building, and the light reflects off the sailboat. It's as if the bright flash made me more awake, and I was pre-verbally amazed that I existed. I was amazed that I was there, not there, but that I was. The baby is sitting in front of this pool at two years of age, and it's this amazement that never left me. All the details are crystal clear. I realized that, if I ever shared that, it would be taken as silly, but I always cherished it inside.

N: Why do you suppose it would be taken as silly?

Q: Because two-year-old babies aren't suppose to do that.

N: Who says?

Q: There was no sense of being that baby. That was part of it, the ridiculousness of supposedly being this baby didn't register at all.

N: Has the Existence changed since then?

Q: No, it has not.

N: Just the body has.

Q: Well, it didn't seem like my body then.

N: That's right. It is bodiless Existence, and you are still there.

Q: Yes, it seems that no time has passed.

N: Time is of the mind and of the body. Existence is mind-free and bodiless. The wondrous Existence still is. Everything you thought of as yourself since then has been just so much dream.

Q: The bhava then was amazed fascination, like an enjoyable shock.

N: So, what can be silly about that?

Q: I love it. (laughter) I've never shared it before, just because of insufficient confidence in the ears that would hear it.

N: That is why it is not worthwhile to follow the trait that developed later of caring about the opinions of others. Is the Existence moved one way or another by the opinions of others? Its wondrousness is self-evident. The memory part of the objective phenomena, what was sensed at the time, is superfluous. The Existence is not a product of memory. It is timelessly the case. In light of this you may want to revisit the opening verse of *Saddarsanam, the Truth Revealed,* by the Maharshi.

Another Q: Ideas about ethics that I hold sacred are really manifestations of being selfish or egotistical in terms of what I think is right.

N: What is it that is truly right, truly good?

Q: I know that to be abiding in an egoless state is good for me.

N: From that abidance streams forth everything that is true, good, and beautiful, satyam-sivam-sundaram. Certainly, it is right only to do unto others what you would have them do unto you. So, what is it that you want?

Q: I want to feel free.

N: Do you know the way to find this freedom? Then, that is good, that is right. See others as you should see yourself. If you would thus see others and truly see yourself, that would suffice.

Q: I should not see others as projections in my mind, who I think they are or who I think they should be.

N: Who do you think they are, and what do you think they should be?

Q: I think it has to do with who I think I am and who I think I should be.

N: Alright. What do you think you are and what do you think you should be?

Q: It fluctuates. If I am inward-turned, I know who I am, and I know what I should be, but, if I am attached, I don't really know.

N: Do you know what causes attachment?

Q: Sometimes I do, and, sometimes, if I blind myself, I don't seem to know.

N: What makes the difference?

Q: If I am earnest in my inquiry or my devotion, the truth is in some ways invisible, but Grace makes it visible and makes it known and knowable. Grace is always there, but I also have to avail myself of the Grace as well.

N: When you are cognizant of the Grace, can you proceed in any other way than what is true, good, and beautiful? When you thoroughly know the source of happiness, attachment becomes impossible. As for what is unsatisfactory, just ensure that you are free of what is other than the good, Siva. Then, you will naturally respond appropriately. Be free of confusion regarding what is the cause of happiness, be clear about what the nature of others is by being aware of the nature of yourself, and always treat others as you would have them treat you, or better. So, it is not that there are no ethics; you must know the core of them.

Q: Have them pure.

N: There is something in you that is truly you that is entirely blemishless. Its stainless nature is beyond taint at anytime. Be keenly aware of that. That is absolutely indivisible. It is one and absolute. Devote yourself to that entirely. Know that entirely, and, then, of course, others will be seen as yourself. Upon this depend all of the ethics.

Another Q: I get into trouble thinking that my happiness is objective. I know the place of happiness because I am reminded of it, but I forget it.

N: Have you ever experienced happiness outwardly? Have you ever seen happiness, heard happiness, touched some happiness, tasted happiness, or smelled some happiness? (laughter)

Q: No, but I keep trying. (laughter)

N: You try because you know something. What do you know about happiness that you continue to try for it? Even if there is the least speck of it missing, you try for it. What do you know?

Q: I know that happiness has to exist.

N: Happiness exists, in perfect fullness, and it is your natural state. The moment that you feel even a speck of it is missing, you search for it. It is an intuitive search for your own Self, since Bliss is identical with Being. The desire for happiness springs up from the depth within. When you experience happiness, it is the within-ness, itself, that shines as happiness, and the place where it shines is also within. Within is not in the body and not in the senses.

Q: If I could see that depth in any experience, that would help to clarify where happiness comes from. When I have objectified it, my mind is outward and unquestioned at that point.

N: Is there anything obstructing the inquiry? Is there anything preventing you from turning within? Must one wait for a certain time or opportunity to turn within? Are you not free to do so all the time? You are absolutely free, and you are free to find the freedom.

Q: That is interesting, but the chocolate cake or whatever is there looks darn good.

N: Chocolate cake can give you a sweet sensation, and, if you eat too much of it, it can give you another type of sensation, I suppose. But can it give you happiness?

Q: Every aspect of anything involved with the chocolate cake involves the body, senses, and mind. However, what you are saying is that there is another aspect that shines in the experience, which I am not seeing.

N: If you eat some chocolate cake in your dream and you feel happy about it, from where does the happiness come?

Q: Definitely not from the chocolate cake.

N: It is just like that in the present waking state, which is only another dream. Trace where the happiness has its source, from where it seems to rise.

Q: It is definitely not the body. I should not say definitely, because I become confused and "snookered" all the time.

N: Do you become confused by the things, or do you confuse yourself?

Q: Not by the things. I confuse myself.

N: So, the things really do not enter into it at all, do they? They neither give you the happiness nor do they take it away.

Q: I lend happiness to the object.

N: The object does not exist anywhere outside of your own mind.

Q: Just like the chocolate cake in the dream.

N: The entire world is like that. If the world is within the mind, in what is the mind? The objects are not real, and the mind, also, is not real. Trace the happiness to its source. There is the Reality. The Consciousness that knows the happiness is the happiness. It is your Being, which is nothing that appears in this waking state or that appears in the dream state. With a body or without a body, with the senses or without them, it is the same. Knowing yourself to be That, what does it matter if there is chocolate cake or not? The appearance and disappearance of the entire world is insignificant in That.

Q: What you are discussing, though, is complete detachment. The only thing that keeps illusion going is a belief in happiness in the external, objective something.

N: Detachment can be spoken of in a variety of ways. At first, it can be spoken of as "becoming detached," which has its root in jnana, or knowledge, specifically the knowledge of where happiness is. That makes a man detached from every worldly thing, and he is happy inside. Detachment can also be spoken of in terms of being the nature of Consciousness, which is the witness of all of this universe and of all the minds in it, and which remains unmoved by any appearance and by the disappearance of anything. For That, even life and death are the same. Then, there is absolute detachment. For the unborn, there is no creation. There is just Brahman, and Brahman alone. There is nothing else to which it can become attached. It is and alone is. One who proceeds with the beginning winds up at the end. In the end, you find that the end is the beginning.

Another Q: What determines ultimate release? If that light is the same, changeless, and brilliant, and a two-year-old has even less thoughts than now, far less than what we might have as adults, what prevented that two-year-old from waking up from the brilliance of that light?

N: The question is good but supposes that there are existent individuals, some of whom are not awake and some of whom are awake. The supposition is that there are some who are unenlightened to their nature and some who are enlightened to their nature, but Self-Realization is characterized by the Knowledge that there has never been an individual. Individuals do not wake up to spiritual truth. You wake up from the dream of individuality and leave it behind.

Q: Why wouldn't that have happened for that little two-year-old?

N: The idea of it happening, or an occurrence, is based on the same illusion as the individual. What is to happen and for whom? If you determine your own Existence, seen in its own Light, know by your own Light what your Existence is, you will see that it was not young and is not now older. It was never two or any other age and was never in darkness. The idea of another state other than the Reality is an illusion, yet when we attempt to know the illusion for what it is, it vanishes because it is utterly unreal. That which existed then exists now and always. (Silence) If you want the question answered at the level of which it was asked, which is not the final answer, it must be said that depth of inquiry, depth of knowledge of one's Self, makes the difference.

(Then followed a recitation in Sanskrit and English of verses of the *Brihadaranyaka Upanishad.*)

(Silence)

Om Shanti Shanti Shanti Om

Being is Knowledge

Satsang, August 22, 2010

(Silence)

Om Om Om

(Silence)

N.: Sri Bhagavan gives the instruction, "Know yourself." In this Knowledge, Being, itself, is the Knowledge. It is undivided Knowledge, nondual Knowledge, in that it has no alternative, and there is no division between the knower and the known. If you know yourself, your Being is found to be birthless, imperishable, undifferentiated, entirely formless, without condition, without state, immovable, immutable, and eternal. If you do not know yourself, the "you" that does not know does not exist, for the Self is only One without a second. Your Existence is invariably singular. There are not two selves. The Self is only One.

Inquire within, "Who am I?" Abandoning any tendency to misidentify with the body or its attributes, with the senses, and with the mind—abandoning the tendency to misidentify with what is objective and not the Self—inquire deeply, "Who am I?"

In the book entitled *Who am I?*, the Maharshi says that silence is that in which no "I" arises, in which no "I" appears. In the book entitled *Talks with Sri Ramana Maharshi*, he says that silence is "I." How can he say both? Silence is that in which there is no "I," and silence is "I." That in which misidentification with the body is gone and in which there is no false assumption of individuality is your true Self. That is Silence, the "I"-less true "I." To know yourself is to abide in Silence as Silence. The Knowledge is Being; Being is self-luminous. Examine your existence. It is self-luminous and requires nothing else in order to know itself. At just such a depth, you should know your own nature.

One true "I" exists. There is only one Self and not a multiplicity of selves. There is neither a multiplicity of selves outwardly, which would be imagined only in relation to the body, nor is there a multiplicity of selves inwardly, as if there would be parts of you, such as higher and lower, a true Self and a false self, a real Self and an ego self, and so forth and so on. The Self is only One. By profound, constant inquiry, know this Self. It is this very Self that the Upanishads declare to be Brahman.

You cannot hear it, you cannot see it, and it is not possible to study it as a topic. This has to do with your very Being. When ignorance appears, there is the need for true Knowledge. Realizing true Knowledge by knowing yourself, ignorance is found to be nonexistent, and steady Knowledge is found to be the very nature of your Existence, Being-Consciousness-Bliss.

Dive within and realize That which alone is truly real.

Q.: Is another name for the Self "Consciousness"? Can we say that the Self is Consciousness?

N.: Yes, you can say that.

Q: The tendency is to exist as something between all of the existence of the universe and one part.

N: As you are, all are. Are you one? Are you two?

Q: The eternal vision is constantly manifested and expanding.

N: According to the experiencer, so is the view. In the eternal, there is no difference whatsoever. For the unborn, there can be no talk of creation.

Q: Where is the course of the lila?

N: It is according to the viewer of it. If God sees God with God's own eye, is there lila?

Q: The greatest capacity of Consciousness seems to dominate the lesser capacity of Consciousness in the totality that exists in that lila.

N: What do you mean by "Consciousness"?

Q: I am talking about the manifestation of the part. It seems that you are there and I am here, and it seems to be that you are the Master and I am the disciple, and, during this entire time, we are talking about One.

N: Who says all that? Who sees all that?

Q: One part of the whole, for it is the mind that dwells in duality.

N: The idea of a part is also just a thought. Inquire for whom are all these ideas: parts, wholeness, manifested, unmanifested. If we inquire for whom these are and know ourselves, all the differences prove to be nonexistent.

Q: So, the objective of the inquiry is to center in the Self?

N: It is the Knowledge of the Reality as it is and nothing less. The Knowledge is of the very nature of Consciousness. Consciousness is self-luminous and, for Consciousness, there is nothing other.

Q: There is philosophy and books, schools and trains of thought. For the nations, the forgetfulness of all these parts prevails in the world of mundane, mischievous behavior, miscomprehension, and misunderstanding. Where did all this chaos come from?

N: You have summed it up: all of that is just a misunderstanding.

Q: This misconception occurs in so many millions of millions of creatures.

N: The idea of "millions" is also a misunderstanding.

Q: My looking into the misconceptions as a witness of all these is part of my inquiry. Then, "Who am I?"

N: If there is the deep inquiry "Who am I?" so that Self-Knowledge shines, there is no more misunderstanding. The root of such imagination proves to be absent.

Q: And that is the lila?

N: Call it by any name. First inquire; then say what is.

Q: I had better inquire really well. (laughter)

N: Yes, you should do so to the best of your ability.

Q: I don't want to deceive myself.

N: You won't. You will not be happy unless you know yourself.

Q: I think that I am being blessed. Many people don't like the happiness. As the misconceptions vanish, I become an easy target, because, the bigger the Consciousness, the more responsibility there is.

N: Remain without attachment, and you will have equanimity. Realize the nature of the Self, the pure Consciousness, as it is. Then, we can see about all these other things.

Another Q: Other than lila, is there anything else that explains the origin of misunderstanding and misconceptions? Is Self-inquiry a prerequisite to ask the question about it?

N: There are ever so many explanations, and he offered one referred to as "lila." Someone else may give some other explanation. The explanations are only as real as that which they are trying to explain. Is illusion real? Any explanation of illusion is bound to be as illusory as the illusion itself. The explanations are only to wean us from the illusion and not to give us some solidified idea that this really happens.

Other than inquiry, how else to know oneself? Without knowing oneself, how could one know what is real?

Q: We have seen many saints who worshipped a personal God that were able to achieve enlightenment. They did not talk about inquiry. They talked only about a personal God and becoming absorbed in prayer and worship. How did they achieve? I want to know how should we explain their enlightenment?

N: It needs no explanation. It is proof in itself. Absorption is the key. We can say that the Knowledge-essence shines in the form of the devotion.

Q: What is the state of a person after achieving enlightenment? In this material world, how will his attitude and outlook be?

N: He will be detached from all worldly things, happy at heart in the Knowledge of himself, which is the highest devotion to God. Whether we speak in terms of knowledge or devotion, the ego-notion dissolves. Its utter dissolution is complete absorption. That is the goal and nothing less. If that is realized within, one abides at the very source of all that is true, good, and beautiful.

Q: He will have conquered all the internal enemies, such as anger, and will have no ill-will and no animosity.

N: Ill-will, animosity, anger, etc. have their root in ignorance. Where there is duality and the belief in one's ego and the egos of others, such can arise. When the ego is absorbed or utterly dissolved, such become impossible.

Q: So, there isn't a practical technique of dissolving the ego?

N: What can be more practical than the inquiry as prescribed by the Maharshi, "Who am I?" Your Existence you have with you always. You always exist. It is not an inert existence; it is a knowing Existence. Grace is already there in abundance; it is limitless. If we turn within and make an earnest attempt to know ourselves, this is the most practical of practicality.

Q: Do we need to concentrate on any particular spot of the body?

N: Concentration on a particular spot of the body is not necessary, but one should get to the very root of that concentrative power.

Q: The object of concentration should be?

N: On the nonobjective. After all, one wants to know the Self, not a part of the body or some objective phenomenon.

Q: Is that the soul?

N: What do you mean by "soul"?

Q: The knowledge of God

N: Then, that soul is infinite and eternal and only One.

Q: It is not very easy. (laughter)

N: Sri Ramana wrote in verse, "Self-Realization is easy, the easiest thing there is." The difficulties prove to be only imaginary. They seem solid, but, when we make an earnest attempt to dive within, their apparent solidity dissolves. There is really nothing obstructing the Reality, nothing in the way of God, and nothing preventing one from knowing oneself. The obstacles prove to be illusory, composed of imagination, maya. Sri Bhagavan defined maya as "that which is not."

Q: The mind always wanders away. When we try to bring it back, again it wanders. What is the best way to bring it back?

N: You know that it wanders. What is it that so knows? No matter how long and how far it wanders, something knows before the wandering, during the wandering, and after the wandering is over. Something knows, and that something is more you than wherever the mind wanders. Know this "something" that is shining and unmoving.

Q: That means that one has to transcend the mind.

N: Yes. What is referred to as inquiry is entirely mind-transcendent. Likewise, the Knowledge is mind-transcendent.

Another Q: The body never announces itself as the body. The world is the same way. It is in my terms that it is "this" or it is "that." The Maharshi says that before I worry about all those things, find out about myself who is the one naming all of those things. It is a redirection that I am familiar with, but it is very striking and very fruitful.

N: Yes, you name all those parts. You conceive them. Their existence depends on your awareness of them, or your conception of them if you know the world is within the mind. They do not stand up and declare their own reality. You say, "I am such and such" and "this is such and such" and between "I" and "this," the two poles of duality, is stretched all of the illusion. Of the two, "this" depends on "I." The Maharshi said, "What is the use of knowing all else without first knowing oneself." He then added, "What else is there to be known when oneself is known."

If there is an "I," there is "this." Is there an "I"?

Q: That would be something that would be named, as well. It comes before the others, but it's on the same footing.

N: What, then, is real? There is Reality. It is not something, and it is certainly not nothing. The Reality comprehends itself. Brahman knows Brahman. Even all that is regarded as illusion is only That. You have known That as all this. The knower, the knowing, and the known are entirely just That—Brahman. Brahman is the only Self that there is. There is no other kind of Self.

Another Q: Everything that Ramana and the scriptures say about my nature is true, accurate, and understates what the experience of one's Self truly is. The unclarity, the doubts, and the questions are solved when I inquire. When

I actually inquire, everything that needs to be known becomes obvious in a way that I would not have predicted from the mind's point of view in advance.

N: If it conformed to one's preconception, what good would it be? None of the spiritual instruction of the Maharshi, scripture, or inquiry conform to one's preconception, that is, to limited conception.

Q: Which is such Grace because, if it did conform to it, it would be so limited that I would not be interested in it.

N: It would not be liberating. That which does not conform to the imagined conceptions is that which liberates one from all the imagined bondage. The best way to learn to inquire intensely is to inquire intensely. Continuity of practice has its own power. Nevertheless, an aspirant can increase the intensity of his desire for liberation by reflecting on what is the true source of happiness. In what way will he be truly happy, without a break and without end? Immortal bliss is found only in one place. There is the desire to know, to increase the intensity of one's practice. Keenly discern what you are attempting to know. If you determine that it is utterly nonobjective, the innate intensity, which is really the vividness of Reality, consumes all else. In essence and substance, inquiry is pure Knowledge. Pure Knowledge, which is nonobjective Knowledge, is only Consciousness. Is the intensity of Consciousness measurable?

Q: Anything of measure would be of the mind, and there is nothing in Consciousness that in any way resembles a mind. If I inquire into what is Consciousness, the answer is the Consciousness, and that I know directly. Do you have any more good questions?

N: What do you need to know?

Q: Nothing, but I love when you ask questions like that. It is like when the rishis gathered to hear Dakshinamurti's silent teaching. Even though there is nothing really to hear,

I want to hear it over and over and feel that Knowledge continuously and without end. So it is when you ask questions like that.

N: The questions are expressive or indicative of the same ancient Silence. Silence is perpetual. All the terms used to express the essential teaching are, in truth, only that same Silence. When the Maharshi was manifestly silent, there was Silence. When He spoke, there was still the same Silence.

The spirit and purpose of the questions are that one should not take for granted any bondage or any ignorance. Bondage is only ignorance. Ignorance is only false supposition. The suppositions seem to survive only due to lack of inquiry. If light is brought in to search for darkness, what happens to the darkness? Being nothing, it vanishes. So, if you think "this is," it is wise to first determine if it is so. Since the view of "it is" depends on the definition of "I am," it is best to inquire "Who am I?" There is no need to affirm the Truth. It is sufficient if the false is questioned. Then, the Reality, which is there always, stands self-revealed. To see the rope that is actually there, it is enough to question the illusion of a snake that was superimposed upon it through imagination. Imagination being put to an end, Reality is self-evident, and you, yourself, are the Reality.

Another Q: Is that why the Self is inconceivable and always new?

N: The inconceivable is realized with a Knowledge that is only Being.

Another Q: My purpose is to be bliss.

N: Alright. How do you propose to be bliss?

Q: By forgetting about the linear progression of all these events that my mind wants to chronical-ize. I can forget all those definitions and say, "That's just an illusion."

N: It is not forgetting in the sense of loss of memory, but forgetting the definitions.

Q: Yes. It's remembering who I am, rather than all the contrived memories and experiences.

N: It is remembrance of who you are. Who you are must always be the same and is immovable. It is not subject to varying perspectives, but simply is as it is, always. The tendency to return to a limited definition is only so long as one feels the definition is valid or has some degree of validity. When it is known to be entirely false, purely imagined, there is nothing in it for you, and you do not return to it, or, rather, you no longer conjure it up.

Q: I try to remember that I am bliss, I am joy, and I am peace. I try to remember not as a matter of doing but just being that.

N: You are bliss, and you are intuitively drawn to your nature. Affirmation of it will not make it more so, but, if you deeply inquire as to what your very nature is, curious to know your very Being as it is, and, in the course of such, you cease to misidentify, that suffices, and your nature as Being-Consciousness-Bliss stands self-revealed. As long as there seems to be someone who goes in and out of that, the one who attempts in earnest to seek it, inquire to see what his definition is. Whatever definition is false—some thinking, some doing, etc.—abandon it by knowing that it is not really "I." Continue until the irreducible substrate alone remains. Bliss knows itself. It has no need to affirm itself. It is so solidly itself that there is nothing contradictory to it.

Another Q: It is said that it is necessary to purify the mind, to strengthen the mind. Is there any special technique to purify and strengthen the mind? Or is it that by just inquiring "Who am I?" the mind automatically becomes purified and strengthened?

N: The latter is the case. The inquiry is sufficient.

Q: To strengthen the mind?

N: To strengthen the mind and to purify the mind. What else is purification but abandonment of the mind's imagination, the darkness of ignorance? What else is strength of mind but the ability for it to remain in its source without being differentiated as a "mind." This comes by inquiry to know oneself. Any other practices employed for the purposes of strengthening and purifying the mind work to the extent that they contain this same knowledge-essence, which inquiry is composed of solely. Otherwise, if one engages in some other practice and merely does so mechanically without this knowledge-essence, what good comes of it? Where there is this knowledge-essence, the diminishing of egotism, there is success.

Q: How to overcome the obstacles in the way?

N: What are the obstacles?

Q: The mind always roams in the future or roams in the past, and it doesn't stay in the present. Normally, the mind doesn't stay in the present. That is the obstacle.

N: The past, the present, and the future are all equally unreal. Consider them like the past, present, and future of a dream. The Reality is timeless and is not the past, not the present, and not the future. Being mind-transcendent, the Supreme Reality is time-transcendent. That which transcends time and the mind is your true abode, your true Self. Inquire into the true Self to know it as it is. There is no obstruction between yourself and yourself. There is no gap or difference.

(Then followed a recitation in Sanskrit and English of verses from *Ashtavakra Gita.*)

(Silence)

Om Shanti Shanti Shanti Om

Immeasurably Vast

Satsang, October 23, 2011

(Silence)

Om Om Om

(Silence)

Truly, your Self is only Brahman—the immeasurably vast, absolute Being. Such a vastness is it that it is actually utterly transcendent of time and space. It is eternal and truly infinite. This alone is your very Existence, and, apart from this Existence or different from this Existence, there is no other existence for you or for anything else.

It is only misidentification that seems to overlook this nature of the Brahman-Self and, through imagination, superimposes the limitations of what is not the Self—what is not Brahman—upon yourself. This does not change your nature; your real Being is immutable. It is never modified at any time, but, due to such illusion, where there is infinite Being-Consciousness-Bliss, there seems to be an "I," objects, ignorance, and suffering.

For whom is such superimposition? Whose ignorance or misidentification is it? The idea that there is someone for whom it is, is, itself, the misidentification, for, in reality, the Self does not misidentify. In reality, nothing is superimposed upon Brahman. It remains ever just as it is—infinite and perfectly full.

Sri Bhagavan says that all other thoughts, all concepts of differentiation, start with the notion "I." The "I" is an incorrect assumption, and whatever is based upon it is similarly not true. Any limitation you can imagine, any bondage that you can conceive for yourself, is based completely on this notion of "I," while the "I," itself, is merely an imagined superimposition upon the vast, absolute Existence of Brahman—the real Self.

Ignorance has no substance and no validity, yet belief in it gives rise to the experience of bondage. It is pseudo-bondage, but, when in it, one does not know that. Absence of such ignorance—that is, true knowledge of one's Self—is liberation from all of the imagined bondage. How is liberation brought about? It is brought about by Knowledge and by inquiry. No activity of the body, speech, or mind can accomplish this. Knowledge shows what the Reality is and thereby liberates one from the unreal.

How to attain this Knowledge? This, then, is the question. The Knowledge is actually innate, and it will shine in your experience fully without the least trace of obscuration as soon as the misidentifications are abandoned. So, you inquire into the nature of your very Existence, your very Consciousness. You discern what limitations are being superimposed upon your nature. You know something is a superimposition if it is not eternal. You know that it is a superimposition if it is changeful. You know that it is a superimposition if it results in a sense of limitation or bondage. You know that it is a superimposition if it is anything but the infinite Brahman—Sat-Chit-Ananda—Being-Consciousness-Bliss. Discern such misidentifications and then inquire, "Who Am I?" and realize what you truly are. The moment you fully discern that ignorance is ignorance, it ceases to exist.

Such is the nature of maya or illusion; it has only a seeming existence. The ignorant one does not actually exist. The ignorant one and his ignorance are both imagined, a product of misidentification or superimposition of what is unreal upon the real. They seem as if actual but are not so. The only reality that actually exists is the Brahman-Self. Inquire in the deepest recesses of your nature as to what you truly are. Discerning and casting aside each misidentification, you will in turn find the one who misidentifies also to be of the same nature. What exists is one Self—Brahman—and that eternally is just as it is. In this, there is the Bliss of immaculate perfection—the immortality of eternal Being. It is the Knowledge of the self-luminous Consciousness. For That, there is no other, no alternative. If you think otherwise, even by a trace, inquire to know the nature of the thinker. Continue to inquire until you know with certainty, beyond any possibility of doubt, that the immeasurably vast Brahman is the only Reality, and that the only Self.

Q.: There is a spiritual urge that is very beneficial at a stage that I might call "the urge to repair." Does it consume itself if purely followed or is it actually something to disidentify from? It implies that there is something to repair.

N.: Why do you have that assumption?

Q.: With gross misidentifications, I could consider successfully releasing them as a kind of repair.

N.: If there is any sign of imperfection, there is a natural yearning to find perfection or to return to it. It is an intuition of your actual nature, isn't it?

Q.: So, would it consume itself or would it actually have to be let go of consciously?

N.: Trace the feeling to its nature, and then neither side which you have proposed is applicable. If it is an intuition of the innate perfection or the perfect fullness of the Self and that this, indeed, is your natural state, which is why you wish to find it or return to it, or wake up to it, would there be any need to get rid of that? Could it really be said to extinguish itself? Not truly. Yet, it is possible to realize the Truth in which no imperfection needs any repair for it does not exist. If you are limited, you must pull off those limitations, but are you truly limited to begin with? Such an inquiry completely removes the false limitations and, furthermore, shows that they never actually came to be. So, then, does such desire to be free of limitation—desire for Liberation—get thrown aside?

Q.: Fulfilled would be a better term.

Another Q.: The phrase, "Ignorance has no validity," like so many things that you say during a satsang, is an entry point to Reality.

N.: The "entry" is always a matter of setting aside, or the destruction, of some ignorance. Then, you find that you already are within—where you want to be. Indeed, you are the place itself.

Ignorance has no validity. There is not a drop of truth in any kind of limitation. The seeming solidity of ignorance is entirely borrowed from one's own Reality. When something imaginary is superimposed upon a substrate, the substrate is the only solid thing there. Any apparent solidity, vividness, or substantiality found in that which is superimposed actually belongs entirely to the substrate, and such does not actually leave the substrate and go into the imagined part. It is just like that with the Self, which is true and ever solid, and ignorance, which is never valid. We should perceive the falseness of ignorance from top to bottom: the falseness and its details, the various names and forms that it appears as, and the falseness of its basis, which is the one who can be ignorant.

Q.: Can I be ignorant?

N.: You can not be ignorant and be Brahman at the same time.

Q.: The one that would say that it is ignorant is not another "I." If it is not another "I," there is not a second, which is the invalid assumption of individuality.

N.: It seems to assume itself, but that is not possible. The ego, or "I," is not truly the knower, which is pure Consciousness. Since it is not the knower, it can neither know other things nor can it know itself. If the ego is the root of ignorance and it cannot know itself and it cannot know anything else—further ignorance—what does that say about the entirety of ignorance?

Q.: "I" is not an experience like an individual "I" is experienced, which is experienced like an object. The experience that knows that there is no ignorance is not an experience experiencing itself as an object. There is no objectivity in that. There is something that comes before experience.

N.: The Self is a matter of direct or immediate experience, which is nonobjective. In this, experience and Knowledge are the same thing, and that experiential Knowledge is identical with one's Being. The certainty of it is without comparison. The more deeply you inquire into the one who is ignorant, who is the basis of ignorance, who is the one who appears in the various guises of the names and forms of ignorance, the more you discover that he is absent. There is one Knower, which is of the nature of pure Consciousness. There is one Self. There is not an ignorant self and a true Self. There is no second knowing entity. Consciousness is the only knower. For that One, there is never any ignorance. Another one does not actually exist.

Another Q.: As we go from the knowledge of the process to the state where we want to be, is that by practice or Grace or is it a combination?

N.: Yes, all of them. Practice is necessary, but it is by Grace that one practices. The Grace that is needed is already there. It is not to be created anew, but it is ever-existent. If you understand the practice to be one of Self-inquiry, which is making one's vision entirely nonobjective, you understand what needs to be understood. If you pursue such inquiry, all illusions will be burnt up. What now appears as a process is actually the end shining in your present state. The end appears as the means. The Knowledge appears as the inquiry. Be sure that, inquiring "Who am I?", you make your vision entirely nonobjective and stay firmly with that. If you start to think of something else or conceive of the inquiry as a mental process to quiet thoughts or something similar, you should immediately inquire, "For whom is this view? For whom is this idea?" and thereby dive deep to abide as that which the Maharshi refers to as "the Heart," which is the self-existent, quintessential Being.

Another Q.: On Friday night, I was tired. It could be related to some sickness. It is interesting to try to inquire when the mental faculty is not sharp. I am not sure if it actually makes a difference. To understand and to retain concepts is harder, but inquiry isn't that. Because I believe, or give credence to the idea of, myself as being thought, I know there are some limitations.

N.: Do you rely on thought to know that you exist?

Q.: No. I just know.

N.: This interior knowledge of existence is the actual place of inquiry. Physical tiredness, illness, and mental fatigue are inconsequential to the actual inquiry. Be certain that your inquiry is entirely nonobjective and that it does not become any kind of mental practice. It is not a repositioning of one's thoughts, but it is ceasing to misidentify with any thought.

Q.: The meditation was on the passage from the Maharshi that says that the dead are doing fine and it is the living that grieve, so one must destroy the ego and any outgrowths of the ego. I notice the outgrowths. You mentioned to inquire into the Sat-Chit-Ananda and remove the objectivity and misidentifications. Noticing the misidentifications seems to partake of the inquiry.

N.: The desire to be free, the power that discerns where there is delusion, the light by which one eliminates the delusion and sees his way clear, and the absolute Being that thus remains are all one and the same. Yes, one must kill the ego, but the best way to kill it is to seek it. Finding it to be unreal is complete death. Nothing is as dead as something that never actually came to be. (laughter)

Q.: What we believe in as life must be questioned. It is merging, somehow, this reality with the body.

N.: How do such merge? How can we combine the real and the unreal? Such is the so-called combination of the Self and what is not the Self.

Q.: I thiink that there is not a combination, and it is just believed to be a combination. Is there really a combination? Is there unreality there?

N.: Can you combine the unreal and the real? Is there a real unreal to combine with it? If you keep going in this direction, you must ask if the idea of a combination is real or unreal.

Q.: If I were making a recipe and took nonexistent ingredients and threw them into a bowl and mixed them…

N.: No one is going to be fed that way. (laughter)

Q.: If there is something in the bowl already and I mix them up, do I create anything new or different? Essentially, is that what you are saying?

N.: Yes, you have the recipe. (laughter)

Q.: That is important to understand. I forget that though. You point to the one who forgets, and that one has to be inquired into.

N.: If one forgets his real nature, he has to remember, but how else to remember That except by abiding as That? This being so, there is no actual forgetfulness or remembrance. There are not two. The idea that the Self is remembered or forgotten by another self should be questioned. There are not two knowers. So, an individual can neither remember nor forget. You are not the ego, or individual, and most certainly not a mind or a body. This Knowledge gets rid of the entire recipe. With this Knowledge, there is not even a bowl in which to put the recipe ingredients. (laughter)

Q.: The cook gets laid off permanently. (laughter)

N.: The cook becomes cooked. (laughter)

Q.: It seems you have merged everything into that recipe. There would not be anything separate in the end.

N.: Your real Self does not mix with anything, and a second self has not come to be. Deep inquiry reveals this. Where there is no second self, or ego notion, there is, similarly, no world-notion, no one bound, and nothing to constitute the bondage.

(Then followed a recitation in Sanskrit and English of verses from the *Brihadaranyaka Upanishad.*)

(Silence)

Om Shanti Shanti Shanti Om

(Then followed a Tamil recitation from *Song of Ribhu*, chapter 13)

The Self is Brahman

Satsang, January 29, 2012

(Silence)

Om Om Om

(Silence)

N.: The Self is Brahman. There is no other kind of self. Brahman is the Self and nothing objective to be imagined, conceived, or perceived. To realize the supreme and everlasting bliss of Brahman, you must realize your identity as that. Such realization consists of Knowledge—nonobjective Knowledge. This is not something perceived through the senses or conceived in thought, but it is transcendent, nonobjective Knowledge in which knowing is Being.

Of jagat-jiva-para—the universe, the individual, and the Supreme—Sri Bhagavan said, "These three appear as if three only so long as the ego is there." In egoless Knowledge, that is, in the Reality as it is, there is no such differentiation. Of the three—oneself, the universe, and the Supreme—the definitions attributed to oneself determine the form or definition of the others. So, if there is misidentification with the body, one then imagines an external world or universe. In relation to the body, the eternal, the infinite, that is, the Supreme, appears as if something else different from oneself. But, are we bodies? Dive deep into the nature of your Existence—your very Self. "Self" signifies Existence, itself. Inquire to know the real nature of "I," the real nature of the Self. What is your Existence? Can it be a body? If you are not a body, can you have beginning or end, birth or death? Can you have location? Can you be the performer of any action? All those qualities and characteristics pertain to a body, but your Being is not a mere body.

If you are not the body, what is the world? The Maharshi said, "Has anyone ever seen the world without a body?" The world, external, and internal, lose their meaning and cease to exist as such if you know the truth that you are not the body. If you are not the body, where are you, and when are you? Spaceless and timeless is Being. Is this Brahman, or is this yourself, or is there no difference?

Within the mind is conceived the mental image of the Supreme and the mental image of a world to which is attributed another concept that such are external. Are you the mind? Are you in the mind? Is there a second knowing existence apart from Consciousness to be called "a mind"? If you are not the mind, everything conceived within the mind does not pertain to you and cannot be a definition of you. You remain, existing as the inconceivable. In That, the inconceivable, there can be no differentiation, for difference is merely the thought of such and not a transformation or division in Reality. Reality is pure, absolute Existence, or Brahman.

The very idea, the barest assumption, of existing as an individual, as an ego, should be inquired into. Who am I? Existence is only one. Duality is a product of imagination. There cannot be two existences for you; there cannot be two selves. So, you cannot at the same time be Brahman and a limited individual. You cannot be the Self and an ego simultaneously. Nor can you oscillate back and forth between those two, for Existence ever exists; it is as it is. You never cease to be. That which is changeful cannot be you. So, whatever you truly are you are always.

What are you always? Before birth, all through life, and after death, what are you? Waking, dreaming, and deep dreamless sleep, what are you? With a body, without a body, with the senses, without the senses, with thought, without thought, the "I" imagined, or the cessation of such imagination, what are you? Who in truth are you?

In the Sastras, the Self is declared to be of the nature of Sat-Chit-Ananda—Being-Consciousness-Bliss. Know your Being by the light of this innermost Consciousness, and the innate Bliss shines unveiled. Inquire. Inquire until the certainty of this, the Truth, is self-evident. There is no one else to be ignorant of it. Such is Self-Knowledge. Inquire.

Q.: Master, Sat-Chit-Ananda expresses itself in day-to-day life. I know the chair. There is existence. I use my own light, which is Chit, work hard at knowing, and I experience peace. That is my experience in day-to-day life experiencing other things. My understanding is not clear, for I have to work hard to find something existing, and then eventually I get peace. Can you throw some light on that?

N.: If you must go through the senses by which you perceive the chair in the waking state of mind, there is much hard work, as you referred to it, to see what is, but consider your own existence. Do you require any work to know that you exist? Do you do anything to exist?

Q.: No.

N.: This Existence is always and is one without a second. Making your vision nonobjective is the way.

Q.: Does the chair have an existence different from my existence?

N.: Does the chair declare its own existence, or do you say that it exists?

Q.: I say.

N.: The chair does not exist always, but you exist always. What does this tell you?

Q.: That I am continuous. My Existence is continuous.

N.: Your Existence is continuous, and the chair has no existence apart from you.

Q.: The objects always require attention. I give attention to the objects. There are so many objects in the world that exist, and I want to know the existence of everything.

N.: Do you want to know the Existence of everything or the form of everything?

Q.: Form.

N.: The imagining of form can go on endlessly, but the only thing that is actually there is pure Existence, which is unformed. To know the unformed Existence, know yourself. The thoughts, "The chair has my existence," "Another object has my existence," etc., are not eternal. They are expressions of knowledge, not the knowledge itself. Make your vision nonobjective. The chair is nothing but the thought of it. The thought is nothing but the knowledge of it. This is so much so that there is no "it;" there is just knowledge. The knowledge is inherent in the knower. What is his nature?

Q.: Some objectless knowledge. That is what I have heard, but I have not understood it completely.

N.: Yes, you are objectless Knowledge, or pure Consciousness. As for the chair, it is like a chair seen in last night's dream. To pass through one's dream saying, "This is also myself, this is also myself," is fine, but it is better to wake up. Then, what happens to the chair? As long as we consider objects, there is the definition of being a perceiver. Find out if you are a perceiver. The perceived rises and falls and depends utterly upon the perceiver. There is no perceived apart from the perceiver. Find out the nature of the perceiver. If he is found to be unformed Consciousness, there is no perceiver, perceiving, and perceived. Where such differences vanish is true Knowledge.

Another Q.: I am so grateful to have satsang and to be able to hear the truth. It is when I can practice most deeply. I can read spiritual texts conceptually or non-conceptually. If the text is read conceptually, I really do not understand it. When it is read non-conceptually, though, it is a description of my experience. Do I approach inquiry in the same way? When I inquire, "Who am I?", am I seeking to find a concept of myself or am I directly inquiring into the essence that I know as "I"?

N.: Who would select either? Is he a concept?

Q.: Yes, he is a concept.

N.: Then, he cannot do anything. He is just an inert piece of imagination. Inquiry is of the nature of Knowledge. The end appears as the means.

Q.: If the end appears as the means, does it mean that I have to start at the end?

N.: Yes, if the end is oneself, you start with yourself. You start with your Existence, and where you start is where you end.

Q.: If I start with my Existence, there is no start. In the experience of existing, I don't start existing because I start inquiring. It is more that I stop thinking that I am something else.

N.: Sri Bhagavan said, "You un-realize the unreal."

Q.: It is reeling back the dream of being another.

N.: Alright. The Self is ever existent. It is eternal. Knowledge, or Realization of the Self, must necessarily be of the identical nature. It is referred to as nondual, because of its absence of difference, its absence of duality, its absence of division, and its absence of an alternative. Seek eternal Knowledge. It does not have a beginning, for whatever begins ends. Seek the reality of Being, which ever is. This is what satsang, scriptures, and the rest are for.

Q.: You said something, but I can't remember the words.

N.: That is alright. Just express your own understanding.

Q.: You say that, in order to realize the Self, my identity must be one and the same as that Self. Does something else exist other than that?

N.: That the Self can be known only by the Self is, after all, self-evident. Another would be non-Self, and the non-Self cannot know the Self.

Just as there is only one Existence, forever indivisible, so there is only one Knower, one Consciousness, and not a multiplicity of such. There are not two of you that one could be ignorant of the other and then come to know the other. Existence, Consciousness, is only one. The entire assumption—a bare supposition—that you are something else, an "I," a "mind," that supposedly is a second knowing entity, should be questioned and thoroughly examined. As long as that supposition is not inquired into, the Self will seem to be at a distance, at least subtlely so, or unrealized. If, through deep inquiry, that false assumption is abandoned, there remains no one else not to know the Self, and the Truth of the Self is then self-known. Thus, Self-Knowledge.

Q.: It is questioning any assumption of "another" right where it appears to start. Does it ever actually occur?

N.: For whom would it occur?

Q.: It couldn't occur for the Self.

N.: It cannot occur to itself because that is redundant. There is not a third one, because that arises only after the "I." Let your inquiry be thorough, deep, and persevering. "Who am I?"

Another Q.: Does Brahman of which you are speaking have a beginning?

N.: The eternal, the timeless, cannot be spoken of as beginning or ending.

Q.: I read that Brahman has a beginning. I am not the body; nor am I the mind. I know that they have a beginning and an end, and there is Brahman, which is absolute Truth.

N.: If it is absolute Truth, it can have no beginning or end. That which is before the beginning and after the end, which knows about the beginning and the end, which itself is beginningless and endless, understand that to be yourself, to be Brahman.

Q.: Does it have to do with the inconceivable?

N.: Find out. That which is conceived has a beginning and an end.

Q.: So the Self is inconceivable, and that is who I am. That is the position of absolute purity or Being.

N.: That is right.

Another Q.: How do cause and effect work in the waking state? There is an element of time in it. In deep sleep, there is no cause and effect, but, in the waking state, thoughts come—this is the cause of this, this is the cause of that. I try to deconstruct cause and effect in my inquiry.

N.: Regarding that which appears objectively, subtle as one's thoughts or gross as things sensed, you can infer cause and effect, but does your Being have a cause? Is Being an effect?

Q.: I will have to inquire regarding that.

N.: If you inquire, you will find yourself to be beyond all causality. The waking state is said to be the effect, and deep sleep is the cause. You are beyond all three states. The same one who exists in deep sleep, when there were none of these waking state considerations, still exists now. If you seem to be caught up in these things, what has happened? Your nature has not changed, but some misidentification, composed of imagination, seems to be active. Such starts with the very notion, the mode, of "I," aham vritti. One should search for that, find that, and get to the root of that.

Q.: The "I" comes up again and again in the waking state. When I assert myself as the witness, something is going on, and there is no simultaneity.

N.: You may not be able to have simultaneous ideas, but Consciousness, which is the ever-present, silent witness of all that is ever known and experienced, is continuously present. The instruction regarding the witness is not meant to be interpreted as, "Think that you are the witness." Rather, it means to know yourself to be the nonobjective Consciousness, the unknown knower of all that is known, as the Upanishad declares. You are Consciousness. Speaking of Consciousness in relation to all else, which is to be negated, it is called the witness. By itself, it is just absolute Existence.

You see the "I" come and go. You see the world come and go. What is this witness that sees the subject and the object come and go, but that does not come and go? Identify yourself as that and not with an "I" or with an object.

Q.: Thank you, Master, thank you.

Another Q.: My state of mind changes. You described the inquiry step-by-step, taking down the ideas regarding the body, the world, and the mind, just by your questions. To understand the questions requires some mental faculty, but, past that, the actual inquiry does not seem to require the mental faculty.

N.: The actual inquiry is mind-transcendent. It is not mental. Such is true Knowledge. The means of expression, the words used, etc., may require the senses and mind, but they are incidental. The actual inquiry—the actual Knowledge—is beyond words and thoughts. Thus, the opening phrase of Dakshinamurti Dhyanam, "Revealing the Supreme Truth of Brahman in eloquent silence."

Q.: Yes, the Truth could not be touched by the obscuring factors of thought. You quoted the Maharshi as saying, "Un-realize the unreal." It makes more sense now because the un-realizing comes with deep experience, from this Dakshinamurti silence. Is it the only way?

N.: By this silence, all the doubts were resolved for his disciples, which means that their egos were proved to be nonexistent. The ignorance was negated. Silence is that in which no "I" arises. The Maharshi revealed this. Where there is no "I," can there be any veil, any dullness, and any delusion?

Q.: That dullness needs someone for whom it pertains.

N.: Discrimination cannot be truly regarded as a mental activity, for if you discriminate between thought and yourself, how can that be a thought? Fine discrimination involves the clarity of Consciousness, which can never be obscured. The gunas refer to the mind and the senses. You are beyond all of that.

Q.: From the ego sprouts all this other stuff. I give it reality, and that is the mistake. Then, I appear to become affected by these different states, but it is only an appearance.

N.: Discern the nature of the one who experiences such. When you know dullness or when you know agitation, tamas or rajas, or, when you know sattva, the light by which you know is invariable. The light, your Existence, does not change. It does not become part of those qualities. Superimposition of the unreal upon the real does not make the unreal even one bit real. There is not a trace of the snake in the rope.

Q.: It is so important to divest myself of that identity.

N.: Yes.

Q.: With the slight grasp of, or slight belief in, that identity, it seems to be real.

N.: Yes. The smallest, infinitesimal speck of the real attributed to the unreal makes the entire unreal seem as if real. Such is a testimony to the power of Reality. It does not prove any solidity in the unreal, even momentarily so. The apparent reality in any illusion has only one source. This source is you. Every experience seems real for a while and then passes. The sense of reality remains, but the form of the experience changes.

Every condition and state of mind seems as if real momentarily and then passes. There is nothing special about the momentariness; that is also unreal. What is it that can apparently lend the force of its reality endlessly, never be extinguished, and which ever is just as it is? Though apparently lending its reality, yet it remains unmodified, just as the rope is the only substantial thing in the snake. The rope is not modified into a snake, and the snake does not really come to be. So it is with the conditions and experiences, both external and internal, that you think you have. Who knows all of that? What is his existence? Aside from his knowing of it, the "this" aspect has no existence. Who knows?

Q.: The knowing of?

N.: Everything.

Another Q.: So, devotion has no division.

N.: Devotion has no division, and the purpose of devotion is to remain in the state free of division.

Q.: So, a devotee who has pure devotion is one who realizes the Self, because there is no division of Existence.

N.: That is so. Otherwise, if he puts himself up as being separate and distinct from the God that he worships, he makes too big a deal over himself, does he not? Where the identity of being separate dissolves, devotion is at its sweetest.

(Then followed a recitation in Sanskrit and English of verses from the *Annapurna Upanishad.*)

(Silence)

Om Shanti Shanti Shanti Om

(Then followed a recitation in Tamil from chapter 19 of the *Song of Ribhu.*)

ॐ

Other SAT Publications available are:

- ~The Song of Ribhu (The English Translation of The Tamil Ribhu Gita)
- ~The Ribhu Gita (The English Translation of The Sanskrit Ribhu Gita)
- ~A Bouquet of Nondual Texts
- ~Origin of Spiritual Instruction
- ~Essence of Enquiry
- ~Self-Knowledge
- ~Self-Realization
- ~Timeless Presence
- ~Svatmanirupanam, The True Definition of One's Own Self
- ~The Four Requisites for Realization and Self-Inquiry
- ~Nirvana Satkam, Six Verses on Nirvana
- ~Nirguna Manasa Puja, Worship of the Attributeless One in the Mind
- ~Saddarsanam and An Inquiry into the Revelation of Truth and Oneself
- ~Advaita Devatam, God of Nonduality
- ~Essence of Spiritual Instruction
- ~The Quintessence of True Being
- ~Ever Yours in Truth, Nome

For a complete list of books on Advaita Vedanta and the Teachings of Sri Ramana Maharshi, please contact the publisher:

SAT TEMPLE
SOCIETY OF ABIDANCE IN TRUTH
1834 OCEAN STREET, SANTA CRUZ, CALIFORNIA 95060
(831) 425-7287
www.SATRamana.org
sat@cruzio.com

www.ingramcontent.com/pod-product-compliance
Lightning Source LLC
Chambersburg PA
CBHW060906300426
44112CB00011B/1358